Smoldering Ashes

A book in the series
Latin America Otherwise:
Languages, Empires, Nations
Series editors:
Walter D. Mignolo,
Duke University
Irene Silverblatt,
Duke University
Sonia Saldívar-Hull,
University of California
at Los Angeles

SMOLDERING

CUZCO AND THE CREATION OF REPUBLICAN PERU,

ASHES

CHARLES F. WALKER

1780–1840 ✵ DUKE UNIVERSITY PRESS   DURHAM AND LONDON 1999

© 1999 Duke University Press
All rights reserved
Printed in the United States of America on acid-free paper ∞
Typeset in Adobe Caslon by Tseng Information Systems, Inc.
Library of Congress Cataloging-in-Publication Data appear
on the last printed page of this book.

FOR

NANCY WALKER

ZOILA MENDOZA

MARÍA E. MENDOZA WALKER

CONTENTS

L*atin America Otherwise: Languages, Empires, Nations* is a critical series. It aims to explore the emergence and consequences of concepts used to define "Latin America" while at the same time exploring the broad interplay of political, economic, and cultural practices that have shaped Latin American worlds. Latin America, at the crossroads of competing imperial designs and local responses, has been construed as a geocultural and geopolitical entity since the nineteenth century. This series provides a starting point to redefine Latin America as a configuration of political, linguistic, cultural, and economic intersections that demands a continuous reappraisal of the role of the Americas in history, and of the ongoing process of globalization and the relocation of people and cultures that have characterized Latin America's experience. *Latin America Otherwise: Languages, Empires, Nations* is a forum that confronts established geocultural constructions, that rethinks area studies and disciplinary boundaries, that assesses convictions of the academy and of public policy, and that, correspondingly, demands that the practices through which we produce knowledge and understanding about and from Latin America be subject to rigorous and critical scrutiny.

Smoldering Ashes looks at the dying years of Spanish colonial rule and the early years of the Republic from the vantage point of Cuzco's native peoples. Indian and Creole joined in the struggle against colonialism, but their visions of nationhood collided; the version of republicanism championed by the elite would ultimately allow Creoles to maintain their position of privilege. Indigenous anticolonialism imagined a more equitable society modeled on the Inca empire. While mindful of their joint challenges to Spanish rule, Charles Walker underscores how the contradictions splitting apart Indians from non-Indians significantly shaped the emerging Peruvian state.

By shifting analytical focus from the elite to Peru's Indian peasantry, Walker forces us to recognize native peoples' decisive role in constructing the new Republic even as their political intentions were ultimately thwarted. Like other contributions to the series, *Smoldering Ashes* draws on subaltern and postcolonial studies. And, as a work of critical history, it reminds us that the political struggles between Indian and Creole that took place over 150 years ago weigh on the present.

Walter D. Mignolo, Duke University
Irene Silverblatt, Duke University
Sonia Saldívar-Hull, University of
Southern California

ACKNOWLEDGMENTS

I have accumulated so many intellectual debts in the last decade that I should be facing IMF sanctions. I only hope that I have reciprocated to some degree with all of the people mentioned below, as well as with those who are not acknowledged. I owe a great deal to the people of Cuzco and San Jerónimo. Guido Delrán, Isabel Hurtado, Lucho Nieto, Gabriela Ramos, Marisa Remy, Henrique Urbano, and Pilar Zevallos are among those who made work at Centro Bartolomé de Las Casas so fruitful. My students at the San Antonio Abad University taught me a great deal, particularly in the grim days of the late 1980s. Special thanks to members of the Taller de Historia who pitched in with research assistance: Margarita Castro, Eduardo Luza, José Luis Mendoza, and Margareth Najarro. For the last ten years, my "summers" in Cuzco have been greatly sweetened by the friendship of Miryam Quispe and of Thomas Krüggeler, always generous with his knowledge of Cuzco. Since our years working together in the Archivo Departamental del Cuzco, Kathryn Burns has been a great friend. I also thank Marisol de la Cadena for a careful reading of my work and for her support. One of my greatest debts to Cuzco is the enduring friendship of Iván Hinojosa. No one has taught me more about Peru or made me enjoy it more than Iván.

This project began at the University of Chicago. Bernard Cohn pushed me to pay special attention to language and the use of space, while Friedrich Katz forced me to think comparatively. John Coatsworth has never ceased to favor and impress me with his characteristic intelligence, commitment, and kindness. Many of the ideas in this book were developed in discussions with him. Nils Jacobsen of the University of Illinois shared with me his tremendous knowledge of and enthusiasm for Peruvian history. He continues to be a valuable supporter and friend. In Chicago and beyond, Michael Ducey, Michel Gobat, Laura Gotkowitz, Roland Hsu, and Aldo Lauria have been superb friends and critics. Since those days, Peter Guardino and Rich Warren have read countless drafts of these chapters and have always encouraged me with their comments as well as their own work.

Ruth Borja, Manuel Burga, Marcos Cueto, Neus Escandell-Tur, Emilio Garzón, Luis Miguel Glave, Manuel Glave, Pedro Guibovich, Christine Hünefeldt, Marta Irurozqui, Elia Lazarte, Maruja Martínez, Aldo Panfichi, Franklin Pease, Mariana Pease, Victor Peralta, Scarlett O'Phelan Godoy, and Nuria Sala i Vila have helped me in different stages of this project. The late Alberto Flores Galindo encouraged me, and I, like so many people, miss him. Through the years, the Mendoza family has supported me in many ways. I'd particularly like to thank Don Eduardo and Doña Zoila for their loving kindness. Carlos Aguirre has been a dear friend and important collaborator in the last ten years, and I frankly don't know what I'd do without him and his wonderful family.

I would like to thank the people of the Archivo Departamental del Cuzco—in particular, Jorge Polo and Horacio Villanueva Urteaga—the Centro Las Casas Library, particularly Mary and Julia, the Archivo General de la Nación, the Biblioteca Nacional, the Archivo Histórico Militar, the Instituto Riva Agüero, and the Archivo General de Indias. Félix Denegri Luna opened his library to me, sharing his knowledge of Cuzco and Peruvian history. Antonio Acosta not only facilitated work in Spain but also made both Cuzco and Seville more enjoyable.

My colleagues have confirmed the reputation of the Department of History at the University of California, Davis, as a congenial place. Lucy Barber, Bill Hagen, Ted Margadant, Barbara Metcalf, Alan Taylor, and Clarence Walker gave me invaluable comments on the manuscript. Ben Orlove also has been a generous friend. Above all, I'd like to thank Arnold J. Bauer, who has read every chapter several times. Arnie has improved my prose, clarified my arguments, and kept me smiling. I could not ask for a better mentor. Students here who have assisted me include William Ayala, Patrick Barr, Keith Heningburg, Albert Lacson, Claudio Robles, Leticia Rosado Russell, and Adam Warren. Jason Newman completed the index. I have also benefited from the suggestions of a number of fine scholars outside of Davis, including Cristobal Aljovín, JoAnn Kawell, Peter Klarén, Brooke Larson, Florencia Mallon, John Rowe, Linda Seligmann, Matt Shirts, Steve Stern, Enrique Tandeter, and Ann Wightman. Paul Gootenberg has offered advice for years, and Eric Van Young has provided valuable comments on several chapters. Tulio Halperín Donghi has inspired me since my undergraduate days.

I quickly learned why fellow Latin Americanists encouraged me to approach Valerie Millholland at Duke University Press. She has led me through the intricate world of academic publishing with grace, humor, and enthusiasm. I would also like to thank Mark McLean for the maps and Annie Barva for her fine copyediting. Fellowships from the Wenner-Gren Foundation, the American Philosophical Society, the National Endowment for the Humanities, and the Tinker Foundation allowed me to conduct research in Cuzco and Lima. At the University of California, Davis, I have counted on fellowships from the Humanities Institute, the provost's office, and the Committee on Research. I would also like to thank Dean Barbara Metcalf and Assistant Dean Steve Roth of the Social Sciences Division, as well as Kevin M. Smith, Vice Chancellor for Research, for generous publication support.

I have a wonderful family who has always supported my passion for Latin America. Mary pushed me to have a broader vision of the world, and my brother, John, who read the manuscript, has always been there for me. Maggie has spoiled me for decades, and I appreciate her love even if I never admit it. Finally, I would like to mention the three women to whom the book is dedicated. My mother, Nancy Walker, has always been my greatest booster, and I want to thank her for her unwavering love and support. My wife, Zoila Mendoza, has taught me more about life than anyone else and has always believed in me as a historian. My daughter, María, brings constant joy. To them, my love.

SMOLDERING ASHES

"Cuzco is the only place where you can gain a true idea of Peru."—Juan Pablo Viscardo y Guzmán, 1781

"The only word to sum up Cuzco adequately is evocative."—Ernesto "Che" Guevara, *The Motorcycle Diaries*

On May 18, 1781, horses dragged José Gabriel Condorcanqui into the central plaza of Cuzco. A local leader who claimed descent from the last Inca ruler of the sixteenth century, he had taken the title Tupac Amaru II to lead the largest rebellion in colonial Latin America. Backed primarily by Indians, the uprising had spread throughout much of South America and had nearly overthrown the Spanish. Six months into the fighting, however, colonial authorities captured Tupac Amaru II and several other key leaders. The punishment meted out to the rebels reflected the scope of the uprising and the panic of Spanish authorities. Tupac Amaru was forced to watch the execution of his comrades and family members, including his wife and key confidante, Micaela Bastidas, whose tongue was cut out before she was strangled. Executioners then tortured José Gabriel at length and tied him to four horses to be quartered. When his limbs did not separate from his torso, he was beheaded. The arms, legs, and heads of José Gabriel and Micaela were displayed throughout the viceroyalty.

Sixty years later, on November 18, 1841, the Cuzco caudillo and president of Peru, Agustín Gamarra, was killed when attempting to rouse his troops in Bolivia. Some contend that one of his own soldiers shot him. General Gamarra had participated in all of the major political events in the region since 1815. He had fought on both the loyalist and rebel sides in the War of Independence (1809-24), invaded neighboring countries, conspired in and put down coup attempts, and held the Peruvian presidency for two terms, 1829-33 and 1839-41, as leader of the conservative coalition. Throughout his political and military career, this quintessential caudillo maintained a strong base in his native Cuzco.

These two deaths bracket the narrative of this book. The lives of Tupac Amaru II and Agustín Gamarra symbolize the challenges of converting Peru from an ethnically diverse but highly stratified viceroyalty into an independent nation. In these sixty years, people fought for a variety of options to Spanish colonialism, with republicanism finally taking hold. The Indian leader of a mass uprising in the twilight of Spanish colonial rule and the conservative mestizo caudillo at the dawn of independence confronted many of the same obstacles. They had to address the sharp divisions between Peru's Indian majority and non-Indians, as well as other social and geographic tensions, such as the animosity between coastal Lima and highland Cuzco. Above all, they had to search for ways to reconcile the demands of disparate and contentious groups into a formula for the seizure and practice of power. In the pages that follow, I show that the practice of caudillismo and its relationship to state formation—in Peru and throughout Spanish America—can be understood only through a careful examination of the desires and political efforts of the lower classes and of their relationships to regional and national political movements.

Throughout this book, I demonstrate that the vast population of highland Indians—often understood to be passive and usually presented as an anonymous mass rather than as individuals—is the key to understanding the turbulent transition from colony to republic. In fact, from the Zapatistas in southern Mexico to the indigenous movements in Bolivia and Ecuador, they remain today at the center of struggles over nation-state formation. Indians played important and often overlooked roles in the mass movements that fought (and defended) Spanish rule and clashed in the caudillo-led civil wars decades later. Indians not only followed leaders such as Tupac Amaru and Gamarra, but also influenced the movements' platforms by negotiating the terms of their participation. Historians have far too often accepted contemporary views that deemed Indians incapable of political consciousness and indifferent to the battles over the state.[1]

I argue that local, regional, and "national" political struggles can be understood only when studied together. Community-based struggles were connected to and affected broader political movements in two ways. First, members in the community—and at times the entire community—would couple their opposition to a particular authority or a set of policies with a broader coalition, as was the case in hundreds of Indian communities during the Tupac Amaru uprising, but also during less tumultuous and historically visible periods. Second, Andean communities used less confrontational tactics to resist the onerous demands of the Bourbon and republican states. For example, they took abusive authorities to court with surprising success. I demonstrate that they not only defended their political and economic rights, but limited the course of action that political groups could take in the Andes. These efforts help explain why, despite their claims to omnipotence, the colonial state and the republican state could not freely impose their programs on Andean society.

Similarly, I also emphasize that the debates about postcolonial Peru were not limited to elite ideologues. I show that ideological battles over the nature of colonial and postcolonial society are at the heart of Spanish American state formation and nation building. The interplay between national identities and those based on region, ethnicity, religion, and other markers shape politics in the early republic as much as it does in the late twentieth century. To address these questions, theorists have increasingly emphasized how diverse groups "imagined" or "invented" the nation and how the state implemented its particular vision.[2] In recent years, scholars have explored how different groups, elite and nonelite, constructed opposing notions of nationalism.[3] In Peru, ideologues crafted a definition of Peruvian citizenship that excluded the vast majority of the population. The exclusionary policies and discourses that characterize the Andean republics today can be dated from this period. However, Indians and other lower-class groups also participated in these discussions, and in doing so, they contested the narrow notions of citizenship and political rights propagated by elite groups.

In this study, I examine the intricate and difficult relations among national ideologies and policies, regional political movements, and the lower classes. These different spheres need to be integrated in order to understand the difficulties in nation-state building that Spanish America encountered. Integrating them requires both a careful reconstruction of political movements that pays attention to a variety of tactics beyond insurrection and collective mobilization, and an examination of diverse ideological debates. I show how political movements included or excluded the dark-skinned lower classes, and how they were, in turn, influenced by and affected these groups. Subaltern political movements are neither autonomous nor fully dependent.[4] Examining the connections and misconnections between "peasant politics" and multiclass regional and national movements illuminates Spanish America's difficult postindependence history.

A program that stresses the role of the lower classes and highlights ideological battles can be accomplished only by paying close attention to the political battles themselves. Far too often, the dizzying change of presidents and other signs of turmoil after independence in Spanish America have led scholars to interpret the postindependence period as mere chaos or as elite machinations and lower-class failures. Anecdotes about several politicians simultaneously claiming the presidency in Peru or statistics that show a dozen presidents in a decade serve as symbols for political and social backwardness. This book, in contrast, seeks to illuminate the logic and nature of these struggles. Although postindependence caudillos largely agreed on republicanism as the proper form of government in Peru, they incorporated strands of federalism, regionalism, and even Inca revivalism into their programs. Even as they apparently abandoned the Constitution when they seized power by force, they aligned with political parties and created multiclass movements. Examining the Gamarra movement highlights the ideological and social complexity of caudillo coalitions.

The related theoretical fields—political culture and the new cultural history—lend an explanatory hand. These schools have reinvigorated political history by examining how political behavior and language changed, rather than by searching for winners and losers. Both schools grant politics a certain autonomy, instead of seeing it as merely a product of broader structural processes, particularly economic. They also pay close attention to language, discourse, and practice, searching for patterns of behavior as well as shared and conflicting views on how politics was to be practiced in a particular period.[5] Latin Americanists who read studies on European cultural history envy the availability of sources and wonder whether such studies are possible for a period marked by turmoil in a region that has not always carefully preserved historical documents.

My experience demonstrates that such analyses of politics and culture in this period and region are possible. After I had conducted eight months of research in the Cuzco Departmental Archive, an employee mentioned the Velasco Aragón Collection locked up in an adjacent room. After removing a great deal of accumulated junk, dust, and miscellaneous books, we uncovered dozens of bound volumes containing newspapers and political pamphlets from the nineteenth century. These sources allowed me to explore the practice and rituals of caudillo politics, and to examine how the Gamarristas, the followers of General Agustín Gamarra, created and sustained a coalition in Cuzco and how it operated throughout Peru.[6] I look not only at mass political uprisings such as rebellions and civil wars, but also at elections, celebrations, and military campaigns. In the midst of civil wars, the groups vying for control of the state—which included a surprisingly broad section of civil society—competed for followers by expressing their views in the streets and in the active press. Throughout Spanish America, historians are dusting off old sources and discovering new ones that highlight politics, culture, and society.[7] I emphasize the need to link the study of public rituals such as parades and elections and discourse with the examination of the power struggles at the heart of caudillo politics. Scholars of political culture in Spanish America have too often separated political practices or rituals from material interests and battles over the state. Such a separation not only overlooks changes in political culture through time, particularly in the transition from colony to republic, but also lessens the explanatory power of cultural approaches to postindependence state formation.[8]

THE LOWER CLASSES AND CAUDILLOS

This book builds on current efforts to place the lower classes at the center of history. Taking advantage of the vast amount of research in "peasant studies" in recent decades, scholars from a variety of disciplines are correlating local histories or the "little tradition" with large processes such as state formation.[9] They explore how local, regional, national, and transnational trends intersect and affect one another. Accenting the reciprocal nature of this relationship, these studies demonstrate not only that national trends modify local society, but that local or regional spheres influence national politics and identity creation. They recognize that "the move in social history away from state politics, and toward a focus on the 'small people,' has often gone too far by dropping the state out of the picture."[10]

Throughout this book, I maintain that peasant and caudillo politics were not separate fields, but intimately linked. Caudillos relied on peasants, and inhabitants of the countryside often found themselves embroiled in political struggles. I contend that only by linking these two areas of study can the difficult path to political stability and state formation in Spanish America be understood. With few exceptions, political turmoil enveloped the nascent Spanish American republics. Throughout the continent, military chieftains fought for the control of the state. In some cases they formed alliances against the leading political groups, which were usually divided into liberals and conservatives; in many other cases they joined with them. Some fended off lower-class subversion, whereas others championed populist movements. Some remained in national office for decades, but others led small, isolated local movements. Through the analysis of the Cuzco caudillo Agustín Gamarra, this book attempts to understand why and how caudillos predominated.

The question has long troubled Spanish Americans. Dating from Domingo Sarmiento's classic study of Facundo Quiroga (1845), caudillo analysis constitutes a prominent form of national self-examination, an enduring genre of Latin American literature that stretches from Sarmiento's nineteenth-century romanticism to the literary boom of the 1960s and beyond.[11] Caudillos are the subject of countless novels, biographies, and social scientific essays, serving as lively metaphors for national problems and even national potential.[12] In this sense, as a symbol of "strong man" politics, caudillismo is not limited to the military chieftains prominent in the nineteenth century. The study of caudillos addresses enduring problems of instability, fragmentation, and disunity that outlasted the military leaders themselves.

Scholars have approached caudillismo in many ways. Richard Morse presented the military strongmen as a key element of postindependence efforts to resurrect Spanish patrimonialism.[13] Others contend that the lack of experience with self-government in the Spanish colonies and the deleterious effects of the long wars of independence hindered political stability and placed the military in a position to assume authority.[14] Social scientists frequently cite the continent's economic problems as another cause of political instability.[15] In order to explain the difficulty in establishing stable political institutions and thus the rise of caudillismo, some emphasize regional conflicts. According to this view, elegantly espoused by John Lynch, the caudillo emerged to represent politically and economically backward regions threatened by centralism or to control lower-class insurgency in this context of political disorder.[16]

One element missing from these works is a detailed examination of how caudillos built alliances, constructed programs, and ran the state. Despite the centrality of caudillismo to understanding Spanish America, few studies have concentrated on how caudillismo functioned. The bureaucratic structures and cultural projects created by figures such as Gamarra endured far longer than the caudillos themselves; they marked state and society for decades, if not centuries. For example, the tax system dating from the 1820s lasted for decades, and Gamarra's conservative "Cuzco First" discourse resonates even today. Consequently, I examine how Gamarra created his movement in Cuzco, stressing the administrative and ideological mechanisms of the postcolonial state. I focus on the question of why such diverse groups as the elite, the middle sectors, and the lower classes supported or opposed particular caudillos. This analysis seeks to fulfill Joseph and Nugent's plea to bring the state back in without leaving the people out.[17]

I emphasize the influence of ideological struggles dating from the eighteenth century on the nature of postcolonial Peru. The caudillo-led civil wars were not simply power struggles between greedy military officers. Throughout the country, they involved intense debate in the press and in public forums about the postindependence state, particularly the questions of political stability and the role of the lower classes. Government representatives and their allies inculcated their notion of state and society—their cultural project—through different policies, performance, and the press. I follow how these views were disseminated and contested by different sectors of Cuzco society, from the urban elite to the rural peasantry.

CUZCO AND ITS PEOPLE

The former center of the Inca Empire, the city and region of Cuzco affords a particularly rich case for analyzing the political culture of modern Latin America. Cuzco-based movements led the initial struggles against Spanish domination and, after independence was won, against

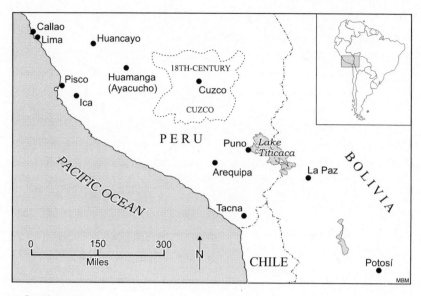

1. Southern Peru

efforts to centralize power in the capital, Lima.[18] These movements proposed diverse counterhegemonic ideological projects, all of them involving an Andean utopia. By invoking the Inca Empire, people in Cuzco attempted to create alternatives to colonialism as well as to coastal domination. These "invented traditions" ranged from revolutionary change, with Indians at the top of the social pyramid, to Incan monarchism—with an "Inca" replacing the Bourbon king, but social hierarchies otherwise remaining in place.[19] These diverse projects failed not only because of opposition in Lima and other regions but because of the tensions and disagreements between Cuzco's urban population, particularly mestizos, and the rural Indian majority. Nonetheless, I show that even if not put into practice, these projects shaped efforts to build a postcolonial state and define who were to be deemed citizens. Gamarra himself incorporated the Incas into his discourse. In fact, I examine the transition of Inca revivalism from a revolutionary platform during the Tupac Amaru uprising to one that bolstered a conservative caudillo in the early republic.

Second at this time only to Lima in terms of population and of economic and political power, the city and region of Cuzco were at the

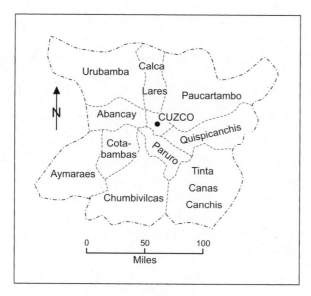

2. Cuzco in the Eighteenth Century

forefront of the anticolonial uprisings, the caudillo wars, and the tensions between coastal Lima and the Andes. In 1827, the department of Cuzco had approximately 250,000 people, up to 40,000 of them living in the city of Cuzco. Peru as a whole had a population of about 1.5 million.[20] Bounded by the upper provinces (*provincias altas*) to the south, the Amazon basin to the east and north, and Ayacucho and Arequipa to the west, the department consisted of eleven provinces, including the province of the city of Cuzco. The political boundaries of Cuzco—what in 1784 became the intendancy and in 1824 the department of Cuzco— have remained largely the same from the late eighteenth century until today, with only minor changes to the south and the west.[21] The political analysis at times spills over from the communities, towns, and city of Cuzco to include other areas of Peru and Bolivia, thus demonstrating the benefits of a regionally focused study that keeps both local and national societies in sight.

Most accounts of Cuzco past and present emphasize three distinct areas: the majestic city of Cuzco with its Inca "ruins" next to and under Spanish churches and colonial architecture; the imposing mountain ranges and narrow valleys running north and south; and the "exotic"

Amazon jungle to the east. More specifically, in the eighteenth and nineteenth centuries the region was divided into approximately half a dozen production zones, mainly according to altitude and proximity to markets. Livestock was raised in the high ranges in the upper provinces in the districts of Chumbivilcas, Cotabambas, and Canas y Canchis to the south, most of which are at least 4,000 meters (13,125 feet) above sea level. The region surrounding Cuzco—the districts of Anta, Paruro, Quispicanchis, Urubamba, and Calca y Lares—was noted for its grain production, the latter providing much of the Cuzco market.[22] The fertile valleys surrounding the city of Cuzco supplied foodstuffs, and mills located primarily in Quispicanchis and in Abancay to the northwest produced the region's textiles.[23] Sugar was grown primarily in the western districts of Abancay and Aymaraes. Paucartambo, particularly the areas bordering the jungle, was the center of coca cultivation, although production from Urubamba and Calca y Lares increased in the eighteenth century. In the early republic, the lowlands to the east (referred to as the "frontier of the savage Indians" in the maps of the period) remained largely in the hands of Amazon peoples with cultures distinct from highland Indians as well as from the Spanish-speaking population.[24]

Between Lima and Upper Peru (which became Bolivia in 1825), the region of Cuzco maintained important ties to the coast as well as to other Andean areas. Cuzco producers marketed most of their sugar and textiles in Upper Peru, particularly the mining city of Potosí. Muleteers returned with a variety of goods—above all, mules. Cuzco merchants also traded actively with Arequipa, Ayacucho, and Lima. These circuits, as well as more localized ones, centered on the constant traffic on the Royal Highway along the Vilcanota River. Commerce was not the sole link with other regions. Several important religious pilgrimages brought Andean people together.[25] Mail routes give an idea of the distance from other regions. In 1834, three routes linked Cuzco with the outside. Mail carriers left Cuzco twice a month for each route: the five-day trip to Arequipa; the week-long journey south to Puno, where mail from Bolivia was gathered; and the all-important thirteen-day trip to Lima. To reach Lima, the carriers proceeded to Ayacucho to the northeast and from there down to the coast.[26]

Socially, the division between Indians and non-Indians shaped Cuzco society more than anything else in this period. In fact, at the heart of this study are the racial dichotomies that persisted and even strengthened in the republic. In 1827, approximately 75 percent of Cuzco's population was Indian. They constituted approximately half of the city of Cuzco's population.[27] In 1845, 84 percent of the Indians registered in the tax rolls lived in communities—some located in the city of Cuzco—and the remaining 16 percent in haciendas.[28] The boundaries between Indians and non-Indians were by no means impermeable.[29] Nonetheless, people in Cuzco constantly used the term *Indian* to refer to the Quechua-speaking inhabitants of the Andes, rural and urban.

Who was an Indian? Centuries of miscegenation and cultural crossing meant that physical appearance or phenotype was not an adequate marker of "Indianness." Cultural markers included the Quechua language, simple clothing, a potato-dependent diet, rustic production techniques, and adobe housing. Authorities in the late colonial and early republican periods actually employed a number of words to refer to the indigenous rural population: *naturales* (naturals), *peruanos* (Peruvians), and more often *indios* (Indians). For the state, *Indian* was ultimately a fiscal category. Authorities espoused a tautological definition of what constituted an Indian: one who paid the Indian head tax and, in colonial times, fulfilled a series of other obligations, such as *la mita*, the labor draft. With a few exceptions such as the *caciques* (the ethnic authorities) and priests' assistants, all male Indians between the age of eighteen and fifty paid the tax, whereas non-Indians were exempt. Until its abolition in 1854, the head tax anchored racial definitions in Peru. In the period of study, Indians did not reject this category en masse. Although people challenged Peru's racial categories and used divergent understandings of what being an Indian meant, non-Indians and Indians themselves constantly used the term *Indian*. Independence did not weaken the bifurcation of Peru into Indians and non-Indians.[30] In Peru, the lines dividing Indians and non-Indians were more sharply drawn than in the other center of colonial Spanish America, Mexico, and intermediate groups, although important, were comparatively less significant.[31]

The other end of the social spectrum, the elite, changed from 1780 to 1840. Many of the region's prominent merchants and hacienda owners were ambitious Spanish immigrants who had arrived in Cuzco in the eighteenth century. They established business and political networks by marrying into powerful families and lending money to and paying bonds for colonial authorities. Like their brethren throughout the continent, they managed a diversified portfolio, centering their interests in the city of Cuzco. A search for Cuzco's dominant class takes us to the neighborhoods around the Plaza de Armas, the central plaza, rather than into the haciendas throughout the region. Yet the leading families in 1780 — the Ocampo, Ugarte, Guisasola, La Madrid, and Gutiérrez, among others—did not dominate Cuzco fifty years later.[32] The violent Tupac Amaru rebellion, the decline of the Upper Peru–Bolivia market, the defeat of the Spanish, and other factors led many of them to emigrate. This book examines who replaced them and why, and it follows the rise of a new group that weathered or even profited from the long War of Independence and forged ties with Gamarra and other political leaders.

Defining the two social extremes of colonial society, Indians and elites, is relatively easy. Intermediate groups pose greater problems. Although Cuzco had a scant black population, the mestizo population was large, making up almost a quarter of the region's population. These diverse people appear throughout this book. Individuals located economically, culturally, and politically "between" the Spanish and Indians—such as merchants who did not have the contacts or capital of the elite and residents of the small towns along the Royal Highway and the poorer neighborhoods of Cuzco city—participated as leaders and followers in the Tupac Amaru and Pumacahua rebellions. After independence, legislators recognized this group by including them in the head tax, as *castas*. Although this new tax encompassed all non-Indians, including affluent merchants and landowners, it affected mostly poor rural workers with a variety of occupations. Opposing political factions in postindependence Cuzco frequently clashed over the place of mestizos in the republic. I pay particular attention to the role of cultural brokers —caciques, parish priests, and muleteers, in particular—who mediated between Indian society and regional and national politics. This perspective illuminates clashing and changing notions about race and society at the center of Peru's difficult transition from colony to republic.

ORGANIZATION

From November 1780 to April 1781, the Tupac Amaru rebels controlled most of southern Peru, nearly taking Cuzco. The rebellion, the subject of chapter 2, stretched from its base in Tinta, just south of Cuzco, to what is today northern Argentina, Chile, Bolivia, and much of Peru.

Rebels destroyed textile mills and estates, banished and occasionally murdered authorities, and in some areas created an alternative state. In all, up to one hundred thousand people died. Closely following the course of the rebellion, I underline its protonational platform. Although multiple ideological currents such as Enlightenment thought, neo-Inca revivalism, and disgruntlement over the Bourbon reforms nourished this rebellion, the leadership emphasized the bonds between all native-born Peruvians and the need to expel the Spanish. Social and racial divisions, however, undermined this platform, as the colonial state's portrayal of the rebellion as a caste war reinforced its military efforts. Although the Peruvian community of Creoles, mestizos, Indians, and blacks envisioned by Tupac Amaru shared an opposition to Spanish rule, they also mistrusted one another, which marked or marred future state formation efforts as well.

The defeat of the uprising and the brutal execution of its leaders signaled difficult times for the rebellion's mass base, Cuzco's Indian population. The state sanctioned harsh anti-Indian measures; ideologues condemned Indians for their backwardness and violence; and local authorities challenged their political autonomy. However, as chapter 3 shows, the colonial state failed to "reconquer" the region after the defeat of the rebels. The state could not greatly increase the tax burden it exacted or dissolve the autonomy enjoyed by caciques, local Indian authorities, because it was reticent to invest in a more effective administrative system. Moreover, fear of another uprising and the region's stagnant economy discouraged the state and non-Indians, who vividly remembered the Tupac Amaru uprising, from attempting to usurp Indians' land and exploit their labor. Above all, I analyze Indians' efforts, especially their use of the legal system, to thwart both the state and interlopers. These lawsuits indicate that local power relations varied greatly from community to community, with some caciques remaining in power and others being replaced by Indians and non-Indians. The difficulties that the Bourbon authorities encountered both foreshadowed and shaped the postcolonial impasse between the state and indigenous peasants. Neither the colonial nor the republican state could impose its will on the Andean peasantry.

From the Tupac Amaru uprising until the Pumacahua rebellion (1814–15), the southern Andes were the site of numerous Indian-based uprisings. After 1815, however, the center of the struggle for independence shifted to the coast and Lima. At this point, patriot forces had to rely on foreign generals, José de San Martín of Argentina and Simón Bolívar of Venezuela, to lead the fight against the Spanish. Chapter 4 examines this riddle by reviewing Peru's long War of Independence, 1808–24, from the perspective of Cuzco. I show that by 1815 social divisions had crippled the movements based in the southern Andes. At this point, the Indian population had not only been ravaged by war but also found their hopes dashed. Disillusionment set in. Not only do I highlight many peoples' attachment to Spanish rule; I show that people in the southern Andes contemplated, and in some cases fought for, other alternatives such as Inca revivalism and reformed modes of monarchism, refashioning these alternatives according to their political traditions and goals. Contrary to the Whiggish and nationalist historiography, the replacement of Spanish rule with a republican system was not inevitable.

Chapter 5 studies caudillismo and postindependence state formation by examining Agustín Gamarra's coalition in his native Cuzco. After switching from the Spanish to the patriot army in 1821, he became a general, Cuzco's first prefect, and twice president of Peru. In Cuzco, Gamarra created a heterogeneous coalition. Using the military, the militias, and the subprefect office to foster loyalty and disseminate his program, he gained the support of military officers, influential priests, local Indian authorities, and much of Cuzco's common people. His movement created an authoritarian ideology that stressed Cuzco's claim to political and economic preeminence based on its former role as the center of the Inca Empire and its importance during the colony. In addressing the why and how of caudillismo, I stress the social complexity of his coalition, the important connections between local, regional, and national political movements, and the need to take seriously the ideological debates of the period.

Chapter 6 examines how caudillo politics worked on the ground and how political culture changed after independence in the city of Cuzco. I explore the public sphere—specifically, the press, festivities, and military campaigns and intrigues. People debated and fought over control of the state and the relationship between the republican state and civil society. Although only a small minority of Cuzco's population was literate and both major parties postulated a restricted notion of politics, these debates and struggles over the state involved surprisingly broad sections of urban society, including the illiterate. In studying how political groups communicated their platform in the press and the streets, I contrast Gamarra's success in creating a regional coalition to his liberal opponents' failure to build a Cuzco-specific program. By incorporating the adoration of the Incas into his program, Gamarra drew from the most significant political symbol of the region. Because of their aversion to monarchism, which they associated with the Incas, and their emphasis on European ideologues, liberals could not ground their efforts in such a vivid historical precedent. Gamarra's success in building a broad coalition steeped in local customs and linked to a national movement provides important clues regarding the endurance of authoritarianism in modern Spanish America.

In the final chapter, I focus on the central question confronting Peru's postindependence politicians: what should be done with the Indian majority? The strapped republican state quickly reinstated the Indian head tax, thus resurrecting the keystone of Spanish colonialism and racial divisions in the Andes. Non-Indian authorities emphasized the backwardness of Indians and their lack of interest in politics, thereby justifying their own exploitative intrusions. Once again, however, the state could not impose its will in the countryside. On the one hand, the unstable nature of the state and Cuzco's declining economy hindered the neocolonial efforts of the Gamarristas. Political turmoil impeded authorities from establishing themselves, while continuing economic stagnation decreased demand for Indians' land and labor. On the other hand, Indians themselves negotiated improved conditions. In essence, they paid the head tax and received some political autonomy and special rights as landholders. Ultimately, even Gamarra could not bridge the division between Indian and non-Indian societies. His failure to recruit Indians for his military campaigns, as evident in the Battle of Yanacocha (1836), led to his demise and epitomized the enduring gulf between the republic of Indians and the republic of Peru.

From 1780 to 1783 the largest rebellion in Spanish American colonial history rocked the Andean region. Initially based in Cuzco, the uprising was felt in an area stretching from modern-day Argentina to Colombia. The Tupac Amaru stage lasted a little more than half a year, at which point the center of rebellion shifted to Upper Peru, what is today Bolivia. The rebels nearly overthrew Spanish colonial power and in doing so radically altered relations among the state, the elite, and the indigenous peasantry. Along with the Spanish Conquest, the uprising constitutes the most discussed phenomenon in Peruvian history and today is remembered and venerated by a variety of groups and organizations.

Despite the enormity of the rebellion and the considerable attention it has received from scholars, the aims and significance of the Tupac Amaru movement remain open to debate. There is no unequivocal answer to the question, What were the objectives of the rebels? Some historians have interpreted the rebellion as a mass antecedent to the War of Independence that would take place in the early nineteenth century. Others have emphasized its Inca ideology, depicting it as a revivalist or messianic movement. Others have not looked so far forward or backward in time, but instead have placed it within the colonial tradition of negotiated political rights. Part of the interpretative problem lies in the ambiguity of the leaders' platform as well as in the breach between their rhetoric and the insurgents' activities. In most of his proclamations and letters, Tupac Amaru advocated a broad, multiethnic movement that sought to cast off the more exploitative practices of colonialism as well as the European exploiters themselves. He claimed to act in the name of the king and the Catholic Church and recruited the support of not only Indians but Creoles, mestizos, and blacks. He never specified what type of polity would replace Spanish colonialism. Although the leadership sought the support of non-Indians, thus emphasizing the movement's breadth and restraint, Indian insurgents often contradicted these efforts by sacking or burning estates owned by Creoles and attacking a broadly defined enemy: those people not considered Indians. These two intimately related features of the uprising—the vagueness of Tupac Amaru's platform and the tensions between a multiethnic and an "Indian" movement—came to the fore repeatedly during the rebellion and help to explain its demise.

An analysis of the Tupac Amaru rebellion can benefit from and contribute to debates about nationalism and colonialism. Most definitions of nationalism emphasize the existence of a unique body of people and the attempt to attain political gains for this body or nation.[1] The Tupac Amaru uprising fulfills the first condition and, as this chapter argues, the more questionable second one. Tupac Amaru addressed his movement to a coalition of social groups perhaps most easily defined in negative terms as all those not Spanish or European. He strove to include mestizos, Creoles, and blacks in his movement, emphasizing their union as native-born peoples mistreated by the Spanish. On the second point, however, the applicability of the concept of nationalism to the rebellion is not so clear. He never specified what form of government would replace the Spanish and combined seemingly contradictory elements such as Inca monarchism, "traditional" colonial practice, and hints of Enlightenment thought. Nonetheless, there is little doubt about his immediate objective: to demolish Bourbon colonialism.

The use of the concept of nationalism for an Indian-based movement in the Andes in the eighteenth century stretches its usual chronological, geographical, and social applications. Tupac Amaru rose forty-five years prior to the independence of Peru and before the nation-state predominated in Western Europe. Moreover, the movement was defeated and thus never put into practice its nationalist project. Therefore, the prefix *proto* must be attached to the terms *national* and *nationalist* to describe the movement. A variety of scholars have questioned whether nationalism could exist prior to nations. Although they recognize the cultural manifestations of broad-based identity, they note that these stirrings

were not translated into political action.[2] Today, most scholars emphasize the imagined or constructed nature of "the nation" and present it
as a discourse grounded in a mythical past propagated by statemakers
and their ideologues, rather than as some type of enduring, primordial
legacy. In this view, nationalism followed the nation-state. Nonetheless, these "imagined communities" did not develop out of a vacuum,
but rather from the reworking of various notions of identity and community.[3] Tupac Amaru embodied a form of protonationalism anchored
in the Andes and the Indian population. This program contrasted with
the platform of the Creole-led movement for independence and with
the ideology of the postcolonial state. This chapter highlights these differences, and argues that the concept of a Peruvian nation needs to be
pluralized.[4] The book follows the tangled relationship between Andean-
based and Creole nationalisms.

In recent decades, numerous scholars and schools have attempted to
free the examination of nationalism in Asia, Africa, and Latin America
from the constraints of a model largely developed for and in Europe.[5]
Although the rich scholarship on anticolonial movements in Asia and
Africa offers a sharp critique of Europe-centric perspectives and fascinating comparisons for Latin America, it is not easily transferable
to Latin America, however. Again, timing is essential. Independence
in Latin America came in the early nineteenth century, but in Africa
and Asia not until the twentieth.[6] In general, the first great wave of
nation building—independence in Spanish America in the early nineteenth century—has not been sufficiently examined in the literature on
nationalism and (anti)colonialism.[7] The analysis of the rebellion of Tupac Amaru can shed light on this process.

PRECURSOR, INCA, OR TRADITIONALIST?
TUPAC AMARU AND HISTORIANS

The uncertainty about the nature of the Tupac Amaru movement reflects the highly ideological nature of its treatment by historians. The
uprising has been at the forefront of diverse interpretations and debates
about Peru's past, present, and future. No period has featured as promi-
nently in the debates about what is Peru and why it is so highly divided
than the years of the War of Independence, when insurgents in Peru
had to rely on foreign armies to defeat the Spanish. The analysis of the

Tupac Amaru movement confronts both questions. Within these enduring debates, three interpretations of the movement can be found: as an antecedent to independence, as an Inca revivalist project, and as a massive but traditional form of political negotiation. This chapter demonstrates that these interpretations need to be combined within the concept of protonationalism.

Some scholars have presented the rebellion as an Indian precursor to the Creole-led War of Independence in the early nineteenth century and thus have incorporated Tupac Amaru into the pantheon of nationalist heroes. This view gives the Andes and the Indian population a presence in the struggle for independence, which was based on the coast and led by non-Indians. In the 1940s, Boleslao Lewin, the Polish-Argentine author of what is still the best narrative history of the movement, emphasized Tupac Amaru's anticolonial spirit and actions, and called for a rethinking of independence in light of the mass rebellions and revolts in the Andes in the eighteenth century.[8] More recently, the Velasco Alvarado regime in Peru (1968–75) presented Tupac Amaru as the initiator of Peru's unfinished revolution, a project to have been culminated by Velasco Alvarado himself.[9] Guerrilla movements in Uruguay and Peru have adopted his name.

These interpretations straitjacket the Tupac Amaru rebellion, however. The rebellion is seen as a mass forerunner to the overthrow of the Spanish and the creation of a Creole-led nation state, a very different social movement in a very different context. Spain, its American colonies, and, in fact, the entire world changed dramatically between 1780 and 1820. The Bourbon kings lost their hold on their colonies and for a few years on Spain itself, and the selection of political options for the seditious widened greatly with the French Revolution and other insurgencies. In light of the context in 1780, it is not surprising that Tupac Amaru did not overtly call for some sort of democratic republic in the southern Andes. Nor should it be assumed, as it often is by the precursor school, that Tupac Amaru sought political independence like the "patriots" of the early nineteenth century. As I demonstrate in this chapter, the rebellion did not call for freedom from Spain or the creation of an independent republic. The leadership never clarified the exact form an alternative state would take, and the movement certainly should not be subsumed within the Creole-led nationalist movements. Finally, the nationalist perspective also overlooks the problematic relation between the uprising and the War of Independence. The Indian-based movement led by Tupac Amaru terrified non-Indians, inducing them decades later to control the lower classes in the fight against the Spanish and fortifying their belief in the need to create an exclusionary republican state. The Tupac Amaru rebellion was not the failed beginning of a long war against the Spanish, but an entirely different movement.

In part as a reaction to the precursor interpretation, the rebellion has also been presented as an effort to resurrect the Inca Empire (the Tahuantinsuyo). In the eighteenth century, a revival of interest in the Incas took place among descendants of the Inca monarchs as well as among common Indians.[10] The Incas undoubtedly constituted the most important referent for the rebels. José Gabriel insisted on his Inca lineage and adopted the name of one of the martyrs of the conquest, Tupac Amaru, to whom he was related. Two related cautionary points need to be made about neo-Inca nationalism. First, as in any invented tradition, the understanding of the Inca Empire and its usage in social and political movements varied greatly between different social groups. For some members of the "royal" Inca families in Cuzco, their devotion to the Incas paralleled their resistance to Bourbon attempts to limit their prerogatives as a special colonial corporate group. The representations of the Incas sought to affirm their rights as negotiated with the Habsburgs in the sixteenth and seventeenth centuries. For the Indian masses, the Incas could have a more subversive meaning as a world free of colonialism and exploitation. The Bourbon state even used the Incas to justify its own project. In this period, different ways of understanding and using the Inca Empire circulated quite freely in the different social and cultural spheres of Cuzco. Tupac Amaru himself moved in these different spheres, which enabled him to mix the different perspectives on the Incas.[11]

Second, some historians have presented the fascination with the Incas as another indication of enduring Andean memory and tradition.[12] Yet the invocation of the Tahuantinsuyo did not emerge out of some long-term memory, but rather from a reworking of colonial discourse. Their evocation was not external to colonial power relations and ideologies. Although the neo-Inca revival is an important factor in the movement's ideology and timing, it alone is not a sufficient explanation. The rebels did not look solely to the past. Their movement was firmly anchored in the present, addressing contemporary concerns and incorporating late eighteenth-century ideologies. Whereas the nationalist interpretation forces the Tupac Amaru into the nation-state mold, a tendentious anachronism, the Inca revival perspective can overlook the complex political and social objectives of the uprising.

A third perspective does not look to the Inca past or the republican future, but instead places the uprising firmly within the tradition of negotiated relations between the state and the indigenous peasantry. John Phelan has demonstrated how, in the wake of the Tupac Amaru uprising, rebels in New Granada, what became Colombia, based their movement on the venerable "long live the king and death to bad government" motif. The so-called Comunero rebels contended that the state's actions had broken this pact, an unwritten constitution, and thereby jeopardized its legitimacy. In short, the rebellion sought to retain traditional relations rather than overthrow the state.[13] Tupac Amaru's rhetoric partially supports this interpretation as it emphasized allegiance to the king and the legitimacy of the uprising within the colonial pact. Colonial discourse, however, could be subverted: using these terms did not necessarily support colonialism itself. More importantly, as Alberto Flores Galindo has insisted, the rebels' *actions* contradict this interpretation. They were not prepolitical or conservative: they had "undeniable anti-colonial intentions."[14] By executing officials and ransacking estates and mills, the rebels stepped beyond mere renegotiations of the colonial pact. At the same time, they recruited all non-Europeans. No clear alternative to colonialism existed, and they thereby combined Inca restoration, dual monarchies, and fragments of anticolonial thought, but they sought to overturn colonialism in the Andes. The violence that marked the beginning of the uprising, its planning, and its extension throughout and beyond the Peruvian viceroyalty indicate that it was more than a local incident targeting a specific authority or particular abuse. The Tupac Amaru uprising almost immediately surpassed the boundaries of the more typical revolt.[15]

The eighteenth-century Andean rebellions should not be framed, therefore, solely as failed antecedents to independence movements akin to other mass insurgencies of the Enlightenment era, or as backward-looking restorationist projects, or as more, albeit grandiose, revolts. Instead, these perspectives need to be unified. Although the social base and ideology of the Tupac Amaru uprising were vastly different from the independence movement decades later, it was nonetheless anticolonial. The incorporation of the Incas did not preclude a radical anticolonial movement in line with events in Europe, the United States, and, in the near future, Spanish America. Rebels in the Andes incorporated various traditions and discourses in their questioning of colonial rule. Throughout the rebellion, participants sought to create a mass, anticolonial movement. The uprising must be judged on its own terms, rather than in relation to what occurred decades later in the War of Independence. The rebel leadership, their mass base, their platforms, and the wider global context itself in the Americas and Europe were radically different than those of the Spanish American rebellions of the early nineteenth century. The rebellion itself must be analyzed closely; attention must be paid to what the leadership and the masses sought by participating in the rebellion, which in turn requires understanding the economic, political, and social context of Cuzco in 1780.

CONFLICTS AND CONTEXT

The Bourbon reforms dramatically changed relations between Andean society and the state. Dating from the beginning of the eighteenth century, this series of modifications was implemented in Spain's American holdings primarily during the reign of Charles III, 1759–88. Influenced by Enlightenment thought and compelled by frequent wars with the French and the English to extract more revenue from the American colonies, the Spanish state centralized its colonial administration and increased its demands on the population. Dismantling the Habsburg system, it reduced the number of American-born individuals in the administration and tightened control of the different administrative units. Watched over by the vigilant Bourbons and their key ally, Lima's merchant elite, local and regional officials were forced to depend less on negotiation and more on coercion. Caciques, the intermediary between Andean society and the state, were hard pressed to fulfill the growing demands of the Bourbon state without jeopardizing their legitimacy in local society. The state increased a variety of taxes, improved collection methods, and imposed new monopolies.[16]

Changes in jurisdiction diminished Cuzco's economic and political role in Upper Peru. In 1776, the viceroyalty of Río de la Plata was created, separating Cuzco and the rest of Lower Peru from Potosí and the Titicaca basin.[17] In 1778 a "free trade" policy was enacted that among other initiatives opened Buenos Aires to trade with Spain. Silver extracted from Potosí was channeled through Buenos Aires, which, in turn, marketed imported goods not only in Upper Peru but also in Cuzco and Arequipa. Gold and silver was to be minted in Potosí rather than Lima, and unminted precious metals could not be exported to Lower Peru. Therefore, paying for imports from Cuzco such as textiles, sugar, and coca was increasingly difficult.[18] Like their counterparts in Lima, the Cuzco elite complained about these changes, describing their dire economic consequences and the potential social problems that could ensue.

Fiscal demands on the Andean population increased dramatically with the Bourbon reforms. The *alcabala*, a sales tax paid on most goods traded by non-Indians, rose from 2 to 4 percent in 1772 and to 6 percent in 1776. More importantly, Visitor General José Antonio de Areche arrived in 1777 and enforced the tax's vigorous collection. Customs houses were built throughout the southern Andes.[19] In the second half of the 1770s, products such as coca leaves and social groups previously exonerated from the alcabala, such as artisans, were now taxed. By widening the state's fiscalization of almost all trade, incorporating previously exonerated groups and products, and heightening collection efficiency, the Bourbon reforms angered virtually every group in Peru.[20] The changes were not simply economic. Creoles felt excluded from key administrative positions, and corporate groups, such as artisans or members of the church, had their rights and prerogatives reduced.

The Bourbon reforms greatly increased the tax load extracted from Indians—overturning their exemption from certain taxes, raising their rates, and collecting from them more efficiently. In Peru, the colonial state had long depended on the Indian head tax for a large part of its revenue. Augmenting the state's coffers, therefore, required increasing the pressure on Indians. The collection of the head tax skyrocketed after 1750, multiplying by a factor of sixteen in Cuzco between 1750 and 1820.[21] Indians also faced more than increased sales and head taxes. The *reparto de mercancías* or *repartimiento*, forced sales, was another despised institution condoned by the colonial state. *Corregidores*, local officials usually aligned with powerful merchants and producers, were allowed to oblige Indians to buy products, often at inflated prices.[22] The practice was abolished in the midst of the Tupac Amaru rebellion. As discussed in chapter 3, the Bourbons also chipped away at peasant communities' political autonomy. Caciques had increasing difficulty fulfilling the demands of the state while retaining legitimacy in their communities. Also, the Bourbons sought to replace traditional "ethnic" caciques, often with non-Indians, but in doing so, they sparked bitter battles that raged in the courts for decades and occasionally in the streets. Many displaced or threatened ethnic caciques joined the Tupac Amaru forces.[23]

By the second half of the eighteenth century, Cuzco's comfortable place in the Pan-Andean economy was slipping. The Bourbon reforms, however, were not the sole cause of its economic difficulties or of the widespread disgruntlement. The internal weaknesses of the region's economy and the consequent inability to compete with foreign products also contributed. While the Bourbon "free trade" policy did not open the way for a deluge of imports, products from Upper Peru, the Río de la Plata viceroyalty, and overseas increasingly competed with those of Cuzco.[24] The region suffered from overproduction and saturated markets as prices stagnated and even dropped.[25] Competition increased and prices decreased at the very time when demands by the state were on the rise, making for a combustible situation. Cuzco's major economic ventures such as textiles, coca leaves, and sugar were vulnerable because of their dependence on coerced labor, forced sales (the reparto), and distant markets. To paraphrase Nils Jacobsen and Hans Jürgen Puhle, the region's economy was characterized by a backward infrastructure and exorbitant transportation costs in the rugged Andean terrain. The labor supply was inelastic, and producers depended on forced labor.[26] Rebels vividly expressed the antipathy toward textile mills during the uprising when they burned and sacked dozens of them. In 1780, Cuzco's economy was stagnant, if not in decline, and the bulk of the population blamed the colonial state.

In order to explain rebellions like Tupac Amaru's, ideological as well as economic and political factors need to be examined. Countless scholars have shown that uprisings are not mere reactions to objective conditions. Moral or cultural transgressions are equally if not more important in prompting insubordination.[27] The movement's leaders and followers stitched together its ideology from a number of sources. Well into the nineteenth century, Andean rebels combined currents of Enlightenment and anticolonial thought, neo-Inca nationalism, and more traditional appeals that questioned specific abuses rather than the legitimacy of the state. This mixture constitutes a creative combination of ideologies rather than an inchoate and failed strand of Western thought. Throughout the period studied in this book, the search continued for a subversive platform that adhered to Andean culture.

Neo-Inca nationalism was the most evident ideological source for the Tupac Amaru uprising. Throughout the eighteenth century, the descendants of the Inca elite, particularly the royal caciques of Cuzco, venerated the Incas. They not only celebrated their royal heritage but demanded greater privileges than those already granted caciques.[28] Particularly important for this resurgence was the history of the Inca Empire by Garcilaso de la Vega, *Comentarios Reales,* first published in 1609. The prologue by Andrés González de Barcia in the second edition from 1723 included a prophecy quoted by Sir Walter Raleigh that Inca rule would be restored with the aid of people from England. José Gabriel, who was often referred to as "El Inca," cited this work in his legal efforts to confirm his title as cacique in Lima in the 1770s.[29] On April 13, 1781, shortly after the capture of Tupac Amaru, the bishop of Cuzco, Juan Moscoso, wrote that "If Garcilaso's *Commentaries* had not been the reading and education of the insurgent José Gabriel . . . if these and other lessons of a few renegade authors about the Conquest had not made such a strong impression on the traitor, he would not have undertaken his detestable rebellion."[30] After the rebellion, authorities vigorously censored Garcilaso's work.

As is the case with all nationalist myths, Inca nationalism was the basis for diverse political projects. Ethnic caciques—a category that included distinguished members of the city elite, relatively prosperous entrepreneurs such as Tupac Amaru, and hard-pressed local authorities in distant communities—incorporated the Incas into their opposition to the centralization campaign by the Bourbons. As Flores Galindo has argued, the Indian masses also developed their own interpretation of the Inca Empire, "an egalitarian society, a homogenous world consisting only of *runas* (Andean peasants) in which there would be no great merchants, no colonial authorities, no haciendas, no mines, and those who were then pariahs and wretched would again determine their own destiny . . . the world upside down."[31] The romanticization of the Inca Empire could be used to demand equal rights for the Indian nobility or to justify overthrowing colonialism. Both views would be expressed during the uprising.

Less is known about other ideological influences. People in Lima and Cuzco in the 1770s discussed new ideas emerging primarily from events in Europe and the United States. Yet they did not develop into full-fledged protonationalist beliefs until the publication of the *Mercurio Peruano* in the 1790s, and they only manifested themselves in mass insurrections in the early nineteenth century. Even then, Enlightenment thought and other revolutions as models did not have absolute influence, but instead were combined with other ideologies. Nonetheless, the bits and pieces of Enlightenment thought and the growing dissatisfaction with colonialism rubbed off on Tupac Amaru. They can be considered influences on or sources for, more than causes of, his development as a rebel and ideologue.[32]

In 1777, Tupac Amaru arrived in Lima, where, according to his wife Micaela, "his eyes were opened."[33] He stayed near and apparently frequented the University of San Marcos, where the censorship of the reading and discussion of Enlightenment thought was often circumvented. He befriended Miguel Montiel y Surco, a mestizo from Oropesa, Cuzco, who had visited England, France, and Spain and was an enthusiastic reader of Garcilaso de la Vega. Montiel y Surco introduced José Gabriel to other critics of Spanish colonialism, specifically Creoles opposed to Areche's policies.[34] We can only hypothesize about other possible ideas and influences encountered by José Gabriel. In Lima in this period, intellectuals increasingly questioned the validity of scholasticism, the traditional educational doctrine.[35] Although José Gabriel had access to information about the independence movement in the United States, as the newspaper the *Gazeta* published detailed accounts, it did not constitute an important symbol in the rebellion. It was referred to with more frequency in other conspiracies and revolts in the 1780s.[36] In the latter half of the century, Europeans and Americans fought bitterly over scientific accounts by authors such as Cornélius De Pauw that presented the Old World as superior to the New. Peruvian intellectuals followed and commented upon these debates, but did not play an active role. These discussions, though, could have invigorated José Gabriel's distaste for Europeans.[37] On the other hand, the Creoles' lack of interest in the Indian population—and perhaps their uneasiness with a highland cacique such as José Gabriel—could have strengthened his resolve to lead a Cuzco-based Indian struggle. In sum, he had access to bits and pieces of Enlightenment thought and protonational yearnings, which contributed to his anticolonial leanings.

Other more immediate factors need to be considered in order to understand the Tupac Amaru uprising, particularly José Gabriel's own path toward rebellion. José Gabriel Condorcanqui was born on March 10, 1738, in Surimana, approximately fifty miles southeast of Cuzco. His father, who died in 1750, was the cacique of three towns in the district of Tinta—Surimana, Pampamarca, and Tungasuca. José Gabriel studied in the prestigious school of San Francisco in Cuzco, run by the Jesuits for the offspring of caciques. He inherited 350 mules and used these to work the Cuzco to Upper Peru route. Owning mule trains provided him important contacts throughout this region. As cacique he held the right to land; he also had modest mining interests and coca fields in Carabaya, to the south.[38] He could thus be considered a member of the colonial middle class, with strong ties to the lower and upper classes. He spoke Quechua, which bonded him not only with the Indian majority but also with noble Indians and the many non-Indians who spoke Cuzco's lingua franca. As a cacique of royal Inca lineage, he was a member of a privileged class. For example, he and Gabriel Ugarte Zeliorogo, a distinguished member of Cuzco's city council, called each other cousins, considering themselves part of an extended family.[39] In 1760, he married Micaela Bastidas Puyucahua, a mestiza from Pampamarca, near Tinta, who would be an important commander during the uprising. They had three sons—Hipólito, Fernando, and Mariano.

José Gabriel's enduring problems with authorities over his claims to the cacique office and his extended legal battle over his rights as the descendent of the last Inca deeply embittered him. They also gave him important experience in Lima and elsewhere in using the courts and employing his rhetorical skills about his rights and the exploitation of Indians. In 1766, after years of delay, he was granted the position of cacique that his father and then his older brother had held. Yet in 1769 it was taken away from him, only to be returned in 1771. Conflicts with successive corregidores of the Tinta province, Gregorio de Viana and Pedro Muñoz de Arjona, prompted these delays.[40] It is not surprising that, a decade later, the rebellion targeted corregidores with particular vehemence.

Beginning in 1776, Tupac Amaru battled in the courts with Don Diego Felipe de Betancur over which of them was the legitimate descendent of the last Inca, Tupac Amaru, beheaded by Viceroy Francisco Toledo in 1572. Betancur sought to confirm his royal heritage in order to gain the marquisate of Oropesa, a rich fief dating from the seventeenth century. José Gabriel attempted to prove his descent through his father's family in order to gain prestige and enhance his position in colonial society. Whether he sought to prove his claim to be an Inca in order to justify an uprising that would replace the Spanish monarchy with an Inca one is difficult to ascertain. What is clear is that his dealings with the legal system frustrated him. He spent much of 1777 in Lima pleading his case in the courts and to all who were interested.[41] In this period, he also petitioned the viceroy that the Indians of his *cacicazgo* be exonerated from the mita, obligatory labor, in Potosí, noting the terrible working conditions and the lack of men in his district. The recently arrived visitador general, José Antonio de Areche, rejected this request. José Gabriel persisted, gaining the support of other caciques of the Tinta provinces (Canas y Canchis), but again was rebuffed. No decision had been reached in his suit with Betancur when the rebellion began in November 1780.[42] At this time, Tupac Amaru had sufficient motivation to turn against the Spanish state; he also had the contacts and respect necessary to lead a mass rebellion.

In the years preceding the rebellion, the church and the state in Cuzco clashed in a virtual civil war, a situation that could be considered the division within the ruling class that precipitates many social revolutions. In general, the Bourbon state had challenged the Catholic Church's influence in the Americas by expelling the Jesuits in 1767 and much more closely supervising the church's finances. In Cuzco, the conflict was personalized in the clash between two key participants in the Tupac Amaru uprising—the bishop, Juan Manuel Moscoso, and the corregidor of Tinta, Antonio de Arriaga. Moscoso provided some of the most detailed accounts of the uprising in his attempts to absolve himself from accusations of supporting the rebels. The hanging of Arriaga by Tupac Amaru marked the beginning of the rebellion.

In 1779, Moscoso, recently appointed bishop of Cuzco, requested that all priests along the Royal Highway present detailed summaries of the state of their parish. Only the priest of the town of Yauri, Justo Martínez, failed to comply. In late 1779 and early 1780, Moscoso sent commissions to investigate, but their arrival sparked riots in Yauri and Coporaque, towns in the upper provinces to the south of Cuzco, with each side blaming the other for the violence. Moscoso claimed that Arriaga, in an attempt to defend his political and economic interests in the region, directed the resistance to the church representatives. Arriaga contended that Moscoso had overstepped his jurisdiction and supported subversive activities in the region. They both appealed to well-known aversions of the Bourbons: Moscoso to the dislike of omnipotent local officials and Arriaga to the opposition to seemingly disruptive priests. Just when the matter had reached the courts, Arriaga was executed by Tupac Amaru. The timing bolstered the accusations that Moscoso had aided the rebels, so he spent the following years defending himself from these charges. During the rebellion, he wrote lengthy and hostile reports on the uprising and raised money for royalist forces.[43] The church-state division resurfaced during the uprising when many priests supported the rebels.[44]

Dozens of riots and revolts took place in the late 1770s and 1780 in different areas of the Andes, several of them just months before the outset of the Tupac Amaru rebellion. The ones that occurred in Arequipa and the city of Cuzco in 1780 expressed the widespread furor over the fiscal reforms imposed by Visitador Areche. As multiethnic movements employing an eclectic ideology, they clearly paralleled the Tupac Amaru movement. Although some indications that José Gabriel himself was involved in these uprisings are questionable, the revolts themselves no doubt influenced the nature and timing of the uprising that began in the Tinta province in November 1780.

In the late 1770s, Visitador Areche supervised the severe tightening of the tax system. He raised taxes—in particular, the alcabala, the sales tax—expanded the number of products and merchants encompassed by these taxes, and improved collection procedures. The changes were rapid and drastic.[45] The measures affected virtually everyone in late colonial society—including estate owners, displaced Creole authorities, lower-class merchants, and Indians. The fact that the new rates and the customs houses targeted merchants helps explain the surprising speed with which news, rumors, and general disgruntlement were spread. In this era, merchants linked different regions not only with products but with information. It should not be forgotten that Tupac Amaru himself owned mule trains. The fiscal reforms of the 1770s prompted different forms of insubordination. In 1774, a riot broke out against the recently inaugurated customs house in Cochabamba, Upper Peru. A disturbance took place in Maras in the Urubamba province outside of Cuzco in 1777, and groups attacked the customs house in La Paz in 1777 and

1780.[46] The riots or conspiracies in Arequipa and Cuzco in 1780, however, were the most important antecedents for the Tupac Amaru uprising. On January 1, 1780, a handwritten lampoon, a *pasquinade,* was affixed to the cathedral door in Arequipa, which proclaimed: "Quito and Cochabamba arose / And why not Arequipa? / Necessity obliges us / To take the life of the customs house administrator / And all those who gave him refuge / Watch out!"

On January 5, more pasquinades were placed. One was directed against Arequipa's corregidor, Baltasar de Sematnat, who had offered a five-hundred-peso reward for the arrest of the author of the January 1 verses. It read:

> Take care of your head
> And also your companions'
> The señores customs officials,
> Who without charity
> Have come to this city
> From distant foreign lands
> To tear out our entrails,
> Without pity moving them,
> To all see us exclaim:
> Because it is certain and true
> That if there is not an example
> Of killing these thieves,
> They will strip us clean;
> And thus, noble citizens,
> In your hands lies
> The chance to enjoy without taxes
> All your possessions,
> Taking the lives of these
> horrible, infamous robbers.
> . . .
> But we only say, Long Live,
> Long Live the Great Charles III
> Death to his evil henchmen
> and also to bad government.

The verses initially attacked the individuals who were executing the new tax policies but exonerated the Spanish Crown: "We put lampoons / No, We Don't Deny It / But Without Disobeying King Carlos."[47] Yet the "long live the king and death to bad government" mode, so common in insurgent thought in the early modern period, did not persist. Pasquinades found on January 12 asked, "For how long, citizens / of Arequipa, are you to be / the target of so many taxes / forced upon you by the King?"[48] The anonymous author also contrasted the Spanish and English monarchs: "The King of England / Loves his Subjects / In contrast to Spain / I speak of King Carlos."[49] Other verses complimented England as well, at a time when Spain had secretly allied with France in order to defend its holdings in North America and to regain Gibraltar. Although moderately successful overseas, Spain was unable to defeat the British navy in Gibraltar. The lampoons also referred to replacing Carlos III with an Inca king, Casimiro.[50]

The pasquinades were most pointed about recent fiscal policy, denouncing the customs houses and the sales tax, and ridiculing and threatening those who carried out these policies.[51] They clearly sought to induce a wide sector of the population to participate in the protests. The lampoon directed at Sematnat ended, "Do not be afraid / Oh, noble citizens / help us with your efforts / Noblemen, plebes, and elderly."[52] The pasquinades combined different elements of anticolonial thought—the critique of the king's wayward representatives and subsequently of the king himself, Inca restoration, popular religion—and specific grievances (such as the one about customs houses) in what one author calls "a search for political alternatives to the colonial state."[53] The rebels were not alone in using verse. Defenders of the status quo replied in a long poem that described recent "criminal" events and posed the question, "What is this, Ignorant Plebes / What fantastic nonsense / has stained in an instant / the loyalty of so many centuries?"[54]

The "rebellion of the pasquinades" moved beyond rhetoric. On January 5 and 8, guards noted strangers on horseback and on foot passing through the city at night. The numbers of these phantom riders increased in the following days, compounding the fear of violence prompted by the lampoons. On the thirteenth, a group attacked the customs house. Underestimating the opposition, Juan Bautista Pando, the administrator of the customs house and the primary target of the lampoons' barbs and threats, refused to alter his energetic collection efforts. On the fourteenth, a crowd of approximately three thousand rebels again attacked the customs house, ransacking its offices. Pando and his colleagues barely escaped. Corregidor Sematnat's impromptu abolition of Areche's policies did not appease the growing band of rebels, described as a motley group of mestizos, Indians, and some whites.[55] In the following days, riots continued as groups attacked the corregidor's house and the jail. On the sixteenth, a militia unit held the city against the rebel forces with great difficulty. Once the city was secured, however, they rounded up suspects, and hanged many of them. Government forces singled out for punishment nearby Indian towns suspected of supporting the disturbances.[56]

Some documentation suggests that Tupac Amaru was present in the Arequipa disturbances.[57] Even if the evidence is not true, his political designs were no doubt influenced by these events. News reached Cuzco quickly. Already on January 14, a pasquinade appeared in Cuzco, stating, "Arequipa Victorious / Arequipa spoke before Cuzco, head of this kingdom, where no one heard the pleas of the poor; but it is now time to compete with our cries, Long Live the King and Death to Bad Government and Tyranny."[58] The document complained of royal monopolies and the new taxes, and derided Areche. Appealing to the city's enduring rivalry with Arequipa, it ended, "It is better to die killing than live suffering and we should not be less than those of Arequipa."[59]

In January 1780, a customs house was established in Cuzco. It drew the ire of a broad segment of Cuzco. One document called the employees "subtle thieves," complaining that they subjected Indians to particular exploitation and abuse.[60] The city council noted nervously the growing number of lampoons against the customs house, which it claimed "had prompted the tumult in Arequipa." Describing the threat posed by the urban plebeians and the population of Cuzco's fourteen provinces, the council called for patrols, instructing them to pay special attention to questionable gatherings.[61] Their suspicions were well founded.

On March 13, an Augustinian priest, Gabriel Castellanos, alerted the authorities about a broad conspiracy in Cuzco that he had been told about in confession during Lent. Pedro Sahuaraura, the cacique of Oropesa, also apparently betrayed the conspirators.[62] The leaders were quickly apprehended. Eleven out of twelve were Creoles or mestizos, while one was an Indian cacique, Bernardo Tambohuacso Pumayala, from the nearby town of Pisac. Four of them were silver makers, and several were estate owners—both occupations affected by the recent fiscal vigor.[63] In their testimonies, the defendants repeated the thrust of the lampoons—their opposition to the customs house and resentment toward Lima and Spaniards—and conceded that the movement sought to incorporate Creoles, mestizos, and Indians. Connections can be found with the Tupac Amaru movement as some of the accused, or their relatives, participated in the larger rebellion months later. Tupac Amaru's brother-in-law, Antonio Bastidas, claimed that when the rebel leader "knew that Tambohuacso had been hanged, he said that he couldn't understand how the Indians let this happen."[64] Arriaga and others accused Bishop Moscoso of abetting the Plateros ("silver makers") rebels, deepening the animosity between the corregidor and the bishop.[65]

In Upper Peru, a massive uprising alternately paralleled, joined, and contravened the Tupac Amaru rebellion. The Tupac Katari rebellion was actually a succession of uprisings. From 1777 to 1780, the community of Macha, in the Chayanta province near Potosí, fought the corregidor, the non-Indian cacique, and other local authorities in the courts. The leader of the Indians, Tomás Katari, who claimed to be the community's legitimate cacique, was imprisoned in late 1779 and then liberated by force en route to trial. The community took their case to the high court in the city of La Plata. By mid-August 1780, relations between Indians and local authorities became increasingly violent as the corregidor was captured and then freed. Both sides contended that they had the support of viceroyalty authorities and were forced to use coercion to implement these rulings. In September, Katari declared himself governor of Macha and led the expulsion of non-Indian authorities from the region. He emphasized his submission to the Crown and presented his efforts as the justifiable implementation of rulings by the *audiencia*. On January 15, 1781, however, he was assassinated. His brothers, Dámaso and Nicolás, initially replaced him as leaders, and in March, taking the name Tupac Katari, Julian Apasa assumed command of the increasingly widespread rebellion in Upper Peru. It remains unclear whether José Gabriel had ties to Katari in November 1780.[66]

THE GREAT REBELLION

Despite the disturbances in Cuzco, Arequipa, and elsewhere in the late 1770s and early 1780, the Tupac Amaru uprising took the colonial state by surprise, especially the corregidor of Tinta, Antonio de Arriaga. On

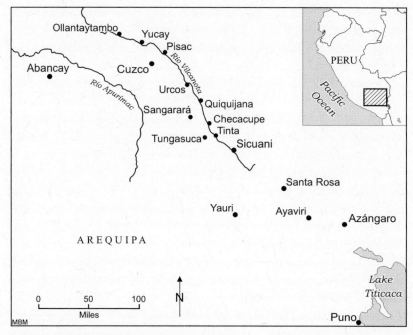

3. Major Sites of the Tupac Amaru Rebellion

November 4, in the home of the priest of Yanaoca, Carlos José Rodríguez y Avila, Arriaga and José Gabriel celebrated Saint Charles's feast
day—the priest and the king's name day. Although José Gabriel and
Arriaga were on cordial enough relations to break bread together, they
had fought for years over José Gabriel's cacique rights.[67] Feigning that
he had an unexpected but urgent errand in Cuzco, José Gabriel left
early and with a group of his followers waited for Arriaga on the road
to Tinta. They ambushed him that evening, taking him and three aides
to a cell in Tupac Amaru's house in the town of Tungasuca. They forced
Arriaga to write letters to his treasurer, requesting money and arms
(with the contrivance that he was planning an expedition against pirates
on the coast), and subsequently to a colleague for shackles, a bed, and
the keys to the Tinta town hall. Under duress, he also ordered that all
inhabitants of the region meet in the town of Tungasuca within twenty-
four hours. Arriaga's imprisonment was initially kept secret from Cuzco
authorities, and Tupac Amaru succeeded in gaining the money, arms,
supplies, and audience necessary to launch the revolt.[68]

An unusual observer, Santiago Bolaños, a Genovese sausage maker who lived in Sicuani, described the events of these days. Upon arriving in Tungasuca, where thousands were already congregated, he asked about Arriaga and was told of his imprisonment in Tupac Amaru's house. Bolaños thought, "it [Arriaga's imprisonment] must be following a supreme order," but he overheard some people comment that it was "by order of the King."[69] Bolaños's Spanish friends told him that the punishment was perhaps due to Arriaga's crimes as governor of the Tucumán province in the Río de la Plata viceroyalty.[70] On November 9, "in Spanish and the Indian language" Tupac Amaru instructed the Spaniards, mestizos, and Indians to line up in columns, then allowed them to disassemble. The following day, they marched to the sounds of drums and fifes to a knoll where gallows had been set up. One witness calculated that there were four thousand Indians, all armed with slings. A *cholo* (a mestizo with cultural ties to both Indian and Spanish cultures) began to read a proclamation in Spanish, but was instructed to read it in Quechua. Bolaños requested a translation. The document stated that "Through the King it has been ordered that there no longer be alcabala, customs, or the Potosí mita and that Don Antonio Arriaga lose his life because of his harmful behavior." Another witness explained that Tupac Amaru called Arriaga "harmful and tyrannical" and pledged to "raze the *obrajes* [textile mills], stop the mita to Potosí, the alcabala, customs, and the reparto de mercancías, and that Indians be freed to live in union and harmony with the Creoles."[71] At this point, when the rebel leaders had mobilized thousands of troops and espoused a belligerent rhetoric, it is clear that their plans went beyond punishing a venal authority and negotiating improved conditions.

Rebels led Arriaga to the gallows. In the first attempt, the rope broke, temporarily saving him. When the executioners replaced it with one used for roping mules, the execution succeeded. Bolaños heard rumors that Tupac Amaru intended to destroy textile mills and capture six more corregidores, and that he threatened to chase anyone opposing him throughout the entire kingdom. Bolaños returned to Sicuani confused by the events he had witnessed. He decided to stay in town but was convinced by Don Ramón Vera, the holder of the local tobacco monopoly, to flee as soon as possible. Although Bolaños might appear dimwitted, many individuals who had witnessed the hanging of the corregidor were unsure at this point what was to follow. As one report noted, "the unimaginable cruelty of a Corregidor executed in the center of his province by one of his subjects, and by his beneficiaries and confidants, in the presence of those who respected and feared him" flabbergasted the troops.[72]

Tupac Amaru took immediate and decisive action. Early on November 12, his forces, estimated in the thousands, reached Quiquijana, the capital of the Quispicanchis province in the Vilcamayo Valley. The corregidor, Fernando Cabrera, had already fled, indicating the rapid spread of rumors. Tupac Amaru heard mass and returned to Tungasuca. On his way, he attacked the textile mills of Pomacanchi and Parapicchu. He opened up the jail housed in the mill of Pomacanchi and, after asking if the mill owner owed anyone money, distributed some of the cloth and thousands of pounds of wool to his brother, Juan Bautista Tupac Amaru, a priest, and his Indian followers. One report noted that "the resentful Indians were about to burn the mill, cheered on by the prisoners."[73] Indians despised the mills because of their despicable working conditions and their use as jails. Also, the obrajes played a central role in the reparto because their owners acquired wool at artificially low prices and sold fabric at high ones. A number of priests received José Gabriel on his return to Tungasuca. One, however, wrote him a letter, questioning whether the Crown had actually sanctioned his activities. Tupac Amaru answered sharply, ending his letter on this ominous note: "I can see that you have a great deal of affection for the thieving corregidores, who, without fear of God, imposed unbearable jobs on the Indians with the reparto, robbing them with their long hands. Some priests joined in, and they will be expelled from their jobs as thieves, and then they will know my power."[74] On November 12, the town council met in Cuzco to discuss the "horrible excess" in Tungasuca.[75] News of Arriaga's execution had arrived.

The corregidor of Cuzco, Fernando Inclán Valdéz, established a war council that included some of Cuzco's leading citizens. They raised funds and on November 13 sent an emissary to Lima to request aid. Don Tiburcio Landa organized a company composed of local militia members, volunteers from Cuzco, and approximately eight hundred Indians and mestizos procured by the caciques of Oropesa, Pedro Sahuaraura and Ambrosio Chillitupa. On November 17, they reached Sangarará, a small town north of Tinta. Reports vary about the events of the next twenty-four hours, but both those sympathetic to the rebels and those loyal to the colonial state seem to have agreed that the Tupac Amaru forces routed Landa's forces.

According to one report, when the sentinels reported no sign of the enemy, Landa's company camped for the evening, more concerned about an impending snowstorm than the enemy. At four in the morning, they awoke to find themselves surrounded. Landa and his troops took refuge in the church. Tupac Amaru commanded them to capitulate and instructed the priest and his aide to leave. When these instructions were disobeyed, he ordered all Creoles and women to abandon the church, indicating that an attack was imminent. Landa and his forces prevented anyone from leaving, and several died in the ensuing chaos. Their gunpowder caught fire, burning much of the church's ceiling and causing one wall to cave in. By now desperate, they fired their cannon and charged. Greatly outnumbered and outpositioned, hundreds of Landa's troops were killed. The report calculated 576 dead, including more than 20 Europeans. Twenty-eight wounded Creoles were treated and freed.[76]

The survivors who fought for the Spanish gave a more detailed account, blaming Tupac Amaru himself for the damage to the church and for the violence. Bartolomé Castañeda contended that upon arrival, Landa secured the support of Indians from Sangarará. He also claimed that the commanders realized the enemy was near and debated about whether to set up camp on one of the surrounding hills or to settle in or near the well-fortified church. They chose the church and sought refuge from the cold evening, which proved to be a fatal mistake. Tupac Amaru's troops slipped into the adjoining cemetery and bombarded the enemy with rocks from their slings. Landa's artillery was useless because of the walls separating them from the cemetery.[77] One soldier was killed in the stampede into the church. Castañeda claimed that the Tupac Amaru forces deliberately set the church on fire. Desperate, many of the soldiers confessed to the busy priest. When forced to abandon the church, they were killed by stones and spears. Castañeda saved himself by hiding in a small chapel. He calculated that at least three hundred of his comrades died, most of them subsequently stripped by the Tupac Amaru troops. He guessed that there were six thousand Indians in the surrounding hills and far-reaching support for the rebels in much of the region.[78]

An account given by the chaplain of Landa's forces, Juan de Mollinedo, provides more details about the Sangarará battle and depicts the panic and hatred felt by the troops. In his report, he notes that an award was offered in Cuzco for Tupac Amaru, dead or alive, which spurred Landa's company to hasten their expedition. After Landa had won the debate over whether to set up base in the church or outside of town, false alarms woke up the troops several times. Mollinedo describes the frustration when the Indians took the adjoining cemetery and reports that one soldier was blinded by a rock propelled from a sling. He details the heroics of Landa and other leaders, who fought on after they were shot. Many were killed by the fire in the church, blamed on Tupac Amaru, and those men who fled "the voracious flames fell into the hands of the no less voracious rebels. The universal slaughter, the pitiful groans of the dying, the bloodthirstiness of the enemy, the fragments of flames—in short, everything that occurred that unfortunate day provoked horror and commiseration, sentiments never felt by the rebels; blinded by fury and thirsty for blood, they only thought of stabbing all the whites."[79] Mollinedo tabulates 395 dead in the battlefields, plus an incalculable number incinerated in the church. He puts Tupac Amaru's forces at twenty thousand Indians and four hundred mestizos. After some mistreatment at the hands of his captors, Tupac Amaru himself freed Mollinedo in deference to his role as chaplain.

Sangarará was an overwhelming but in some ways costly victory for Tupac Amaru. In defeating a well-armed contingent from Cuzco, he demonstrated to his growing number of followers their collective military might and added hundreds of firearms to his arsenal. The events in Sangarará were told and retold throughout the region, but the Spanish quickly incorporated the debacle into their propaganda. In Cuzco, Bishop Moscoso excommunicated Tupac Amaru for the "atrocious crime" of burning a church, and from this time forward, the colonial state never tired of presenting him as a sacrilegious traitor.[80] Moreover, the state propagated an interpretation of the Sangarará battle similar to Mollinedo's account: thousands of bloodthirsty Indians murdered non-Indians who had taken refuge in a church. Although this presentation of the uprising as an irrational caste war impeded Tupac Amaru's efforts to gain the support of Creoles and other influential non-Indians, in the short term the Sangarará battle gave him an air of invincibility that commanded respect and support from the Indian masses.

By mid-November, people throughout the Cuzco region, and soon elsewhere inside and outside of the Peruvian viceroyalty, wondered who the rebels were, what they were after, how strong they were, where they were based, and who supported them. In constant edicts and letters to emissaries, Tupac Amaru addressed many of these questions. In this initial phase, he pledged in the name of the king to expel all corregidores and Spaniards and to abolish a number of exploitative institutions. His proclamations invariably began with some variation of "I have royal orders." For example, an edict dated November 15 began, "the King has ordered me to proceed extraordinarily against several corregidores and their lieutenants, for legitimate reasons that are for now reserved."[81] Rebel leaders gradually shifted away from invoking the Hispanic monarchy and began to call upon the Incas. After the battle of Sangarará, José Gabriel and Micaela commissioned a portrait that presented them as the Inca king and queen (qoya).[82] In the edicts and speeches, however, Tupac Amaru and the other leaders emphasized their goal to remove wayward officials and their support for King Charles.

These communiqués need to be read critically. The rebels' insistence on their support of and by the king did not necessarily legitimate colonialism or indicate José Gabriel's "reformist" demands. Any subversive movement usually attempts to maximize its support without attracting the unbridled opposition of the state. In this case, Tupac Amaru sought not only to incorporate as many people as possible, but also, with his moderate and even vague rhetoric, to delay the full-scale wrath of the colonial state. This interpretation, however, implies a level of intentionality that cannot be confirmed. It would be more correct to understand his rhetoric as a subversion of dominant paradigms. A variety of scholars working with the concept of hegemony have demonstrated that the discourse of counterhegemonic projects does not come from outside the dominant discourse, but rather turns it on its head.[83] José Gabriel and other commanders emphasized that their "rights" within colonialism had been systematically breached. They were not attempting to return to some sort of benevolent Habsburgian pact, but rather trying to defeat the Bourbon project. Using the very discourse of colonialism made their movement even more seditious. The vagaries of colonial rule and the disjunction between discourse and practice made it easy prey for this type of subversion. For example, the term *bad government* clearly lends itself to a variety of understandings; it is polysemous. Fighting in the name of the king did not necessarily mean adhesion to colonialism. Examining the rebels' actions can help clarify the significance of their rhetoric. In this case, when the rebels were destroying estates and chasing authorities, the struggle was blatantly subversive.

Tupac Amaru created a protonational ideology that sought to unite all of the different ethnic groups born in Peru against Spaniards or Europeans. He and other ideologues repeatedly presented the Creoles and mestizos as *paisanos,* or compatriots. They did not address a *patria chica,* a narrow homeland, but rather the entire Peruvian viceroyalty and beyond. On November 21, Tupac Amaru underlined his aim not to harm the Creoles in any way, but rather "to live [with them] like brothers, congregated as a single body, destroying the Europeans."[84] They presented Spaniards, *chapetones,* as the enemy. In a document calling for recruits, he complained of "hostilities and abuse coming from Europeans."[85] In the midst of the Sangarará battle, Tupac Amaru decreed that he would "extinguish" the reparto and Europeans, and retain only the head tax, which would be decreased by 50 percent. Mollinedo considered this decree devious propaganda to isolate the Spanish from the Creoles and mestizos.[86] The exact definition of the enemy varied during the rebellion as some Indians extended its meaning to include all non-Indian exploiters.[87] Nonetheless, Tupac Amaru attempted to unify all non-Europeans in the struggle against colonialism.

Tupac Amaru and his commanders moved quickly to expand their base throughout the region to the south of Cuzco. They instructed caciques in Azángaro, Lampa, and Carabaya to "put up gallows, grab corregidores and other Europeans, sequestering all their goods you can find."[88] Countless edicts were sent to explain the rebels' motives—emphasizing their efforts against corrupt authorities and their support for the king—and to call on Indians to join them. Caciques and other intermediaries were used to read these documents to the mostly illiterate Indian masses and to recruit them. Communications were also sent to Upper Peru, northern Argentina, and Chile. The insurgent forces multiplied rapidly, from six thousand in mid-November to upwards of fifty thousand by late December. In late November, one fearful writer commented in a letter to the Cuzco corregidor that Tupac Amaru's army "grows by the minute, its courage increasing in light of its triumphs."[89]

The rebels counted on travelers, above all muleteers, and swift soldiers for coordination and espionage.[90] *Chicherías,* taverns featuring corn beer, were important sites for conspiracies, rumors, shared frustrations, and during the rebellion, strategy sessions. Located along the different trade routes and within the city of Cuzco, these taverns not only put Indians and non-Indians into contact but also linked different regions through talkative travelers.[91] Despite its rapid expansion, which had provoked such panic among Spanish forces, the movement faced problems common to guerrilla insurgents, however. They lacked basic supplies—in this case, food, alcohol, and coca leaves—and were armed mainly with spears, knives, and slingshots.[92] One anonymous document describes how thousands of rebels were slaughtered "because they are simpletons who don't realize that with a sling you can't take on Juan Fusil [John Musket]."[93] They also suffered from disciplinary and communication problems as the leadership found it increasingly difficult to control the actions of its soldiers.

Micaela Bastidas, Tupac Amaru's wife, was in charge of logistics. For many observers, she was the superior commander. After the victory in Sangarará, Tupac Amaru decided to consolidate his forces in the south before turning his attention to the center of colonial power in the Peruvian Andes, the city of Cuzco. He sought to increase his numbers and prevent attacks from Arequipa and Puno. In early December, he commanded the capture of Lampa and Azángaro, cities near Lake Titicaca, and of Coporaque and Yauri, cities in Cuzco's upper provinces. Micaela remained in Tungasuca, by this time the movement's headquarters. She coordinated with the different elements of the movement, organized the movement of supplies and troops, and kept close tabs on her husband, urging him to hurry the attack on Cuzco. On December 6, she wrote him that the soldiers were getting restless and would soon return to their towns. She warned him to be careful and noted her desperation: "I am capable of turning myself over to the enemy so they kill me, because I see your lack of enthusiasm about such a grave affair, thus putting everyones' life in danger, and we're in the midst of the enemy and not only are our lives in danger, but thanks to you those of my children and the rest on our side."[94] She sought to take Cuzco before reinforcements arrived from Lima. Micaela Bastidas did not hold such an important position merely because of her marriage. Many other women formed part of the rebellion's leadership. For example, Tomasa Condemayta, the *cacica* of Acos, organized and led troops. On December 9, she complained that with "the Inca far away," the movement was weakening.[95]

Although the Tupac Amaru forces had proceeded to the Lake Titicaca area after they hanged Antonio de Arriaga, their base remained in the Vilcanota Valley to the southeast of the city of Cuzco, where the rebellion had begun. Bishop Moscoso called the Vilcanota Valley "the throat of all the kingdom" and the "nerve center of the revolution."[96] Particularly important were the provinces of Quispicanchis, Chumbivilcas, and above all Canas y Canchis (or Tinta), where Tupac Amaru "had complete support of his home province."[97] Linking Cuzco with Upper Peru, the Royal Highway ran along this river. Many of the communities that supported Tupac Amaru actively participated in the transregional commercial circuit. As Flores Galindo has noted, members of these communities do not fit the stereotype of miserable, impoverished peasants.[98] Tupac Amaru himself was from this region, worked his mules there, and had extensive business and family contacts. He had close ties to dozens of caciques, who proved to be important supporters.[99] He counted on three overlapping recruiting advantages: kinship ties throughout the Vilcanota Valley; connections with other caciques, many of whom had worked with him and followed his legal efforts; and contacts throughout the region due to his work as a merchant and his duties as a cacique to procure mita laborers for the Potosí mines. Resistance to the movement was based in the city of Cuzco and in the Sacred Valley to the north of the city, where the majority of the caciques opposed Tupac Amaru.

The movement's leadership was socially heterogeneous. O'Phelan Godoy counted nineteen Spaniards or Creoles, twenty-nine mestizos, seventeen Indians, four Negroes or mulattos, and three of undeclared ethnicity among those individuals who were tried for directing the rebellion. They came from more than a dozen different provinces in Peru, and a few were from Chile, Río de la Plata, and Spain.[100] One loyalist accused Tupac Amaru of bringing in "Indians, and mestizos and Creoles, who he fools with the fallacy that he will not harm them or damage the Church, and that he will pursue and exterminate only Europeans."[101] Among the seventy most prominent defendants, fifteen professions or economic activities can be found—with farmers, artisans, and muleteers making up just more than half of the total. These data confirm the argument by many authors that the leadership was formed by a colonial middle class, a group that, although not poor, was excluded from powerful economic and political circles.[102]

Community Indians made up the bulk of the Tupac Amaru forces, primarily established *originarios* (natives) rather than *forasteros* (outsiders). As noted, most came from the Vilcanota Valley. Women were well represented in both the leadership and the fighting forces.[103] The rebels' motivations are more difficult to pinpoint. Their hatred for the colonial state and its representatives was made quite plain in their actions. There is no doubt that the heightened demands of the state helped spark the conflict. The rebels were not, however, merely reacting to state policies. Much of the fighting was personal as they punished abusive corregidores and caciques, or burnt down textile mills, acting on local conflicts that in many cases had been developing for years. As is usually true of peasant movements, their fervor waned as they moved farther away from their own communities and grievances. Yet Tupac Amaru did manage to organize units that moved throughout the Cuzco region. Although part of their motivation was no doubt the spoils of war, they were not mere criminals as the Spanish state contended.

The case of the unfortunate Esteban Castro highlights how disgruntlement over colonial policy, the appeal of Tupac Amaru himself, and circumstance brought some people into the conflict. Structural changes and local conflicts are not the only factors that need to be considered to explain rebel activities. One of Tupac Amaru's emissaries chanced upon Castro, a muleteer, in late November and asked him to patrol the hills of the Quispicanchis province. After a couple days of tedious sentry duty, Castro decided to tag along with Tupac Amaru supporters from different towns in the Vilcanota Valley. He dropped out after a few days, though, because his mule was tired, and he returned to his hometown of Surimana, where he was subsequently captured. When asked why he joined the rebels and thus broke with "the legality of our Catholic King," he responded, "because a decree was published that expressed that there would no longer be corregidores, repartimientos, customs, and alcabala, and that only he [Tupac Amaru], as a little King, would have to be obeyed." Castro then claimed he abandoned the movement by December 1780. Although he denied that he supported Tupac Amaru, he did note that when he was a sentry, "he felt like grabbing all the Spaniards that passed that road and sending them to the Pomacanche textile mill." If Castro was downplaying his role in the rebellion in order to save himself, he did not succeed in camouflaging his hatred for Spaniards and the mills. He was hanged.[104]

After the Sangarará battle, panic swept the city of Cuzco. Authorities brought out the two most venerated religious images in Cuzco, Señor de los Temblores (Our Lord of the Earthquakes) and Mamacha Belén (Our Lady of Bethlehem), for processions to ward off the rebels and, more realistically, to discourage the lower classes, including the city's substantial Indian population, from supporting the insurgents. In a letter dated November 17, Bishop Moscoso expressed contempt and nervous distrust toward the lower classes, sentiments that lingered in the region for decades.[105] He noted that although "Indians should not be censured due to their imbecility and rudeness, I have put decrees against the Rebel on the doors of all the churches in this city." He contended that "all of this help is needed quickly to protect this city, which is the key to the kingdom. Cuzco lacks arms and people who use them, as only Indians, cholos, and mestizos abound here, and they, sympathetic to the larceny of the Rebel, will abandon us and pass over to the other side."[106] On December 1, the corregidor of Cuzco estimated that he could count on only twelve or thirteen hundred troops to defend the city, whereas Tupac Amaru had more than forty thousand as well as reserves coming from the provinces to the south. He doubted that an attack could be withstood.[107] The residents of Cuzco were not alone in their fear. For example, an official of Abancay, the province west of Cuzco, described the "panicky terror" of the people in nearby towns. Other authorities nervously chronicled the throngs joining the rebels, the intimidation of royalists, and the speed of José Gabriel and his forces. They feared for their lives.[108]

When the rebels entered a town, they often jailed royalist officials, including caciques, and set up fear-inspiring gallows. For example, when Tupac Amaru and six thousand Indians reached Velille in the Chumbivilcas province on November 27, they sacked the house of the corregidor and distributed his belongings, named new authorities, opened up the jail, and destroyed the roll used for punishment.[109] As the waters began to rise with the onset of the rainy season toward the end of the year, the rebels took control of many bridges. They also watched over roads and trails, thus gaining the upper hand in communications and intelligence.[110] Toward the end of 1780, however, Tupac Amaru's seemingly inexorable offensive slowed slightly. Royalist forces finally showed themselves capable of confronting the rebels, and the intense propaganda against José Gabriel and his "hordes" began to take effect. Moreover, reinforcements were soon to arrive. On December 20 and 21, the rebels were defeated outside of Ocongate in the Quispicanchis province. The outnumbered government forces used their firepower to divide the insurgents and kill hundreds of them. Bishop Moscoso, who provided the best account of this battle, chided the rebels for their wanton violence, describing how they had murdered all the "Spaniards" they had come across, regardless of age or gender. The corregidor's soldiers displayed the heads of some of the rebels on lances, exhibiting them in the streets of Cuzco. Moscoso applauded this action, deeming it "very opportune for warning the plebians, and for correcting in part their bad attitude."[111]

Pro-government letters and reports, many of them widely disseminated, depicted the Indians as cowardly thieves who temporarily joined the movement in order to loot and pillage, and Moscoso emphasized that the rebel troops were undisciplined. This interpretation sought to ease the panic caused by rumors of from fifty to one hundred thousand rebels controlling Cuzco's southern provinces and soon turning their attention toward the city itself. Casting the rebels as violent criminals rather than as subversive rebels, it also justified full-scale repression against them and discouraged non-Indians from supporting them. Yet Moscoso also noted that by avoiding direct confrontation with royalist troops and by retreating quickly, "like flies swatted away from a plateful of sweets," the rebels were difficult to defeat. He described their guerrilla tactics with frustration and good military sense.[112]

On December 17, Tupac Amaru returned from his foray into the Lake Titicaca area. Two days later, when he heard reports that auxiliary royalist troops were on their way from Buenos Aires, he finally heeded Micaela Bastidas's insistent call to attack Cuzco. He left Tungasuca with four thousand troops, recruiting en route to Cuzco. The rebels reportedly sacked numerous haciendas. Tupac Amaru's contemporaries, as well as generations of scholars, have criticized him for the delay in attacking Cuzco. They contend that if he had heeded Micaela, the outcome would have been different, but his intent was to extend territorial control and prevent a counterattack from the south before he confronted the bulk of the Spanish forces in the key city of Cuzco.[113]

News of the rebels' approach petrified much of the city's population. One commentator noted that the arrival of royalist troops only confirmed the rumors of the subversives' strength. The government attempted to control and limit information circulating in the city of

Cuzco about the Tupac Amaru forces.[114] The royalist forces were not unprepared. In December, Moscoso led a successful drive to raise money for the city's defense. Reinforcements arrived from Abancay, and more importantly, a well-armed expedition from Lima reached Cuzco on January 1.[115] Many citizens called for a negotiated settlement as they nervously wondered about what the urban lower classes would do when the city was attacked. The arrival of reinforcements tipped the scales to favor the view of the hard-liners who rejected negotiations.

Tupac Amaru began the siege of Cuzco on December 28. His original plans for a pincer movement were frustrated when columns led by Diego Cristóbal Tupac Amaru and Andrés Castelo were prevented from reaching the city.[116] He stationed his troops on a bluff to the west of the city and sent negotiators to the city council with a letter calling for immediate surrender. The document noted his Inca blood and the actions he had taken against the corregidores. He listed his plans as the suppression of the corregidor office, the end of the reparto, the nomination in each province of a conscientious Indian mayor, and the creation of a *real audiencia* in Cuzco.[117] The city council and Bishop Moscoso rebuffed his envoys.

After more than a week of frustrated negotiation and skirmishes, the main battle for Cuzco began on January 8. The rebel forces sought to besiege the city and to control the northern entryway that linked Cuzco with the grain-producing valleys to the west and Lima. Militia troops, particularly the merchants' battalion, charged up the steep hills surrounding the city to confront the insurgents, and diverse companies stopped the rebels' occasional charges toward the city. Thousands of loyal Indians from Paruro bolstered the royalist forces. The cannons and artillery used by the rebels repeatedly misfired because of the treachery, according to some, of one of the few Spaniards who fought for the rebels, Juan Antonio de Figueroa. On January 10, the rebels, numbering thirty thousand according to one report, withdrew. Casualties had been light on both sides. Numerous hypotheses have been presented for this turn of events. The royalists had placed thousands of Indians at the front line, and perhaps Tupac Amaru wanted to avoid their slaughter. He apparently wanted to take the city without violence, to enter triumphantly, which was impossible at this moment.[118] His troops were also dangerously low on food, prompting many to slip away in the evenings.[119] Although the rebellion was far from over, the Spanish now went on the attack.

After the failed siege of Cuzco, Diego Cristóbal Tupac Amaru led an offensive to the north and east of Cuzco—to Calca, Urubamba, and then Paucartambo. The royalist cacique, Mateo García Pumacahua, pursued him. José Gabriel returned to Tungasuca, while some of his more adept commanders campaigned in the upper provinces to the south. At this point, divisions within the Tupac Amaru forces became apparent. In late January, Micaela received reports that several towns in Chumbivilcas had turned against the rebels. Other commanders sent her prisoners accused of spying for the government.[120] Diego Cristóbal complained about the excesses of his troops. Official sources gleefully publicized reports of large-scale desertions, particularly among non-Indians.[121]

Flores Galindo has identified two forces within the rebel movement that were increasingly at odds: "the national project of the indigenous aristocracy and the class (or ethnic) one that emerged in the course of the rebels' struggle." Their different uses of violence widened this schism between the leadership and the followers. Tupac Amaru and Micaela knew that attacks against Creoles and especially against priests, women, or other "noncombatants" would drive non-Indians away, thus making a multiethnic movement impossible. Yet they were unable to control the diverse groups that operated under their banner, a weakness exploited by the government.[122] Tupac Amaru, Micaela, and the other commanders led forces that executed Spanish authorities, sieged haciendas and textile mills, and attacked those who attempted to stop them. Rituals such as the execution of Arriaga highlighted Tupac Amaru's regal power. The rebels' use of violence harmonized with their presentation of the uprising as an effort against malevolent colonial practice, their wrath limited to the wayward Spanish. The Indian masses, however, at times employed a much broader definition of the enemy, one that could sometimes include all non-Indians. The violence itself thus went beyond the mere extermination of the enemy.

In order to understand better the violence of the rebellion, the military encounters themselves need to be reviewed. Despite the high number of troops on both sides, guerrilla incursions more than large-scale battles characterized the confrontations. The topography of the Andes, with its high peaks and narrow valleys, helps explain the low numbers of combatants in any given battle. The rebels preferred the higher passes and trails, using their knowledge of the terrain and recognizing their inferiority in arms.[123] In many of the rebels' victories, they seized a town, estate, or mill with little opposition. In others, they attacked in waves. Spanish accounts emphasized the persistence of the rebel attackers and the painful effects of their main weapon, slings. They also stressed the importance of women in collecting rocks to be flung and in slowing royalist charges with sharpened animal bones in fierce hand-to-hand combat.[124] The royalist commander Pumacahua, the cacique of Chincheros who would return to prominence in 1815, helped turn the tide against the rebels by adopting the guerrilla strategy they had used so successfully.

Even in the heady period before the siege of Cuzco, Tupac Amaru's forces occasionally disobeyed his commands to control their violence. In November of 1780, in the aftermath of Sangarará, the Indians of Papres, Quispicanchis, stoned to death the Creole cacique of Rondocan, despite the fact that he supported the insurgents. One report claimed that they killed him because he was not an Indian.[125] Dressing in Spanish attire was often considered sufficient grounds for being killed in some rebel-controlled areas. Indian supporters of the rebellion threatened all *puka kunkas* (rednecks), the Quechua nickname for Spaniards.[126] In late December, as the rebel forces approached Cuzco and confronted the troops ably led by Pumacahua, they were accused of atrocities in Calca in the Sacred Valley. According to one royalist commentator, "they cruelly killed every male and female Spaniard they came upon, classifying as Spaniards or mestizos all those who wore shirts: and, what is even more horrible, they lewdly took advantage of all the attractive women, killing them afterward and going on to the greater impiety of having sex with the cadavers of other women."[127]

By February, the Tupac Amaru forces were on the defensive in the region around Cuzco. Inspector General José del Valle arrived at the end of the month with two hundred well-trained soldiers from the fixed battalion of Callao. Del Valle and Visitor General Areche sought to appease the Cuzco population by abolishing the reparto and the customs houses and by offering a pardon for rebels who gave up arms immediately.[128] By March, they commanded fifteen thousand troops, divided into six columns. Most of them were Indians.[129] At this point, Tupac Amaru confronted not only a much stronger royalist force and divisions within his own troops, but also logistical problems in securing sufficient clothing and food. One rebel commander complained that his troops were "naked."[130]

On March 9, del Valle left the city of Cuzco, leaving behind a small contingent to defend the city. In Cotabambas to the south, the fifth column defeated two of Tupac Amaru's more able generals, Tomás Parvina and Felipe Bermúdez. Both Creoles died. Most of the royalist troops proceeded along the high slopes to the west of the Vilcamayo Valley in pursuit of the rebellion's leader. On March 21, a traitor slipped out of Tupac Amaru's camp to warn del Valle of an imminent surprise attack. His troops moved their camp and fended off a dawn assault. Del Valle believed that without the warning, his forces would have been decimated in "another catastrophe such as that of Sangarará."[131] On March 23, the bulk of the royalist forces positioned themselves outside of Tinta, near Sangarará. In the following days, both sides suffered from a low supply of food and from the unusually cold weather as snow fell on the poorly provisioned soldiers. The royalist forces surrounded the rebels camped in Tinta and attempted to starve them out. On April 5, the rebels tried to break through, yet failed. Tupac Amaru managed to flee, crossing the Combapata River to the town of Langui, where he believed that Colonel Ventura Landaeta would hide him. Soldiers eager to claim the twenty-thousand-peso reward followed him, however, and captured him on April 6. On April 14, well-armed soldiers marched Tupac Amaru, Micaela, other family members, and much of the rebellion's leadership into the city of Cuzco.[132]

The capture of José Gabriel and his inner circle did not end the rebellion. Diego Cristóbal assumed the leadership of the rebellion as it shifted to the south to the Lake Titicaca area and Upper Peru. Andrés Tupac Amaru, a distant nephew, also commandeered important forces. Diego Cristóbal's proclamations were more blatantly anticolonial than José Gabriel's. The rebels' actions also became more radical as they attacked non-Indian groups largely left untouched in the Tupac Amaru phase. Violence committed by both the rebels and the royalists forces reached new levels. In Upper Peru, Julian Apasa took command of the Katari rebellion after Tomás Katari was killed in January 1781. Although Kataristas and Tupamaristas combined forces to lay siege to the city of La Paz in July and again in August 1781, tensions between them impeded their unification. Nonetheless, insurgency continued into 1783 in Upper Peru and the Lake Titicaca area. In the Cuzco area, however, the capture and execution of the leadership meant the end of the uprising.

This chapter has attempted to show that the rebellion was a proto-national movement aiming to overturn Bourbon colonialism. Although differences emerged between the leadership and the masses, most evident in the varying uses of violence, they agreed on the need to attack or expel local and regional authorities as well as the beneficiaries of the system, such as estate and textile mill owners, and to abolish key colonial impositions, such as the reparto and the sales tax. The division should not be exaggerated. Tupac Amaru II began his movement by publicly executing a well-known (and loathed) corregidor. Almost immediately afterward, the rebels went on the attack. The leadership did not want to negotiate improved relations with the state; they sought to overthrow it. José Gabriel's invocation of the Spanish king and the idea of placing himself as a new emperor should not be discounted as backward looking or conservative. It is anachronistic to question the political nature of the movement simply because it did not espouse some type of republican platform. At this time, almost a decade before the French Revolution, republicanism was barely taking hold in political discourse in the United States.[133] In Peru, it was not put into place until the 1820s, after decades of fighting and intense debate among the forces who fought against the Spanish, many of whom favored some type of monarchical system to replace Bourbon rule. Further complicating the situation was Creole intellectuals' omission of "the Indian problem." José Gabriel did not find in Lima compatible intellectual and political currents or supporters for an Indian-based anticolonial movement. No clear postcolonial alternative existed at this time, so Tupac Amaru sought to build one.

Nor should the bulk of the fighters be presented as followers of timeless Andean practices or "irrational" violence. They fought because of their enduring dislike for Spanish colonialism, personified by the corregidor and other authorities who were so often attacked in the rebellion. The insurgents' disillusion had increased in the years before the rebellion because of rising demands from the state despite Cuzco's economic stagnation. Local conflicts and political practice need to be examined for a full understanding of rebel behavior: the insurgents were not mindless followers of a charismatic leader. Nonetheless, although not always in agreement, the leadership and the rebel forces shared the goal of overturning Spanish colonialism.

Although the three interpretations of the uprising reviewed in the introduction to this chapter contribute to understanding it, they in fact need to be combined. The precursor view correctly interprets the rebellion as anticolonial. However, both Peru and Spain changed radically between 1780 and the independence period, 1810–25. Moreover, the relationship between the Tupac Amaru uprising and the long campaign for independence also needs to be taken into account. As seen in the following chapters, the Great Rebellion (the Tupac Amaru uprising) hardened racial tensions in Peru, making a multiethnic movement more difficult. The interpretation that emphasizes Inca identity correctly stresses it as the most important symbol for the rebellion. Yet this symbolism needs to be viewed as an "invented tradition" rather than as a primordial memory. The people of Cuzco remembered and memorialized the Incas in different ways, and the incorporation of the Incas did not necessarily contradict or impede a more modern, "national" project. Finally, the "long live the king" interpretation correctly places the Tupac Amaru rebellion in a tradition of negotiated rights. By the 1770s, however, with Visitador Areche implementing the Bourbons' escalating demands, this strategy had reached its limits. Despite a moderate, almost confused discourse, Tupac Amaru was not negotiating with but rather attempting to overthrow the state. The Tupac Amaru rebellion must be understood in light of eighteenth-century political culture: greater tensions evident in the increasing number of revolts, diverse invocations of the Incas, and the emergence of new ideological and political currents. It was a protonational movement that confronted and was undermined by the contradictions of colonialism in the Andes.

What does this analysis contribute to the understanding of nationalism? Above all, it emphasizes the need to pluralize the subject and discuss multiple nationalisms that overlapped, intersected, and at times even combined. In Spanish America, the Creole bourgeoisie were not the only ones who could imagine an alternative to Spanish colonialism and to demand their rights under the guise of nationalism.[134] Tupac Amaru's movement created an Andean and Indian-based platform that did not disappear with the defeat of the rebellion. Similar movements arose in subsequent decades, and Peru's difficulties in nation and state formation can be understood only by examining the relationship between this rebellion and those of the ultimately victorious Creole state makers. Applying the concept of nationalism (or protonationalism) to the situation does not imply that the Tupac Amaru movement was the forerunner of independence: it involved a vastly different social group (leaders and followers) acting in a different period, using different means and different rhetoric, and presumably possessing different goals. Yet the Tupac Amaru movement had a vision of a postcolonial society and sought to implement it through a social revolution. Analyzing the movement does not merely offer a social history of the ultimately insignificant losers. The movement radically altered social relations and even Peru's historical course in the coming decades, if not centuries.

Why were the rebels defeated? A number of factors need to be considered in answering this question. In strict military terms, the Spanish superiority in firearms and José Gabriel's hesitation to attack Cuzco stand out. Flores Galindo, though, has delved into more important factors—in particular, the divisions within colonial society that, although in some ways prompted the uprising, eventually led to its demise. The Tupac Amaru rebellion could not count on the support of a majority of the caciques or of the Indians in the region. The reasons for caciques' opposition include antagonism toward Tupac Amaru and his extended family, fear of losing their advantageous standing in colonial society, and the incentives and threats presented by the colonial state and army. Supporting the rebellion was extremely hazardous, as many authorities would painfully discover in the ensuing months and years. Similar explanations can be offered regarding most Indians' reluctance to support the rebellion. Although many were prevented from joining the rebels by their cacique or the overseer of the estate where they worked, others simply did not agree with the rebellion or were afraid to fight. Indians were by no means a homogeneous group: regional, ethnic, and class conflicts divided them.

Despite a concerted effort, Tupac Amaru never managed to recruit Creoles, blacks, and mestizos en masse. The Bourbon reforms had antagonized a wide spectrum of society, from the most downtrodden to the affluent. The rebel leadership recognized and shared the frustration of Creoles and mestizos marginalized by the favoritism toward the Spanish or shackled by the economic reforms. Yet the rebellion never became a multiethnic, anticolonial movement. Many reasons for this failure can be found, but the very divisions fostered by colonialism are especially important. Members of the "middle class" such as provincial merchants, although infuriated by the Bourbon reforms, feared a mass uprising.

Their fear stemmed more from their concern about the loss of their favorable position in society than from their concern about a caste war. As would be evident in the long War of Independence, vast sectors of the intermediate groups so important in anticolonial struggles equivocated. In late colonial society, class, race, and geographical divisions intertwined in what Flores Galindo calls the "colonial knot."[135] For example, although Indians never fought in unison, non-Indians dreaded such an occurrence. In the uprising, racial tensions weakened class solidarity, and class self-interest wreaked havoc with racial unity. In propaganda against the rebellion, the Spanish state trumpeted these divisions.

The Spanish knew that they had been fortunate to capture José Gabriel. Manuel Godoy, the first minister and confidant of Charles IV, noted in his memoirs that "no one ignores that the entire Viceroyalty of Peru and part of Río de la Plata were nearly lost in 1781 and 1782."[136] Areche boasted that when sentencing and punishing the defendants, he would use "all the forms of terror necessary to produce fear and caution."[137] Horses dragged José Gabriel, Micaela, their oldest son Hipólito, José Gabriel's uncle, and five associates to the gallows in Cuzco's main plaza. The spectacle began with five hangings. Then José Gabriel's uncle and son had their tongues severed before execution at the gallows. After Tomasa Condemayta was asphyxiated with the infamous garrote, Micaela had her tongue slashed. The garrote did not work because of her thin neck, so executioners strangled her with a rope. Having witnessed the deaths of members of his family and of his movement's inner circle, Tupac Amaru was taken to the center of the plaza. Executioners cut his tongue off and tied him to four horses in order to be quartered. When the rebel leader's limbs did not separate from his torso, Areche ordered him beheaded. His head was exhibited in Tinta, his body in Picchu—the battlegrounds of the siege of Cuzco—where it was burned, his limbs in Tungasuca and Carabaya, and his legs in Livitaca and Santa Rosa.[138]

Repression did not end with the bodily punishment of the rebels. The state campaigned to root out all cultural elements of the neo-Inca nationalism that had emerged in the eighteenth century. Before the capture of José Gabriel, Bishop Moscoso made a series of recommendations to Visitador Areche in April, most of which were carried out. He called for the destruction of all portraits of the Incas and for the prohibition of clothing associated with the Incas, certain dances, the use of "Inca" as a last name or title, literature that questioned the legitimate .

rights of the Spanish monarchy in the Americas (with harsh punishment for readers of subversive material), and customary law. Moscoso also censured at length the work of Garcilaso de la Vega.[139] These measures and others, such as curbs against the use of Quechua, were implemented in the following years.

The brutal executions of the leaders of the rebellion, the widespread repression of Andean culture, and an open disdain for Indians among key ideologues in the years following the Tupac Amaru uprising would seem to portend terrible times for the Andean peasantry. The indigenous peasantry of the southern Andes—their rebellion defeated after it inflicted grave losses and even humiliated the colonial state—would confront the unbridled hatred and desire for vengeance of the state and sectors of the elite. Yet in the decades following the Tupac Amaru rebellion, the final forty years of colonial rule, the Spanish were not able to impede new uprisings, dismantle Indian political autonomy, or even increase taxes and other exactions to the extent that they wished. A reconquest of the Andes following the defeat of the Tupac Amaru and Tupac Katari rebellions did not take place. Moreover, the search for an Andean-based anticolonial movement continued. Chapter 3 examines how lower-class groups resisted the punitive measures and fierce anti-Indian spirit in the wake of the great Andean uprising.

For the Indians of the southern Andes, particularly those who witnessed the execution of Tupac Amaru and his supporters and the display of their dismembered body parts, the brutal defeat of the rebellion portended terrible times ahead. A somber mood pervaded the city on the day of the grisly, carefully planned execution. Some interpreted a sudden downpour as a sign of distress by the sky and the elements.[1] The uprising had demonstrated the vulnerability of the colonial state and had forced it to spend a great deal on stopping the rebels. Combined with the Bourbon's incessant desire to increase the revenue squeezed from its American colonies, the fury caused by the rebellion would prompt physical and cultural repression, as well as increased fiscal and labor demands. Caciques confronted harsh punishment and efforts to eliminate the office altogether. The rebellion also intimidated non-Indians, particularly the Spanish and Creole elite, and encouraged them to temper their complaints about Bourbon colonialism and to think twice about alliances with the lower classes. In this period deemed "the Great Fear," the dividing lines between Indians and non-Indians, and between the Andes and the coast, hardened.

Yet the aftermath of the rebellion did not produce an unrestrained assault on Indians' economic resources, a multiplication of their tax and labor burden, or a loss of their culture. Although rabidly anti-Indian tracts were written, and plans to punish, watch over, and incorporate the Indians were discussed, a "second conquest" of the Andes did not take place.[2] Defeating the rebels on the battlefield proved to be easier than implementing the changes conceived by the Bourbon state. The state's attempt to impose new authorities, heighten its demands, and in general rationalize the bureaucracy at the cost of Indians' autonomy and economic well-being faced persistent and often successful challenges. This chapter examines how relations between the peasantry and the state were remade in the wake of the rebellion.

Several factors account for the Bourbon failure to weaken Andean culture and to reorder relations between Andean people and the state. First, there were contradictions and deficiencies in the reforms themselves and in their implementation. Although the colonial state achieved its primary goal to increase the amount of revenue extracted from the American viceroyalties, it did not create a notably more efficient bureaucracy that might have weakened local power groups and tightened the connection between state and society. Divisions within the colonial state and the Bourbon's opposition to spending money on its colonies hindered the reforms. Second, the region faced economic problems. Although the economic stagnation prompted difficult times for indigenous peasants—active producers, merchants, consumers, and taxpayers—it also eased external pressures to appropriate Indians' resources, particularly land. Finally, efforts by the Indians themselves constituted the most important obstacle to the Bourbon reconquest of the southern Andes. Indians flooded the courts to impede the imposition of outsiders in the cacique office and to question authorities' abusive behavior.

A review of more than one thousand criminal trials has shed light on a number of issues: the relationship between rebellion, resistance, and hegemony; the contradictions of the Bourbon project; and the social complexity of late colonial Andean society. This chapter examines the question of whether the use of the legal system buttressed colonialism or served to question and even weaken it.[3] The trials indicate that armed rebellion and the use of the courts are not contradictory, opposed strategies—resistance on the one hand, submission on the other—but rather fall along a continuum. In fact, Cuzco in this period demonstrates the intimate relationship between armed rebellion and the use of the courts. In the lawsuits, peasants highlighted the contradictions and fissures of the colonial state. Although the fear of another rebellion intensified the state's punishment of suspected insurgents and its repression of Andean culture, it also made the state sensitive to charges of official misbehavior that could spark another uprising. Peasant communities could use this concern to their advantage; it could also, however, be used against them.

As described in chapter 2, executioners tortured, humiliated, and executed José Gabriel, Micaela, and dozens of their supporters in public rituals in April 1781. Their body parts were disseminated throughout the Cuzco region to confirm their defeat and to warn the population of the dangers of sedition. Visitor General Areche deemed that news of the execution be widely propagated, "thus stemming the diverse ideas that have spread among almost the entire Indian nation, full of superstitions that make them believe in the impossibility that they be given the death sentence."[4] Repression did not stop at this point because the rebellion itself had not ended. Diego Cristóbal led the continued insurrection, now focused in the Lake Titicaca area to the south. After months of negotiations, when hostility between the Tupamaristas and the Kataristas prevented a broad alliance and undermined both movements, he accepted a pardon in late 1782. In March 1783, however, soldiers arrested him and hundreds of others, including sixty-three members of his family. Whereas most of the prisoners were simply banished, Diego Cristóbal was dragged by a horse, tortured with burning tongs, and hanged. His mother had her tongue cut out. According to one author, Viceroy Agustín Jáuregui sought to "wipe out the whole Inca family."[5]

The state did not limit its punishment to the movement's leaders. Events in Santa Rosa, located on the Puno side of the La Raya mountain range that separates the Lake Titicaca region from Cuzco, exemplified the brutal repression applied in the wake of the uprising. On June 22, 1781, royalist forces approaching the town were met by Indians "asking to be forgiven." The soldiers ordered them to return to the town and then instructed all adults to congregate in the middle of the plaza. Some frightened Indians ran, many of them taking refuge in the church. All of the town's population, however—even an "old Spaniard," Indians who had fought for the Crown, and the carriers of the platform with the effigy of Saint Rose that had been brought out for divine protection—were forced into the plaza. Every fifth man was executed "in about an hour and ten minutes."[6] Similar occurrences took place throughout the region.

Punitive measures went beyond the ritualized extermination of the leadership and the execution of suspected rebel sympathizers. The Bourbon state sought to undermine Pan-Andean solidarity by removing indigenous authorities considered loyal to Tupac Amaru, weakening the cacique office in general, prohibiting Inca Garcilaso's *Comentarios Reales,* and banning dances, dress, and artwork associated with Indian culture. Authorities called for the "extirpation" of Quechua and the Castilianization of the Andes.[7] Many of Bishop Moscoso's proposals to curb the invocation of the Incas and to eliminate other elements of Andean culture—part of his hysterical and self-conscious denunciations during the uprising—were put into practice. In a region recently wracked by what authorities considered a caste war, the Bourbon's efforts to strengthen the state and homogenize the population assumed a particularly urgent and ethnocentric character.

From 1780 to 1786, the Madrid lawyer Benito de la Mata Linares was the most important official in Cuzco. He served as an advisor to Visitador Areche during the uprising, presided over the trial and execution of Tupac Amaru and the subsequent repression, and was Cuzco's first intendant from 1783 to 1786. Mata Linares incessantly warned of the threat of another uprising. In 1781, he deemed that Cuzco was populated only by "traitors and cowards," implying that although the entire population had supported the rebels, some were too pusillanimous to convert their support into action. In 1783, he cautioned that the city's "fidelity has not been assured," and two years later he instructed authorities to "prevent that a spark touch off the *smoldering ashes*" of Cuzco.[8] Viceroy Teodoro de Croix echoed Mata Linares's concern and his fire metaphor when he wrote in 1786 that with the memory of Tupac Amaru still fresh, "you must not trust anyone who has not proven his zeal, fidelity, and love for the King, especially if he is someone of distinction among the Indians; it would be very easy for them to light the flame of rebellion, which while seeming to be entirely extinguished, still gives signs of life from time to time."[9]

These warnings were not idle expressions of lingering postrebellion paranoia. Signs of deep indignation and possible subversion continued to appear. In 1783, a short-lived uprising in the Quispicanchis province, news of the Katarista uprising in Upper Peru, and a rebellion in the Andean town of Huarochirí, outside of Lima, disturbed Cuzco royalists. In December 1784, authorities reported a conspiracy by Cuzco's Indians. A carpenter, Clemente Barrientos, claimed that plans had been made, once again in chicherías, to kill all of the city's Spaniards. On a central street, an Indian had supposedly dumped a dead Spanish woman "with a bruised face and swollen leg," the first victim of the violence. Although guards strictly patrolled the streets and arrested a few suspects, the conspiracy could not be confirmed.[10] In May 1786, however, lampoons placed in churches and other public places confirmed the presence of dissidents in Cuzco. The first lampoon censured the king, vindicated Tupac Amaru, and described an uprising involving Huamanga and Arequipa. Weeks later, another one asked, "Brothers, when will you wake up? You should expect nothing from a King so distant that he is unknown, except for the reports of these mandarins. . . . you must decide—arms are not lacking—and thousands of men pine for freedom." It referred to a "type of republic" that would be created and the promised aid of "two powerful potencies," presumably England and the United States. Above all, it complained of favoritism toward the Spanish over Creoles.[11]

The posters thus conjured up colonial authorities' preeminent fear: a mass uprising that invoked Tupac Amaru and counted on support from Spain's enemies. Mata Linares blamed a small group of renegades for supposedly subverting the plebians. Although the lampoons stopped appearing, anonymous letters were sent to the viceroy complaining of abuses by authorities.[12] The rumors and posters indicated the resentment over the colonial state's heavy-handed policies and, as Mata Linares and other officials nervously noted, the possibility of more insurgency. Spanish authorities worried that another uprising in Cuzco, a distinct possibility, would fatally weaken the colonies' defenses, particularly against the English. In 1786, Mata Linares wrote, "If Spain were to lose Buenos Aires and Lima to foreign invaders, the empire could remain intact if control were retained of Cuzco, but, with Cuzco lost, all the kingdom will be lost since the sierra is the shield of all this America."[13] This concern over the military consequences of another uprising in Cuzco continued until independence. Ironically, the Spanish based their last stand in Cuzco as Viceroy José de La Serna governed there from 1821 to 1824.

BOURBON REFORMS WITH A VENGEANCE

In the wake of the Tupac Amaru uprising, the Bourbon state continued its parallel efforts to centralize the colonial administration and to increase revenues. In 1784, the French intendant system was introduced in Peru. Eight intendancies were created, with the intendancy of Puno transferred to the Río de la Plata viceroyalty.[14] It was believed that intendants would be able to keep a closer eye on their regions than authorities would in Lima. Conscious of the fact that the corregidores' abuses had been a major cause of the indigenous revolts in the Andes throughout the eighteenth century and that these authorities' economic activities had impeded revenue collection, the Crown replaced the corregidores with subdelegates who were to be supervised closely by the intendants, who in this case were based in Cuzco rather than distant Lima. In order to discourage financial entanglements between subdelegates and local power groups, the authorities were promised adequate salaries. The Bourbons sought to replace the power of priests, caciques, the wealthy, and authorities with a stronger link between local society and the viceregal state. In Peru, the Bourbons succeeded in what they considered as their primary objective: to increase the revenue they extracted from their American holdings. They failed, however, in their efforts to place autonomous authorities throughout the viceroyalty and thus reshape political and economic relations. Local politics continued to resemble practice under the Habsburgs. The introduction of the intendant system did not break up local networks of economic and political power or uproot Indians' political autonomy. Although the changes set off strong centrifugal tendencies, the Bourbons did not modernize the state in the way that they intended.

Several factors explain the Bourbon's inability to transform relations between local society and the colonial state in the Andes. The reforms themselves were not a cohesive, unified set of policies.[15] They constituted a late reaction to the Iberian Peninsula's decline in Europe, during which revenue necessary to modernize the administration was repeatedly used for immediate, usually military, needs. A sharp schism separated the content of the reforms and their application. This schism is most evident in the fact that despite the insistence on the need to prevent a recurrence of the abuses of the old corregidores, the intendancy system did not result in the establishment of centrally controlled, acceptably paid officials. Moreover, conflicts among governmental officials at different levels (the king, the viceroy, the intendant, and the subdelegates) hindered effective administration. In post-Tupac Amaru Cuzco, the incongruities and inconsistencies of the reforms were particularly flagrant. The fear of provoking another peasant uprising and concern over hindering tax collection tempered the more draconian repressive impulses.[16] Authorities abandoned policies designed to renovate the state (and, above all, to collect greater revenue) because of their short-term economic or political cost. Furthermore, the colonial state did not know whom it could trust. Not only were the peasantry and the church out of favor, but the Cuzco elite was divided and also seen as potentially rebellious.

The Crown's inability to create a more efficient political administration reflected the ambiguities of Bourbon policies. Despite the replacement of corregidores by subdelegates, corregidor-like practices continued. Because of the subdelegates' lack of economic resources and low status, they were perceived as feeble underlings of the intendants. In order to accumulate resources and respect, and thus to establish their power, they often forged crooked and exploitative alliances with caciques, priests, and others. The subdelegates often engaged in local, generally monopolistic, and blatantly exploitative economic practices.[17] Increased pay would not have automatically done away with corruption and exploitation. Controlling local officials constituted an immense challenge in the vast districts of the southern Andes, where a high proportion of the economy was based on the exploitation of the indigenous population as consumers, taxpayers, producers, and laborers. In Cuzco, the inefficacy of the Bourbon reforms meant that traditional practices and authorities, particularly ethnic caciques, endured.

CACIQUES AND LOCAL AUTONOMY

The ambiguities of Bourbon policy are particularly evident in the fate of the caciques. Since the sixteenth century, the caciques constituted the pivotal figure in the relationship between the state and indigenous society. These chieftains collected tribute (directly or through representatives), organized the fulfillment of other fiscal and labor obligations, and generally enforced social order. Yet in the eighteenth century, these officeholders faced three interrelated pressures that threatened them individually and jeopardized the office itself. First, they confronted increasing competition for their positions from other local Indian nobles and outsiders, which resulted in long legal battles. Second, they had a more and more difficult time fulfilling the heightened demands of the Spanish state without endangering relations with local indigenous society. Third, proposals were made to abolish the office itself, particularly after the Tupac Amaru rebellion. Because of these pressures, by the late eighteenth century no single type of cacique or cacique-society relationship predominated. Rich and poor caciques, respected and repudiated caciques, Spaniards, creoles, mestizos, and Indians alike held the office. Their economic standing and legitimacy in the eyes of Indian peasants, non-Indians, and the state varied greatly. Yet, in general, Indians preferred the traditional ethnic caciques to outsiders named by the intendant and fought for the existence of this office, which they understood as central to their relative political autonomy. In many cases, they succeeded in defending their ethnic caciques.[18]

The Spanish state questioned the position of the cacique for a number of conflicting reasons. For some critics, the caciques constituted an outdated relic that encumbered efficient administration. Many worried about their potential as political subversives. Others called for limitations on the caciques' powers in order to curb their abuses of the Indians. On the other hand, some defended the office as both legitimate and expedient. These opposing views on the caciques surfaced with the Tupac Amaru rebellion. After the uprising, Visitador Areche advocated abolishing all cacicazgos other than those held by persons who had demonstrated their loyalty to the Crown, an abolishment that would have included even caciques who had remained neutral during the rebellion. He sought to replace them with elected governors and mayors.[19] His plan was not enacted; instead, bitter legal and local struggles over the control of the office ensued. The contradictions between punishment and appeasement and between administrative modernity and tradition that characterized Bourbon ideology and policy were once again brought into the open.

In convoluted legal battles involving key authorities and institutions, Areche's measures were slowly diluted. A 1790 royal decree from the Council of the Indies amended previous regulations and limited the prohibition of caciques to individuals who had supported Tupac Amaru. Caciques who had remained neutral either because they chose to do so or because the rebellion did not extend to their jurisdictions were no longer subject to removal.[20] In 1798, Cuzco's real audiencia prohibited subdelegates from naming *caciques gobernadores* in "Indian towns," thereby defending ethnic caciques. Many temporary caciques were replaced, whereas other non-Indian local authorities merely stopped using the title cacique.[21] Nonetheless, changes with the introduction of the intendancy system in 1784 included eliminating the caciques' role as tax collectors, thereby severely limiting their relevance within the colonial system.[22] Data from the criminal trials, discussed later in this chapter, indicates that *alcaldes varayoks,* Indian mayors, slowly replaced the caciques in this function. Ethnic caciques confronted the competition not only of Indian officials but of non-Indian authorites who were usually in alliance with higher officials. What happened to caciques at the local level varied greatly, thus demonstrating the discrepancy between Crown policy and its application in the American colonies.[23] It is clear that many ethnic caciques managed to hold on to their position despite the hostility of the colonial state.

An 1806 document depicts the coexistence of contradictory notions and policies regarding the cacique. In a list of thirty-nine cases presented to the real audiencia concerning cacicazgos, candidates for the office employed divergent rationales. Many, such as Juan Huacoto from the town of Cupi in the province of Lampa, stressed their "blood right." Others, such as Don Simón Callo of Sicuani, requested restitution because they had been suspended after the Tupac Amaru uprising. Some were clearly not hereditary caciques. Don Gregorio Roldán de Deza—candidate for cacique in Asillo, where a centuries-long conflict over the office continued—bluntly pointed out the increase "to your Majesty in money as well as tributaries" during his brief tenure.[24] Officeholders and aspirants understood and manipulated the contradictory notions of the period about the cacique office in terms of qualifications and duties. In the trials over the office, one side frequently emphasized inherited rights and tradition, whereas the other extolled the expediency of having a Spaniard rather than an Indian in charge of local government.

Numerous rifts divided Cuzco, and no single group assumed local power with the faltering termination of the cacique office. Some ethnic caciques managed to hold onto office, but others, usually outsiders, became powerful. Priests, militia leaders, subdelegates, and Indians vying for the office of mayor allied and fought for power alongside or against caciques. The Tupac Amaru rebellion and subsequent Bourbon policy complicated an already complex division of power.[25] The ambiguity of official policy inadvertently tended to support traditional practices and leave a great deal of room for political maneuvering. In the context of intermittent international war, conflicts between different levels of government in Spain and Lima and between the real audiencia, the intendant, and the subdelegates within Cuzco, plus the general contradictions in Bourbon thought and policy, members of the economic and political elite were not the only ones with motive and ability to question or disobey the orders of the viceroy, the real audiencia, or the intendant. Yet before the efforts of the peasantry are examined, Cuzco's late colonial economy is reviewed in the next section.

THE ECONOMY

The economic situation of the indigenous peasantry of the Southern Andes also seemed bleak in the wake of the Tupac Amaru uprising. A vindictive state sought to increase their already heavy tax burden and was willing to break traditional colonial practice by allowing outsiders to encroach on *ayllus'* land (Indian communities). Moreover, the region's economic woes adversely affected the peasants, who were important producers and consumers. Yet in the final decades of Spanish rule, the state did not impose its demands at will, nor did outsiders assume control of huge tracts of land. Like its early republican successors, the Bourbon state was unable (and largely unwilling) to enforce the demands of the regional elite, mainly because it had little to spend, mistrusted its divided supporters, faced warfare at home, and juggled divergent notions about the most expedient relationship to be fostered between the state and the Indian masses. Also, the stagnation of the region's economy diminished outsiders' interest in usurping community land. In order to understand the regional economy, three factors should be considered: (1) the effects of the Tupac Amaru uprising, (2) the jurisdictional changes imposed by the Bourbons, and (3) the general economic situation of the region.

In the Tupac Amaru uprising, haciendas and obrajes were damaged and destroyed, formidable numbers of people were killed, wounded, or uprooted, and sources of credit disappeared. The rebellion left ample evidence of the vast physical devastation caused by both sides. Archival sources indicate the dire consequences of the rebellion in terms of population displacement. A tax collector in Cotabambas noted in 1786 that agricultural production slumped in 1781 and 1782 because "many were absent because of their fear of the rebellion, and some because they had joined the campaigns." A cacique accused in 1786 of collecting tribute from the exempt claimed that he was making up for the dead from the Tupac Amaru rebellion.[26] A recent study of the tithe in the region found a sharp decline in agricultural production and the ability to collect this tax from 1780 to 1783, but a return to previous levels thereafter.[27] There is little doubt that the damage was extensive. By itself, however, the rebellion cannot explain Cuzco's economic difficulties. Other areas recovered relatively quickly despite massive physical damage and socio-economic disruption. The Tupac Amaru rebellion simply exacerbated an already serious situation.[28]

In the 1780s, the colonial state continued implementing policies that diminished Lima's virtual monopoly as entrepôt for the trans-Atlantic trade and Cuzco's central marketing and production role for Upper Peru. In 1784, the intendancy of Puno was transferred to the Río de la Plata viceroyalty. Moreover, the "free trade" policy opened the vice-royalties of Río de la Plata and Peru to European imports. These poli-cies did not induce a deluge of imports or create economic barriers that crippled southern Peruvian production, however. Cuzco products con-tinued to find a market in Potosí. According to one study, "the division between the Río de la Plata Viceroyalty, in which Potosí was located, and the Peruvian Viceroyalty, enacted in 1776, did not in any way mean the creation of a border impeding commerce. The Peruvian intendan-cies of Arequipa, Cuzco, and Lima furnished more than 50 percent of the American products sold in Potosí in 1793."[29] The Bourbon reforms did portend two related, century-long processes: the increasing impor-tance of maritime rather than overland transportation and the decline of Andean trade circuits linking Upper and Lower Peru. Both trends threatened Cuzco's economic and political importance.

As discussed in chapter 2, the uprising and the Bourbon administra-tive and economic reforms were not the only causes of Cuzco's economic crisis. The internal weaknesses of the region's economy and the conse-quent inability to compete with foreign products also played a major role. The case of textile production in Cuzco, central to its economy, illuminates the predicament of the Cuzco economy. After the Tupac Amaru rebellion, the *chorrillos* or smaller production units prospered, but many obrajes languished.[30] The mills' wretched labor conditions and backward technology limited their ability to compete. Obrajes de-pended on convict labor, which allowed the convicts to pay debts and make restitution and provided the state with an alternative to maintaining prisoners in the perennially overcrowded and inadequate jails. Despite the pay, however, prisoners dreaded this fate. In 1792, one Indian's lawyer pleaded against the "cruel penalty of the mills."[31] Although a review of European workshops in this period would also unearth exploitative practices and miserable working conditions, the obrajes of Cuzco were not only backward technologically, but also housed their workers under guard in appalling conditions compounded by inadequate or at least unappetizing food. In the context of late colonial and republican political instability, these conditions made the obrajes vulnerable to internal and external sabotage and even destruction. Owners lived in constant fear of a repetition of what happened to the owner of the Guaro obraje during the Tupac Amaru rebellion, where "the workers themselves were the first ones to begin sacking."[32] This insecurity would plague the mill owners throughout the first half of the nineteenth century.

Producers of Cuzco's other major products, such as sugar and coca, faced difficulties similar to those faced in the textile industry. Their dependence on distant markets and on an unstable, often coerced labor force made them vulnerable to workplace turmoil, and the absence of stable political authority created optimal conditions for protest or flight. Short of capital, they also faced growing competition from other regions. Arequipa increasingly provided sugar for Upper Peru, and coca cultivation expanded in the Lake Titicaca region. From the middle of the eighteenth century, the prices of agricultural products stagnated at low levels. Price series on corn from 1720 to 1795 demonstrate a steady decline in prices.[33] The grain market, for example, was saturated in the post–Tupac Amaru period. Depressed during the final colonial decades, sugar and coca production in Cuzco stagnated in the first half of the nineteenth century.[34]

The economy at the local level, particularly in the indigenous communities, cannot simply be deduced from this general portrayal of economic decline. Conditions varied between regions. Even within a particular community, important differences emerged. Two broad trends, however, can be gleaned from a variety of sources. On the one hand, Indians' tax obligations skyrocketed, mainly because of improved collection mechanisms. As discussed in the previous chapter, tax collections in Cuzco increased sixteenfold between the 1750s and the early 1820s.[35] This increase constituted the primary cause of economic distress for Indians and the primary achievement of the Bourbon reforms in the eyes of the state. On the other hand, economic hardship was mitigated by local control (in some cases recuperation) of land and other resources by rural, mainly indigenous communities.

Three factors must be considered in order to evaluate the real impact of the increasing tribute revenues. The first is population growth. One scholar calculates a 0.4 percent annual growth rate for Cuzco for the 1689–1786 period, which would mean a growth of 133 percent within a seventy-two-year period. Another found a range of annual growth rates from 0.6 to 1.3 percent in the late colonial and early republic, with an 0.82 percent rate for the 1791–1850 period.[36] Although the lack of even approximate figures of the number of dead from the Tupac Amaru uprising makes any estimate hazardous, even such crude calculations as these indicate that part of the increase in tax revenues can be attributed to demographic growth.

Second, much of the increased tax revenue originated from improved collection procedures. Thus, some of the increase came from the pockets of corrupt collectors rather than tribute-paying Indians. More frequent and effective revisions of the tax rolls after the 1780s, the *revisitas,* reduced fraud and evasion.[37] A third factor was the prohibition of the reparto. In the districts of Cuzco in 1754, corregidores were permitted to sell goods via the reparto with a total value of 961,900 pesos. The actual incomes from the forced sales were often higher, with markups approaching 300 percent.[38] In 1754, only 15,898 pesos of tribute were collected from Cuzco. As proponents of the abolition of the reparto insisted, the sale of overpriced goods diminished the Indians' capacity to fulfill other obligations, particularly tribute. Although certain officials continued the practice after its abolition in 1780, the burden of purchasing overpriced goods was nevertheless reduced, thus freeing money for tribute payment.[39]

Not only were Indians receiving low prices for their products, but the economic stagnation of Cuzco in this period meant that alternative sources of income were scarce. The growing population of landless drifters reflected the economic difficulties the peasants faced and the disruptive effects of the Tupac Amaru rebellion. In 1790, Pablo José Oricaín decried the high numbers of Indians that roamed "together with their families and livestock, under the pretext of bringing the animals from one pasture to the other. They wander around carrying some short sticks; wherever they find a source of water and sufficient pasture they build a temporary shelter until the residents of that place oblige them to render services or rents . . . and in this manner they migrate from one place to the next."[40] He calculated that one-third of the Cuzco diocese's population was poor, and two-thirds of these eighty thousand souls were gravely so. A fraction were beggars, including "very many Spaniards."[41] Peasants' fateful vulnerability to short-term crises, whether man-made or climatological, also attested to the difficult economic times. In the Andes, with its difficult topography and capricious weather patterns, misfortunes could rapidly become life-threatening catastrophes.[42] In late colonial Cuzco, the increased fiscal obligations coupled with the region's general economic stagnation made for very difficult times for much of the Indian population.

The economic crisis did have some positive consequences for the rural indigenous population. As numerous historians have noted regarding the early republican period, outsiders had little incentive to infringe on land and other resources in the midst of an economic downswing. Nils Jacobsen argues that in the period between the Tupac Amaru uprising and independence, Azángaro communities gained in the centuries-long battle over effective control of lands.[43] The same argument can be applied to Cuzco. In contrast to what occurred with Mayan Indians, land-grabbing elites did not usurp great tracts of property from the Indians of the southern Andes in the final colonial decades.[44] The potential for renewed violence, the ambiguity of state policy and action, and the bleak economic situation discouraged outsiders from investing time, capital, and potentially their lives to usurp land, force sales, or coerce labor. As the next section's analysis of the court cases proves, these practices continued, but to a lesser extent and intensity than would have been the case had the trans-Andean economy offered greater opportunities for profit. Of course, political uncertainty, elite squabbles, and economic malaise are not the only explanations for the hesitancy of the state and non-Indians to assault ayllus' relative autonomy and economic resources. Indians in the Cuzco region aggressively defended these rights, mainly through the legal system. Taking advantage of the Bourbons' uneasiness about another mass rebellion and the government's related efforts to rebuild its relationship with the tribute-paying masses, the peasantry hampered the abuses of old and new caciques and of other authorities through the extensive use of the legal system.

In the wake of the Tupac Amaru uprising, ayllu Indians employed a host of strategies to defend their political autonomy and economic resources—including horizontal and vertical alliances, threats of violence, passive resistance, and, above all, lawsuits. In hundreds of trials, Indian peasants denounced the abuses of local authorities and often questioned their right to office. In a period when Indians and others were constantly reminded of the physical, economic, and cultural costs of a failed rebellion, they used the legal system to take advantage of the state's fear of another uprising and its will to constrain local officials. Their repeated use of the legal system reflected their belief that it worked.[45] These trials constituted an important weapon of the peasantry, and the records of the trials provide valuable material for historians. They illuminate the conflictual relations between authorities and the peasantry; illustrate different tactics used by the lower classes; and shed light on the relationship between legal maneuvers and rebellions, and on how hegemony is constructed and contested inside and outside of the courtroom.

In their lawsuits to counter the post–Tupac Amaru Bourbon "reconquest," Indian peasants not only contested the reforms but reshaped relations among local authorities, the state, and themselves. Several authors have used the concept of moral economy to review relations between the peasantry and the state in the eighteenth century. Stemming from work by E. P. Thompson and developed by James Scott in terms of the peasantry, this concept emphasizes "relations, rooted in unwritten but understood norms of conduct and reciprocity, [that] gave cultural meaning to the more formal agreements that required the native people to render service and tribute to the colonial state in exchange for access to rights and resources that allowed them to maintain their way of life."[46] Tristan Platt, among others, refers to this unwritten agreement as the colonial pact.[47] What requires emphasis is that this pact was not the conservative force that some analysts imply—an ethereal constraint on indigenous resistance that emanated from centuries past; it was instead constantly negotiated and remade. At any point in Andean history, the meaning of "reciprocal relations" was in daily contention. The concept of moral economy can easily be interpreted in such a way that it blurs internal divisions and conflicts within the peasant community.

The fact that large segments of an ayllu or community could organize in opposition to an interloper does not imply homogeneity or even long-term consensus. Behind these conflicts lay a series of alliances, glimpsed in many of the trials discussed below.

Indigenous peasants have a long tradition of using the legal system to defend resources and to promote their interests. Recent studies show how Indians used the legal system as early as the sixteenth century, and today the *tinterillo* (pettifogger) is a ubiquitous figure throughout Andean society. Indians maintain a reputation for being litigious, and indeed peasants crowd the courts of Andean cities—suing, defending themselves, and countersuing.[48] As José Gabriel had learned in the 1770s, Lima was a hostile and costly site for a southern Andean litigant. The Tupac Amaru rebels therefore demanded the creation of an audiencia in Cuzco "so that the Indians will have recourse to justice nearer to them."[49] The colonial state fulfilled this demand in 1787.[50]

I examined more than 1,000 *causas criminales,* trial records, from 1783 to 1823: 575 from the real audiencia, 389 from the intendencia, 218 from the cabildo, and 71 from intendencia-provincia. In theory, the audiencia should have served as an appeals court for cases viewed in the intendencia, the main legal institution, and in the cabildo, which handled nonviolent urban transgressions. Yet many cases went directly to the audiencia. In general, it judged the more serious crimes.[51] I found cases from every *partido* (district) of Cuzco as well as Huamanga, Guayaquil, La Paz, and Arequipa. Almost half the cases tried in the real audiencia, the intendencia, and the intendencia-provincia were crimes committed within the city of Cuzco. Other cases came from prominent areas such as Quispicanchis, Canas y Canchis, Chumbivilcas, and Abancay. Not surprisingly, these areas were economically important and had two nuclei of criminal activities: obrajes and trade routes. Higher populations, greater economic activity, proximity to the courts, and generally stronger links to the state's operations and discourse explain here as elsewhere the higher percentage of crimes in urban and economic centers. However, as the cases involving remote, predominantly Quechua monolingual communities demonstrate, the legal system, both its redressive and repressive components, reached deeply into Cuzco's rural society in the late colonial period.

The analysis here focuses on roughly 20 percent of the total cases—those involving behavior by authorities that was considered abusive and inappropriate by the colonial state and/or members of local society. Such behavior was sometimes specifically identified as tax fraud and unjustified imprisonment, but most of the time it was described generically as "abuses." Of course, many cases of abuse never reached the courts. Fear of retribution discouraged many interested parties from lodging a complaint. Also, many conflicts were resolved or dropped at a local level. Abusive conduct was thus much more extensive than trial records indicate, but by the same token the means of recourse for civil society were not limited to lawsuits. In almost all of these trials, a great deal of negotiation and accommodation took place prior to the lawsuit. These lawsuits thus reflect only the visible, recorded aspects of local power relations. What is important to emphasize, however, is that these relations were not limited to the prepotency (a favored term in the Andes, past and present) of authorities, economic elites, and their followers; rather, they involved an elaborate set of codes, actions, and tactics in which all social groups participated.

Several important limitations of criminal trials as historical sources need to be noted. First, despite the use of the courts by every sector of society, a great deal of criminal behavior was not tried in the formal legal system. Local authorities—caciques, Spanish mayors, and Indian mayors—were authorized to punish petty transgressors without formal trial.[52] Violent, seemingly arbitrary behavior that served to buttress the powerful frequently characterized these efforts at local "law enforcement" and social control. Also, much criminal behavior was punished without the intervention of the state, local or viceregal. Court records contain numerous references to private jails in haciendas and obrajes.[53] The elite was not alone in taking justice into its own hands. The local population, including the peasantry, dealt quite harshly with thieves and other transgressors. Although some criminals, such as infamous rustlers, were handed over to colonial authorities, most crimes involving people of the same community were managed directly. The trial records reviewed here thus slight intraclass crimes.[54]

When trial records are used as a historical source, the context of the courtroom must be taken into account. In his study of colonial Mexico, William Taylor points out a series of inherent "distortions" of criminal trials. Colonial employees transcribed, summarized, edited, and, in the case of Peru, often translated the testimonies in the trials. More importantly, the strategies and terminology employed in the courts were shaped by and designed to conform to colonial notions about law and society. Therefore, the explanations provided by the defendants, particularly about their motives, must be interpreted cautiously.[55] In Peru, the gap between peasant society and official colonial discourse and practice was enormous. Although Quechua translators were provided, the courtroom in Cuzco could be a foreign and intimidating site for a highlands peasant. It should be kept in mind, however, that Andean Indians had a centuries-long tradition of court battles and that many of them participated as willing plaintiffs. Coercion against the defendants was apparently infrequent. In colonial criminal trials, a surprising and welcome amount of forthright statements about local society can be found.[56]

Caciques were the primary defendants in the trials against abusive authorities in late colonial Cuzco. In the real audiencia, they were accused in 44 percent of the cases (thirty-seven cases out of eighty-four); subdelegates in 20 percent; *recaudadores* (tax collectors) in 20 percent; and mayors in 11 percent. In the intendencia (including intendencia-provincias), caciques were accused in 36 percent of the cases (twenty-two out of fifty-eight); mayors in 22 percent; priests, subdelegates, and members of the military in 12 percent each; and recaudadores in 10 percent.[57] Unfortunately, it is not always clear whether the accused cacique was hereditary (*de sangre*) or a newcomer (*interino*). In eleven of the thirty-seven cases against caciques in the real audiencia, explicit mention was made about their status as interinos. These cases include some with the most flagrant and systematic abuses. Indians were the plaintiffs in 72 percent of the real audiencia cases and in 48 percent of the intendencia cases. Their suits were lodged by the *protector de Indios*, but the indigenous plaintiffs testified in every case. Often, they were supported by other authorities such as priests or contending caciques.

THE NATURE OF THE DISPUTES

Of the *abusos* challenged in the courts, two major types stand out. The first type involved systematic exploitation: usurpation of land, tribute fraud, coerced labor, and the forced sale of goods (i.e., the reparto, banned in 1780). The allegations often included reports of wanton violence and "immoral behavior" such as adultery or polygamy. Although usually concentrating on a particular authority, the accusations generally mentioned the complicity of others. The second major category of abuse was violence against or imprisonment of a commoner by an authority. The fact that the beating or imprisonment was often preceded ("provoked," according to the defendant) by a confrontation over the authority's misbehavior indicates that these two categories were related: exploitative practices were often backed up by violence, and economic gain and coercive social control constituted integral elements of local power.

Almost every possible combination of abuses can be found. In fact, it was unusual for a single allegation to be lodged because these practices were usually related. For example, a subdelegate in Quispicanchis was accused of forcing Indians to work for him for free at an obraje and at his house, charging exempt Indians the head tax in order to pocket the money, and replacing authorities with his friends and relatives.[58] Another subdelegate reportedly worked with an accountant and a cacique to sell unwanted or overpriced mules, dried potatoes, corn, and coca leaves to Indians. This enterprise allowed him to demand free labor and the use of extensive community lands.[59] A recaudador became violent when Indians resisted working at his chorrillo, and another sent laborers to work at a prominent friend's estate.[60] An *alcalde mayor* in Vilcabamba usurped the position of cacique and exaggerated his subjects' debts in order to force them to work in the mines.[61] An individual who served as alcalde mayor, recaudador, and cacique of Ocongate sent Indians to work in coca plantations in the Paucartambo valley, sold overpriced mules, iron, and other goods in exchange for the best livestock valued at "very low prices," and excluded Indians from the tax rolls even though he charged them tribute. His father was rumored to have conducted similar operations, thus "keeping the courts always busy."[62] In 1817, plaintiffs accused the subdelegate of Quispicanchis, Juan Tomás Moscoso, of violence, tax embezzlement, nepotism, land and water rights fraud, and attacks against and replacement of the mayor and local judges.[63] These trials clearly depict the close relationship among the different types of exploitation. Authorities used the returns in one type of activity to reinforce another. In this period, "power" was not constituted by controlling a single economic resource such as land, but rather by combining efforts to gain revenue through a number of enterprises with efforts to monopolize political dominance.

Despite the oppressive scenarios portrayed in the trials, in which the term *prepotencia* was frequently used to characterize caciques and other officials, local power emerges in the records as short term and fragile. On the one hand, many of the malfeasants were outsiders who presumably wanted to gain money, allies, and status, and then move on to more lucrative enterprises. They did not attempt to entrench themselves locally. On the other hand, divisions within elite groups and active resistance by the peasantry hindered the accumulation of economic and political power. Even with broad alliances and numerous concessions, a newcomer confronted powerful enemies. For example, local priests challenged many caciques interinos from the beginning of their tenure, and subdelegates faced the opposition of venerable caciques. Despite public displays of power, such as indiscriminate whippings, officials feared provoking the commoners because they depended on them economically and worried about protests being lodged locally or in the courts. In light of the Crown's distaste for wayward authorities, local authorities dreaded the possibility of rumors or accusations about misbehavior reaching intendancy officials. Therefore, beyond the veneer of local omnipotence, the power of local officials in this period remained brittle.

These trials highlight the tangled political alliances in the post-Tupac Amaru era after the creation of the intendancies and the erosion of the cacique office. Such alliances assumed no standard pattern in this period. The subdelegates, weaker than their predecessors because of the proximity of the intendant and the abolition of the profitable reparto, needed the support of the locally powerful. They frequently allied with caciques, either those they had placed in office or acquiescent veterans. They could, however, also align with powerful economic figures, such as hacienda owners, militia leaders, or even priests. In the words of David Cahill, "[the] jockeying for social position in many *doctrinas*—typically involving *subdelegados,* priests, caciques but also military, alcaldes, and *hacendados*—came to be a prominent feature, almost a rhythm, of late colonial rural life in the Cuzco region."[64] I found virtually every possible combination of collusion between subdelegates, priests, caciques, and local authorities in the trials, but certain patterns recurred more often. Interestingly, the patterns of collusion also reveal priests and representatives of the Bourbon state to be increasingly at odds in this period.[65]

Cases against an official were usually part of an enduring, behind-the-scenes struggle over local political power. Often, disputes over the cacicazgo, which had raged for centuries, played an important part. The post-Tupac Amaru purge, the ambiguity regarding the cacique office, and the resulting political vacuum kindled these struggles. The 1806 document mentioned previously in this chapter lists thirty-nine requests for the office of cacique, most of them made by former office-holders.[66] The same document also tallied ninety-three complaints by Indians against "caciques and others," the majority against caciques.[67] The struggles over the cacicazgos were often part of broader conflicts. For example, in the frequent battles between a subdelegate and a priest, each contender often promoted a different nominee for the post of local cacique. Generally, the subdelegate would defend his nominee, a cacique interino, by accusing the other nominee of having supported Tupac Amaru and of engaging in subsequent rabble-rousing. The priest or other defenders of the *cacique de sangre* (also called *cacique étnico*) would harangue the newcomer for disrupting tradition and endangering local stability, insinuating the possibility of a revolt.

Indians were more inclined to accuse caciques interinos than hereditary caciques. The newcomers had weaker ties to the community and thus had fewer constraints on their behavior. Whereas an abusive hereditary cacique and his family faced pressure from friends and associates, a newcomer was concerned more about his relationship with his superiors than about local complaints. One should not, however, romanticize the behavior of the hereditary caciques; numerous cases reveal their misconduct. Inheriting the position did not automatically confer legitimacy in the eyes of the Indians. Yet each cacique's political survival depended on the maintenance of reciprocal relations with indigenous society. If a cacique's Indians resisted fulfilling the state's demands for tribute and labor, he had to make up the difference. His ability to punish transgressors was limited because he and his family members faced the daily consequences of losing the respect and confidence of the local population.

The recently named outsider was more interested in assuring a quick profit. Although good relations with local Indians facilitated his work, gaining the capital he needed to maintain ties to the members of the political and economic elite was generally a greater priority. Also, many caciques interinos aspired to higher office. The origins of the interinos varied (some were true outsiders, whereas others were locals, often mestizos, who used the position to fortify their socioeconomic position), but they were less concerned than the hereditary cacique about maintaining norms of reciprocity and acceptable behavior. It does not take much imagination to realize, for example, that for the Pucará (Lampa province) cacique, who did not speak Quechua and therefore had to rely on a translator, the margin for negotiation with monolingual Indians was small.[68]

Although the imprecision in the use of the term *cacique* prevents any quantitative comparison between complaints against hereditary caciques versus outsiders who held the office (often the difference was not noted and a Spanish last name is not a reliable criterion), the interinos were the objects of the most detailed complaints. In many trials, their legitimacy was explicitly questioned because of their origin. In 1802, plaintiffs in Tiquillaca, Puno, described in great detail the cacica's abuses, contending that "the recently named cacica has become [se ha hecho] a foreigner to this town; she does not allow anyone to have a store or even a produce stand; only she can sell food, and even then at inflated prices."[69] The use of the reflexive verb *hacerse* and the gist of the sentence indicate that "outsider" was not an objective, absolute category referring to place of birth or time of residency, but rather a status dependent at least in part on behavior and attitude. Thus, some caciques interinos and other outsiders saw it in their interest to promote good relations with locals in order to gain their confidence and even support. Perhaps the defendants cited above managed to cultivate good relations with some elements of the local population and not others.

The case of Francisco Martínez reflects the tensions surrounding the cacique office. He actually ran into trouble before officially taking office. In 1785, Martínez, at this point a sergeant of the dragoon militia, was said to have demanded, "as cacique," five reales of a tribute debt from Narciso Santos Mamani, the former cacique of Marangani, Sicuani. Mamani refused to pay, shouting that "if my monarch knew about these outrages against Indians, nobody would dare to commit them." Martínez and his thugs beat up Mamani. The trial evolved around Mamani's purported support for Tupac Amaru in the recent rebellion and his intemperate, subversive nature.[70] In 1793, Martínez became embroiled in another series of lawsuits that questioned his conduct and ultimately cost him his job.

Ventura Aymitumi accused Martínez—cacique interino of the Quehuar ayllu in Sicuani since 1789 and promoted to militia captain—of collecting tribute from exempt Indians, making Indians work on his estate with little or no pay and minimal food, impounding animals, and imprisoning Aymitumi when he protested. Aymitumi descended from a line of royal caciques. In various trials, he described how Martínez forced Indians to work on his "opulent estate" and provided them with only a bit of coca and boiled wheat, although he made great profits marketing his goods in Upper Peru. Aymitumi claimed that Martínez and his guards not only roughed him up, but harassed his extended family.[71] The subdelegate of Canas y Canchis, Don Juan Bautista Altoaguirre, defended Martínez, reprimanding Aymitumi for his lazy, drunken, and subversive spirit: "Occupied by his laziness, he disturbs the tranquillity of the other Indians, seducing them in drunken sessions, like those he held in the recent rebellion in which he was a dedicated traitor, to conspire against the honorable citizens."[72]

In 1795, Martínez had Aymitumi and other Indians arrested, charging that they resisted paying tribute, attacked his hacienda "like in the time of the Rebellion," burned his crops, and killed his foreman. The accusation again centered on Aymitumi's putative support for Tupac Amaru. With the aid of a translator, Aymitumi claimed that this trial was retaliation for his lawsuit against Martínez. He argued that he had been forced to fight for the rebels because his father was a cacique and that he ultimately participated in the campaigns against the rebels in Upper Peru after the death of Tupac Amaru. He again condemned Martínez for forcing Indians to work on his hacienda and for taking their animals. Pascual Fernandez, a field-worker, and several other Indians supported his accusations. Aymitumi sought to regain the hereditary cacique position by garnering the support of the ayllu's Indians. In 1795 and again in 1798, he took Martínez to court for his vindictive conduct, which included the "redistribution" of his land.

In the 1798 case, Martínez was forced to pay the court costs and was warned not to harm Aymitumi.[73] He complained that he was a sick, ruined man, scared to return to Sicuani, where thieves had looted his house. After several more trials involving Aymitumi and Martínez, the latter was removed from the cacicazgo of Quehuar. In this situation, Indians' persistence paid off,[74] yet Aymitumi spent more than three years in Cuzco pursuing these different cases, much of the time in jail, and he never regained the cacique position. Martínez ultimately failed to use his position as cacique to become wealthy and to rise in the colonial bureaucracy. As in many cases, both sides appeared to lose.

In the trials, lawyers and witnesses clearly expressed the prevailing official views of Indians and of state policy vis-à-vis the indigenous population in the late colonial period. Although opposing lawyers in cases
concerning abusive practices against Indians battled in long, often bitter legal struggles, their arguments reveal shared notions about Indians. Enlightened ideas about the possible rationality of the Indians had
not seeped into eighteenth-century legal discourse. From the conquis-
tadors in the sixteenth century to the caciques interinos in the final
colonial decades (and into the republican period), officials argued that
because Indians were irrational and infantile, they needed the guidance
or prodding of outsiders. Conversely, throughout the colonial period,
the state sustained that Indians required protection. Both sides agreed
on the need for intervention in Indian society, but they disagreed on
the nature and agent of this intervention. Non-Indians interpreted the
Tupac Amaru uprising as proof of the urgency of this intervention.

Authorities accused of improper behavior against Indians presented
a forthright defense: if not compelled by outsiders, Indians would re-
cede into idleness and vice. Without coercion or persuasion, they would
produce only for subsistence, purchase little, avoid work on estates, and
fail to pay tribute. They would turn their back on Christianity, return
to pagan rites, and drink too much. Participants in the trials frequently
argued that authorities had to use force with the Indians, a venerable
argument in colonial Peru. In 1793, when charged with whipping and
hitting Indians, a subdelegate downplayed the accusations against him
in the following terms: "These [accusations] are worthy of scorn because the Indians need it because if not punished, they get hopelessly
presumptuous. I know this by experience, which is why I must alert
Your Highness that if Indians are not corrected with whippings, their
arrogance, drunkenness, laziness, absence from Doctrine and mass, and
failure to pay tribute to the detriment of the caciques will be inevitable."[75] In virtually every case charging an official for abusive behavior,
the defendant argued that he had always had in mind the best interests
of the Indians and the Crown and that his endeavors ultimately sought
to facilitate the fulfillment of colonial obligations and to prevent subversion. Usually, the defendants mentioned the necessity of occasional
violence against Indians and their untrustworthiness in the courts.

The *procuradores* (lawyers) or protectores de Indios employed a similar discourse in the defense of Indians. They argued that if not protected by the state, Indians would fall into the hands of exploitative outsiders. The concomitant inability to fulfill tribute and labor obligations was usually implied. When defending an alleged criminal, the protectors contended that the ignorant or infantile state of the Indian led him toward such behavior. In 1820, a procurador defended an Indian accused of assassination by noting his race's immaturity and irrationality: "The Indians' lack of ingenuity, reason, and talent as well as their rusticity do not allow them to discern situations and avoid mischief. This deplorable situation, which excuses them from malice in their actions, derives from their uncivil lives and lack of enlightenment in which they miserably vegetate, making them through privilege a class of minors. All the laws and municipal ordinances treat them leniently, . . . even more so than children."[76] A protector de Indios in Lima and a famed "precursor" of Peruvian independence, José Baquíjano, used similar rhetoric in 1779. In his defense of an Indian who had admitted committing a theft, Baquíjano contended that the defendant's own testimony should be ignored because he was "an ignorant, fearful, lying, inebriated Indian."[77] Alternative perspectives on the Indians in the grim post–Tupac Amaru intellectual environment were rare exceptions.

Litigants in Cuzco emphasized the defendant's (usually an authority) misbehavior and invoked diverse codes of conduct. They most commonly employed a Habsburgian notion of state and society in which authorities were understood to be guardians of Indians, which was part of a pact between Crown and subjects. Litigants would describe the defendant's misconduct, stressing the breach with common practice overseen by His Majesty, the king. Indians also contended that the placement and behavior of newcomers imposed on them violated traditional relations between the state and the indigenous peasantry. This venerable "long live the king and death to bad government" motif was not merely a retrograde effort to resurrect the colonial past. As the Comunero rebellion in New Granada and both the Tupac Amaru uprising and the War of Independence in the southern Andes indicated, it could be used to delegitimize rulers and even to justify overthrowing the state.[78] It had revolutionary potential. Plaintiffs also used a more directly functionalist approach, pointing out that abusive endeavors by authorities diminished Indians' ability to fulfill their tribute and labor obligations. They echoed the state's avowed goal to root out abusive authorities and networks of political and economic alliances, playing to the Bourbon's desire to thwart corrupt intermediaries, improve tax collection, and prevent unrest prompted by unrestrained authorities.

Frequently, the plaintiffs strengthened their case by detailing the defendant's disregard for accepted moral practices. For example, a cacique in Cotabambas was accused not only of fraud and battery, but also of killing "a daughter," stealing from the church, and living in "complete adultery."[79] Captain Vargas, the recaudador of Lamay, was also accused of insulting local mestizos and Spaniards and of abducting women.[80] In an accusation against the Marqués of Cochan, subdelegate of Cotabambas, the plaintiff argued that Cochan lived with another woman besides his wife in "his very own home." Furthermore, "enraptured with the love of his sweetheart, he endlessly endeavor[ed] to find ways to make her rich, which is why he organize[d] prohibited games like dice."[81] Anselmo Hinojosa, cacique of Calca, allegedly not only took land but "disturb[ed] single and married women."[82] For both the plaintiffs and state authorities in Cuzco or Lima, such moral infractions signified the abandonment of acceptable relations with the subject population.[83] These cases indicate that the Indians considered abusive conduct—whether pecuniary exploitation, violence, "immoral" behavior, or a combination—as illegitimate and knew that they could gain the ear of colonial officials at the intendancy level.

Did the use of the courts reinforce the ideological codes underlying Indians' subordinate position in colonial society? Certainly, the legal system served as a key forum for representatives of the state and members of the elite to express and propagate their disdain for Indians. The anti-Indian spirit of the post–Tupac Amaru "Great Fear" looms large in the trials of the era. In terms of whether the Indians accepted this definition of themselves and their position, I would propose a cautious interpretation. Invoking legal terms and strategies that implicitly or explicitly justified Spanish rule and colonial hierarchies does not mean accepting them. Hegemony is not so simple. The use of the legal system reflected and perhaps reinforced these social divisions, but it in no way caused them. The fact that the Indians did not explicitly question in the courts the predominant views of themselves as needy inferiors does not mean that they accepted these views. It means that they knew that they could not challenge such views in their lawsuits and that their representatives did not deem it necessary, expedient, or even correct to do so.

On the other hand, subaltern groups should not be credited with crafty resistance every time they used colonial institutions to their advantage. Although they could benefit from their lawsuits (and could certainly suffer in the courts as well), we cannot assume that they understood their efforts as subversive and thus that they merely ignored the ideological and political ramifications of their use of the courts.

THE DECISIONS AND THEIR SIGNIFICANCE

No sentence was found in 67 percent of the cases in the real audiencia and in 84 percent of the cases in the intendencia. In those cases in which a sentence was pronounced in the real audiencia, removal from office (10 percent of the total) and fines (8 percent) constituted the most common forms of punishment. Court costs, jail terms, and acquittal were ordered in each of three cases. The outcome of the numerous cases with no decision remains a puzzle.[84] The fact that in some cases the defendant was acquitted indicates that no sentence was not the same as a verdict of not guilty. In the cases with decisions, the loss of a position, hefty fines, and other sentences were unwelcome punishments for the guilty.[85] Despite the high number of cases with no sentences, lawsuits constituted a potent threat. The Indians' repeated use of the courts suggests that they considered it an effective weapon.

Whatever the outcome, confronting a lawsuit as a defendant represented a troublesome burden. Not only was it a costly, time-consuming process, particularly because of the renowned corruption and indolence of the Peruvian courts, but a defendant lost legitimacy in the eyes of the state and local society. A trial often publicized shady dealings and political alliances, and the defendant had to organize a defense and confront the charges. The case against him was often bolstered by the participation of long-standing enemies and their allies. A petty charge could thus resurrect decades-old disputes and conflicts. Even if the defendant believed that he had done no wrong and could convince the court, a public reading of the charges against him was unwelcome. As in contemporary Latin America, defending oneself from legal charges of corruption and abuse in colonial Peru represented a potential calamity for an official.

Why was the Bourbon state responsive to lawsuits filed by peasants and their representatives in an area that had recently been the site of a massive rural uprising? Primarily, it was concerned about another rebellion and relied on Indian tribute in its persistent efforts to increase fiscal revenues. The post–Tupac Amaru policy thus combined repression with negotiation. Colonial authorities, conscious that exploitative corregidores and other local officials had helped kindle the rebellion and had often obstructed tax collection, supported the punishment of errant officials. Cuzco's heavily indigenous population contained a large percentage of the viceroyalty's tribute payers. In the testimonies against the officials, the plaintiffs generally stressed the defendants' disruptive behavior and their failure to fulfill their colonial obligations, so the state took notice. Moreover, viceregal officials believed that maintaining control of Cuzco was essential for the defense of Peru. Because of their concern over internal and external threats to security and their search for greater revenues, they had little sympathy for local officials who raised the ire of the indigenous population.

CONCLUSION: PEASANTS, STATE, AND SOCIETY IN THE AFTERMATH OF REBELLION

This study supports the findings of scholars who cast the courts as a Janus-faced institution that both promoted the state and the upper classes' viewpoints and defended their dominance, while at the same time providing a forum for questioning and even subverting this control. The legal system constituted a site of incorporation and contestation.[86] The question whether the use of the courtroom increased the legitimacy of the Bourbon state in the eyes of Indians and other plaintiffs needs to be engaged from two related perspectives: Did it augment their respect for the colonial state and draw them into colonial structures? And did it preempt other forms of mass political actions, namely rebellions? The answer is a guarded no on both accounts. Their triumphs demonstrated to the peasants that the colonial state, or at least certain representatives or echelons, continued to acknowledge their rights to relative political autonomy and to freedom from pernicious interlopers. Yet, at the same time, their defeats in the courtroom and the series of complaints that prompted them to sue in the first place increased their hostility toward the state. It should be remembered that Indians did not always win their legal battles. Not only did they lose many cases, but, more significantly, in many of the trials reviewed here they faced each other on opposing sides, as defendants and as plaintiffs. Political divisions in late colonial Cuzco did pit Indians against non-Indians, but in most cases they pitted Indians against other Indians.

In terms of the relationship between the legal system and social movements, events in the early nineteenth century vividly demonstrated that using the courts did not impede more radical behavior. From 1805 to independence in the 1820s, decades after the Tupac Amaru rebellion, Cuzco was the site of numerous revolts, including the Pumacahua rebellion, 1814–15. The use of the legal system had not prevented the peasantry from taking more direct action. The fact that reliance on the courts from 1787 to 1814 was sandwiched between two massive revolts refutes the argument that "reformist" tactics such as filing lawsuits impeded more revolutionary activities. In fact, the preparation of a lawsuit could mobilize a community, thus facilitating organized protest if legal remedies failed. Rebels would claim that justice had not been served when their plea had been turned down or a favorable sentence not carried out.[87] A lawsuit against authorities did not prevent the very same people from rising up collectively.

What did Indians achieve by using the legal system? I argue that the contradictions of Bourbon policies, the stagnant economy, and above all the indigenous peasantry's use of the courts impeded the implementation of the accelerated reforms plotted out by the revanchist colonial state. Peasant resistance, primarily in the form of lawsuits, constituted an additional and substantial impediment to the changes envisioned by the Spanish Crown. Although not as catastrophic as it might have been, the period did prompt or heighten changes that continued to mark Andean society well into the republican period. Centrifugal forces gained strength as a variety of figures vied to supplant the waning powers of the cacique. A particularly harsh anti-Indian discourse emerged that persisted through the War of Independence and into the republican period. The already formidable schism between the Andes and Lima-based intellectuals widened. Indians did not stand by, however, as these changes took form.

THE LONG WAR OF INDEPENDENCE IN PERU

I n 1808, Napoleon's forces invaded Spain, replacing King Ferdinand VII with Joseph Bonaparte. Spanish liberals resisted, creating provincial juntas that would fight in lieu of the deposed king. They sought the support of the American population, offering in return to improve the colony's status within the empire. By heightening discord in Spain and questioning the legitimacy of the Spanish monarchy, the Napoleonic invasion converted the timid calls for greater economic and political autonomy and the occasional revolts in Spanish America into massive political movements. In Mexico in 1810, an uprising led by Father Miguel Hidalgo y Costilla swept through the Bajío region, attracting more than one hundred thousand followers. After the defeat of the rebels, royalists managed to hold on to power until the 1820s. In South America, two major fronts challenged Spanish rule. José de San Martín led the insurgents from Río de la Plata over the Andes to Chile, while in the north Simón Bolívar commanded forces centered in New Granada, which later became Venezuela and Colombia. Both movements converged in Peru in the 1820s, defeating the Spanish in 1824.

From 1808 until the mid-1820s, debates about the position of the American colonies raged not only in Spain but throughout the Americas. For the population of Cuzco and other regions, this period was marked by dizzying and often contradictory changes as the colonial state alternately reduced, abolished, and reintroduced taxes and other impositions. From 1808 until 1814, several revolts and conspiracies took place in southern Andean cities, culminating in a mass uprising based in Cuzco. With the defeat of the misnamed "Pumacahua rebellion," the focus of the war shifted to Lima and the Central Andes. Not only did the center of the conflict move to the coast, but it increasingly became a war of independence. Whereas in the earlier period insurgents and noncombatants had discussed numerous possibilities, by 1820 only three alternatives existed: the absolutist status quo, some type of reformed monarchism, or independence. Although patriot leaders declared Peru independent on July 28, 1821, the final defeat of the Spanish took place in December 1824 at the Battle of Ayacucho. Few people escaped the war and its reverberations: as soldiers (men and women fighting in different ways for both sides), as providers of supplies (bought at inflated prices or seized without compensation), and as followers of the incessant rumors about the ideological and military battles being waged throughout the Americas.

In recent decades, many interpretations of the Peruvian War of Independence have questioned the population's commitment to freedom from Spain. Patriot forces in Peru ultimately had to rely on outsiders as commanders and soldiers: first San Martín and subsequently Bolívar. The majority of the economic and social elite remained royalist to the end. Whereas in some regions the struggle against the Spanish temporarily camouflaged the antagonisms between diverse social groups with divergent platforms, in Peru the war could not patch over these divisions. Animosity between social and ethnic groups nominally fighting on the same side emerged almost immediately, and regional divisions, above all between Lima and the southern Andes, became increasingly visible.[1] The lower classes formed *montoneros,* guerrilla bands, which often acted quite autonomously and, to the horror of estate owners and other occasional victims, pursued their own vision of "independence."

These issues were at the center of a heated controversy in the 1970s. In 1972, Heraclio Bonilla and Karen Spalding published *La independencia en el Perú,* which questioned the celebratory tone of the commemoration of the 150th anniversary of Peruvian independence. The authors insisted that Peruvian independence had required foreign armies, that the Lima elite had been ambivalent, if not downright royalist, and that the lower classes did not massively support the patriot movement—they were either not interested or not invited. The book prompted contentious discussions and accusations, and the debate remains open more than twenty years after the first edition was published. Scholars largely agree that the struggle for independence was not a cohesive movement that unified Peru's regions, classes, and ethnic groups. Yet others have qualified Bonilla and Spalding's views, noting that certain sectors of the colonial elite did support the independence movement and that guerrilla bands acted throughout the viceroyalty.[2] Alberto Flores Galindo points out that "while it is evident that Independence—in and outside of the city of Lima—was not a social or popular revolution, this does not mean that we should overlook the intervention of the lower classes and, even less, to deny the changes brought by Independence."[3] Focusing on the Indian population, this chapter examines the War of Independence and its legacy from the perspective of Cuzco.

The chapter questions the interpretation that all the conspiracies, revolts, rebellions, and warfare in Peru and the rest of Spanish America from 1808 to the mid-1820s were part of a monolithic War of Independence. Although anti-Spanish sentiments were at the heart of this turmoil, and the end result was an independent republic, no single conflict pitting Spanish forces against Peruvians seeking independence characterized this period. First, as Bonilla and Spalding pointed out in 1972, Peruvians manned both the royalist army and the patriot forces, and both armies counted on outsiders. Interpretations that cast Peruvian insurgents in a fight against Spanish royalists are sociologically incorrect. Second, and more important, dissidents considered a number of alternatives to Spanish absolutism, including even a series of monarchical schemes. Republicanism did not emerge until after more than a decade of debate and warfare. One major problem with the Whiggish or nationalist interpretation of independence resides in its consideration of those who did not fight for an independent republic as either royalist or apolitical. The lower classes, in particular, contemplated a number of alternatives to both Spanish colonialism and republicanism. To understand the role of the Peruvian majority in the long struggle, these alternatives need to be taken seriously.[4]

INSURGENCY IN THE SOUTH

In 1805, Gabriel Aguilar and José Manuel de Ubalde, Creoles born in Huánuco and Arequipa respectively, planned to seize Cuzco and install an Inca emperor. Failing to persuade a Cuzco cacique to take the role, they decided Aguilar would lead the new state. Although short on military strategy, they were long on messianic and providentialist beliefs.

Betrayed before they could initiate military action, they were tried and hanged in a Cuzco plaza in December 1805. Approximately thirty accomplices, mostly priests and professionals, were also tried. The courts deported six of them and freed the others.[5] Spanish authorities interpreted the conspiracy as a dangerous attempt to take advantage of the Indians' attachment to the former Inca capital. A judge wrote that "the capital, Cuzco, is the idol of the Indians, where they revere the ashes of their old sovereigns and where the remains of their old nobility are found. The proclamation of an Inca would have had fatal consequences which is why these traitors [Aguilar and Ubalde] wanted to do so."[6] With the execution of Aguilar and Ubalde, colonial authorities sought to prevent the spread of the conspiracy.

Although Aguilar and Ubalde envisioned radical changes, they did not seek to create a republic. They made clear their plans to resurrect the Inca Empire. In subsequent years, dreams such as these would blend with the war against the colonial government, but not in 1805. Their seemingly fantastic plans, however, influenced other conspiracies outside of the city of Cuzco, which greatly concerned authorities. For example, events in Huarocondo, Abancay, contained all the elements of a full-fledged Andean uprising except that, despite a thorough investigation, it remains unclear whether anything actually happened. On July 19, 1805, Eusebio Lobo, identified interestingly enough as a mestizo who did not know Spanish, met four Indians who were returning from the fields drinking corn beer. He overheard them talk about their anger over what the Spanish took from their wheat crop and reminisce about the "past rebellion"—that is, the Tupac Amaru uprising.[7] Lobo claimed that they discussed "taking the lives" of Spaniards and debated about where to begin the uprising. Days later, one of the Indians, Pedro Díaz, threatened some soldiers in a chichería, drunkenly boasting that he would kill them "because he was a descendent of Llamac Inga and a principal noble." A sergeant imprisoned Díaz and his fellow drunkards.

More than two hundred pages of testimony confirm little about the plan. The Indians mentioned that the revolt would take place on the Day of Santiago (July 25), the patron saint of Huarocondo, and thus the date of a large festival, or on Our Lady of the Angels Day (August 2). Witnesses described an argument between Lobo and Díaz in which Lobo yelled at his Indian wife, and Díaz defended her.[8] The defendants admitted widespread tensions among Indians over the *repartición de trigo,* the monopsonistic system in which colonial authorities controlled the sale and price of wheat.[9] The prosecutors tried to uncover connections with the Aguilar-Ubalde conspiracy, accusing Pedro Díaz of spreading news about events in Cuzco.[10] Although many defendants admitted that they had contact with Cuzco through the marketing of their agricultural products, and one said that a chola market vendor in Cuzco had reported disturbances in the city, they denied any contact with the conspiracy, and prosecutors found no evidence to contradict the suspects. From the sketchy evidence available, it appears that all versions were partially correct. The Indians had grievances and contemplated rebellion, and the accusers exaggerated their case. Real audiencia authorities ascertained to their relief that the purported rebels in Huarocondo had no links with the Cuzco conspirators and freed all the suspects.

By 1808, hostility toward the colonial regime and rumored uprisings were materializing into organized resistance. People increasingly resented Bourbon rule, particularly favoritism toward Spaniards, escalating tax demands, convoluted economic restrictions, inattention to the colonies, and other related grievances. Spain demanded more from its colonies while tightening its political hold. The situation, of course, varied between and within regions: some prospered at the beginning of the nineteenth century, with many individuals benefiting from the prosperity. But a large section of the population suffered from and disliked Spaniards' virtual monopoly on prominent administrative positions, the frequent increases in taxes, and Spain's preoccupation with Europe to the detriment of its colonies. In Spanish South America, discontent was greatest in the economically dynamic but politically peripheral regions such as Río de la Plata. In contrast, administrative centers that benefited the most from colonial centralism, such as Lima, resisted the calls for independence. James Lockhart and Stuart B. Schwartz note that the direction of the campaigns for independence reversed the direction taken in the conquest: "the areas conquered last were the first to rise and themselves aided actively in taking the others, converging on Peru in a mirror image of the sixteenth-century movement outward from that base."[11] Also, influential Enlightenment ideologies increasingly found their way to Spanish America in these years, grounding the platforms of the rebel leadership and inciting the lower classes as well.[12]

Events in Spain beginning in 1808 stimulated malcontents in America. Under Charles IV (1788–1808), Spain reacted to the French

Revolution and the rapidly changing scene in Europe by immersing itself in numerous international wars and heightening absolutism in Spain, thereby undermining the Bourbon reforms at home and in its colonies.[13] In March 1808, Charles IV was forced to abdicate in favor of his son, Ferdinand VII. Months later, Napoleonic forces occupied Madrid, and Napoleon placed his brother Joseph Bonaparte on the throne. Provincial juntas opposed the French invaders and, in January 1809, decreed that the American dominions constituted integral parts of the Spanish monarchy or "nation."[14] People in both Europe and the New World now widely questioned the political legitimacy of the Spanish in the Americas. During the captivity of Ferdinand VII, 1809–14, uncertainty and confusion marked politics in Peru.

In this period, events in Cuzco were closely related to those in Upper Peru. The initial stages in Spanish South America of what became the War of Independence pitted the rebellious Río de la Plata viceroyalty, which included much of Upper Peru, against the colonial military garrisoned in Lima and increasingly in Cuzco. In July 1809, a junta in La Paz, led by the mestizo Pedro Domingo Murillo, called for self-government and attempted to gain the support of the Indian population.[15] Juan José Castelli directed the first major expedition of rebels from Río de la Plata to Upper Peru. On May 25, 1811, amidst the Tiwanaku ruins, he abolished tribute and forced labor and promised to distribute land and establish schools. He proclaimed Indians to be citizens with equal rights.[16] In the same year, several uprisings took place in La Paz, in which Indians participated en masse, and in Tacna, a Peruvian city to the southwest of Cuzco.[17] These events affected Peru more than in military terms as anticolonial ideologies reached the Cuzco area from the south, Upper Peru, and Río de la Plata.

Since his arrival in 1806, the viceroy of Peru, José Fernando de Abascal y Sousa, an adroit strategist and experienced commander, had strengthened the army and militia. His efforts largely prevented neighboring rebellions in Upper Peru and Quito from expanding. He used the southern Andes, particularly Cuzco, as a base to suppress the Upper Peruvian rebels.[18] Abascal assigned the president of Cuzco's audiencia, the Creole General José Manuel de Goyeneche, to be military commander of Upper Peru. Goyeneche led the counterattack, occupying La Paz in October 1810 with an army composed primarily of Cusqueños.[19] Murillo was executed shortly thereafter. Upper Peru was reannexed to

Peru and became the staging ground for the campaigns against Río de la Plata. After 1811, Abascal increasingly depended on a draft, primarily in Cuzco, to man the military campaigns in Upper Peru. Indian commanders Mateo García Pumacahua and José Domingo Choquehuanca led militias composed primarily of Indians, as Choquehuanca drafted twelve hundred men in Azángaro, and Pumacahua counted on thirty-five hundred, primarily Indians from the Cuzco area.

Rumors abounded in Cuzco about the fate of the king, radical changes in Spain, and subversion to the south. In an area where the vast majority were illiterate and no printing presses were to be found, oral culture predominated. Diverse, creative, and often self-serving versions circulated of what had occurred in Europe and what it meant for state-subject relations. Rumors fanned the flames of rebellion and heightened loyalist panic, confirming Ranajit Guha's classification of them as "a universal and necessary carrier of insurgency in any pre-industrial, pre-literate society."[20] In the midst of the Pumacahua uprising, Pumacahua himself, at this point a rebel commander, wrote his adversary, General Juan Ramírez, "Who is the King that you are serving and whose troops you are leading? It is well known that our adored Sir Don Fernando VII no longer exists, and that he was sold to the French nation by the lowly Europeans, and that nothing is known about his whereabouts."[21] As in the Tupac Amaru rebellion, muleteers, parish priests, and other travelers supplied the southern Andes with news and rumors, circulating the information in chicherías, markets, and other stops on their routes. In 1821, the subdelegate of Carabaya, Manuel Antonio de Gómez, summarized the ubiquity and power of rumors spread by and about the insurgents. He described how in southern Peru, particularly in markets, people discussed the imminent fall of the monarch, the concomitant implementation of the Constitution, the corruption of the colonial army, the strength of San Martín's forces, the collapse of Buenos Aires, and so on. He despaired that 90 percent of his jurisdiction had accepted the patriots' views.[22]

Many people interpreted the changes in Spain as the opportunity to seek a more equitable relationship within the empire or even to take justice into their own hands. A conspiracy in Huaroc, Quispicanchis, in 1809 had many of the same elements of the events in Huarocondo four years earlier: drunken plans, quixotic outsiders, and Indian resentment. Mariano Soria, a cobbler and member of the Quispicanchis militia, overheard Indians discussing plans for an uprising. On a Sunday festival day, at the sign of a cough by an Indian dance leader, the Indians would kill the cacique, Don Juan Bautista Bellota (clearly not an ethnic cacique or even Indian), and any Spaniard who defended him. If troops arrived from nearby Urcos or Andahuaylillas, the rebels would attack them. If more substantial forces came from Cuzco, the insurgents would take to the hills and "tire and frustrate them." The plan included burning houses and demolishing buildings to slow the troops. The rebels intended to hang Spaniards "from the willow trees and the beams of Don Ignacio Solar's house." They planned a feast under the trees afterward.[23] To pay for expenses, they would ransack the town's houses, even that of Margarita Colina, whom they considered a "rich Indian." They would seize "the tribute money and gifts that, since the death of the King, the caciques kept for themselves."[24] They claimed to have the support of the entire southern Andean region and direct links with the Tupac Amaru rebels, boasting that "all the people from Quiquijana to Puno have agreed to join the rebellion, including Manuel Bastidas of Tungasuca, the brother of Micaela, the wife of the first insurgent José Tupac Amaru."[25]

Soria was the source of these elaborate plans. He later asserted that he was drunk when he repeated what he had heard. When questioned a second time in the trial, he changed his story. He claimed that he had overheard some Indians talk about how difficult it would be to pay tribute and fulfill labor duties because of the bad potato harvest. These Indians had given him numerous glasses of corn beer and rum, and shortly thereafter he drank more at a friend's house. With his "head hot with drink," he had proclaimed that certain individuals and all the women would be hanged from the willows. He did not remember revealing military plans. He blamed everything on his drunkenness, arguing that the ideas came "out of his mouth but not his heart." The real audiencia showed leniency, sentencing him to only six months in jail.

Perhaps these elaborate plans were the product of Soria's drunken imagination. The short jail sentence and the absence of any contact with or even a mention of political movements elsewhere indicate the event's isolation and insignificance. The trial demonstrates, however, both widespread popular discontent and government authorities' concern over any hint of an Indian-based uprising. This case and the one in Huarocondo indicate that the grumblings of many Indians, whose voices are rarely heard in the archives, transcended dislike for particular authorities and approximated a general repudiation of those defined as Spanish. It seems unlikely that these rumors were the mere fictional product of elite anxiety. The Pumacahua rebellion a few years later would confirm government fears.

The already firm connections between political developments in Spanish America and Spain tightened with the establishment of the Cortes de Cádiz, which governed Spain and its colonies from September 1810 until the restoration of Ferdinand VII in May 1814. Representatives from America, selected by *vecinos* in convoluted elections, participated with full voting privileges.[26] Peru had the right to twenty-two seats, but only eight elected officials arrived, and five alternates were elected in Cádiz. In some regions, elections were not held. In others, such as Cuzco, the representatives could not find the means to pay for the expensive three to four month trip to southern Spain.[27] In 1812, the Cortes promulgated a constitution that converted Spain into a constitutional monarchy, decreasing the powers of the king and increasing those of the Cortes. The Cortes reforms included freedom of the press and the abolition of Indian tribute and the Inquisition. Delegates argued strenuously about the role of the Indian in elections for the Cortes itself and, more importantly, in Spanish America's future.

The Peruvian population avidly followed the development of the Cortes and Spain's 1812 liberal Constitution. Events in Spain did not just inspire middle- and upper-class reformers. Contemporaries wrote with amazement about the lower classes' interest in the Constitution and the dissemination of political ideas. One observer noted that support for the Constitution was so great that "even the plebeians carried little written pieces of the Constitution because it was scarce, and they did not have the resources to get it."[28] On December 11, 1812, Cuzco received the Constitution with three days of festivities, which included fireworks, bull fights, public theater, and other popular attractions.[29] The news of events in Spain extended far beyond the city of Cuzco. In April 1811, authorities in the town of Paucartambo publicized the establishment of the Cortes with a procession down the main street, including proclamations, drums, and whistles, and by posting the decree in prominent places.[30] In the next couple of years, active participation in elections and other novel reforms legislated from Spain complemented and competed with outright insurgency in the southern Andes, prompting optimism and confusion. Indians played an active role in these reforms. In the end, however, their confidence in constitutional reform was dashed. Discussions in Cádiz foreshadowed the early republican authorities' uncertainty and ultimate neglect of the issue of what role Indians should play in the Americas.

In the final decades of colonial rule in Peru, writers who opposed Spanish colonialism had difficulty creating an alternative perspective on the Indian. An official discourse predominated that was part of the "Great Fear," which emphasized Indians' backwardness, their stubborn reliance on elements of their material culture, such as housing and clothing (and thus their resistance to the market), and their proclivity to alcoholism. These views contended that Indians were extremely poor and subordinate because of their natural defects, rather than because of their social or political situation.[31] Contributors to the key protonationalist paper of the period, the *Mercurio Peruano*, 1791–95, either reiterated this negative vision or by and large remained silent regarding the Indian population. Only a few intellectuals challenged the grim post–Tupac Amaru perspective. They agreed that the Indians were poverty-stricken and oppressed, but argued that social and political practices by authorities or local elites, rather than some sort of primordial inferiority, caused the Indians' oppression. This alternative view remained timid and largely isolated, however. Throughout the long War of Independence, insurgents addressed the question of Indians' place in a postcolonial future. They repeatedly vacillated—apprehensive about Indians' potential as citizens and, above all, about the consequences of weakening colonial power structures. The Cádiz Cortes were not an exception.

The Creole representatives in the Cortes defended the Indians' right to form part of the electing body. They calculated that if Indians were included in the population tally, the number of American representatives would increase and in fact surpass the number of Spaniards. The representatives insisted that the Indians should vote—but not have the right to run for office. They were to be represented by Creoles.[32] More consequential discussions took place about the Indian population and colonialism. Spanish deputies lauded the traditional relationship between the colonial state and Indians, insisting that Indians were irrational beings who required protection from wayward outsiders and did not merit any type of citizenship. The Sevillian deputy José Pablo Valiente was particularly harsh: Indians' "spirit and ingenuity is so small and their propensity to laziness so great . . . that after three centuries of opportune, persistent measures to illuminate them in common ideas, they remain the same as in the Conquest period."

He noted, with greater acuity, that if given the right to vote, the Indians would be represented by their exploiters, Creoles. One newspaper characterized this representation as leading the sheep to the wolf.[33] Some Creoles answered by cautiously defending the Indians' rationality, claiming that it was the exploitative institutions of colonialism, rather than their nature, that oppressed them.[34] These deputies contended that Indians could be "civilized" and incorporated into the wider (non-Indian) structures and material culture. Both sides of the debate agreed that the Indians were too autonomous and needed to be liberated from traditional practice as exhibited in their clothing, housing, and food. Some Creole members, however, contended that Indians would be able to shed their Indian ways and contribute to society.

Two other concerns shaped the debates and would continue to mark policy and ideological discussions for decades after independence. Some opponents of Spanish colonialism realized that the rapid overhaul of traditional colonial practice would subject Indians to the increased depredations of outsiders. All of the deputies, Spanish and Creoles, agreed on the need to "protect" the Indian. For many of the former, this protection justified the continuation of the status quo. Many of the Creoles, in contrast, sought a radical change in the relationship with Spain, including the dismantling of the caste system, but worried about the consequences for Indians. Marked by an enduring paternalistic discourse, this concern tempered some of the calls for reform and divided the Creole representatives. But practical reasons more than idealistic ones slowed the implementation of reforms. The conversion of the Indians into full citizens required the abolition of the Indian head tax. Not only did every echelon of the colonial state in the Andes depend on this revenue, but non-Indians relied on it for financial gain and political prominence. The subdelegates of Puno, for example, lobbied their representative to preserve the tax. This conflict previewed the first half century of the republic: the state abandoning liberal ideals because it relied on tribute both to finance the state and to cement caste-based power relations.[35]

Despite the colonial dependence on the tax, the Cortes abolished the Indian tribute on March 13, 1811. This decree, enacted in the name of equality, reverberated throughout the Andes, greatly influencing the political struggles of the period. Indians were freed from the head tax and granted the right to vote for the *cabildos,* the municipal councils. This meant, however, their inclusion in the sales tax, the further decline of the cacique office in the shadow of the councils, and the loss of the protection of their communal land by the colonial state, which they had received for centuries in return for the head tax. The rapid, unsettling policy changes in Spain and the Americas and the heterogeneity of Andean society meant that the impact of these reforms varied greatly from town to town. Changes in the tribute system disrupted the shadowy networks linking bond-paying capitalists, subdelegates, tax collectors, and local officials. The reforms enacted by the Cortes de Cádiz destabilized local power relations in the Andes.

Elections for local office, cabildo or *ayuntamiento* (town council), in which Indians had the right to vote, threatened the power of non-Indians. In nervous letters and memos, mestizos, Creoles, and Spaniards pronounced the dangers of allowing Indians to vote. Although they stressed a number of negative consequences, they were most concerned by the probability that Indians would displace them.[36] Indians used the elections to rid themselves of or weaken authorities and to resist particular impositions. The elections prompted disputes among and between different social groups—struggles that went beyond a mere Indian/non-Indian dichotomy. The reforms also called for land traditionally allotted to tax collectors to be rented, with the funds to be used for hospitals for Indians. This reform meant not only that communities would lose control of the land or its income, but that outsiders would be allowed to control large tracts. The remaining ethnic caciques fought this measure, ultimately with success.[37]

The head tax constituted the linchpin of colonial society in the Andes, and its abolition prompted great controversy and conflict. Because of the Peruvian viceroyalty's dire fiscal situation, and his own aversion to the liberal reforms of Cádiz, Viceroy Abascal introduced a "voluntary" head tax effective for the final half of 1812. Proponents argued that Indians willingly paid the tribute in order to guarantee their communal land rights. In letters to the king, petitions, lawsuits, and uprisings, however, Indians expressed their opposition to the overruling of the 1812 Constitution.[38] By 1813, Abascal pleaded for a restoration of tribute, deeming the voluntary tax a failure.[39] Reactions to the abolition of tribute highlight the complexity of Andean society. In general, Indians opposed efforts to reinstate the head tax, whereas non-Indians, who relied on the tax for their political power or economic standing, supported such efforts.[40]

The abolition of the head tax eliminated authorities' central role in Andean society, one that provided them ample economic and political opportunities. Opponents to the measures therefore included representatives of the various echelons of the intendancy system, as well as many caciques and other indigenous authorities. Some Indians also fared worse with abolition because they lost their exoneration from the tithe, the sales tax, and religious fees. Many affluent Indian merchants opposed the changes on these grounds,[41] yet the majority of Indians fought the reimposition of tribute. Christine Hünefeldt describes the tide of protests against the efforts to reimpose tribute: first a "written warning, later the mobilization of some groups, immediately afterwards the expansion of the protest to other towns and communities, and finally a confrontation with the Spanish and the death of a subdelegate or intendant."[42]

Events in the Liberal interregnum between 1808 and 1814 further entangled local politics in the southern Andes. News from Spain and the implementation of the reforms prompted a variety of political positions, including absolutism, Cortes reformism, and independence. Political divisions at this point were not limited to those for and against Spanish rule. Indians assumed different positions, either embracing or resisting the reforms and often creatively redefining their meanings. Creole reformers expressed their trepidation over the "dangers" of rapid change, particularly vis-à-vis Indian communities, a concern that would shape the ensuing decade of political turmoil. The impact of political change and instability clearly extended from Spain and the viceregal cities well into the Andean countryside. For example, Indians experienced frequent changes in tax policies in these years, which altered their economic standing and relationship with non-Indians and with the state, and underlined the instability of Spanish rule and the possibility of change. As Indians followed, acted upon, and affected these broader processes, the period witnessed their cautious optimism for constitutional reform. In a context of rapid change and a widespread questioning of colonialism, they perhaps saw an opportunity for increased rights. At the same time, they confronted sustained threats to their political autonomy and economic rights, as well as demands for their taxes and for their bodies as soldiers. This combustible situation exploded with the Pumacahua rebellion in 1814.

THE PUMACAHUA REBELLION: DIVISIONS THAT UNITE, DIVISIONS THAT SEPARATE

Politics in Cuzco in the years following the French invasion of Spain centered on conflicts between the liberal, Creole members of the cabildo and the audiencia, the focal point of Spanish interests. The two sides grappled over the implementation of the 1812 Constitution, particularly the elections for city council. Rumors abounded in the city about foot-dragging by the audiencia and conspiracies by Creoles and the lower classes. In December 1812, Rafael Ramírez de Arellano, a lawyer, disseminated a manifesto signed by thirty-seven Cusqueños alleging that the audiencia had resisted holding elections.[43] In a letter to the viceroy dated April 26, 1813, Mateo García Pumacahua—a prominent cacique who arrived in late 1812 to take office as the interim president of Cuzco's audiencia—described the city's tense political climate and the suspicious activities of certain lawyers, particularly Arellano. He also reported that "members of the plebe devoted to these subjects [Creole liberals] bragged while drunk that they would sack the city during Carnival, to the point that people hid their belongings."[44] The high cost paid by Cuzco for the counterinsurgency efforts in Upper Peru inflamed tensions in Cuzco and animated the Creole liberals.

In October 1813, the audiencia arrested several people for an alleged plot to attack the barracks. On November 5, guards blocked protesters' efforts to take the main plaza to protest the arrests, firing into a crowd and killing two people. Governmental sources depicted more than six hundred protesters inciting the lower classes and the guards. In contrast, a report from the cabildo described a planned massacre, as audiencia thugs shot innocent bystanders, including children.[45] The audiencia deemed the cabildo's criticism unmerited and accused the cabildo leaders of harboring revolutionary sympathies. In early 1814, it ordered the arrest of prominent cabildo members. On August 2, 1814, the prisoners escaped from jail, roused a large group of supporters, and imprisoned many Spaniards. The rebels, led by members of Cuzco's lower middle class, demanded the implementation of the reforms promised by the 1812 Constitution.[46] They also condemned widespread corruption, high taxes, and the number of soldiers taken for service in Upper Peru. José Angulo, the leader of the rebels, contended on August 11 that they did not seek a change of government but merely of governors. In another letter to the viceroy a few days later, he argued that the population of Cuzco, "from its first citizens to the lowly plebe," despised the city's authorities. Angulo emphasized Spaniards' corruption and disregard for the local population and the grief of widows who had lost their husbands in the military campaigns to Upper Peru.[47]

Viceroy Abascal refused to negotiate and ordered the rebels to disband immediately. Angulo, in turn, called for the Spanish to meet the demands of the rebels in Upper Peru and Río de la Plata. By this time aligned with the rebels, Pumacahua was named military commander, and the rebels sent expeditions north to Huamanga and Huancavelica, and south-southeast to Puno, La Paz, and Arequipa. Pumacahua had long been a prominent loyalist. He had collaborated in the suppression of the Tupac Amaru rebellion and of the uprisings that took place in Upper Peru in 1809 and 1810. These achievements, his seniority, and the high standing that loyal cacique families held in Cuzco society allowed him to take the office of president of the audiencia. Yet in 1812 he was replaced. In a bitter letter to the viceroy, he commented that many hated him for his "nature," referring to his Indian heritage.[48] Resentment over his unceremonious removal helped convince the seventy-year-old cacique to return from his estate outside of Cuzco and join the uprising, which he believed remained loyal to King Ferdinand. Although some historians exaggerate his importance because the rebellion carries his name, Pumacahua's prestige and experience did allow him to recruit Indians with great success. One contemporary noted that he "had a decided ascendancy among the Indians, so much so that they called him Inca."[49]

The rebels advanced quickly. A hostile account acknowledged that the leaders ably propagated news of the uprising. This aptitude surprised the writer, Manuel Pardo, as he deemed them ignoramuses "who only know how to hate Europeans and the Spanish Government." He described the leaders other than Pumacahua as "so poor they didn't have enough to eat." Besides depicting the leaders' questionable social background, he narrated the rebels' ability to recruit deserters and veterans from the royalist army.[50] Some loyalist commentators blamed priests for instigating "the ignorant faithful," and others lamented how frightened members of the royalist army spread exaggerated ideas about the rebels' strength.[51] Rumors again became a key topic. Angulo himself noted that "popular rumors tend to distort simple facts" and worried perhaps that popular expectations of the uprising would exceed the objectives of the leadership.[52] Viceroy Abascal complained that "outsiders" blew "to keep the fire lit."[53]

The troops led by José Gabriel Béjar and Manuel Hurtado de Mendoza took Huamanga to the north. Thousands of peasants, many veterans of the Upper Peruvian campaigns and even of the Tupac Amaru uprising, joined the expedition heading south to seek "revenge against the Spanish." An officer of Ramírez's forces contended that the rebels were "fortified considerably on their way with many people who joined them, some through seduction and most with the hope and greed for sacking."[54] When the Puno garrison defected, they provided the rebel forces with soldiers and arms.[55] After gaining control of Puno, the priest Ildefonso Muñecas and Manuel Pinelo directed the bloody siege of La Paz. Pumacahua and Angulo captured Arequipa in November. Rebel proclamations cast the movement as a broad struggle composed of "children of the patria" fighting corrupt Spanish authorities.[56] Rebel leaders took advantage of widespread resentment about old and new taxes, recruitment for the counterinsurgency campaigns, and mestizos' power in rural society. The struggles dating from the Napoleonic invasion of Spain and the Cortes came to the fore in the uprising. For example, although contending that rebel leaders forced him to participate in the uprising, Manuel Ccama, an Indian from an hacienda located in Puno, described how insurgent Indians went to arrest Don José Andrés Monroy, cacique interino, who collected tribute. Clearly, the cacique's crime was collecting tribute at a time when Indians considered it abolished.[57] One notable observer barely lived to tell his story. Indian rebels dragged José Rufino Echenique, future president of Peru, from his uncle's estate in Carabaya, located to the south of Cuzco. At the last minute, a compassionate member of the mob separated this five-year-old boy from the main group, who were then murdered. Echenique claimed that this attack formed part of the anti-Spanish frenzy prompted by the uprising.[58]

The leaders believed that the Río de la Plata rebels (the *porteños*, a

term that means "from the city of Buenos Aires," but that became syn-
onymous with insurgents in the southern Andes during this period),
would defeat the Spanish in Upper Peru. In a proclamation written in
February 1815 in Tucumán, Manuel Belgrano, the Río de la Plata leader,
promised his support to the "pueblos of Peru."[59] The Río de la Plata insurgents failed to hold Potosí, however, and fled. Nor could the Cuzco
rebels count on support from King Ferdinand when he returned to the
throne in late 1814. He abruptly overruled the liberal reforms and refused to negotiate increased political rights for his American subjects.
His return strengthened the resolve of the royalist military commanders and weakened that of moderate Creoles who had initially supported
the constitutional reforms proposed by Angulo.

In November 1814, the Spanish general Juan Ramírez recaptured La
Paz. In March 1815, his forces defeated Pumacahua's troops, calculated
by some at more than twenty thousand soldiers, including guerrillas.
The royalists hunted down leaders of the rebellion and executed them
in front of their troops. Ramírez described the weakness of the rebel
forces. They had only forty pieces of artillery and less than one thousand rifles. Most fought on foot with traditional guerrilla weapons such
as slings, clubs, and lances, and many slipped away during the fighting.
The well-armed Ramírez forces used their experience to divide the rebel
forces, capturing and executing thousands.[60] In Huamanga, one report
described the brave rebels eschewing the use of their few weapons and
preferring hand-to-hand combat. The royalists, on the other hand, used
their weapons efficiently and without compassion. They also burned
towns suspected of guerrilla sympathies, bribed informants, and executed civilians.[61] Showing little compassion, they usually executed one
out of five prisoners and in some cases more. One rebel declared that he
hadn't surrendered because "Ramírez pardoned no one."[62] On April 21,
executioners hanged the Angulo brothers, José Gabriel Béjar, and other
leaders in Cuzco. Ramírez had executed Pumacahua in Sicuani "in front
of the Indians who vehemently loved him."[63]

As in the Tupac Amaru rebellion, many peasants had a more radical program or at least took more direct actions against their enemies.
Indicative of the conflicts that raged between 1808 and 1814, many
communities refused to pay tribute and punished and expelled abusive authorities, often outsiders. The movement continued even after
the defeat of the three military expeditions. Well into 1816, follow-

ing the execution of the rebellion's leaders, guerrillas in the southern "high provinces" (Chumbivilcas and Tinta) and in the Lake Titicaca region kept the Spanish state and the locally powerful on the defensive. On August 15, 1815, the guerrillas' leader, the priest Ildefonso Muñecas, abolished tribute, calling it "barbaric and repugnant for civilized nations; because of the tribute the Indian has been looked upon until today as having a different human nature." Violence increased in this stage, particularly against mestizos.[64]

The documentary evidence leaves no doubt about the massive support for the rebels in the southern Andes. Observers and prosecutors described the recruitment and spontaneous participation of the urban lower classes and rural Indians. A report from the audiencia portrayed the impudent rebel leaders proselytizing among the city's "lowest plebeians, who easily believe anything."[65] A hostile account of the rebels' arrival in Arequipa described the disgust of the "fine, sensible, and genteel Arequipa population upon seeing the haughty and insolent swarm of rough Indians, who surveyed everything with the eyes of barbarian conquerors."[66] With a combination of repulsion and anxiety, one observer noted how "members of the rabble—vagabonds and sans-culottes who don't have anything to lose or anything to support them—joined the Cuzco rebels in order to seize the booty of robberies."[67] The description of lower-class rebels as apolitical criminals seeking easy loot can be found in almost any official description of a rebellion, regardless of the period, and needs to be read critically. Royalists also frequently invoked the threat of a caste war, warning about the Indians' plans to kill all non-Indians. One witness of the fall of La Paz to the rebels called it a "disaster . . . to the poor European people and their goods." He noted how the *cholada* rose up with the Cusqueños to attack, strip, kill, and behead the Spanish prisoners.[68] The memory of the long, bloody battle for La Paz during the Tupac Katari rebellion and the violence provoked by the 1809 juntas heightened the concerns about caste war. Pío de Tristán wrote that the rebels intended to "exterminate from this hemisphere all castes other than that which reestablishes the Empire of the Incan gentiles."[69] These types of claims often included depictions of the violence of the military engagements of the period, both the major battles between the armies and the more obscure local incidents, and thus reflected, above all, the apprehension of the white population over the consequences of a mass rebellion. The specter of Tupac Amaru conjured up images of wanton violence and destruction. The Spanish state manipulated these fears in order to gain the support of non-Indians. Nonetheless, accounts of the rebellion describe brutality by both sides.[70]

Indians' support for the Pumacahua rebellion should not be exaggerated. On the one hand, royalists such as General Ramírez counted on Indian troops.[71] In his memoirs, Abascal noted the importance of troops from Cuzco and surrounding areas in the military campaigns from 1809 to 1815. He presented the Indians' participation on the Spanish side as a sign of their "good disposition toward the Spanish government because they couldn't tolerate the demands of such a long campaign, so far from their homes, without being free of the ulcers formed by the corrosive humor that rebellions form in people's souls and without a determined and constant desire to defend the King's cause."[72] Numerous explanations need to be considered to understand why some Indians fought for the Spanish. In many instances, more than one motive impelled them to join the viceroy's troops. Individuals and communities no doubt believed that gaining the favor of the state through military duty could help them in their conflicts with other communities and outsiders. The local context—above all, battles over political office—shaped these different strategies. Many Indians did not participate on either side. One Indian defendant described how his cacique insisted that the Indians should obey whichever faction occupied the town in order to avoid "more havoc."[73] Ramírez's drastic policy of executing one out of five prisoners discouraged Indians from taking up arms, but it also encouraged active rebels not to surrender. Caution in the midst of violent political struggles, which some contemporaries and analysts have mistaken for apathy, characterized Indians' political behavior well into the republican period.

In the midst of the uprising, the situations in Spain and Upper Peru that had favored the rebels changed, helping explain their defeat. Ferdinand returned to power in late 1814, rapidly overturning liberal reforms and hopes. The Río de la Plata rebels led by General Manuel Belgrano were expelled from Upper Peru in the same year. No second front developed in the south. With the experience of the campaigns in Upper Peru, the colonial troops led by Ramírez overwhelmed the rebels' major military units and rooted out the poorly armed guerrilla groups. Unfortunate timing and the colonial government's effective military measures, however, cannot alone explain the defeat of the movement. Many of the same difficulties encountered by the Tupac Amaru rebels riddled the Pumacahua insurgents. Tensions between the leadership's vision of a multiclass movement and the more radical efforts of the Indian lower classes emerged quickly. Indians envisioned the uprising as an opportunity to expel, in most cases quite violently, despised authorities and to resist the head tax and other colonial exactions. Their actions scared Creole reformers. One observer noted that property owners understood that "the revolution and the war is directed against all those who have property to lose."[74] Also, the intermediary groups that led uprisings for independence throughout Spanish America were weak and dependent on the state in the southern Andes. The caciques had been greatly enfeebled as a class, and sectors of the middle class, although despising Bourbon policies, feared the lower classes and ultimately relied on colonialism for their modest, precarious, but nevertheless "superior" social and economic standing. The rebels could not count on sufficient allies to assume leadership positions throughout the southern Andes.[75]

One striking feature of insurgent activity in the southern Andes is the repeated allusion to the Incas. For Aguilar and Ubalde, resurrecting the Inca Empire was not an ideological backdrop but rather the focus of their conspiracy. Numerous other examples can be found. In the 1790s, ayllu Indians in Oropesa, Quispicanchis, referred to their cacique, Don Marcos Pumaguallpa Garcés Chillitupa, as "Inca" and he called them "Incacuna," the plural of Inca in Quechua. He was accused of sowing discord with the idea "that there are still defenders of the Inca Kingdom, thereby reviving the superstitious character that unbridles the most pusillanimous spirit of the wretched nature of the Indians, who only need the weakest motor to imprison in their spirits the most bloody plans."[76] Years later, the priest of Oropesa claimed that Chillitupa promised Indians that "soon the time will arrive when you will return to your former state [antiguo ser]. . . . Have your slings, clubs, sandals, dried meat, and coca ready to rise at the first warning . . . a descendant of the last Inca will be crowned."[77] In an illuminating and amusing example, one of the mestizo leaders of the Pumacahua rebellion, José Agustín Chacón y Becerra, insisted that Pumacahua himself incorporate "Inca hieroglyphics" on the flag he used in order to emphasize his noble lineage. Pumacahua refused, arguing that it would only be a ploy to gain the respect and support of the Indians.[78] Yet, as a descendent of the Inca emperor Huayna Capac, Pumacahua did don Inca wear and decorum, which reflected, according to two commentators, his interest in being crowned emperor.[79]

These cases support Flores Galindo's seminal argument about the use of the Incas in the construction of diverse counterhegemonic projects in the Andes from the arrival of the Spanish to the twentieth century. They also underline the more sophisticated aspects of what he has called the Andean utopia (aspects misunderstood by some of his critics). The movements that utilized Inca iconography were not autonomous from broader political movements or restricted to Indians. Nor were they looking backward, hopelessly attempting to reverse the conquest. In 1812, a statement by a rebel ideologue captured the affinity between grievances against Spanish colonialism and the longing for the return of the Incan Empire. He noted that "the Indians don't commercialize, nor do they have the freedom in their business that the whites do, and for that reason they said that the son of the Inca would soon come."[80] All the insurgent groups in the southern Andes referred at some point to the Incas, using them to represent an alternative political system. Although each group had a particular, self-serving definition of the Incas, this iconography promoted a common, anticolonial historical consciousness for quite diverse and even antagonistic social groups. The enduring richness of the Incas as a subversive symbol lies in its very ability to transcend social divisions, such as the one between Indians and Creoles. References to the Incas in no way signify an alternative Indian project that could never combine forces with a more moderate, Creole-led movement.[81]

As described in previous chapters, the Spanish had banned allusions to the Incas in songs, dances, and texts. In 1790, Mata Linares warned about the Indians' "natural propensity to subversion and tumult and their great desire to return to the domination of the Incas and thus the possession of the goods that they believe the Spanish usurped, which means that we must fear that they will rebel when they have the chance or some fiend encourages them to do so."[82] This same authority worried that the Aguilar-Ubalde conspiracy would take hold because of the Indians' veneration of the city of Cuzco, the Inca capital. Despite the Crown's efforts, or perhaps because of them, non-Indians and Indians incorporated the Incas into their efforts to construct an alternative discourse to the one promulgated by Spanish colonialism. European and

North American liberal ideologies entering Peru had to be adapted to the southern Andean context, an ethnically segmented colonial center whose political and economic predominance was in decline. Whereas groups not only in the southern Andes but also in Río de la Plata and in the New Granada viceroyalties often invoked the Incas, ideologues in Lima largely failed to incorporate them.[83] This omission reflected how Lima thinkers and policymakers distanced themselves from the Andes, specifically how they overlooked the population's contemporary concerns and their historical elaborations. Although some early republican thinkers did discuss the Incas, in general this gulf between the people and the state—between Cuzco and Lima—would only increase in the early republic. In Cuzco, the Incas would continue as the central historical and political icon.

The defeat of the Pumacahua rebellion hardened ethnic and social divisions in the southern Andes. The events in the liberal interregnum had demonstrated to non-Indians the need to perpetuate social control based on caste hierarchies and to avoid a mass uprising. Indians had seen their hopes for change through liberal reform and then in mass rebellion soundly defeated. The anti-Pumacahua repression increased their dislike for colonialism and, in general, their experience during the long "liberal spring" left them bitter: they endured chaos and warfare that, after a glimpse of change, culminated in the same oppressive political structures. The restored king in Spain expressed no interest in negotiating increased rights for his American subjects.

THE FINAL DECADE 1815–1824

With the defeat of the Pumacahua uprising, the focus of the war shifted from the Southern Andes to the coast, which was not a mere tactical move, but a complete change in leadership, mass base, and platform. Although subversive activities continued in Cuzco after 1815 and the decisive battles were fought in the highlands, Lima became the base of operations for both armies and the focal point for ideological discussions. At this point, the restoration of the monarch diminished the available political options. Previously, many critics of the colonial regime had defended the Spanish king, blaming "bad government" before 1808 and subsequently the French invaders for the unsatisfactory implementation of what these critics considered to be his benevolence. Upon his return, however, Ferdinand squashed reforms and reformists in Spain and the Americas. After 1815, to defend Ferdinand was to defend the absolutist status quo. Therefore, insurgents discussed and fought over three alternatives: a constitutional monarchy, a new monarch, or an independent republic. The interpretation that pits the long war as a clear-cut struggle between loyalists and independence-seeking patriots greatly oversimplifies the struggle. Opponents to Spanish colonialism weighed other options besides an independent republic. The war itself presented new hardships as well as opportunities for resistance, thus shaping how people understood and participated in the tumultuous events of these years.[84]

A Lima-based movement finally achieved independence in the form of a republic. Cuzco, Arequipa, Tacna, and the rest of the southern Andes were not decisive centers of insurgency in this final decade of the War of Independence. In 1816, Joaquín de la Pezuela replaced Viceroy Abascal, who had effectively resisted the reforms legislated from Spain and had controlled the vast Peruvian viceroyalty. Pezuela faced the threat of José de San Martín's army in Río de la Plata and a nearly bankrupt treasury. In 1817, San Martín led his army west over the Andes into Chile, surprising most observers, including Viceroy Pezuela, who believed that San Martín would, as Buenos Aires rebels had repeatedly done, press northward into Upper Peru. From Chile, San Martín threatened to control the sea and to invade Lima.[85]

Support for independence was lukewarm in Lima. Members of the upper classes largely tolerated and even championed Spanish colonialism. They benefited from Lima's primacy in the colonial economy and administration, and feared that a war against the Spanish would prompt the lower classes to rise. Concern over uprisings by the city's multiethnic lower classes—the plebeians, rural workers, and slaves—kept much of the Lima elite in the royalist camp throughout the long War of Independence. The Consulado, the organization of Lima's key merchants, continually donated money to the viceroy's cause.[86] From 1808 to 1820, however, authorities uncovered several conspiracies in the capital, and the viceroy and others expressed concern over the internal threat in Lima. Some prominent members of Lima society attempted to mobilize the lower classes and to consolidate ties with the patriot armies to both the south and north.[87] Guerrilla bands operated around the capital, thus heightening the already severe crisis in the agricultural economy.

Nonetheless, it was only with the arrival of the armies led by José de San Martín and Simón Bolívar that the patriots were able to dislodge the royalists from Lima.

On September 10, 1820, San Martín landed with about four thousand men in the town of Pisco to the south of Lima. The cautious Argentine general planned to advance slowly and wait for Peruvians to rise up. After several weeks, he sent a detachment into the Andes and another up the coast with orders to blockade Lima by land and sea and to recruit soldiers. His adversary, Viceroy Pezuela, emphasized that royalist forces and supporters were to hold on to Lima at any cost. He was deposed on January 20, 1821, and replaced by José de La Serna, who evacuated Lima. By mid-1821, with many towns declaring themselves independent, La Serna and San Martín began negotiations, the Spanish believing that San Martín's monarchical leanings would prompt a favorable settlement. Negotiations broke down, however, and the fighting spread from the coast into the Andes. Guerrilla bands fought throughout the central Andes, attacking the royalist army and its supporters. On the coast, escaped slaves and other members of both the rural and urban lower classes formed small bands that subverted social control on the estates and attacked transportation routes. San Martín's ultimately unfulfilled promise to abolish slavery attracted important contingents of slaves and members of their families who dreamed of freedom.[88] When San Martín withdrew from Peru in 1822, Simón Bolívar took over the leadership of the divided, virtually bankrupt insurgent forces in September 1823. Although independence was declared on July 28, 1821, the Spanish were not really defeated until the Battles of Junín and Ayacucho in June and December 1824.

This final stage of the War of Independence was not a clear-cut battle between Spanish loyalists and Peruvian patriots. The insurgents relied on a sizable contingent of foreign soldiers, and oftentimes Peruvians manned the colonial army and much of its officer corps. The war resembled more a civil war than an "international" liberation struggle. Quick encounters and guerrilla tactics rather than large-scale battles characterized the fighting. Also, sharp internal divisions beset both the royalist and patriot camps. The viceregal forces had to contend with rapidly changing events in Spain. In March 1820, military officers who balked at the risk and cost of the war in the Americas and other liberal forces compelled Ferdinand to restore the liberal Constitution and the Cortes. He was forced out of power, only to be restored again in December 1823. Debates raged within the patriot camp not only about military strategy but also about what type of government should replace Spanish colonialism. The creation of an independent republic was not a foregone conclusion. Military leaders feared that the war had "unleashed" the lower classes, and that social control would be impossible to reimpose. On the other hand, the montonero forces, guerrilla groups backed primarily by the lower classes, believed that they had earned certain rights by fighting in the war, demands that they would press for decades. The debates from this period reflected the uncertainty about Peru's future, particularly the widespread ambivalence about the potential role of the Indian population.

The liberals won the battle within the patriot ranks against the constitutional monarchists as well as the long war in Peru against the Spanish. They also defeated the constitutional monarchists in the press and in public debates, emphasizing that the Spanish would never cede and that alternative monarchs could not be found. The replacement of San Martín, who had monarchical leanings, with Bolívar ratified this victory. In these years of military and ideological battles, the liberals' greatest weakness also manifested itself: their lofty rhetoric had little basis in Peru's complex reality. They spoke from and largely about Lima, barely engaging the rest of the viceroyalty and soon-to-be republic. Republican liberalism would long suffer from its elitist rhetoric, which excluded not only lower-class groups but the majority of the country outside of Lima. Liberal ideologues repeatedly failed to address the Indian question, defaulting to conservatives, who supported and in many senses achieved the continuation of the colonial status quo. Although the liberals won most of the ideological clashes of the era, they stumbled on the Indian question. Their indecision and at times lack of interest cast a long shadow on the republic.[89]

CUZCO AND THE VICEROY'S LAST STAND

In the long decade between the defeat of the Pumacahua rebellion and the overthrow of the Spanish, two men governed the Cuzco region— Pío de Tristán and Viceroy La Serna. From September 1816 to 1822, Tristán, a member of a distinguished Arequipa family, was the president of the real audiencia and often referred to as the "president of Cuzco."

In late 1821, Viceroy La Serna transferred the viceregal government to Cuzco. Throughout his term, Tristán had great difficulty fulfilling all the demands of the viceregal state. In the midst of a severe economic crisis, Cuzco was required to provide money and an increasing number of soldiers for the royalist cause. Insurgents frequently cut off Cuzco from its most important markets in Upper Peru, while severe frosts and drought reduced agricultural production in 1816 and 1817, and an epidemic afflicted the Tinta area in 1817. Early in that same year, Tristán insisted that he could not raise taxes once again; no one had the resources to pay. He repeatedly referred to the annihilation of Cuzco's economy, which he deemed "worthy of compassion."[90]

Other observers also commented on economic difficulties in the countryside and the near impossibility of collecting the head tax. Collectors in Paruro quit en masse in 1819, arguing that "as is well known, recent years have brought calamity and hardships for all people. With this inevitable situation, the number of tribute payers has diminished, some dying of need and others migrating to other towns in search of subsistence."[91] In 1820, the Cuzco city council indicated that late frosts in November had destroyed much of the season's crop. Tristán had particular difficulty finding men for the army. In 1817, he argued that the population was so scarce that only artisans were left to dragoon, and their absence would further weaken the economy. By October, he contended that because he could not find recruits with "established homes," he had to grab those "who, accustomed to poverty and satisfied with less than what is necessary to survive, wander all over America with only a poncho."[92] He developed an elaborate plan to reward Indians who turned in deserters with tribute exemptions, but the plan failed. Tristán also complained that even when he could track down recruits, he could not afford to feed and clothe them.[93]

Colonial policy induced by the war worsened the situation for Cuzco's rural population. The frequent military campaigns against insurgents organized and manned in Cuzco ravaged the weakened economy. An 1821 document calculated that twenty-eight thousand men had left the region to fight against the rebels and that the military campaigns had cost Cuzco more than eight million pesos. The document asserted that due to its diminished population and crippled commerce, Cuzco could not continue to finance the colonial army.[94] The military draft spurred many Indians to abandon their communities. In May 1822, a priest complained that in order to avoid abduction or harassment by soldiers, Indian men in the city of Cuzco disguised themselves as women.[95]

The economy was not Tristán's only concern. Insurgents within Cuzco and from rebel-held territory to the south, west, and north frequently threatened Cuzco. The economic hardships of the period and the hostility to exploitative outsiders motivated the most serious internal challenge—the 1818 rebellion in the western district of Aymaraes. The newly named subdelegate, José Paliza y Magón, had quickly earned the antipathy of the population. Locals resented his efforts to collect the increased Indian head tax (raised by more than 10 percent) and a "voluntary" tax from mestizos. Indians also opposed his efforts to draft more soldiers for the army. When he lowered the price paid for cows slaughtered for dried meat for the armies, his support plummeted even more in this livestock area. Behind these measures lay Paliza's own considerable economic activities involving the illegal and widely repudiated reparto and the monopolization of the livestock trade. In a letter to the Cuzco audiencia, Captain Agustín Pío de Erenda noted that Paliza, "because of some business operations that he has to sustain himself as subdelegate, might be hated."[96] He was correct.

In late August and early September 1818, Indians in the communities of Lucre and Llinqui attacked Paliza's representatives when they arrived to collect the increased tribute. The local authorities tried to arrest the rebels, but failed. The audiencia sent Clemente Casanga, a tax collector and veteran of the Upper Peru campaigns, to apprehend the rebels, but he and his soldiers were threatened and expelled. The rebels marched to Toraya and drank, danced, and threatened the local tax collector to the sound of the church bells. They returned peacefully to Llinqui. On September 15, upon hearing rumors that several men had been arrested because of the revolts, Llinqui community members again besieged Toraya. They freed the prisoners and burnt the stocks in the public plaza.

On the sixteenth, following written instructions sent throughout the region by the rebellion's leaders, Indians from many nearby communities joined the rebels in Toraya. At this point, the Casanga brothers, Clemente and Antonio, were in charge. Although involved in the suppression of the initial skirmishes, numerous mestizos, such as Clemente Casanga, changed sides. Joined by Indians from neighboring towns, the rebels surrounded the capital of Aymaraes, Chalhuanca. At dawn on the seventeenth, armed with slings, sticks, garrotes, wooden swords, and stones, they charged the plaza. The rebels caught Paliza's assistant, Don Francisco Aristumuño, trying to escape over a back wall and knocked him over with a rock from a slingshot. Calling him a thief, they stoned and stabbed him to death. They stoned and clubbed Paliza and his son-in-law, José Torrepico, leaving them for dead. Later, when they found Paliza near death in the house of his assistant, they finished him off with large stones to the head. The crowd sacked the municipal council and the subdelegate's house, taking over seven thousand pesos in tribute money, which they later returned. A long, drunken fiesta ensued with constant screams of "Viva la patria." During these heady hours, one participant happily declared that there would no longer be judges or head taxes.[97]

In a series of meetings, the rebels replaced authorities associated with Paliza and named a commission to negotiate with the real audiencia in Cuzco. The participants communicated their actions to the surrounding communities, many of which had sent representatives. Their demands, although vague, centered on the "bad government" of Paliza and the unfairness of his economic impositions. Yet their plans surpassed a mere reversal of the tax increase or the price decreases. In a document given to caciques and local tax collectors for distribution to their communities, the rebels wrote:

> We are not rising against the Crown or the faith of God, but instead we are defending ourselves against these and other extortions. . . . Our tributes are due soon, and we will pay according to the old custom, 3 pesos 5½ reales, and lastly we will not permit Spaniards [chapetones] to be judges or any other post; they must be from our *criollo* country, . . . and in the case that these orders are not obeyed, we will raise our own troops, and we will go to other towns to remedy the situation quickly, and you will have to suffer. . . . We are now all of the same body, españoles [non-Indians] and tribute-paying Indians.[98]

Their actions and rhetoric went far beyond expelling a repudiated authority.

Despite the cries of "Viva la patria" and their anti-Spanish sentiments, the rebels did not connect with the independence movement elsewhere. Authorities in Cuzco nervously reported the rebels' contacts with dissidents in Huamanga to the north and in Andahuaylas to the west, but these factions never coordinated their efforts.[99] One anonymous patriot in Lima noted that the rebels were "only waiting for some help from the undefeated San Martín," who was still in Chile at this point. The writer mentioned 120 insurgents sent to Huamanga to help the Aymaraes rebels "if necessary," but they never arrived.[100] The rebels' isolation derived in large part from the absence of insurgency in Peru at this point. The year 1818 was a period of relative calm preceding the final stage of the War of Independence, which was marked by the arrival of San Martín in 1820. The Aymaraes rebels did not have effective potential allies. In September, however, they did not appear to feel the need for them. An air of festivity and anticipation rather than dread marked the revolt. Nonetheless, their references and demands demonstrate their awareness of the broader political changes underway throughout the continent.

On September 27, troops led by Leandro Prada attacked the rebels, who responded with guerrilla tactics. Prada did not succeed. The commission formed to negotiate with the real audiencia had never left. After this point, the course of events becomes unclear. On September 30, many Indians swore allegiance to the king in Toraya. Authorities in Cuzco sent more than four hundred men to capture the rebels. They "burned every town, hut, or house on their way."[101] At some point in October, the rebels were defeated. In his memoirs, Pezuela mentions that two thousand rebel Indians and cholos confronted the Cuzco troops.[102] Two rebels were executed in Chalhuanca, their heads and arms remaining on display for days. A military court in Cuzco tried most of the rebels, including the Casanga brothers and other leaders. The defense lawyer argued that the rebels were guilty of sedition but not of rebellion (*sublevación*) because they had targeted an official rather than the king. The courts sentenced Clemente Casanga to five years in jail in Callao. Most of the mestizo leaders were sent to the army, and the majority of the Indians were freed.

Insurgency continued in the Aymaraes region. In 1819, a mob in Oropesa, Aymaraes, violently expelled representatives of the subdelegate who were in town collecting taxes and conscripting soldiers. Santiago Prieto and other mestizo leaders of the incident fled to Ica on the coast and in 1821 joined Agustín Gamarra's insurgent forces.[103] They returned to the area in 1822 and, a year later, were accused of participating in the 1819 events and of having weapons.[104] In October 1821, the royalist commander, José Carratalá, expressed his concern about the "gang of rebels" that had gathered around Aymaraes.[105]

Not all of the incidents in this period constituted serious challenges to the Spanish. In 1819, authorities arrested drunks in several places who had shouted "Viva la patria." When no evidence of participation in the independence movement were found, they were released.[106] The courts, however, dealt harshly with other suspects. In 1819, the audiencia tried Bernardo Tapia and fifteen Indian accomplices for placing seditious lampoons in eleven towns in the Cuzco and Lake Titicaca region. It is unclear what the lampoons said and whether Tapia was deranged or the colonial state simply considered sedition a form of madness, but the prosecutor did emphasize Tapia's eccentricity. One official stated that if Tapia "isn't completely crazy, he's awfully close." The prosecutors noted that Tapia presented himself as "Lieutenant Colonel Commander, Commanding General of the Peoples' Auxiliary Army, Lieutenant Judge, Chief Regent, Peacemaker, Conquistador, Defender of Peru."[107] Tapia claimed that he was in contact with some of the martyrs of the Pumacahua rebellion, that Charles V (1500–58) was on the throne in Spain, and that Ferdinand VII was the natural son of Joachim Murat, the French marshall and king of Naples from 1808 to 1815. Indicative of the need to treat accusations of insanity cautiously, the courts also considered Tapia's recommendation to the Indians not to pay taxes as proof of his mental problems. However, his purported ties with some of the Pumacahua leaders and rebels in Upper Peru weighed heavily against him, and he was hanged in the presence of his Indian accomplices. The lampoons were burnt below him and his head remained on display for days. The prosecutor called for light sentences for the Indians. He argued that because of their "reserved, rustic nature" (rather than any political commitment), the Indians had only failed to turn in the "treacherous patriots" and thus should be pardoned. They received public whippings and jail sentences. Authorities again complained about the endless flow of rumors and mentioned "opinions, gossip, disastrous predictions, criticism, murmurs, and incendiary publications and speeches." The prosecutor blamed "countless rascals for spreading the rumor that we are surrounded by half a million, well-armed patriots."[108]

In September 1820, Tristán wrote a detailed memo to the viceroy expressing his concern that the recently landed San Martín forces would "excite" Cuzco. In the meantime, he increased patrols in the western districts that linked Cuzco with the coast, nervously noting that Aymaraes had already proved itself fertile grounds for dissent.[109] Tristán complained that the people's spirits were "quite altered" due to malicious rumors and speeches, yet asserted that he could maintain order if the military garrison remained loyal. His concern about the troops was justified. On March 22, 1821, some officers rebelled and, led by José Melchor Lavín, took over the barracks and opened up the Cuzco jail. Reportedly in touch with San Martín, the leaders were quickly rounded up and executed.[110] To Tristán's relief, San Martín, although calling Cuzco the "heart of Peru," set his sights instead on Lima.[111]

In late 1821, rebel military leaders began to consider attacking Cuzco. Ignacio Urdapileta y Montoya, a veteran of the Pumacahua rebellion, notified a patriot commander stationed in Lucanas of the "general adhesion" of the Indians in Cuzco's provinces to the independence movement.[112] In September, Tristán reported rebel activity in Chumbivilcas and claimed that the Parinacochas district, located between Cuzco and Arequipa, "is in complete insurrection, and although lacking organized troops, they set a bad example for those around them and hamper our efforts."[113] On October 10, the rebel commander Juan Pardo de Zela wrote, "Now is the time to think about the province of Cuzco because its president, Tristán, has only five or six hundred soldiers and four hundred draftees, and I've been told that he doesn't have one gun to arm them and the surrounding provinces have begun to refuse him supplies. Aymaraes and Chumbivilcas desire my presence."[114] Nonetheless, Tristán managed to prevent the insurgents from taking Cuzco.

After evacuating Lima in June 1821, Viceroy José de La Serna moved the colonial government and much of the army first to Huancayo and then to Cuzco in December. He commanded the Crown's final defenses there until the Battle of Ayacucho in December 1824. The government's presence discouraged anti-Spanish activities but did not completely pacify the region. In 1822, the priest of Mara, Cotabambas, Don Antonio de la Cueva, accused the town's cacique tax collector, Pascual Enrique, of rousing the Indians in the name of the patria. Enrique reportedly said that the Indians "wanted to be independent from the judges who ruled them, both secular and ecclesiastic—they don't want to be subordinate."[115] The priest accused Enrique of ordering the "Indians and the people" of the town to attack him. De la Cueva was spared because the bulk of the population was working the fields. Santiago Infantas, who had been recruiting Indians for the military, supported the priest's claims, but Enrique's wife claimed that Infantas had tried to rape her. Once again, local conflicts assumed broader political trappings.

It is difficult to measure the level of support for La Serna and the colonial government in Cuzco at this time. When the real audiencia invited La Serna in 1821 to move the government to Cuzco, its representatives argued that the city offered easy access to Upper Peru, Arequipa, and Lima, that it housed important secular and religious leaders as well as cultural institutions, and that its citizens had demonstrated their loyalty. As in all manifestos touting the merits of Cuzco from this period and others, the authors invoked the Incas.[116] Throughout his stay, La Serna lauded Cuzco's loyalty. This rhetorical courting between the viceroy and urban elites, however, represented standard political practice. The reports of Cuzco's unflagging royalism must be seen as part of the royalists' constant propaganda campaign, just as the lack of widespread insurgency in Cuzco must be viewed as a reflection of the military presence in the region and the absence of political alternatives.[117]

Politically, La Serna relied on officials who came with him from Lima or from other areas of Peru. Few of his major collaborators resided in Cuzco prior to 1821, and even fewer remained after 1824.[118] Economically, the arrival of the viceroy represented a windfall for a few people because it bolstered the state's demand for certain Cuzco-made goods. Individuals who benefited included textile mill owners and tailors who filled the large orders for uniforms. These beneficiaries, however, encountered difficulty in receiving payment. For the majority of the population, the situation worsened as trade with other regions continued to decline, and the tax burden escalated. In 1823, with the military situation increasingly bleak and the Indian head tax difficult to collect, La Serna demanded the first of a series of "forced contributions." Cuzco merchants "donated" more than twenty thousand pesos but requested that this payment exonerate them from the sales tax. It remains unclear whether any of this money was returned or what type of favors the donors received from the colonial state.[119] Subdelegates accrued huge debts in this period, largely because of the difficulty in collecting the head tax. La Serna dedicated most of the state's revenue to the military, particularly the northern army commanded by José Canterac in the central Andes. With a newly installed printing press, the government ran a propaganda campaign against the rebels. The articles ridiculed the rebels' leaders and exaggerated their defeats and internal divisions.[120]

The Cuzco population suffered greatly during the final years of Spanish rule in Peru. Few could escape the decline of the Cuzco economy or the royalists' constant demands for supplies, money, and soldiers. Gabriel Narciso de León, the owner of an hacienda in Limatambo, thirty-five miles to the west of Cuzco, had a particularly alarming time. When La Serna's troops passed through his estate, they expropriated seeds, alfalfa, clothing, mules, and de León's lone burro. Colonel Justo Vigil responded to de León's protests by calling him a cholo trouble-maker, sacking his house, and chopping down his trees. When de León refused to provide more supplies, Vigil had him dragged behind a horse. He was saved by his family, who begged for mercy. De León claimed that throughout this mistreatment, he never stopped praying for the intervention of Saint Patria. By January 1825, his prayers had been an-swered as the patriot forces reached Cuzco. Whether the republic ful-filled his expectations is uncertain.[121]

IDEOLOGY AND INDEPENDENCE IN THE SOUTHERN ANDES

The rebellions, conspiracies, and anti-Spanish propaganda reviewed in this chapter contradict the idea of social and political tranquillity in the southern Andes in the post-Tupac Amaru decades. Deep divisions marked local society and frequently coalesced with the broader politi-cal struggles of the period. The Tupac Amaru rebellion by no means constituted the beginning and end of mass insurgency in the region. The wide variations in local political contexts—particularly in terms of control of the cacique office—and the volatile course of what became a war meant that southern Andean peasants and other ethnic groups re-sponded in different ways to the opportunities and challenges presented by the spreading insurgency against Spanish rule. Administrative posi-tions continued to provide economic opportunities, political contacts, and prestige—overlapping incentives that made for protracted battles. The struggles over these positions and resistance to the colonial state's demand for taxes and soldiers came to the fore in the mass "Puma-cahua" rebellion.

The insurgency in the Cuzco area cannot be reduced to a struggle for and against independence. After the Napoleonic invasion of Spain in 1808, people in Spanish America debated whether to support the Span-ish insurgents and the Cortes system. In the years after the invasion, the available political alternatives multiplied. Motivated by events in

Spain as well as by insurgency to the north and south, dissidents in Peru contemplated various forms of alternative rule, such as a constitutional monarchy or autonomy without full independence. Others maintained their hopes in Ferdinand. In the Cuzco region, people considered, modified, and fought for these possibilities. The translation of these notions into Andean political culture signified the incorporation of the Incas as a historical and political icon into each of these ideological options. For example, monarchists of different stripes cast the Tahuantinsuyo as a successful, hierarchical kingdom. Yet rebels most frequently invoked the Incas as a model for a radical break with colonialism. In these representations, Indians ruled, a truly revolutionary alternative to colonialism.[122]

Yet the uprisings ultimately failed: the Spanish controlled Cuzco until the end of their reign in late 1824. The causes for the failure of the Pumacahua rebellion, as well as of other southern Andean revolts, and for the absence of large-scale insurgency after 1815 have daunted generations of historians. An explanation requires examining the structural and ideological obstacles that impeded the unification of the highly divided ethnic groups and classes of the Andes. Since at least the time of the Tupac Amaru rebellion, colonial authorities believed that control of Cuzco was the key to defending the extensive Peruvian viceroyalty. In the final colonial decades, viceroys strengthened the military presence in Cuzco—relocating a veteran regiment there in 1783, improving the militias, and increasing the number of Spanish officers and soldiers.[123] When the Pumacahua rebellion broke out, the colonial army counted on its more than five years of counterinsurgency experience in the hostile terrain of the Andean highlands. After 1815, the Crown once again strengthened its defenses in Cuzco. The notable military presence of the Spanish in Cuzco—particularly after 1821, when La Serna transferred the entire government there—discouraged further insurgency. In fact, many people from Cuzco fought for independence outside their tightly controlled homeland, in Upper Peru or on the coast.[124] For an area that had suffered through two brutal anti-insurgency campaigns in less than forty years, the efficacy of repression and its threat should not be underestimated. Nonetheless, the improvement of the repressive capacity of the colonial state cannot fully explain the absence of an effective mass movement in the southern Andes.

Historians have emphasized the fragility of the Creole-Indian alliance in the southern Andes to explain the absence or weakness of a mass independence movement. The specter of the Tupac Amaru rebellion and the atomization of the Indian population frightened the Creoles, impeding a broad-based independence movement in the Cuzco region.[125] Creoles continued to depend on alliances with the Indian elite, but by the nineteenth century these alliances were short term and closely monitored by the Creoles.[126] It is necessary, however, to explore more deeply why rebellions in the southern Andes, real and potential, lacked leaders (Creole, mestizo, or Indian) and to examine carefully Indian participation in the anticolonial movement.[127]

The social bases of local power in the southern Andes varied greatly. The inconsistent post–Tupac Amaru administrative reforms complicated the political situation. The fate of ethnic caciques differed from town to town, and no single pattern of political alliances between new caciques, priests, and subdelegates stands out. The Indian population in the Cuzco region had never been homogeneous, but the fragmentary application and impact of the late colonial reforms increased inter- and intracommunity differences, a fact that helps explain the multiplicity of strategies adopted during the long War of Independence. The caste reductionism that has marked much of the historiography—sweeping statements about Indians, mestizos, Spaniards, and Creoles—exaggerates the cohesion and homogeneity of these internally diverse groups. The absence of large-scale Indian participation in the War of Independence after 1815 does not mean that they were held back by their backward ideology or that they were apolitical or even royalist. The heterogeneity of Andean society in the decades following the Tupac Amaru rebellion impeded a mass southern Andean movement, with the important exception of the Pumacahua rebellion, but it did not prevent individuals, communities, and regions from coordinating political actions.

More than the Creoles' hesitance to raise the indigenous masses or the Indians' ideological backwardness or indifference, the lack of an effective group that could mobilize rural society explains the breakdown of political insurgency in the southern Andes during the War of Independence. In a telling quote, a desperate rebel leader in Upper Peru in 1813 wrote of the anemic social base of the insurgents:

> Due to our government's decrees, the majority of the powerful groups of these provinces must be our enemies. The priests because they have lost their investments, most of their goods, the free

labor of the Indians, and the authority they had over them; the hacienda owners because they don't have sharecroppers or servants; the miners and mining entrepreneurs because they don't have mita Indians, and their work is almost paralyzed; the merchants because they are almost all Europeans, the roads are blocked, and without the draft labor system and tribute, not much money circulates; and the Ecclesiastics because they don't have the donations from Mass. Seeing us weakened, all of these groups, to ingratiate themselves with the enemy and to recover the benefits that they had lost, and due to the general hatred that predominates in these provinces against the lower orders, will conduct an irresistible war against us that will lead us to total ruin. The only friends that we have are the rabble and the Indians, but the former, when active, only promotes robbery and disorder, and its members are too tired and threatened from the blows they have received, and the latter are very weak and do not have character.[128]

The elite groups described by Díez Vélez depended too much on the colonial system to lead a full-fledged independence movement. In contrast to the central Andes, where a frustrated merchant sector with excellent mobilizational capabilities rose against the Spanish, in Cuzco no such sector existed.[129] As noted, the ethnic caciques had witnessed the virtual abolition of their office, and their livelihood depended on demonstrating their loyalty and subservience to the Crown. As the above quote expresses, other groups—such as mine owners, priests, and petty politicians—were too weak and relied too much on the Crown and the benefits of colonialism to risk rebellion. They also feared the lower classes. Of course, some of them did take up arms against the Crown. In the Pumacahua rebellion and the other events described here, muleteers, petty merchants, priests, caciques, and mestizos joined or even led the rebels. But because of the strong presence of the colonial state, whose authorities insisted on the centrality of Cuzco in the defense of the Peruvian viceroyalty, these intermediaries were unable to defeat the colonial armies in the long War of Independence. The lack of leaders hindered a mass movement in the southern Andes.

Since at least the Tupac Amaru rebellion, Andean insurgents had struggled to create an anticolonial ideology rooted in local or regional traditions and beliefs. These centered on the invocation of the Inca Empire, the Andean utopia. Rebels such as Aguilar and Ubalde and others described here creatively united elements of Enlightenment thought, more traditional Spanish American notions of political legitimacy, and the Inca utopia, grounding these ideas in unique, at times fantastic, interpretations of events in Europe and Peru. The invocation of the Incas in no way preempted efforts to align with non-Indian social movements or ideologies. Nonetheless, the southern Andean rebellions were defeated, and Lima insurgents, the eventual victors in the long War of Independence, showed little interest in the Incas as a historical icon. To understand the inability to convert the Andean utopia into a "national" ideology we have to examine the social tensions described in this chapter and in previous chapters: the class and ethnic strains that hindered the mass movements and nudged many of the middle and upper classes into the royalist camp. The Andean utopia was not too exotic, but rather too radical: in these years it was considered the ideological foundation for an Indian or peasant movement.

The victorious Lima-based patriots ultimately finessed the Indian question. Concerned about the effects of the abolition of the head tax on state coffers and on caste hierarchies, they oversaw its revival. In general, leaders of the nascent Peruvian state had little knowledge or interest in the Andes. The republic began with the Indians' role undefined: were they to be citizens or subjects who, following the colonial status quo, constituted a different social category with different rights and obligations? As the next few chapters demonstrate, this question and others like it were answered by the continuance of colonial practices. This continuity did not mean, however, that nothing changed with independence or that Indians and other lower-class groups were marginalized from the sharp political battles of the period. As during the struggle for independence, even when excluded from mainstream social movements and parties, Indians utilized different means to defend their rights, including those rights they believed they had earned with independence. The blend of fighting and negotiating that characterized the long War of Independence in Cuzco also carried over into the republic.

"To study Gamarra is to understand the national spirit, to place its culture, to discover its mentality, to open the sociological panorama of the country."—José María Valega, *República del Perú*

"A caudillo is like a magnet: he lives to the extent that he attracts."
—Eduardo Galeano, *We Say No*

On December 9, 1824, patriot forces defeated the royalists in the Battle of Ayacucho, forcing them to capitulate. Fifteen days later, Agustín Gamarra, promoted to general and named by Simón Bolívar as Cuzco's first prefect, arrived in his native city. Not only would Gamarra be the major figure in the creation of the republican state in Cuzco, but he played a central role in Peru's tumultuous political life for decades following independence. Mariano Felipe Paz Soldán scarcely exaggerated when he wrote in 1913 that the lives of Gamarra and his childhood acquaintance, ally in the 1820s, and subsequent nemesis, Andrés Santa Cruz, "are the complete history of Peru from 1820 until 1841; there is not a single page and perhaps even a single scene in which these two do not appear."[1]

Gamarra fought in the War of Independence, first for the Spanish and, after January 1821, as a leader of the patriots. In 1824 he participated in the decisive Battles of Junín and Ayacucho that brought about the end of Spanish rule. He was involved in the endemic political intrigues of the 1820s and 1830s—abetting the expulsion of Simón Bolívar in 1825, masterminding the fall of the liberal president General José de La Mar in 1829, and spearheading the defeat of the Peru-Bolivia Confederation implemented by Santa Cruz in the late 1830s. The efforts against La Mar and Santa Cruz cleared the path for him to become president. His terms as president from 1829 to 1833 and from 1839 to 1841 constituted high points for the conservatives, as the alliance he led was called. He commanded invasions of Colombia in 1829 and of Bolivia in 1828 and again in 1841, at which point he met his death in the Battle of Ingavi.

Agustín Gamarra was a classic caudillo. Although the term can be broadly used as a synonym for dictator, it refers more precisely to the military leaders who ruled Spanish America in the nineteenth century. Military chieftains fought for the control of the state, in some cases forming political alliances against the major political groups and in many others alongside them. Throughout most of the continent, members of the military controlled the state for long periods of time.[2] Different types of chieftains emerged. Many caudillos led national political coalitions with civilian and military participation, but others commanded regional movements that stubbornly resisted centralist control. Whereas many caudillos fought on a conservative platform, fending off lower-class subversion and liberal utopianism, others such as Rafael Carrera of Guatemala championed populist movements. Some remained in office for decades, whereas others led small, isolated local movements that scarcely affected national politics. The caudillos' social bases, ideologies, and impact varied greatly in the nineteenth century. Yet under their different guises, military leaders dominated politics in postindependence Spanish America.

Exactly why caudillos predominated has long troubled Spanish Americans and scholars who study the region. Often, this question is simply posed as, What went wrong? In the nineteenth century, writers emphasized the personal traits of the caudillo, often casting them as symptoms of "national" defects or attributes. Sharply partisan, at times hagiographic, these accounts extolled a caudillo's magnetism or blamed his heavy-handedness for the country's problems. In other words, these portrayals focused on the caudillo himself as the explanation for the country's political situation.[3] In Argentina, Domingo Sarmiento's classic study of Facundo Quiroga posed the challenge facing Spanish America as a struggle between barbarism—the caudillos and their rustic followers—and civilization. His influential work established caudillo analysis as a prominent form of national soul-searching.[4] Virtually every major caudillo has been depicted in multiple biographies.

In line with the general trend of these biographies, authors have both lauded and vilified Agustín Gamarra. In the mid-nineteenth century, Felipe Pardo y Aliaga described him as "affable, generous, well-educated, and eloquent to the point that with one word in Quechua, he could make 12,000 Indians suddenly kneel down."[5] In contrast, José María Valega wrote in the 1920s that "the psychology of this Cuzco soldier indicates, politically, the terrible defect of his race that psychiatrists call moral weakness."[6] Taking a more ambivalent position, in 1941 Luis Alayza Paz Soldán deemed Gamarra a "black angel."[7] Although few historians take seriously interpretations that stress only individuals and their alleged personal attributes (often cast in the biographies in essentialized racial categories or in relation to the vague term *charisma*), they have returned to a fruitful examination of the caudillos themselves — in particular, their relationship with their followers as well as the highly partisan accounts of their deeds by contemporaries and historians. Their careers and their political coalitions also deserve attention. The biographical literature about the caudillos not only demonstrates a great deal about each republic's ideological and political currents, but also provides a wealth of information about postcolonial politics.[8]

This chapter focuses on how the caudillo state operated. Caudillos did not rule in lieu of a state, but instead worked alongside governmental institutions. Although Gamarra manipulated the civic and military realms of the Cuzco state, he did not completely control the state. Certain spheres of the state achieved a surprising level of autonomy, which explains their survival well past the fall of a particular caudillo. I concentrate on how Gamarra used state institutions to build a coalition and on the nature of the state that he helped create. The caudillos' efforts shaped state formation in Spanish America for decades. By using overlooked publications, I also examine the Cuzco-based ideology of Gamarra's coalition. As much as his military prowess, clientelism, or power politics, his authoritarian platform, which promised to restore Cuzco to its previous primacy, explains his success in creating a base in his homeland. In some cases echoing and in others altering conservative discourse that emanated from Lima, Gamarra's supporters created a Cuzco-specific ideology that attracted a broad following and vexed the movement's opponents.

Civil war wracked Peru for decades following independence from Spain. In the political turmoil of the nineteenth century, the division between conservatives and liberals constituted the most visible fault line. Gamarra, Antonio Gutiérrez de La Fuente, and Felipe Santiago Salaverry stood out among the leaders of the conservatives, while José de La Mar and Luis José Orbegoso led the liberals. Although all of them were generals, both groups and in fact each caudillo led political alliances with connections throughout the country. The outline of this division can be traced to the long War of Independence. Conservatives (often called authoritarians, primarily by their enemies) were the followers of those more reluctant to overturn Spanish colonialism, whereas the liberals continued the struggle of the more ardent fighters for independence and of the supporters of a republic rather than a constitutional monarchy. Most influential politicians in the early republic, 1820 to 1850, formed part of a generation that emerged during independence. The majority of the generals that ruled Peru in these years received their military and political baptism during the war against the Spanish, many of them switching to the side of the patriots only when the Spanish were on the verge of defeat.[9]

Conservatives called for a strong centralized state, protectionist trade policies, and the maintenance of colonial corporations and ethos. Despite the high number of foreign advisers, ideologues, and military officers in their ranks, conservatives were xenophobic. They vilified liberals for their supposed favoritism toward foreigners and their application of "imported" ideologies that resulted in political turmoil. The liberals, on the other hand, sought a less centralized state with sharp restrictions on the power of the president. They favored a more open trade policy and the drastic reduction of rights granted to corporate groups. Although liberals were less chauvinistic and militaristic than their conservative counterparts, they did not propose radical social changes. Tulio Halperín Donghi notes their "adhesion to a hierarchical image of society . . . excluding from early Spanish American liberalism any democratic motive."[10] They chided the conservatives for attempting to defend and rebuild colonial structures and for opposing democracy. Although their key leaders were active in Congress, the liberals depended on weak, malleable military leaders such as La Mar and Orbegoso to lead the struggle against the conservatives. Many of the liberal ideologues were priests.[11]

Political struggles in nineteenth-century Spanish America did not always follow neat partisan lines. Some politicians bridged or even crossed back and forth between the conservative and liberal camps. In the Andes, Andrés Santa Cruz, who led the Peru-Bolivia Confederation from 1836 to 1839, is particularly striking. He ruled like a conservative, favoring authoritarian policies and a strong centralized state, yet implemented liberal trade policies. In fact, Generals Gutiérrez de La Fuente, Santa Cruz, and Gamarra had similar political views and careers, and they worked together closely in the late 1820s, yet fought incessantly throughout the 1830s. Opportunism as well as the uncertainty about the nature of republican Peru help explain the blurring of lines between the key political groups and the shifting positions of key caudillos. The division between different factions remained fluid, as did political affiliations in this unstable period.[12]

Federalism also complicated the liberal/conservative distinction. Gamarra led the centralist conservatives based in Lima, yet he maintained a strong coalition in Cuzco grounded on anti-Lima regionalism. Geographically, the conservatives were based in Lima and the northern coast, but liberals were strongest in the south, particularly in Arequipa.[13] However, many individuals, social groups, and even entire regions did not fit easily into this north-south pattern. Moreover, conservatives and liberals did not fully control their bases: Lima conservatives faced constant opposition from Lima liberals (both elite and lower class), while the southern Andes was never solidly liberal. The civil wars of the period did not simply pit the southern Andes against Lima and the north. Political factions changed constantly in this turbulent period as people joined and left coalitions and as conservative and liberal platforms evolved. Nonetheless, the liberal/conservative division constituted the central dividing line, even in the chaotic periods when several caudillos vied for the presidency.

Gamarra represented one consistency among these slippery social and geographic markers of the period. Carrying the banner of the conservatives, he participated in virtually every political struggle of the period. To understand him, we must know his story well before independence. Arguments among historians about the life of Agustín Gamarra begin with his birth in Cuzco on August 27, 1785. Most biographers agree that his parents were Fernando Gamarra, a notary, and Josefa Petronila Messía. Some contend that his mother was an Indian—an allegation made during his lifetime with clear pejorative intent. The allegation that he was the son of a priest, Father Saldívar, provoked even greater controversy.[14] In the press in the 1830s, satirical attacks against Gamarra ridiculed his lineage. For example, the caustic "New Natural History of Tyranny in Peru" classified him as "an indigenous quadruped and an animal."[15] He studied in one of Cuzco's best schools. His defenders have emphasized his knowledge of Latin and Quechua, contending that he had a copy of the work of Horace in his pocket when he was killed in battle in 1841. He entered the San Francisco monastery but left in 1809 to join Goyeneche's army. His contemporaries and biographers cast him as either an arriviste half-breed or a renaissance man who could bridge the Quechua and Spanish worlds.

Gamarra gained important combat experience and contacts during the War of Independence. He did not excel in the battlefield, however, which indicates that caudillos did not necessarily gain power because of their military prowess. He participated in the campaigns against the Río de la Plata and Upper Peruvian rebels and, in 1814 and 1815, fought against the Pumacahua rebels in Cuzco and Arequipa under the command of General Ramírez. In 1815, he led a guerrilla movement against the rebel commander Salas. He ascended to colonel and, after a stint as treasurer of Puno, became the head of the First Regiment of Cuzco in 1818. At this point, he began to contemplate switching to the insurgents. Viceroy Pezuela suspended him for suspected ties with the rebels, including Martín Güemes in Salta, Argentina, and for participating in several conspiracies. Although Pezuela eventually reinstated him, Gamarra continued to be monitored for patriot sympathies.[16] In January 1821, he presented himself to the commander in chief of the rebel forces, José de San Martín, who recognized his rank as a colonel and put him in charge of a battalion soon to depart for the central Andes.[17] James Paroissien, a British confidant of San Martín, deemed this appointment a smart move "because he [Gamarra] is a native of Cuzco and speaks Quechua perfectly. Furthermore, he knows how to treat those people."[18] His contacts in Cuzco proved valuable. For example, in 1823, rebels from the Aymaraes district in western Cuzco stole eight muskets and joined his forces on the coast.[19] Gamarra, however, had little initial success as a rebel commander. He was a better politician than general.

Table 1. Peruvian Executives, 1821–1842, and
the Political Role of Agustín Gamarra

Executive	Years in Office	Gamarra's Position
José de San Martín	1821–22	Began military career
Governing junta:	1822–23	Helped overthrow junta
General José de La Mar		
Manuel Salazar y Baquíjano		
Felipe A. Alvarado		
Marshall José de la Riva Agüero	1823	Initially supported
José Bernardo de Torre Tagle	1823	?
Libertador Simón Bolívar	1823–26	Supported, then opposed
General Andrés Santa Cruz	1826–27	Supported
General José de La Mar	1827–28	Helped overthrow
General Agustín Gamarra	1829–33	PRESIDENT
General Luis José de Orbegoso	1833–34	Opposed
General Pablo Bermúdez	1834	Supported
General Luis José de Orbegoso	1834–35	Opposed
General Felipe Salaverry	1834–36	Allied with, then opposed
Marshall Andrés Santa Cruz	1836–39	Opposed
Marshall Agustín Gamarra	1838–41	PRESIDENT

In March and April 1821, Gamarra failed to confront the outnumbered Spanish troops led by General José Carratalá outside of Jauja, thus allowing them to recapture the Mantaro Valley, a core area. The royalist troops slaughtered hundreds of suspected guerrilla supporters and converted the region into a base against San Martín's forces on the coast. General Juan Antonio Alvarez de Arenales complained bitterly and asked San Martín to decommission Gamarra.[20] Thereafter, Gamarra's alleged errors in the patriots' defeat in the battle that took place in the La Macacona hacienda in mid-1822 near Ica led to his temporary suspension. A commission cleared him, however, of the accusations of military incompetence.[21] In late 1822 and 1823, alongside Santa Cruz, he led the second intermediate campaign to the south that ended in costly defeat for the patriots. Nonetheless, Gamarra rose in the ranks of the patriot army and continued to embroil himself in the political intrigues of the period.

As the military situation worsened for the insurgents in 1823, Andrés Santa Cruz and Gamarra waged a successful campaign to replace the governing junta with José de la Riva Agüero, an event often defined as Peru's first military coup.[22] Members of Congress never recognized Riva Agüero and instead supported the aristocrat José Bernardo de Torre Tagle. Simón Bolívar arrived in Peru on September 1, 1823, in the midst of the debilitating struggle between Torre Tagle and Riva Agüero. Given supreme powers, Bolívar gained the support of members of the Congress and of key military commanders such as Santa Cruz and Gamarra (table 1). Gamarra was named chief of staff and participated in the Battles of Junín and Ayacucho. The pact between Bolívar and the Peruvian officers lasted until the defeat of the Spanish in 1824, but then quickly eroded.[23]

FATHER PATRIA: THE CHALLENGES OF THE POSTCOLONIAL STATE

Authorities such as Gamarra shared with the general population their uncertainty about what was to come in the wake of Spanish rule. Although the royalist army had been soundly defeated in Peru and would be expelled from their last stronghold in Upper Peru by the middle of 1825, the exact nature of the new polity remained unclear. Calls for a constitutional monarchy had been stifled throughout Spanish America by the middle of the 1820s, although they would periodically return.[24] Authorities and most of the population believed at this point that Peru would become an independent republic. The organization of this postcolonial republic, however, remained undefined. The new state faced a myriad of problems, as the novelty and reality of independence set in. Even before victory in Ayacucho, the different Lima-based governments had accumulated massive debts that undermined budgets and tainted foreign relations for decades. The wealthy had withdrawn their money from Peru, while the war itself destroyed production centers. Also, the royalist government had left the treasury depleted.[25] Pressing uncertainties fostered political conflicts for decades: How was Peru's sharply differentiated society to be remolded? What place would Indians have in the republic of Peru? How was nascent Peru to finance its huge debt from the destructive War of Independence? Were Bolivia and Ecuador to become independent nations or return to Peru in some federalist formula?

Cuzco presented particular difficulties. Since the Pumacahua rebellion, the region had not collectively confronted the Spanish. Outside of Cuzco, few people understood how massive the 1814–15 uprising had been, and Tupac Amaru had receded into a distant memory for most.[26] Once established in Cuzco, Viceroy La Serna had used his portable printing press to bombard the enemy with propaganda that emphasized the area's loyalty. In 1825, therefore, many patriot leaders as well as their followers questioned the region's commitment to independence. Moreover, its economic situation was bleak. The region had not benefited from its role as the last stronghold of the Spanish; to the contrary, it had been stripped of a great deal of money, supplies, and soldiers by a viceregal state with little to offer in return. In a letter to Gamarra from December 1826, two important Cuzco treasury officials described the long hours they had spent attempting to replenish the region's coffers. They vilified the Spanish for "taking funds, ruining records, and removing papers."[27] The breakdown of Cuzco's trade routes during the long war had crippled the already weakened economy as Cuzco's "exports" to Upper Peru diminished. Indicative of the economic stagnation, the population of the city of Cuzco remained at approximately thirty-two thousand from 1791 until 1825, and even declined slightly by the 1840s.[28]

In Cuzco, Gamarra needed to revive the region's fiscal system, establish new republican institutions, and prevent the outbreak of pro-Spanish insurgency. He succeeded on all counts. With admiration, envy, or distaste, contemporary commentators and generations of historians have noted the efficiency of the Gamarra government in Cuzco. The republican state was rapidly set up, with Gamarra firmly in charge. Throughout his entire career—as prefect from 1825 until mid-1827, as commander of the armies that invaded Bolivia and then Colombia, as president and then chief opponent of the Peru-Bolivia Confederation, and once again as president—Gamarra maintained a strong base of support in Cuzco. His achievements in implementing republican structures stand out in light of the severe economic crisis faced by the Cuzco regime. The analysis of Gamarrismo—in particular, how Gamarra used patronage and a chauvinistic platform to build a regional base—helps explain the mechanics of caudillismo. It shows that despite the seeming anarchy of frequent civil wars, the regional and national states continued to function. A look at Gamarrismo in Cuzco also helps us to address the question of the political significance of independence. Leaders of the postindependence Cuzco state attempted to forge a new relation between state and society, but in many regards, after much negotiation and a few dead ends, they ultimately resurrected colonial relations.

THE BUREAUCRACY, THE CHURCH, AND FINANCES: ADMINISTRATIVE CHANGES AND CONTINUITIES

In terms of administrative structures, consistency more than radical change characterized the transition from colony to republic. The jurisdictional divisions of the intendancy system were largely maintained as Peru was organized into seven departments, which were in turn divided into provinces. Three departments carried names honoring the war: La Libertad (Trujillo), Junín (Tarma), and Ayacucho (Huamanga), the latter two commemorating the main 1824 battles.[29] Prefects and subprefects replaced the intendants and subdelegates. In fact, for at least a decade, people used the terms interchangeably, referring for example to the subprefects as subintendants. Cuzco's eleven partidos, including the city (El Cercado), were converted into provinces.[30]

Frequent invasions and warfare shaped Peru's external borders in these years and marked Peruvian politics into the 1840s. Border conflicts continued well after Bolivia and Ecuador became independent republics in 1825 and 1830 respectively. For example, Gamarra took advantage of the invasion of Bolivia in 1828 to strengthen his forces. In the following year, he aligned temporarily with Generals La Fuente and Santa Cruz to use the disastrous war with Gran Colombia as a pretext to overthrow the liberal president La Mar, a war in which Gamarra again demonstrated his questionable military skills.[31] Schemes to reunite Bolivia and Peru or to form a separate political entity linking the southern Andes and Bolivia repeatedly failed. The newly defined borders were not based on natural boundaries, and they did not reinforce cultural or ethnic divisions.[32]

City and regional politics evolved around the city council and the prefecture, while, in contrast to the colonial period, the courts held less sway. Although the Cuzco council supported the Gamarrista line of protectionism, it frequently clashed with Gamarra himself and his protégés.[33] Diverse federalist, monarchist, and parliamentarian plans were defeated in the course of the early republican decades. The *juntas departamentales,* councils of provincial notables, constituted the most important federalist experiment. From 1828 until their abolition in 1834,

4. Peru in 1829

these councils sought to promote regional economic development.[34] Political instability fostered a high degree of de facto regional autonomy. Although in no sense did the regional governments become independent or divorced from national politics, the regional prefects held a great deal of bargaining power vis-à-vis the Lima-based government. In turn, provincial capitals such as Cuzco monopolized regional power.[35] The military struggles themselves and the flow of funds to and from Lima maintained the link between regions and center. The constant threat of armed opposition and perennial fiscal crises forced the national government to rely on the regions for military and monetary support. The central government's dependence (and its related inability to repress the hinterland) provided departmental governments with a great deal of power. Gamarra exemplified this provincial power, as he built political alliances that would endure into the 1840s.

The new legal, fiscal, and municipal structures largely replicated their colonial predecessors. Gamarra immediately lobbied for a cautious transition, invoking the need for stability, as conservatives continually did. On December 30, 1824, he decreed that although the real audiencia would close until further notice, the municipality would swear loyalty, and judges would continue to use current laws "as long as they are not opposed, implicitly or explicitly, to the new current system of government." In the same decree, he encouraged judges and other authorities to scrutinize and discourage anti-Spanish sentiments and actions: "detesting by character, philosophy, and religion any idea that upsets the peace between Peruvians and Spaniards, judges will scrupulously proceed in regard to insults and injuries that arise, perhaps from the tensions caused by the war, making it known that mutual and sweet harmony between one another will be the seed of good order and common prosperity." [36]

Gamarra's first measures, therefore, barely altered the existing colonial structures. The grave financial crisis faced by the Bolívar-led government, as well as the uncertainty about what type of national political system would be implemented and whether it would endure, discouraged radical administrative reforms. Foreign creditors and the victorious armies demanded payment. Yet financial concerns and general uncertainty were not the only reasons for clinging to the status quo. Gamarra himself and his authoritarian brethren did not envision or desire radical change. The conservative Spanish writer Mariano Torrente observed events in Cuzco under Gamarra with satisfaction, noting that "in the midst of this terrible crisis, this capital gave unequivocal proof of sensibility and respect toward Spanish authorities and other individuals involved with the defeated forces." [37]

In his stay in Cuzco from June 25 to July 26, 1825, however, Simón Bolívar decreed laws that confronted colonial institutions. He abolished the office of cacique and Indians' obligation to perform personal duties for authorities, and ordered the redistribution of communal land held by Indian communities. As seen in chapter 7, these laws were generally not put into effect: some caciques retained power; Indians continued to toil as servants; and communities retained much of their land.[38] Ignoring the Tupac Amaru uprising, Bolívar awarded pensions to the descendants of the leaders of the Pumacahua rebellion.[39] He also inaugurated a number of schools and charitable institutions for orphans, the disabled, and the elderly, funding them with the rent from the expropriated properties of Cuzco's convents and monasteries. These reforms embodied two key elements of Bolívar's republicanism: his dislike for the church and his confidence that state-sponsored institutions could "remake" the disadvantaged. His reforms not only hurt the church economically, but also encroached on its customary role in education and charity. Two of his innovations—the Colegio de Ciencias y Artes (School of Sciences and Arts) for boys, a merger of the Jesuit schools San Bernardo and San Francisco, and the Colegio de Educandas for girls, one of Peru's first secular schools for women—continue to operate today.

The schools' longevity and dynamism were the exception to the fate of most of Bolívar's reforms. The charitable hospices confronted serious economic problems shortly after Bolívar's departure from Cuzco. Not only did the convents and monasteries challenge the expropriations in the courts and resist turning over property and rents, but the region's weakened economy meant that the estates and urban properties produced far less money than expected. Also, although the more conservative Gamarra continued to protect the schools, he allowed the demise of the charitable institutions. He disagreed with the philosophy of state-sponsored personal rejuvenation and objected to the expense of these institutions and the tensions they prompted with the church. In the mid-1830s, however, the liberal Orbegoso attempted to resuscitate the charitable organizations founded by Bolívar.[40] Even the schools prompted controversy. Conservatives blamed the suicide of two students in the 1830s on the liberal and thus immoral ideas propagated by the schools.[41]

Gamarra immediately found himself at odds with the hierarchy of the Catholic Church in Cuzco. He managed, however, not only to withstand their opposition but, eventually, to gain their support. Although Cuzco's bishop, Father José Calixto Orihuela, had backed the Spanish until their defeat, he participated in the celebrations of late 1824 and 1825, calling for his parishioners to adhere to the republic. Nonetheless, he complained vigorously when Gamarra began to tamper with the jurisdictional borders of the diocese and with church finances. Relations deteriorated when Gamarra demanded in February that the bishop remove paintings from the cathedral that depicted Saint James (Santiago) and the Holy Virgin miraculously saving the Spaniards in battle against the Incas. The prefect contended that it would be "disagreeable" for the soon-to-arrive Bolívar to see portraits displaying divine intervention on the side of the Spanish.[42] Orihuela refused, but Gamarra had them taken down in April.

Relations with the church worsened notably with the arrival of Bolívar and with his expropriations and secularization efforts. Orihuela and others accused the state of supporting the work of freemasons and

Calvinists, whereas in publications such as the *Ecclesiastical Censor* pro-government writers countered that the church hierarchy sought the return of the Spanish.[43] Gamarra claimed victory in this first battle when Orihuela resigned in September of 1826 and was replaced by the more conciliatory Father Antonio Torres. In 1826 and 1827, Gamarra opposed the election of two priests, Eugenio Mendoza and Pedro José Leyva, as congressmen for Tinta, claiming that the elections had been fraudulent and that both priests continued to oppose independence from Spain. He carefully presented them, however, as exceptions to the church's loyalty to the republic, but after many legal battles and a flurry of accusatory pamphlets, he ultimately relinquished the fight.[44] From this point, Gamarra eschewed anticlericalism, counting on the support of the church in his two presidencies. Bolívar himself had backed off from his initial skirmishes with the church and had instructed Gamarra to avoid conflicts because "disagreements with them are always baneful; friendship always advantageous."[45] In Cuzco, problems with the church during Gamarra's reign rarely surfaced after 1827. In 1842, Father Bartolomé Herrera, one of Peru's major conservative ideologues of the republican era, extolled Gamarra at his funeral, comparing him to Jesus and other Christian martyrs.[46]

Finances represented the most pressing concern for Gamarra and other authorities. The nascent state needed to replenish its coffers and create a viable tax system. Urgency encouraged tradition rather than radical change. On August 11, 1826, Bolívar reinstated the Indian head tax that he had abolished the previous year, renaming it the "contribution," and, as discussed at length in chapter 7, Gamarra fully supported its return.[47] The Indian tax provided more than half of the Cuzco prefecture's annual income between 1826 and 1845. Although they caused great controversy, a number of direct taxes targeting non-Indians never amounted to a significant part of the treasury's income, usually less than 10 percent.[48] Two major sources of funds for the colonial state, levies on mining and the sales tax, also produced little income. Mining revenues plummeted in this period, and the unpopular alcabala was abolished in 1826. Other colonial holdovers—such as the tax on Official Sealed Paper (the forms necessary for all bureaucratic dealings) and the *noveno* (the state's share of the tithe)—and different types of loans provided additional revenue. With notable speed, the Gamarra-led Cuzco state government established an effective tax base.[49] With similar efficiency,

Gamarra spent these resources to strengthen his political base in the region.

Cuzco's economic future was not promising at this point. The region had been fortunate to avoid the wartime destruction that had befallen other areas. Daniel Florence O'Leary noted that "the city has suffered very little in the course of the revolution."[50] Yet he also commented upon Cuzco's isolation, complaining that, although blessed with abundant natural resources, the department of Cuzco was "almost incommunicado from the coastal provinces because of the lack of roads."[51] The constant warfare of the following decades, the creation of Bolivia as a separate republic, and the increasing importance of maritime transport rather than trans-Andean journeys aggravated Cuzco's isolation. Arequipa rose as the center of the southern Andean economy, and Cuzco lost much of its share of the Bolivian market. Except for a few momentary resurgences, the sugar and textile industries languished in the first half of the nineteenth century. Of the colonial export economy's staples, only the coca trade recovered and even expanded, and demand for wool rose in the 1830s, the faint beginning of the "boom" of the latter half of the century.[52] Tax collectors in the countryside bitterly echoed complaints from producers about the continually depressed prices for foodstuffs and the dispersion of the Indian population due to hard times and frequent military drafts.[53] Artisans in the city of Cuzco confronted competition from other southern Andean cities, such as Puno and Arequipa, as well as from an increasing number of imported goods.[54] The demand for land in the Cuzco region also remained stagnant throughout much of the nineteenth century.[55]

GAMARRISMO IN CUZCO

Gamarra proved himself quite capable in one of the most important tasks for authorities in the infant republic: selecting people for government positions. Through adroit nominations and the careful cultivation of these allies, he created an enduring base of powerful supporters in Cuzco and its provinces. The analysis of caudillismo needs to shift its attention from the battlefields and reconsider the state, as middling officials such as subprefects and militia leaders proved more important for Gamarra than military officers and guerrillas. Caudillos operated through the state, not around it.[56] In Cuzco, the lack of insurgency in the decade prior to independence meant that there was no clear-cut division between patriots and loyalists. Unlike in Lima, there were no groups of veterans demanding compensation in the form of political office or prominent loyalists posing problems. The War of Independence had not polarized Cuzco as it had Lima and the central Andes. Although many authorities named by Gamarra had been active supporters of the Spanish until the very eve of independence, others had fought against the Crown in the Pumacahua rebellion. Gamarra did not make a concerted effort to exclude individuals associated with the Spanish state. Some of Gamarra's appointees continued in the positions they had held under the Spanish, whereas others worked for the state for the first time.

Politicians and ideologues in Lima criticized Gamarra for incorporating too many royalists in his list of subprefects. In May 1825, Bolívar wrote to Gamarra and expressed his concern about the high number of *capitulados* being given administrative and military positions.[57] In a long response, Gamarra noted "the difficulty in discovering the true merits of those subjects who will be destined to the different positions of the state," but he denied any sort of favoritism and defended the patriotism of his appointees. He summarized the merits of his eleven subprefects: five of them had fought for the insurgents in the Pumacahua rebellion, two were sons of leaders of this rebellion, one had fought under Bolívar, one under Santa Cruz (Tomás Becerra, also a veteran of 1814), one under Gamarra, and one in the Battle of Ayacucho. Only José Mariano Ugarte, the subprefect of Quispicanchis, lacked patriot military credentials. Gamarra described him as "an honorable lawyer. He has not had the opportunity to serve the patria actively, but he has performed many services. Nor did he serve the past government. But his father was taken to Spain for being an insurgent." In contrast, General Antonío José Sucre complained bitterly in 1825 that as subprefect of Quispicanchis, Ugarte had attempted to avoid feeding patriot troops and their horses.[58] Throughout Peru in the decades following independence, many loyalists assumed important political roles, particularly as supporters of the conservatives. After the Battle of Ayacucho, some Spaniards and veterans of this particular battle were expelled from the country, but loyalists who were not Spanish or did not participate in the final military campaigns were not ostracized. It should not be forgotten that Gamarra himself switched sides late in the war, in 1821.[59]

Gamarra's ability to recruit and maintain loyal protégés permitted him to create a steadfast base in Cuzco. Three institutions proved central to Gamarrismo in Cuzco: subprefects, civil militias, and the military. Subprefects linked Cuzco's hinterland with the regional and national states, which greatly depended on these authorities' ability to collect taxes. Because of the centrality of the Indian head tax, the subprefects' efforts made or broke regimes. Gamarra carefully monitored them, rewarding individuals who proved loyal and efficient, and punishing others. Being a subprefect under Gamarra generally represented a crucial step in a long career. Gamarra relied on subprefects not only to collect tax revenues, but to recruit soldiers and provide supplies in times of civil war (almost the norm from 1825 to 1845). They also observed opponents and disseminated political information and Gamarrista propaganda. They and their subordinates linked the rural population, which was composed primarily of indigenous peasants, with regional and national political events.

The position of subprefect provided a series of privileges. Above all, this official had access to thousands of pesos that could be invested and lent, so he would hold on to tribute money as long as possible, hurrying taxpayers and collectors and delaying delivery to Cuzco. Through various subterfuges, he could also keep more money than the percentage granted him according to the law. For example, Santos Valer, a tax collector in Canas, inflated the number of deceased in his towns in his official reports, but continued to collect full tribute and divided the money with the subprefect.[60] Cuzco and Lima officials insisted that subprefects and their dependents were unqualified and ineffective. Many complained of the scarcity of literate candidates for positions such as collector. In his 1831 presentation to the Congress, Finance Minister José María de Pando decried the lack of competent subprefects: "The most qualified citizens refuse to give up their own business ventures to take over this laborious job that does not even provide them the proper decency." In a proposal reminiscent of the Bourbons' halfhearted efforts to professionalize provincial authorities, Pando recommended providing the subprefect a guaranteed income in order to attract better candidates and discourage corruption.[61] Most critics emphasized the subprefects' penchant for pocketing as much money as they could for as long as possible. In 1832, Finance Minister José Serna quoted a "sage economist" who contended, "It is not a big deal to establish a tax and to get it from the taxpayer compared to the difficulty in assuring that it reaches the treasury after passing through the hands of the tax collectors."[62] Although Gamarra relied on the subprefects politically, he also supervised them closely to guarantee that tax revenues reached Cuzco.

THE MILITIAS

The militias constituted the core of Gamarrismo in Cuzco. They controlled local society by incorporating new members into the government and monitoring any threat of opposition. They also served as veritable military academies because outstanding members of militia units frequently entered the army under the tutelage of Gamarra and his major supporters. Gamarra promoted the development of the militias, originally established by Bolívar in early 1825, and ordered all men between fifteen and fifty years of age to enroll. Between 1827 and 1835, seventy-four regiments were formed in Cuzco.[63] In 1831, boasting about the growth and improvement of the militias, Prefect Juan Angel Bujanda summarized the discipline and order of the different regiments commanded by a who's who of Gamarrismo: Gregorio Lugones, Juan Ceballos, Felipe Infanta, and Juan Luis Oblitas.[64] The career of Augustín Rosel typified the careers of key Gamarra backers in Cuzco: subprefect and militia leader from 1825 to 1834, military commander against Orbegoso and Santa Cruz in 1834 and 1835, persecuted outcast during the Peru-Bolivia Confederation, and powerful insider during Gamarra's 1839–41 regime, "the Regeneration." Rosel's prominence should not be confused with omnipotence. He and other subprefects did not escape long trials over tax debts during the friendly Gamarra governments or in Santa Cruz's government.[65]

High-ranking positions in the militias represented important avenues to political and economic gain. Militia officers had access to political and military figures and thus opportunities to accrue local power. They provided the regional government with an important social base and military force. In the early republic, the prefect selected the commanders, who in turn nominated a long list of officials and assistants. An 1830 decree called for the commanders to be "citizens of known fortune" in order to assure their troops' upkeep.[66] Prefects frequently lauded militia commanders for donating uniforms, arms, or horses. In 1831, Domingo Farfán, the commander of the cavalry militia in Quispicanchis, sent an eight-page summary of his nominations for thirty-five vacant positions ranging from captain to field assistant.[67] Filling these positions and directing the militia provided the commander a loyal, well-armed base of support as well as economic opportunities. These officials could promote their own interests when buying provisions. Also, the recruits worked in the officers' various enterprises and enforced social and labor control. Prominent textile mill owners often held important positions in militia regiments.

An 1832 document supporting Pedro Cano's promotion depicts the importance of the militias in the consolidation of the Gamarra coalition and the mechanisms used by individuals to gain political favor. The document summarizes Cano's activities after independence. From 1824 until 1831, he held the position of governor of the third district of the Tinta province, "aiding the united and national armies whenever they passed through the southern part of the Cuzco department, efforts that have kept him for so many years in this position." He was also mayor of Tinta, Tupac Amaru's base, for three years. In September 1829, he became captain of the Fourth Company, Second Squadron, of the Tinta militia. He reputedly "uniformed his entire company at his own expense and disciplined them with great dedication." During the so-called Esobedo uprising in Cuzco in 1830 (discussed more fully in chapter 6) he prepared his troops, "maintaining them at his own cost in order to oppose the efforts of the agitators; he alerted the authorities immediately about his willingness to fight, gaining the compliments of his commanders."[68] He also provided the national army with recruits and donated two hundred pesos "to the Nation." For the construction of the Combapata Bridge, he gave three horses and "donated the labor of more than one thousand workers" as well as his own. The author compliments Cano for "always having seen aiding the public good as his first duty." In 1834, Cano was named congressman.[69]

Imbued with the militaristic nationalism characteristic of caudillo rhetoric, this document illustrates the relationship between local authorities and the departmental state. Cano periodically provided recruits, provisions, money, and laborers, thus pleasing his commanding officer Juan Ceballos, a prominent Gamarrista, as well as more highly placed authorities. In turn, he received the opportunity to climb in the military-state hierarchy and accumulate a great deal of local power. His ability to gather one thousand workers derived from his position as a militia officer. Cano represented the echelon linking subprefects with local society. Like him, many of those nominated by Anselmo Vera for the office of subprefect in 1832 in a similar document had been governors, mayors, tax collectors, and other local officeholders.[70]

The militias consistently fought on behalf of Gamarra. During the Gamarra presidency, the distinction between the military and the militias became blurred because Gamarra incorporated many regiments into the national army. During the La Mar government, one contemporary claimed that in Cuzco "Gamarra acts in complete independence. He disobeys the orders of La Mar, and he promotes, licenses, punishes, and gives titles without authorization. He increases the numbers of battalions and squadrons."[71] The senior judge of the Cuzco Supreme Court complained in 1827 that Gamarra would not allow military officers (apparently even militia officers) to testify in court and would grant them immunity reminiscent of colonial corporatism. Despite the complaints of the courts and of the Cuzco junta departamental, the officers' virtual immunity continued.[72] The results of Peru's conflicts with its neighbors to the south and north in 1828 also greatly favored Gamarra. He increased the size and strength of the army in the south in order to invade Bolivia in 1828. He succeeded in destabilizing the Sucre government and returned to Peru with an improved reputation and a fortified military base: the Army of the South. The disastrous war with Colombia decimated the Army of the North and led to the ouster of La Mar by Gamarra, La Fuente, and Santa Cruz. Ironically, Gamarra's poor performance on the battlefield strengthened him politically.[73] In an 1830 letter written near the Bolivian border, Gamarra recognized the importance of the militias and their virtual fusion with the military: "the minister of Bolivia has been shocked by the sight of so many people and so many members of the civil militia, uniformed out of their own pocket so that they are indistinguishable from the veteran soldiers except for their lack of arms."[74]

From 1830 to 1835, Gamarra continued to increase the number of militias in the Cuzco region. By 1833, the province of Urubamba alone had twelve militia companies stationed in the larger towns as well as in outposts in the area leading to the jungle.[75] Gamarra relied on these units to repress the growing number of rebellions. In July 1833, for example, the Paruro Battalion helped defeat an uprising in Ayacucho.[76] In the midst of the 1834 civil war, Gamarra converted the civic companies of Quispicanchis into the Quispicanchis Battalion with putative full recognition from the national army. He extolled their "model morale and discipline" and named two renowned Gamarristas, Martín Gavino Concha and Pascual Aranabal, as commander and major. In 1834, many important Gamarristas commanded militia units in Cuzco, which proved to be Gamarra's most important military base in the ephemeral Cuzco Federation.[77] Santa Cruz carefully monitored Gamarra's actions. In early 1834, in a letter to General Domingo Nieto, Santa Cruz argued that Gamarra sought to "occupy all of the Sierra, concentrating forces in Cuzco, where he has ample supplies." After defeating Gamarra in August 1835, Santa Cruz wrote to Orbegoso that "the damned Gamarra and his proselytes, who have greatly increased in number here in Cuzco, where we were received worse than the Spanish, have been permanently annihilated."[78] In February 1836, he dissolved all of Cuzco's militias.[79] The militia leaders and most of the militias themselves, however, would return to prominence.

THE MILITARY

Both contemporaries and historians have called Gamarra's first presidential term a military oligarchy.[80] The military reform law of December 1829 represented the single most important measure by Gamarra to aid and gain supporters throughout the country and to marginalize potential opponents within the armed forces. Intended to cut government expenditures on the military and to calm the concerns of Peru's neighbors, the law reduced the number of officers. Although foreigners and veterans of the Spanish army were supposed to be the first suspended from active duty, through various means Gamarra convinced many prominent Peruvian-born military leaders to "reform"—that is, retire. Gamarra's critics increasingly accused him of favoring foreigners ("los suizos"), charges that the active anti-Gamarra press echoed.[81] Gamarra sagely noted in a letter in 1830, "With the *reformados,* it's necessary to be very careful."[82] Although Congress changed the law in 1831, Gamarra continued to favor his allies regardless of their nationality. Opponents unsuccessfully conspired against the Gamarra government throughout his tenure. Intrigues by the reformados constituted several of the more important of the seventeen conspiracies that Gamarra faced during his four years in office.[83] In 1833, he promoted more than a dozen officers, and all of them fought for him in 1834 when he attempted to remain in office.[84]

Gamarra gained important political support by arranging for the military to buy its cloth for uniforms from Cuzco textile mills. Not surprisingly, the region's two prominent *obrajeros* from this period, Gregorio Lugones, owner of the Amancay mill in Paruro, and Ramón Nadal, owner of the Lucre mill in Quispicanchis, enthusiastically backed Gamarra. In 1826, "wanting to foster the factories of this department," Gamarra ordered that one hundred thousand varas (approximately eighty-four thousand meters) of wool cloth (*bayetón*) from Cuzco be purchased annually for the army. He also requested material for thousands of uniforms for troops throughout the country and two thousand pairs of shoes.[85] In 1827, he demanded that soldiers' shirts be made from Cuzco fabric, thereby "conciliating the comfort of the troops and that of the inhabitants of the Cuzco department."[86] For the following fifteen years, Lugones and Nadal filled countless commissions for cloth.

From 1825 until 1835, the government placed frequent orders with Lugones. He often complained that he could not fill orders until he received the money he was owed.[87] The most common payment procedure was for a prefect-level authority to order a subprefect to pay the mill owner from the tribute money already collected. In 1834, claiming that "there is not a cent in the national treasuries," the Cuzco prefect instructed the subprefect of Tinta to give Lugones an unspecified advance. Financial problems in the same year forced the government to reduce the request of forty thousand varas to thirty thousand. The subprefects of Cotabambas and Paruro were ordered to pay 3,840 and 3,000 pesos respectively.[88] In 1831, an explosion and ensuing flood in Lugones's Amancay obraje killed three hundred and destroyed the installations. Prefect Bujanda claimed that Lugones's finances were in a "deplorable state" and lobbied to grant him the Sahuasahua hacienda and chorrillo in Paruro, which formerly pertained to La Merced Convent. When authorities turned down this extreme act of favoritism, Lugones began renting Sahuasahua in 1833.[89] From 1830 until at least 1834, Lugones was the commander of the Paruro militias.[90] Controlling a large group of soldiers, volunteers, and conscripts could benefit the owner of a labor-intensive activity such as the textile mills. Yet Lugones was not an intransigent Gamarrista. He continued to sell fabric to the government during the Peru-Bolivia Confederation, 1836–39. A representative of Santa Cruz had approached him in late 1835, coyly noting that "I believe you are an idolater of the law."[91]

Ramón Nadal, on the other hand, resolutely supported Gamarra, staking his fate on the Cuzco caudillo. Born in Salta in what became Argentina, Nadal had been a colonel of the loyalist army and was captured in the Battle of Ayacucho. Gamarra sent him to Cuzco in late 1824 to propagate news of the defeat of the Spanish. Nadal quickly transformed himself from a virtual prisoner of war to an influential military officer and businessman. In 1827, nominating him to command the Chumbivilcas militias, Gamarra argued that Nadal, "despite being a capitulado, has a very good disposition, talents, conduct, and does not lack patriotism . . . in part thanks to the family relations in this city [Cuzco] through his marriage to a woman from a respected family."[92] Nadal had married into a well-known Cuzco family, the Garmendias, and owned the Lucre textile mill in the same province.[93] In 1830, Bujanda recommended him for the position of colonel of the regiment of the civic militia in the important province of Quispicanchis. In 1834, Nadal became the colonel of the Chumbivilcas cavalry. Although his support for Gamarra was well known, he managed to continue in business during the Peru-Bolivia Confederation.[94] After the Gamarra-led defeat of the Peru-Bolivia Confederation, authorities commended Nadal for stymieing the troops of General Francisco Paula Otero, an important pro–Santa Cruz military leader. In 1839, Nadal organized important public ceremonies in Cuzco in favor of Gamarra. By 1840, he was commander general of the department, one of the three highest officials in Cuzco.[95]

Gamarra's efforts to create a strong base were not limited to filling key political positions, the militias, and the military with his supporters. He also employed the tax system to recruit, reward, and punish. In the 1834 civil war, he used tax exemptions to compensate his defenders. In early May of that year, Prefect Bujanda relayed Gamarra's message that individuals from Quispicanchis and Paruro would be exempted from the casta tax in return for their "distinguished service to the patria."[96] A few days later, Bujanda promised vecinos blancos (white citizens) exemption from the same head tax if they fought for the Gamarra forces as guerrillas or in the militia.[97] Prefects also used tax collection debts as a means to attack enemies. After each regime change, the incoming administration scrutinized the records of former officials. For example, upon Gamarra's defeat to Santa Cruz in 1835, the Santa Cruz general Blas Cerdeña instructed Cuzco treasury authorities to verify the finances of all Gamarrista subprefects.[98]

All of the subprefects named by Gamarra faced lawsuits about their use of tax money—lawsuits initiated not only by Santa Cruz but by Gamarra himself. During his administration, some of Gamarra's most loyal followers were brought to court to justify their debts as subprefects. Not only did the treasury maintain a certain amount of autonomy that allowed them to prosecute debtors, but Gamarra himself proved willing to take his loyal authorities to court because these lawsuits kept them under his control and provided much needed revenue when they paid their debts. In 1833, while Gamarra was still in the presidency, Prefect Bujanda was taken to court over debts from when he was subprefect of Urubamba. He blamed the "perverse enemies of order" for the ordeal. No decision was reached, but the fact that the preeminent Gamarrista in Cuzco had to defend himself in the courts questions the notion of an omnipotent caudillo.[99] For political survival in this tumultuous period, money often mattered more than the support of a particular authority.[100]

Cuzco politics in this period should not be understood solely as a division between Gamarristas and liberals. Although many individuals did not participate in the endemic political struggles, others served and even supported both sides. Pablo Mar y Tapia exemplified the ability of many to dodge the high cost of political ostracization. Beginning in 1804, Mar y Tapia held important positions in Cuzco's colonial administration, including procurator of the real audiencia. He aided the Crown in the fight against the Upper Peruvian rebels and the Pumacahua rebellion, and, in 1816, he replaced Agustín Chacón y Becerra as notary of the intendancy. After independence, Mar y Tapia succeeded in overcoming any obstacles posed by his prominence during colonial rule. He owned several haciendas and one of Cuzco's finer houses, Casa del Almirante, where he hosted General Sucre, President Orbegoso, and President Santa Cruz. In 1825, he organized the reception for Bolívar, thereby winning Gamarra's praise, and in 1826, he represented Paruro in Congress.[101]

Mar y Tapia preferred Gamarra's political rivals. In July 1834, the pro-Orbegoso prefect Juan Bautista Arguedas named Mar y Tapia as treasurer, a position he held until March 1835. Arguedas noted that Mar y Tapia had been "the target of persecution" by the previous regime.[102] Nevertheless, Mar y Tapia regained the support of Gamarra. Remaining outside the constant political struggles of the late 1830s, he returned to his position as notary in 1839. The constant turmoil and sharp rhetoric of the caudillo struggles did not mean that Cuzco society was neatly divided into political camps along caudillo lines.

GAMARRISTA IDEOLOGY: CUZCO FIRST

Through more than a decade and a half of conspiracies, coalitions, coups, and military campaigns, Gamarra positioned himself as Peru's leading early republican conservative. He quickly joined the opposition to Bolívar, who had originally nominated him prefect of Cuzco, and in the late 1820s led the efforts against the liberals. He assumed the presidency in 1829 and held it until 1833. The defeat of Santa Cruz in 1838 and Gamarra's return to the presidency constituted a high point for Peruvian conservatives. The 1839 Constitution—classified by one historian as Peru's "most embarrassing document of nineteenth-century republican history"—defended slavery, centralized power in the presidency, and eliminated any remnant of social reform.[103] President Gamarra supported all the common causes of nineteenth-century conservatives: protectionist trade policies, severe social control measures, centralist institutions, and xenophobia. The Gamarra coalition in Cuzco demonstrated one notable characteristic of politics in early republican Peru: the firm connections between regional and national movements.

In his efforts in Cuzco, in Lima as president, or throughout the country and over its borders in his numerous military campaigns, Gamarra perpetuated one central trait of his movement: authoritarianism. He and his followers blamed the country's ills on indecisive and inapplicable institutions such as the Congress or the juntas departamentales, and they presented Gamarra, a strong, effective executive, as the solution. For example, in an obsequious letter to Bolívar written in 1826, Gamarra noted that "the people do not want unworkable theories; they want to get out of poverty and rest from the wars that have oppressed them. The freedom to speak and write without obstacles is insignificant to the present civilization. In one word: all of America needs a vigorous government."[104] Authoritarian ideologues emphasized the evils of partisan politics and blamed the liberals for Peru's instability. An anonymous writer claimed that "the anarchists do everything through liberalism."[105] In 1839, the pro-Gamarra newspaper, *Cuzco Libre*, cautiously celebrated the defeat of Santa Cruz in similar terms: "Peru is now free from foreign domination, but not from the tyranny of political parties, of quarrels, of triviality, of senselessness, . . . and the force of ambition."[106] Authoritarian ideologues argued that cliques of liberal politicians, strangers to Cuzco, impeded the unification of Peru under the aegis of Gamarra.

In Cuzco, the debates and accusations between liberals and conservatives (or Gamarristas) paralleled the debates being held in Lima. Through the active press (discussed at length in the following chapter) people in the provinces read and commented on the works of Lima ideologues. Papers published in Cuzco, Ayacucho, Trujillo, and elsewhere not only transmitted news from Lima, but also informed readers in Lima about the provinces. While the flow of news and ideological debates moved from Europe and the United States to Lima and from there with great strength to the hinterland, a persistent counterflow allowed provincial movements to influence intellectual and political circles in the capital. In Lima, Cuzco, and elsewhere, conservative writers heralded the benefits of a strong, stable government and condemned the liberals for leading Peru into anarchy. For example, in 1833, Gamarrista writers called their enemies "anarchic liberals," and "damned sans-culottes."[107] The first issue of the pro-Gamarra newspaper, *La Aurora,* opened with a story entitled "Revolution," which began by calling these liberals "the ruin of los pueblos."[108]

Gamarra supporters charged that the liberals sought to place a new oligarchy in power. In order to underline the closed, elitist nature of the liberals, they labeled them a club or a partido, used in a clearly derogatory sense. In a pamphlet addressed "to the inhabitants of Cuzco," the Gamarrista prefect (and at this point a Salaverry supporter) Martín de Concha declared, "You will not know any more parties: they have fled with the enemies of order, those with the name servile, liberals, outsiders, and foreigners: we are now all children of the patria and friends."[109] Liberals in turn criticized the conservatives for returning Peru to a colonial-like despotism and Gamarra for corruption and cronyism. An 1833 pamphlet decried that "due to a deplorable fatality we have seen that in these times Gamarra has concentrated all the elements of conspiracy and disorder in this department, and has taken from obscurity men that surround him to be his slaves and to sustain at any cost his horrible domination."[110] The central issue dividing the liberals and conservatives was whether republican institutions—such as elections, Congress, freedom of the press—could take hold in Peru.

Gamarra did not propose the same program for Cuzco as he did for the nation. During his term as prefect and the subsequent period, when Bujanda and other protégés carefully maintained his support in the region, Gamarra offered what could be called a "Cuzco First" platform. Gamarrismo emphasized this caudillo's predilection for his native land, touted in chauvinistic rhetoric and materialized in different types of favoritism. Focusing on the painful contrast between Cuzco's glorious Inca past and its stagnation in the early nineteenth century, Gamarra cast the region's decline as a result of the encroachment and discrimination of outsiders, particularly political forces from Lima, Arequipa, and Bolivia. He and his colleagues thus disseminated a hyperbolic discourse that emphasized his birth in Cuzco and his desire to return it to its previous preeminence. Virtually every text that formed part of the celebrations of 1824 and 1825 extolled his Cuzco origins. In 1835, announcing his return to Cuzco, a broadsheet declared, "COMPATRIOTS: today I have stepped on the sacred soil of my birthplace after a year of absence. Everywhere, even in the midst of extreme danger, you always remained in my memory and in my heart. Crossing over from Bolivia, I was instructed that the cradle of the Incas was occupied by an insolent soldiery and suffered unmerited humiliations; I decided to fulfill the most gratifying of my duties."[111] Gamarrista discourse in Cuzco repeatedly emphasized his allegiance to his homeland and the former prominence of the region.

Political tracts stressed the purported grandeur of the region during the Inca and colonial periods. When they contrasted the discouraging present situation with the past, Gamarrista ideologues conflated the Inca Empire and Cuzco's political and economic strength in the colonial period. Writers and speakers presented the Incas as a symbol of Cuzco's former grandeur, not referring in any substantial way to the Incas themselves or to their descendants. At times, references to the Incas transcended mere Cuzco chauvinism to substantiate historically the merits of authoritarian rule. For example, an 1827 critique of corrupt authorities in the republic extolled the order and morality of the region from the time of the Incas until the defeat of the Spanish. The author attributed the order and morality "not to the sciences that illustrated them or the leniency of [the Incas'] sage laws: but rather the fatal rigidity of these laws, the assiduous work they dedicated to them, and the tireless vigilance of the chiefs in punishing any small negligence, these are what gave all of those who pertained to the Inca Empire clarity and sparkle."[112] An 1831 pamphlet deriding the liberals asked, "Why do we want more social pact than that established by our Incas? What could be more rational than one orders and all obey?"[113] Gamarristas interpreted the Inca Empire as a model of hierarchy and social control, an interpretation that other conservatives developed in the nineteenth century.

An American diplomat in Lima warned the secretary of state that Gamarra's use of the Incas formed part of his efforts to establish a monarchy in Peru. In February 1834, Samuel Larned, the U.S. chargé d'affaires, wrote, "There can be no doubt of the intention of Gamarra and his partisans, to establish a monarchical government in Peru;—under the sway of this personage; who claims to be descended from the Incas;—and which claim is substantiated, in as far as his personal appearance is concerned;—for it is evident therefrom, that he is an almost unmixed descendent from the aborigines of this country."[114] General Orbegoso, who had been deposed by Gamarra and whose forces fought Gamarra's in a civil war at the time the letter was written, had lobbied Larned about the dangers posed by Gamarra. Although the accusations about Gamarra's supposed monarchical leanings can be dismissed as mere liberal propaganda, the mention of the Incas rings true. Gamarristas consistently invoked the Incas. For example, in mid-1835, at the end of the Orbegoso-Gamarra civil war that led to the Peru-Bolivia Confederation under Andrés Santa Cruz, a Gamarrista colonel distributed a pamphlet that read, "Compatriots: Peru is dislocated and will perish, the victim of the party's aspirations, unless you rebuild it with its own elements. Will the Rome of America, opulent Cuzco, the cradle of the great empire that must be the common center of all Peruvians, coldly consent in its dissolution and demise?"[115] Gamarra and his followers reconfigured into their conservative platform the enduring interpretation of the Inca Empire as a symbol of resistance and rebirth. Whereas in the colonial period the Incas had served as a utopian alternative for different rebels and revolutionaries, including the Tupac Amaru and Pumacahua rebels, they constituted a key icon for the Gamarristas in postindependence Cuzco. Liberals in the region could not or did not employ the Incas to the same degree or success.

Gamarra constantly reminded the Cuzco population of the benefits of having a loyal native son in office during volatile times. His favoritism to the region was most visible in the business he directed to Cuzco textile mill owners and tailors. Throughout this period, these entrepreneurs championed the campaign for protectionist trade policies.[116] Writers from this period invariably blamed Cuzco's economic crisis on the free trade policies that undermined the region's textile mills. In 1830, Cuzco merchants resisted the establishment of foreign merchant houses in their city. They decried the "invasion" of foreign goods, which they claimed was destroying obrajes and chorrillos and putting people out of work. Clearly interested in fending off foreign competition, Ramón Nadal led the protectionist charge, lamenting the "furious war" waged by foreigners against national production and the potential ruin of "the land of the Incas" if the "insatiable Europeans" were given a free hand. Not surprisingly, the Gamarra-led national government sided with the Cuzco merchants.[117] Many groups from Cuzco interpreted the free trade policies espoused by the liberals as a threat to their textile production and as a boon for coastal merchants. One writer in 1829 blamed imports allowed under free trade for the region's "reduction in public revenues, the weakening of agriculture, the paralysis of commerce, the obstruction of monetary circulation, the lack of currency, the annihilation of public and private credit, fear, distrust, and what is more sensitive and painful, the 50,000 families that previously dedicated themselves to and were maintained by manufacturing cloth and textiles . . . are now indigent and desperate, as are the muleteers used to transport these goods."[118]

Gamarra also addressed the animosity in Cuzco toward other key regions: Lima, Arequipa, and Bolivia. In 1836, the U.S. consul in Arequipa deemed that Cuzco should be the figurehead capital of a confederation because its inhabitants "are of a jealous and turbulent nature."[119] Cuzco's inhabitants shared with their southern Andean neighbors a long-standing distaste for Lima centralism, a sentiment that had animated the series of revolts throughout the region in the late colonial period.[120] A French traveler who visited Cuzco in 1834 observed that its residents, "like those of La Paz and other Andean cities, do not like people from the coast and profess for them a disdain for what they believe is their usury."[121]

Cusqueños also mistrusted Arequipa because they feared that Cuzco would lose its traditional economic and administrative supremacy in the south if the liberal schemes emanating from Arequipa were enacted. Andrés Santa Cruz provided vivid testimony of the animosity between the two regions. In June 1834, he wrote to his cabinet with evident frustration that not only were Gamarra and Orbegoso irreconcilable enemies, but so were Arequipa and Cuzco because "each wants the annihilation of the other." The following month he noted that "Arequipeños do not want to form part of a family with Cuzco."[122] Gamarra had also constantly roused anti-Bolivia sentiments in Cuzco, particularly against Santa Cruz. Usually, analyzing a "region's" political perspective can exaggerate cohesion. In the case of early republican Cuzco, however, Gamarra succeeded in creating a broad alliance that defined its goals in opposition to other major cities and their leaders.[123]

CONCLUSION: THE INCOMPLETE STORY

As outlined in this chapter, Gamarra created a strong base in Cuzco. Throughout his career, he promoted this relationship, favoring Cuzco whenever possible. The military support that he received from Cuzco in times of trouble demonstrated his success. His nationalist rhetoric and promises to recapture Cuzco's glory resonated well in this depressed region of declining economic and political importance. He expertly integrated the maximum symbol of Cuzco grandeur, the Incas, into his platform, thereby gaining the support of groups ranging from urban elites to the Indian masses. The fact that he was born in Cuzco helped him, particularly vis-à-vis his opponents, who had suspect backgrounds: the Bolivian Santa Cruz and the Ecuadorian La Mar.

The examination of Gamarrismo in Cuzco sheds light on the mechanics of caudillismo. It displays how Gamarra used patronage and other methods to gain supporters and how he and his followers crafted a platform. It also illuminates the functioning of the early republican state. Despite almost constant civil wars, it continued to collect taxes and operate. It spent most of its revenues on the military and the bureaucracy, allotting much less to education and "charity," services offered by the church until Bolívar's reforms in the mid-1820s. Like countless biographies of nineteenth-century military leaders, however, this analysis does not tell the full story of caudillo politics. Taken alone, it neglects the complexity of early republican state building.

This review of Gamarra's career exaggerates the ease with which he ascended to power. At various times, he was suspended from the military, defeated in civil war, exiled from Peru, betrayed by supporters, and nearly killed in battle, which was his ultimate fate in 1841. Even in Cuzco, he faced constant military and ideological opposition. From 1825 to 1841, his liberal adversaries denounced him and his coalition in the press, and challenged his platform. They planned and in a few cases carried out conspiracies, coups, and uprisings, usually in cahoots with forces outside of Cuzco. The following chapters examine the role of civil society in the caudillo struggles. Chapter 6 focuses on the city of Cuzco, particularly the changes and continuities in political practice or culture. Chapter 7 examines the role and fate of Cuzco's majority, the Indian population, in the early republic.

"Peruvian society has a character all its own; its taste for the exaggerated and the miraculous is extraordinary."—Flora Tristan, *Peregrinations*

Two contradictory images of Cuzco and much of caudillo-ruled Spanish America in the decades after independence can be conjured up. On the one hand, Agustín Gamarra created a virtual political fiefdom in his homeland. As outlined in the previous chapter, he established a network of increasingly powerful loyal authorities throughout the department, built up the militias, tamed the church, disseminated a Cuzco-specific program, and muzzled his opponents. Many contemporaries and scholars, most writing from Lima, reinforced this image of Gamarrista omnipotence. On the other hand, when he was president, Gamarra confronted more than a dozen conspiracies, coup attempts, putsches, and revolts. In the chaotic 1833–36 period, control of Cuzco shifted at a dizzying pace as Gamarra left the presidency, attempted to retake it with no success, and ultimately lost in battle to Santa Cruz. His opponents did not limit their challenges to the battlefield or to the command of the prefect office. Throughout these years, an opposition press belittled him and his conservative project. Close attention to political events in this period demonstrates the fragility of his power and the fluctuations in postindependence politics. Although Gamarra built a substantial coalition in Cuzco, he and his followers faced frequent challenges and in several periods lost political control of the region.

Therefore, neither the image of the entrenched dictator nor that of incomprehensible tumult satisfies. Caudillismo did not replace politics, but instead constituted a unique form of politics that involved the military, organized political groups or parties, and much of civil society. This chapter examines how caudillo politics worked in the city of Cuzco from 1825 to 1840—in particular, any differences from and similarities to politics in the colonial period. It emphasizes political culture, or what in Cuzco in this period were convoluted and acrimonious battles over defining "rules of political behavior."[1] Keith Baker provides a broad definition of political culture: "the set of discourses and practices characterizing that activity in any given community. Political culture comprises the definitions of the relative positions from which individuals and groups may (or may not) legitimately make claims one upon another, and therefore of the identity and boundaries of the community to which they belong (or from which they are excluded)."[2] The concept of political culture moves beyond structural explanations for the outcome, or the "winners," and takes the struggles themselves seriously. Caudillo-led political coalitions vied to define the parameters of the new republic. The political conflicts themselves were not just mere means to take control of the state and impose a vision of the republic; instead, they were key sites for defining the rules and codes of postcolonial political practice. People fought in the battlefields, the courts, the press, and the streets not only to defeat the enemy and seize the state, but also to determine how groups could use these different sites to shape social and political relations.

The analysis of political culture in this period leads to the question of public opinion and public space. Jürgen Habermas defines the "public sphere" as the space where people come together "in a debate over the general rules governing relations in the basically privatized but publicly relevant sphere of commodity exchange."[3] Geoff Eley provides an even more concise definition: "a sphere which mediates between society and state, in which the public organizes itself as the bearer of public opinion."[4] Habermas's theories and countless works elaborating on and criticizing those theories have emphasized the importance of the public sphere in modernity and the development of bourgeois societies. These works have shed new light on reading, civic associations, and daily life, particularly in cities.[5] Analysts have elaborated Habermas's concepts in relation to groups presumably excluded from this eminently "bourgeois" arena: the lower classes and women. Simply put, most historians prefer the use of the plural "publics."[6]

Spanish America's public space would seem anemic in the nineteenth century. The dominant classes employed an exclusionary view of who merited citizenship and what groups could form "public opinion." Indians, blacks, the casta lower classes, and women were excluded from formal politics, and de facto regimes often ruled, so the relevance of "public opinion" would appear minimal. Literacy rates remained low compared to the rates in Europe and North America, and civil associations developed slowly.[7] Yet the case of Cuzco indicates that discussions and clashes over the nature and control of the state moved beyond the sphere of the military and the elite. Despite their nominal exclusion from participating in "rational" debates and institutionalized struggles over the state (e.g., elections and formal political groupings), lower-class groups followed the lively debates in the press and frequently participated in the turbulent political struggles. Leaders of coalitions mobilized the masses when politics took to the streets in festivals, demonstrations, and riots. After following and in some cases participating in the ideological and military conflicts, the lower classes, women, and other groups normally deemed unworthy of (and uninterested in) formal political participation did not easily forgo politics. The public sphere widened at times despite the best intentions of the state and of leading political factions.[8]

In order to apply concepts such as political culture and the public sphere developed in or about Europe to a colonial or postcolonial context, particular attention must be paid to forms of knowledge and practice that separated or united the colonized and colonizers. Of greatest interest are the gray areas that linked different groups and about which the struggles over the meaning and control of colonialism often centered. The case of Cuzco questions the validity of sharply drawn lines separating popular and elite culture and delineating the Indians from the non-Indians. There was a great deal of play and overlap in the space between oral and literate cultures, between the religious and secular, and more specifically between Quechua and Spanish.[9] Here, I stress the relationship between oral and written modes of communication because it raises a central issue in examining politics in a society in which the illiterate were the majority.

The previous chapter outlined the programmatic differences between conservatives and liberals, but the question of how politics operated in the republican period requires more attention. These two groups did not maintain tightly organized, public institutions in the sense that each had an internally organized party with an institutional base or clear procedures. Instead, they organized and conspired behind closed doors, in salons, living rooms, and the barracks.[10] Jorge Basadre uses the term *moments* to describe periods when the activities of the political groups came to the fore, with evident leaders and goals. Cuzco in the early republic supports Basadre's argument that the press, the military campaigns, and Congress served as points of cohesion, even in periods of seemingly little political activity. Liberals and conservatives constantly promoted their programs and their leaders and attacked those of the opposition in widely disseminated newspapers and pamphlets. Leading politicians crisscrossed the country in political and military campaigns.[11]

Two characteristics mark Cuzco liberals. First, they opposed Gamarra. This opposition could be seen as substantiation of the cynical contention by one nineteenth-century general who claimed that Peru had only two parties, "the persecuted and the persecutors."[12] Undoubtedly, some members of the opposition to Gamarra in Cuzco were bitter by their exclusion from office, and if the state could have afforded it, they probably could have been co-opted. Many of the liberals, however, remained critical of Gamarra and never sought a position. Indicative of the surprising autonomy of certain realms of the state, some public officials opposed Gamarra but retained their positions in the bureaucracy. This division between Gamarra supporters and opponents reflects above all the power attained by Gamarra in Cuzco: his movement set the agenda for early republican politics. Individuals opposed to him conglomerated under the liberal banner.

Ideological differences with the Gamarristas distinguished Cuzco liberals. Unlike their opponents, liberals emphasized republican institutions such as the Congress, the juntas departamentales, and the courts. They sought a less centralized state, with sharp restrictions on the head of state, and favored a more open trade policy and a reduction of rights granted to corporate groups. Whereas authoritarians stressed their nationalism, liberals presented themselves as more cosmopolitan, relying much more on foreign, primarily European, ideologues in their literature. Cuzco's liberal periodicals—such as the *Fiel Compromiso* ("Faithful Commitment") and *Remitido para Todos* ("Sent for Everyone")—frequently reprinted articles from foreign newspapers on political theory and international events. The articles described occurrences in Spain, France, or Mexico and discussed Bentham, Constant, or Rousseau. The staid summaries or transcriptions about European intellectual currents contrasted greatly with the heated debates about regional politics, however.

Conservatives and liberals could also be differentiated by their answers to questions about the nature of Peruvian society and about the proper relationship between its diverse groups and the state. The leading ideologues of both factions believed in a hierarchical society, supporting slavery and the Indian head tax. Nonetheless, the conservatives defended these institutions and a closed political system much more energetically than did liberals. In contrast to the conservatives, the liberals had faith in an eventual unification or homogenization of society under the aegis of a decentralized state that would sponsor educational reforms, normalize practices, and set up charitable institutions. For example, Cuzco liberals defended the establishments created by Bolívar, such as the girl's school and the orphanage. The conservatives, on the other hand, believed in an authoritarian state upholding order and social divisions. The question of the role of the church did not separate these two groups. Although the liberals had some anticlerics in their ranks, many of their leaders were priests.[13] In sum, the liberals cannot be defined as democrats. They were, however, noticeably less retrograde than the conservatives.

Both groups presented political stability as their goal, but in their platforms they differed on the means used to attain it. Conservatives stressed action in the midst of instability, justifying de facto regimes in the name of order and in the face of external and internal threats. Liberals presented commitment to the Constitution, the legal system, and elections as the path to political stability. This distinction between the two groups was especially apparent in how they criticized one another. Conservatives cast liberals as elite snobs, more grounded in European intellectual currents than in Peruvian reality. Liberals depicted the conservatives as oligarchs who, in an approach reminiscent of colonial patronage, used favoritism and the armed forces to advance their own personal interests. This sharp distinction, however, broke down in the world of caudillo politics. Above all, liberals used the very methods for which they condemned the conservatives: they conspired, expelled the enemy when they were in power, relied on the military, and manipulated elections. Caudillo politics resembled the rough-and-tumble worldview of the conservatives much more than the legalistic vision championed by the liberals. This chapter examines why the liberals succumbed to such practices, whether by force or choice.

Cuzco city professionals constituted the largest bloc of Gamarra opponents. Gamarra's favoritism toward sycophantic followers frequently came at the expense of these professionals, so many of them opposed the concentration of power in Gamarra's retinue and, in general, supported the liberals' call for change. When naming groups or agencies opposed to Gamarra, liberal writers mentioned members of the Supreme Court, the municipality, other governmental agencies such as the mint or the printing press, and teachers. In practice, these personal grievances and ideological beliefs coalesced.[14] Political groups in early republican Cuzco, however, do not divide easily into socioeconomic categories. Political factions cannot be differentiated merely by economic activity. Most members of Cuzco's political elite were both professionals and landowners. The purported schism between the "traditional" hacienda owners and the "modern" urban professionals emphasized by some analysts does not apply to the situation in Cuzco.[15] Furthermore, Gamarra excelled at creating a heterogeneous group of supporters. Key Gamarristas included the nouveau riche, professionals, artisans, members of the colonial elite, and large sectors of the lower classes. Both the Gamarra alliance and the opposition cut across occupational and class lines.

EVERYDAY POLITICS: ELECTIONS, PLOTS, COUPS,
PUTSCHES, AND REBELLIONS

In the caudillo period, political groups incessantly fought over the control of the state. In fact, turmoil characterized politics as Peru averaged more than one president per year during the two decades following independence. Chaos often reigned as several statesmen simultaneously claimed the presidency and civil wars raged throughout much of the country. Many caudillos broke alliances and the law to seize power. Yet behind the chaos and bald power struggles lay important disagreements about the relationship between state and society. Examining these episodes in detail demonstrates the nature of these debates and helps to trace the networks linking national political groups, regional coalitions, and individuals in the provinces. A review of a few conspiracies and revolts displays how caudillo politics worked, as well as the differences and similarities in liberals and conservatives' political culture.

Caudillo politics was not limited to intrigue and coercion. Elections constituted innovative public events in the early republic. At first glance, the franchise seems surprisingly broad in nineteenth-century Peru because it included most non-Indian taxpaying men. Indians, in fact, could vote for local authorities. Nonetheless, an indirect and complicated electoral system kept a small group of wealthy men in the larger cities firmly in control of the results. In primaries, secular priests, public employees, and adult male citizens who owned property and paid taxes, and who had resided in the parish for two years, selected electoral representatives from an exclusive list of candidates who met these same qualifications and counted on an annual income of five hundred to six hundred pesos.[16] This group in turn elected congressmen. Not all representatives, however, were elected. For example, the municipality suggested candidates for district governors, from which the junta departamental selected.[17] Elections constituted just one more political arena, neither insignificant nor paramount, in the early republic. Gamarra learned how to manipulate them, although not always with success.

In late 1825, Prefect Gamarra annulled the results of congressional elections. Although he specified a number of irregularities, he mainly objected to Bishop Orihuela's efforts to favor loyalist priests. New elections in November, however, saw two priests chosen, Eugenio Mendoza and Pedro José Leyva, both of whom would be thorns in Gamarra's side.[18] The 1833–35 civil war that culminated in the Peru-Bolivia Confederation began when Congress selected Orbegoso rather than Pedro Pablo Bermúdez, Gamarra's handpicked candidate, to become president. Controversies about elections recurred periodically in Peru. Virtually every coup was done in the name of the Constitution, as the instigators claimed that the governing party had broken electoral rules and thus had lost legitimacy. Yet unlike in Mexico, elections did not prompt widespread debate about democracy or about the role of the brown-skinned lower classes in the republic.[19]

The struggle between Gamarra and Santa Cruz marked Peruvian politics for more than a decade following the overthrow of President La Mar in 1829, and closely tracing these battles illuminates the nature of caudillo politics. Gamarra held the Peruvian presidency from 1829 to 1833. After nearly two years of civil and international war, Santa Cruz defeated him in the Battle of Yanacocha in mid-1835, thereby clearing the way for the Peru-Bolivia Confederation. Gamarra then led the opposition to the confederation and assumed the presidency in 1839. He met his martyrdom in battle in Bolivia in 1841. Throughout this enduring clash between these childhood friends and former military allies, each endeavored to control Cuzco. For example, in 1829, Santa Cruz and his allies helped engineer the overthrow of Gamarra officials as one of the first stages of a frustrated plan to bring Santa Cruz to power. In the next few years, his supporters plotted incessantly in Arequipa, Puno, and Cuzco.[20]

In their publications and actions, the Gamarristas abandoned the explicitly federalist leanings that they had previously manifested. Instead, they reverted to their emphasis on order and on Cuzco's right to economic and political prominence. This shift reflected Gamarra's increasing power in both Lima and Cuzco, as well as the growing tensions between him and Santa Cruz. After 1829, the former allies sought, or at least were associated with, distinct projects. Santa Cruz promoted a confederation of Peru and Bolivia, whereas Gamarra "defended" Peru's borders against such a plan and contemplated the possible return of Bolivia to Peruvian control. His Cuzco-centric nationalism garnered broad support in the region. He also insisted on his campaign to bring order to the anarchy caused by the liberals. In the name of order, Gamarra and his supporters consistently defended their conspiracies against and disruptions of the government.

The conspiratorial activities of Santa Cruz and his cadre of supporters became clearer in the August 1830 "Escobedo" uprising. In mid-1830, President Gamarra contemplated legislation that would have prohibited individuals born outside of Peru from assuming the presidency, thereby denying Santa Cruz the possibility of attaining that office. In May, Prefect Bujanda tightened security in Cuzco because, he claimed, "false and alarming rumors" abounded in Cuzco, the result of secret meetings of men and women.[21] Both conservatives and liberals decried "secrecy" in politics. In this case, conservatives did so not to maintain transparency and the supremacy of legitimate institutions, but instead to prevent political efforts from moving beyond the groups and institutions they controlled. Bujanda's suspicions were well founded. At dawn on August 26, a small group from the Callao Battalion led by Colonel Gregorio Escobedo entered the prefect building by feigning to deliver urgent mail. Joined by soldiers who had been hiding behind the grandstand erected for a bullfight in the Regocijo Plaza, they imprisoned the slumbering Bujanda and other officials and took control of the military barracks. The leaders promised the soldiers pay raises and improved conditions. In a municipal meeting that evening, Escobedo and his supporters deposed Bujanda, arguing that he oppressed Cuzco and that his selection had not been approved by the junta departamental, as the law instructed. One observer remarked that the rebels sought to install "a federalist government or one that is the most analogous."[22] Escobedo proclaimed La Fuente as president. Most analysts, however, see the hand of Santa Cruz behind the rebellion.[23]

The next day, with the support of militia units and civilians, a counterattack was staged by military officers who had eluded capture. In the partisan words of one author, "Without class, social condition, gender or age distinction, as soon as bullets were heard, the people ran to [the recently freed] Prefect Bujanda and other loyal officials to demonstrate their solidarity."[24] By evening, the rebels had been routed. Although several of the leaders were killed in the gunfire, and others were subsequently executed, Escobedo escaped. Gamarra left Lima in early September and arrived in Cuzco a month later. The city celebrated his arrival for days, with a mass, speeches, and poetry.[25] Participation in the Escobedo uprising seems to have been limited to disgruntled officers and soldiers and to a small group of anti-Gamarra politicians and professionals, all linked to Santa Cruz. It expressed, however, the opposition to Bujanda and the enduring federalist yearnings in the city of Cuzco. The uprising's defeat allowed the Gamarristas to justify their authoritarian style in the name of maintaining order against wayward military officers. It reinforced their reputation as effective rulers while weakening liberals' denunciations of them as military oligarchs. They had maintained stability and the Constitution by defeating a barracks uprising.

In the remarkably chaotic 1833–36 period, liberals and Gamarristas attacked each other in the press and, when in power, purged the opposition from governmental office. The events took place in the shadow of dramatic changes across the country. From December 1833 to April 1834, Gamarra and Orbegoso fought in a civil war; Orbegoso won the first round. Even with Gamarra defeated and exiled, however, Orbegoso faced widespread opposition from different conservative factions. When he left Lima to put down insurgents in the south in early 1835, General Felipe Santiago Salaverry rebelled and installed an authoritarian government. By the middle of the year, Salaverry, Gamarra, Orbegoso, and Santa Cruz (at this point the president of Bolivia) were negotiating with each other to form coalitions. Gamarra returned to Peru in June 1835 and established the ephemeral Central State of Peru in Cuzco. In August, Santa Cruz entered Peru and defeated Gamarra in the Battle of Yanacocha. Six months later, he defeated and executed Salaverry, and soon thereafter established the Peru-Bolivia Confederation.

In Cuzco, liberal writers decried the hesitancy of Gamarra's opponents in rising against him. In July 1834, when Gamarra was not in power in Cuzco or in Lima, and thus vulnerable, an anonymous journalist using the pseudonym "the Impartial" wrote, "I do not believe that there are only four Liberals in Cuzco; that would mean that only these very few and well-known people have worked efficiently and actively to the point that they were persecuted, ambushed, and oppressed by the Government of the Tyrant." This self-criticism buttressed the contrast frequently made between the diligent conservatives, willing to risk their lives and to break some laws in order to take power, and the urbane and ineffective liberals. This author blamed the continual presence of key Gamarristas in Cuzco for the liberals' reluctance to act publicly and condemned the latter for their lack of initiative. He then turned to the conservatives' supposed venality. Complaining that only Bujanda and Lucio de la Bellota had been expelled from Cuzco, the author argued that other Gamarra supporters were enjoying themselves on their estates, making money, and waiting to return to power.[26] In response to the reference to the liberals as "sans-culottes," the author argued that Cuzco's liberals could afford to buy undergarments but were not rich because they didn't steal. Liberals frequently denounced the conservatives for disregarding the Constitution and seizing power for personal gain.

Many of the battles from this period pitted one realm of the state against another. Some conflicts, like the disputes of the colonial period, were over rank and public decorum. For example, a lawsuit was filed against a judge for using a "raised feather" in a hat that he wore to mass. The judge, Domingo Eugenio Yepes, recognized that it was inappropriate apparel for his position but claimed that he had bought it that way and thought it was acceptable in light of Peru's "liberal government," which enforced codes "very different than the old etiquette defined by despotism." The courts responded that anyone could buy a general's jacket but could not wear it in public. The case also reviewed the conduct of several military officers who in the same mass had taken seats reserved for members of the Supreme Court. The clash between the liberal court and the Gamarra officers over their relative position and rank in the new republic had thus reached the highly symbolic realm of pews in the church.[27]

These squabbles should not be dismissed as mere Old Regime corporatist infighting. They constituted an important aspect of the struggle between liberals and Gamarristas. The courts and the juntas departmentales supported the liberals in this period, whereas the prefecture remained a bastion of Gamarra's movement. The former attempted to implement liberal education and welfare policies and defended the autonomy of the state from Gamarra's efforts to centralize power. The prefecture patronized the Gamarristas and put into practice Gamarra's tax and police policies. Although these struggles often centered on personal disputes and arcane rules of public etiquette, they represented an important battleground for the major political conflicts of the era.

Once in power, liberals attempted to weaken the Gamarristas' hold on Cuzco. In June 1834, the pro-Orbegoso general Domingo Nieto wrote Cuzco's prefect that "no measure is more urgent or of a greater interest for the maintenance of public order and the consolidation of patriotic institutions than that of removing a great number of the functionaries of this part of the Republic from the jobs that they received from the past administration in exchange for their disregard to liberal principles and their complicity in the perfidious schemes by that disorganizing faction against the law and the Nation's liberty, particularly in Cuzco where Gamarra has long tried to concentrate his elements of conspiracy and disorder that he organized around himself."[28] Nieto presented ridding Cuzco of Gamarra's allies as a crucial step for restoring order. Invested with "extraordinary faculties" by President Orbegoso, Nieto authorized Prefect Arguedas to remove the Gamarristas from office. After Gamarra's defeat in Yanacocha in August 1835, the pro–Santa Cruz general Blas Cerdeña ordered that Gamarra's officers be rounded up "because they wreak havoc in the country through seduction, rumors, and their secret opposition to the Santa Cruz government and the United Army, and finally, not having occupations, they become bums and derelicts."[29]

Both liberals and conservatives justified their conspiracies and expulsions of the opposition in the name of order. The liberals believed that order would be achieved by maintaining the supremacy of the Constitution and republican institutions. Conservatives emphasized the maintenance of a strong, stable government that would defend national and regional interests. To attain these visions of order, each group needed to conspire and, once in power, to expel members of the opposition. When out of power, each group attacked the other's "despotic" ways, only to assume that very same behavior once back in control. As seen in the previous chapter, regime changes prompted turnover in the upper realms of the administration—particularly in prefects, subprefects, and at times the heads of the municipality, the mint, and the treasury. When a new president took office, not all authorities lost their positions, and some components of the state, such as the courts, maintained a surprising degree of autonomy. Nonetheless, the twists and turns in the Santa Cruz–Gamarra battle prompted advancements and banishments, which hardened political lines.

Gamarra's dominance in Cuzco can be explained by his notable political talents, which dovetailed with Cuzco's yearning to return to prominence. Social and economic factors, as well as Gamarra's own efforts in his homeland, help elucidate his success. The explanation also needs to delve into the political culture of the place and period. In light of the constant conspiracies and frequent civil war, the conservatives' willingness to assume power by force and their emphasis on strict order over chaos had a much greater chance of success than the liberals' abstract insistence on freedom and their invocation of the right to conspire and fight for power in order to defend the Constitution in times of emergency. As seeming anarchy reigned and republican institutions languished, the conservatives' call for draconian efforts to prevent anarchy found a larger and larger audience. Liberals, on the other hand, had to convert what they considered emergency measures — conspiracies and civil war — into the mainstay of daily politics. By the 1830s, many people looked askance at their emphasis on the Constitution and the law, seeing these as unrealistic or at least unfulfilled. At the same time, they viewed the liberals as equally conspiratorial as their opponents. Stripped of the veneer of legality and forced to fight in the trenches, the liberals were outmatched by their conservative foes. Political turmoil ultimately favored the conservatives.

THE PUBLIC SPHERE: UNITING THE PEOPLES

The republican period began in Cuzco and in most of Peru with widespread festivities. The grandiose celebrations for Gamarra, Bolívar, and other dignitaries combined speeches, masses, dances, and public revelry. The organization of the festivities and the speeches themselves reflected political leaders' notion of postcolonial Peru. These authorities sought to define communities and to create social and political boundaries, the core of Keith Baker's definition of political culture. They did not envision an integrated society; instead, they continued to differentiate Indians and non-Indians. Although these groups and their celebrations commingled, authorities understood them as separate groups — divided in the past, present, and future. In early republican Cuzco, authorities made little effort to instill republican values among the city's largely Indian lower classes. In contrast to certain sectors of the intelligentsia elsewhere in Spanish America, the Cuzco elite did not believe that the lower classes could be "symbolically whitened through education, through the influence of the press and civilizing literature."[30] To use Benedict Anderson's terminology, Cuzco's "creole pioneers" could not imagine anything but a racially divided society. They attempted to control the urban lower classes' activities in the streets but made little effort to incorporate or "improve" them. Gamarristas did not believe in the civilizing capabilities of the state and considered the Indians irredeemable. Liberals expressed more confidence in the possibilities of state-sanctioned reform. They shared with conservatives, however, the idea of Peru as a segregated country, populated in large part by wayward Indians.[31]

The city of Cuzco went to great lengths to celebrate independence and to demonstrate its republican spirit. On December 24, 1824, thousands greeted Gamarra in Zurite, thirty-five kilometers west of Cuzco. After hours of speeches and festivities, he reached his hometown late on the same day. A recently inaugurated newspaper that became the official government publication, *El Sol del Cuzco*, described in glowing terms the arrival of "Cuzco's son": "This virtuous soldier, deeply marked by the ancient splendor and current depression of his homeland, never forgot during the dangers of the war all that he owed to Cuzco. In the midst of his enemies in Oruro or the extremes of Peru, the image of Cuzco presented itself to his soul. . . . Marching from the battlefield, he received sincere testimonies of gratitude and affection."[32] The author described Gamarra's speech to the Indians in Quechua: "Hearing for the first time their language from an authority . . . reminded the primogenitors of Peru of their sad history. Gamarra watched them cry and, before finishing his speech, cried with them."[33] Indians celebrated with dances, many of which had been banned by the Spanish because they invoked the Incas. William Miller, an Englishman who rose to the rank of general in the patriot army, described the almost daily "processions . . . in which their masks, their grotesque party-coloured dresses, and their lofty ostrich plumes, contrasting with the sad plaintive style of their music, formed a most interesting and illustrative exhibition." He also noted with bemused irony that many women, public employees, and military officers—who had only days before vociferously supported the Spanish—partook in the dances and parties held for the nascent republic and its first prefect.[34]

The festivities continued when the general of the victorious armies in Ayacucho, Antonio José de Sucre, reached Cuzco a few days later. Cuzco luminaries reiterated their gratitude in countless speeches and held several dances for Sucre and his officer corps. Simón Bolívar merited even more speeches and pageantry when he arrived in Cuzco on June 25, 1825. Bolívar's confidant, General O'Leary, wrote that "nothing can be compared to the magnificence demonstrated in the ancient capital of the Incas."[35] Shortly before his arrival, Bolívar himself had raised expectations by writing, "Peruvians! Very soon we will visit the cradle of the Peruvian Empire and the Temple of the Sun. Cuzco will have on the first day of its freedom more pleasure and more glory than under the golden rule of the Incas."[36] Not only did the city give the "Liberator" a crown with sumptuous jewels but, according to *El Sol del Cuzco,* the mythical founder of the Inca Empire, Manco Capac, also sent his greetings from the tomb.[37] One observer commented on the "extraordinary exaggeration" of a monument built in honor of Bolívar.[38] Public and private ceremonies continued for a month, and in the words of one journalist, "This capital could not have given more convincing proof of its patriotism."[39] In 1826 and 1827, Cuzco celebrated El Día de San Simón in honor of Bolívar.

Authorities sponsored these festivities to demonstrate the attachment of Cuzco, the refuge of the last Spanish viceroy, to the newborn republic and its maximum authority, Simón Bolívar. They also reflected sincere jubilation over the end of the war and, for many, the defeat of the Spanish. Yet public festivals also represented an enduring and central form of politics in Cuzco past and present. In the festivities and demonstrations, political groups disseminated their programs, glorified their leaders, and criticized the opposition. Celebrations organized for the arrival of important political figures or for momentous events such as the declaration of independence aimed to legitimate the state, inculcate republican values, and incorporate broad sectors of the population by means of ritual.[40] In this period, Cuzco staged almost daily political or religious festivities. The French traveler Etienne de Sartiges considered the "taste for religious as well as political spectacles" the "characteristic feature of Peruvians."[41] His countrywoman, Flora Tristan, described "scandalous spectacles" in Arequipa. Deeming them more pagan than the spectacles of the Middle Ages, she commented, "It is from these festivals, remarkable for their splendour, that the Peruvians derive their chief happiness, and I fear it will be a long time before their religion has any spiritual meaning for them."[42] Dozens if not hundreds of religious and political celebrations shaped life in Cuzco.[43]

The festivities did not end with Bolívar's departure. In the ensuing years, Gamarra celebrated his arrivals and victories with pomp and merriment, creating a cult of Cuzco rather than of the nation-state.[44] His celebrations represented a frequent and important part of Cuzco politics, and they help explain why liberals remained in his shadow: he never failed to reiterate his ties to the region. Pamphlets described his sorrow upon leaving Cuzco and his joy when returning to his homeland, the land of the Incas.[45] The four-page "Description of the Fiestas Held in This City in Celebration of the Birthday of His Excellency, President of the Republic, Don Agustín Gamarra" from 1832 provides a vivid picture of the festivities and political culture of Cuzco in this period. The celebration itself illustrates Gamarra's success in grounding his movement in a rhetoric and activities that resonated in his homeland. The festivities also highlight the search for a postcolonial political idiom and the continually bifurcated vision of Peru, Indian and non-Indian.

CELEBRATING THE SON OF THIS SOIL

The festivities began on Gamarra's forty-seventh birthday, August 27, 1832, with a play at the School of Sciences and Arts that Gamarra, "author of Peru's independence and peace," had helped found. Street music, the illumination of the city, and steady bell ringing made for a spirited evening. On the following day, representatives of the city's corporations and an unusually high number of "common people" attended a mass in Gamarra's honor. The priest paid Gamarra the ultimate compliment by describing how the church and society required and counted on a protector in the sky as well as one on the ground, "both efficient and accredited in their respective power."[46]

This event demonstrated the slow pace of secularization. The church and Catholicism played a central role in everyday life, including political ritual. Unlike in revolutionary France, celebrations of the republic in Peru did not emphasize the rise of the state and the weakening of the church—a transition from the sacred to the secular.[47] The regional state did not attempt to hinder or modify the almost daily religious festivals and processions, which continued to shape life in Cuzco. After his initial conflict with the archbishop, Gamarra only occasionally challenged the central role of the church in public culture. Conflicts did not arise over religious rituals, and the church actively participated in the political festivals. In their speeches, priests endorsed the republic, or at least the regime in power, and authorities invoked the church and confirmed their own faith. Visits to Cuzco by Bolívar and other dignitaries invariably began with a Te Deum at the cathedral. In Peru, the transition from the veneration of the sacred to the cult of the nation-state occurred very slowly, if at all. Peruvian nationalism, in fact, developed hand in hand with the Catholic Church.[48]

Subsequent events in the celebration of Gamarra's birthday dramatized the support for him among the major state institutions. They also reiterated one of the key tropes of Gamarrismo: a militaristic state based on the (invented) traditions of the Incas. After the mass, representatives from the Supreme Court, the municipality, the Santo Domingo Convent, the university, the seminary, and the high school greeted Gamarra in the prefect office located on the Regocijo Plaza. A reception followed that culminated in a mass toast to a portrait of Gamarra. That evening the Cuzco Battalion staged a drama at the large San Bernardo house, demonstrating that "the military character is the most appropriate for such spectacles," according to the anonymous author of the description. The military not only fought wars and frequently ran the state in the early republic, but also, as this quote indicates, had an important cultural component. Before the play, an actor emulating Mars greeted the patria. Musicians played a song that "graciously emulated the sad rhythm of the Gentiles (Indians) while following the rigorous rules of art in compass and movement." Traditional Andean music could be presented in state-sponsored rituals if adjusted to the supposed rigors of "art" or what in later years would be called the "Western tradition." A "hysterical" one-act farce followed the performance.[49] On August 29, military and civic leaders attended an opulent banquet in the prefect building. The narrator defended the luxurious menu, contending that such food built "lasting friendships."

While ostentatious banquets and exclusive dances continued, the organizers began to hold more popular events. These rituals emphasized Gamarra's allegiance to both Cuzco and the nation, again fusing celebrations of the military and the invocation of the Incas. Several bullfights were held in the next few days, and many of the bulls were adorned with silver and weavings. Participants paid homage to Gamarra by stressing once again his power, his ties to the region, and his defense of the nation. The bullfighters and their assistants honored him with flower arrangements that spelled out "Peru" and "Gamarra." The lancers of the Piquiza Battalion staged a particularly colorful presentation. They strung red and white ribbons, Peru's national colors, from their lances to a float shaped as a large grenade with Gamarra's name and the Peruvian coat of arms emblazoned on it. Coins dangled from the grenade. The *chusma* ("rabble") could not resist the temptation to scramble for the money, which resulted in several injuries.

Bullfights sponsored by prominent members of Cuzco society, dances, plays, and a "circus" in the main plaza continued until September 13.[50] In the ceremonies honoring Gamarra, students read proclamations that described his merits and loyalty to Cuzco. The prefect office printed and distributed many of these testimonies. Although most orators read in Spanish, a few spoke in French and Quechua. For example, a "young man dressed as an Inca King" read several paragraphs in Quechua that condemned Santa Cruz and Bolivia, and thanked Gamarra for protecting Cuzco's freedom.[51]

The author of this account of events criticized the bullfights but noted the enthusiasm of the crowd and their efficient organization. He claimed that "the passion of our peoples [pueblos] for this type of spectacle, despite the horrors that come with them, became clear." The use of the plural demonstrated the prevailing notion that the Peruvian nation encompassed many peoples. Few believed in the idea of an integrated or homogenized nation. The junta departamental, the federalist organization that frequently clashed with Gamarra, questioned some aspects of these celebrations. One prominent member, Pablo Mar y Tapia, complained that owners of houses surrounding the Regocijo Plaza where a bullfight was to be held charged outlandish prices for seats in the windows and balconies. Claiming that attendance was mandatory, he noted the city's "general poverty." Prefect Bujanda changed the location of the bullfight to the much larger San Francisco Plaza. The junta departamental also expressed its concern over the unruly parties and fireworks.[52] Another representative of the junta, Gregorio Quintana, called for a ban on bullfights, decrying the "dissipation, waste of time, and superfluous expenses that result from . . . the vulgar amusement of bullfights." Citing Jovellanos and Monteagudo, he contrasted this "barbaric" custom with more orderly pastimes of the enlightened age. Mar y Tapia sympathized with Quintana's critique, yet overruled him. He emphasized that Quintana had overlooked the fact that the bullfights commemorated Gamarra, "the son of this soil."[53] Throughout the Gamarra period, the junta departamental defended the charitable hospices founded by Bolívar and criticized the municipality and the prefect for not keeping the city clean and orderly. In 1832, however, when Gamarra was president, it did not aggressively attack his protégés or criticize the festivities for his birthday.

In a dispute between, on the one side, virtuous liberals questioning the morality and propriety of loud, drunken festivities and bloody bullfights and, on the other, the sponsor of these events, Gamarra, public sentiment clearly favored the Cuzco caudillo. Cusqueños delighted in these fiestas, a passion that continues today. Opponents' objections reinforced the image of them as elitist do-gooders more interested in European trends than in Cuzco reality. The festivities not only provided excitement and revelry, but also projected an image of a resurgent Cuzco. Although grandiose fiestas were held in the 1770s, the number and pageantry of bullfights had diminished in subsequent decades,[54] and the decline of the city and of its festivities went hand in hand in the eyes of the Cuzco population. By sponsoring elaborate festivals, Gamarra attempted to reverse the decline.

Organizers of the celebrations for Bolívar (Saint Simón), Gamarra, and other authorities labored to invent republican symbolism, a postcolonial idiom. Part of the problem lay in the doubts in the 1820s and 1830s about the political and social organization of the republic: the questions regarding what system to adopt and where to mark the nation's borders had not been decided. Speakers did not know who to laud besides the arriving dignitary or what period to exalt in order to personalize the transition from colony to republic. At the same time, they worried about rousing the masses. Cuzco posed particular problems for finding a usable past. The most important fighting had taken place outside of Cuzco and thus commemorations of the war itself seemed extraneous. Glorifying the Incas and contemporary Indians, converted elsewhere in Spanish America into icons of the new republics, was problematic. Although virtually every political, social, and cultural manifesto from Cuzco referred to the Incas, they did not become key symbols of the Peruvian republic.

Of the two political groups, the conservatives proved more adept at incorporating the Incas into their discourse in the early republic. As seen in the previous chapter, Gamarristas presented the Incas as a precedent to their "Cuzco First" authoritarian regime. In contrast, liberals could have cast the Incas as historical proof of Indians' ability to transform —with the guidance of the state—into productive citizens. Sartiges described how "Cuzco gentlemen" passionately discussed the Incas, observing that the "American Party"—that is, the Cuzco liberals— "among whom only a few don't have a little Indian blood in their veins, maintains for the old Peruvian dynasty an affectionate and vivid memory as if only two or three generations had passed since the Conquest."[55] Yet liberals did not incorporate this passion into their platform. Several explanations can be found. The Incas constituted an ubiquitous yet potentially subversive symbol in the region, and Cuzco had been rocked by Indian uprisings that had presented Inca revivalism as their keystone. In its propaganda against the rebels, the colonial state stressed the dangers of Inca revivalism and its development into Indian violence. Fear had not been the only product of the repression following the Tupac Amaru and Pumacahua uprisings. The colonial state had driven a wedge between Indians and non-Indians—banishing, weakening, threatening, and in some cases killing individuals who mediated between these two groups. Moreover, the view of the Incas as monarchs made many liberals question whether they constituted a proper symbol for the republic.

The liberals' cosmopolitanism also encouraged them to look to Europe rather than to the Andean past. They consistently preferred foreign ideologues over the Peruvian reality.[56] Although all Cuzco politicians cloaked themselves in the tradition of the Incas—in which the Tahuantinsuyo figured as anything ranging from an enlightened despotism to a revolutionary democracy—the conservatives did so with greater sophistication and success. In general, however, neither group converted the Incas into an enduring symbol of the republic.

Nor did the speakers and organizers assail the Spanish and colonial rule. Many Spaniards remained in the region and prominent Cusqueños had been royalists until the final defeat of the colonial army. Although the long War of Independence discouraged the romanticization of the colonial period (which decades later many conservatives saw as a golden age), early republican leaders largely maintained rather than broke traditions associated with Spanish rule. In this sense, the problem lay not so much in finding a usable past as in confronting and ritualizing the conformist present. Although postindependence leaders changed street names, shifted holidays, and disapproved of certain artworks, they by and large preserved key modes of colonial rule and social practice.[57] A historian of the festivities for Bolívar perhaps unwittingly captured the continuities between colonial and republican rituals: "The spectacle had the contour of an actual crowning of a King, with the splendor appropriate for the richest and noblest imperial court of Europe. The only difference was that there, tyrants and autocrats tended to be crowned; here, in contrast, the greatest and most qualified champion of freedom was being crowned."[58] Unable to glorify the past, wary about the place of the Indians in the new republic, and concerned about political stability, the early republican intelligentsia emphasized the present.

Public spectacles of the era venerated the political leaders themselves.

More than a celebration of the republic, the festivals in Cuzco honored Bolívar, Sucre, Gamarra, and other caudillos. In exalting these figures' rectitude, strength, and ties to the region and in emphasizing the region's commitment to them, speakers lobbied for even greater support. The focus on the individual reflected, at least in part, the instability of the era. In the context of rapid turnover in office, porous divisions between the major political groups, and weak institutions, the caudillos held together the coalitions. The exaltation of the individual in the early republic recalled the festivals for the king, part of an ensemble of rituals that cultivated the connection between subjects and the monarchy. In the tumultuous early republic, public politics also extolled the individual, stressing his (and occasionally her) direct links with the people.

Were caudillo politics thus a continuation of colonial political culture in different guise? Certainly, the focus on the caudillo himself recalls the honoring of the king. Yet important differences existed. Speeches by and for the caudillos never directly invoked this resemblance. To the contrary, both political groups stressed their attachment to the republic and employed a new vocabulary. The constant criticism of tyranny, foreign control, and oligarchies was unthinkable in public forums during Spanish colonialism. The speeches by authorities in Cuzco in the 1830s would have landed them in jail a decade earlier. Although the invocation of freedom and liberty was utopic in light of the turmoil of the period, and often hypocritical in light of the policies implemented by authorities, this language constituted an important break with colonialism. It provided the prime material for more radical views of postcolonial society.[59] Furthermore, the dominance of caudillos did not reflect the failure of republicanism—a relapse into colonial ways simply because it was impossible to implement a republic. Instead, the caudillos led political coalitions that sought to create postcolonial institutions and policies. In this sense, their break with the Bourbon monarchy is evident.

CUZCO'S JOURNALISTIC ORGY

In Cuzco, the public and largely oral political rituals described above coexisted with and reinforced a rich and much more recent "print culture." In the press, the competing political coalitions imparted their view of Peru's political situation. Newspapers and pamphlets also offered Cuzco people the opportunity to contest and shape these visions of postcolonial Peru. When Viceroy José de La Serna arrived in Cuzco in 1821, he brought a portable printing press, Cuzco's first. In the next three years, it produced newspapers and fliers deriding the patriots and emphasizing the stability of the colonial state. Newspapers, pamphlets, and posters replaced the handwritten pasquinades so important to insurgency throughout the colonial period.[60] Independence did not stop the press. What had been the "Printing Press of the Legitimate Government of Peru" under La Serna became the "free press" virtually overnight. Thirty-four newspapers saw the light in Cuzco between 1825 and 1837. Many lasted only a few issues. Seven had a single issue, seven had between two and nine, and eighteen had between eleven and one hundred. Two lasted for more than one hundred issues—the official papers, *El Sol del Cuzco* (1825-29) and its successor, *Minerva del Cuzco* (1829-34). The press produced innumerable pamphlets and other ephemeral literature, forming part of what one author called Peru's early republican "journalistic orgy."[61] Although the state's control of the main printing press prompted concern and controversies over censorship, opposition groups nevertheless managed to publish widely.[62]

These publications focused on politics. From the 1820s through the 1840s at least, someone who purchased a Cuzco newspaper or stopped to listen to a public discussion of a pamphlet was likely to read or hear about politics. In contrast to North American newspapers of the era, the newspapers in Cuzco and Peru did not concentrate on imparting technical information such as production statistics, mail schedules, or activities in Congress.[63] Instead, the press remained overwhelmingly partisan: virtually every newspaper, pamphlet, and flier can be associated with a political faction. Most of these publications supported or opposed the regime in power, and most articles treated the political battles that gripped the country. The sudden spate of publications in the midst of intermittent civil war greatly increased the interest in reading and gave it a markedly political character. Other forms of readership characteristic of the Old Regime in Europe—such as salon, public, and religious readings—had not developed to the same extent in Bourbon and postcolonial Spanish America.[64] Although religious texts prevailed among literature in the colony, their numbers were small compared to those of Europe and diminished after independence. Unlike in France, the Counter-Reformation did not flood the Andes with pious works.[65]

Readership is difficult to calculate. The literacy rate in the region remained low, well below one-quarter of the city's population and far less in the outlying provinces.[66] With a population of nearly forty thousand, the city of Cuzco had only two schools, Sciences and Arts for boys and Educandas for girls. In 1833, Sciences and Arts had 435 students and Educandas 166, while the university had less than 100.[67] In 1836, the provinces of Aymaraes, Canas, Calca, Paruro, Paucartambo, Chumbivilcas, and Cotabambas did not have a single school. Abancay, Canchis (in the town of Sicuani), and Quispicanchis each had one, and Urubamba several.[68] In his seminal 1833 survey of Azángaro to the south of Cuzco, José Domingo Choquehuanca complained that although Indians sought education—even learning Spanish and sending their children to the cities to take classes—schools had not been established in the countryside, particularly in the areas populated by the indigenous peoples.[69] Yet the limited number of people who could read and afford newspapers and the modest editions of the papers themselves should not be confused with a small readership.

Through the various links between written and oral culture, the newspapers informed far more people, including illiterates, than could read them. As is common today in Latin America, *El Sol* was displayed publicly outside of the School of Sciences and Arts. Individuals standing in the front would read the news aloud, which usually prompted discussions.[70] Those people who bought *El Sol del Cuzco* in the *botica* owned by Don Mariano Torres in front of La Merced Convent or *El Triunfo de la Libertad* in Don Pedro Vargas's store no doubt commented on headlines. The proprietors might also have allowed people to peruse the papers without buying them.[71] Taverns and chicherías served as important meeting points where people disseminated news. As in the periods of rebellion, authorities constantly complained about the rumors that swept through the city. For example, in 1830, Bujanda threatened military trials for treason for "enemies of order and public tranquillity [who] are studiously scattering subversive and alarming news against the government."[72] The constant speeches made by the mobile caudillos and their followers also bridged oral and written culture. Mixed in with public festivities, these speeches attracted large crowds. The speakers disseminated the political language propagated in the press.[73] In a period of constant conflict, information about military battles, economic problems, and imminent invasions took on a particular sense of urgency. The information transmitted in Cuzco's press moved far beyond a small group of political leaders and prestigious citizens.

Writers illustrated the differences between the political groups through tendentious contrasts that emphasized the negative traits of the opposition. Although the insults directed at particular politicians occasionally deteriorated into obscene personal attacks, in general the criticism and veneration harmonized with the ideological differences between conservatives (Gamarristas) and liberals. The distinction proposed by François-Xavier Guerra in his erudite study of Mexico—a distinction between a premodern "war of the words," which replicated the corporatism and rhetoric of colonialism, and a more enlightened journalistic discourse focused on the construction of a consensus around the nation—seems exaggerated.[74] Cuzco's war of the words ultimately centered on debates about the postcolonial state. Conservative writers heralded the benefits of a strong, stable government and condemned the liberals for leading Peru into anarchy. They charged that the liberals sought to place a new oligarchy in power and condemned them for operating within a closed clique. In a pamphlet addressed "to the inhabitants of Cuzco," the Gamarrista prefect Martín de Concha declared, "You will not know any more parties: they have fled with the enemies of order, those with the name servile, liberals, outsiders, and foreigners."[75] The 1829 publication *La Patria en Triunfo* depicted the horrors of a liberal victory: "Peru, if unfortunately it were to listen to the shouts of horror and intrigue with which the apostles of intrigue who roam madly in unfortunate Lima attempt to fool it, if it allows itself to be dragged into this horrid club of spoiled demagogues who speak for the most degrading passions; and finally, if tricked by these dark souls who want nothing else other than slavery, even when they exalt freedom, it will rush into a barbarous struggle, leaving what type of decorous historical legacy?"[76]

The press nourished the almost constant political battles in the city of Cuzco in this era. Through the official paper, the regime in power touted its merits, propagated its program, and attacked its enemies. The opposition press operated in stages. When a regime—the president or the prefect—was firmly in control, articles would cautiously question some aspects of policy or criticize specific individuals, usually not the most powerful. As the regime weakened, the opposition press trumpeted its shortcomings, often chronicling losses in the battlefield or in Congress. This approach reinforced the links between Cuzco and national events. At this stage, the opposition would also heighten its attacks on individuals. Just as the regime was about to collapse, the opposition directly attacked the president and key followers, including the Cuzco prefect and other authorities. Readers (and listeners) learned of events in Europe, Lima, the rest of Peru, and Cuzco in a language that emphasized the ideological differences between liberals and conservatives. The press allowed them to make sense of often bewildering changes and, in many cases, helped draw them into the political frays.

Newspapers were not the only type of publication in Cuzco. Politicians and others used broadsheets and pamphlets to communicate new laws and regime changes. Brief and often hyperbolic, they served to alert and mobilize people. A single literate person could transmit to a large crowd the ideas of a broadsheet. Flora Tristan noted that she had never seen "such agitation" as when a crowd gathered in Arequipa in 1834 to hear the town crier read out a proclamation.[77] Many of the broadsheets found in the Cuzco archive still have the adhesive used to attach them to walls; some even have pieces of plaster from the buildings where they were posted. Political figures produced two types of pamphlets. One type presented a speech, essay, or a description of a festival too long for a newspaper. The topics of this type of pamphlet ranged from the ruminations of a national figure to the humorous treatment of Cuzco politics. The second type contained extended polemics. An individual or group would produce a pamphlet to respond to a newspaper article or some type of declaration. These responses often developed into successive attacks and counterattacks in which the language became increasingly aggressive. For example, two Chumbivilcas political figures, José de la Cuba and Juan Manuel Oblitas, traded insults in dozens of publications.[78] Political figures often published pamphlets to clear their names.

In this period, pamphlets and broadsheets replaced the crudely written pasquinades characteristic of the late colonial uprisings as the key medium of political propaganda. Did this transformation from a productive process accessible to anyone who could write, however crudely, to one dependent on expensive machinery restrict the public sphere?[79] Certainly, printing a document required more skills, money, and connections than writing a poster. The importance of this argument should not be exaggerated, however. First, the government did not monopolize the printing press. Opposition groups had access to it and used it. The sheer quantity of published materials from this period challenges the idea of a restrictive press. Second, nothing prevented the continued creation of lampoons—certainly, the danger was no greater than it was under the Spanish—yet they did not represent important forms of communication in the early republic.[80] More than the threat of imprisonment, the absence of subversive, lower-class movements explains the dearth of pasquinades. The endemic political struggles of the period had at their core the battles between conservatives and liberals, which incorporated a variety of local movements and grievances. In this period, no mass social movement emerged autonomous of the local, regional, and national movements ultimately led by caudillos. Political battles were fought within the parameters of the caudillo wars, which were much wider than many contemporaries and analysts believed.

Newspaper and pamphlets dedicated much of their space, sometimes almost all of it, to personal attacks, often quite vicious. In describing the attacks against her uncle Pío, Flora Tristan claimed that newspapers "are more virulent in Peru than elsewhere."[81] Satire and parody constituted the key idiom of political discourse in this period. In the best known political literature of the period, the Lima conservative Felipe Pardo y Aliaga led a journalistic campaign against the Peru-Bolivia Confederation (1835–39). In notably clever and racist prose, Pardo y Aliaga ridiculed Andrés Santa Cruz's purported "Indian" accent and lineage and his pretension of "invading" Peru. The poem "La Jeta" ("The Face" or "Mug") poked fun at Santa Cruz's features, while the pseudonym given to him, Monsieur Alphonse Chunga Capac Yupanqui, a mixture of French and Quechua names, mocked his predilection for France, which Lima intellectuals deemed ludicrous for an Andean person.[82] Liberals proved just as adept at attacking on these same grounds. For example, writers referred to Gamarra as "His Majesty Guatanaica."[83] Personal attacks predominated in Cuzco as well.

The *Fiel Compromiso* published in 1834 proclaimed that "the government of Gamarra substituted crime for talent; it doesn't know how to fight, only murder."[84] Newspapers and pamphlets frequently included parodies of speeches or diaries. In these parodies, conservatives would emphasize their plans to stay in power through violence, or liberals would admit their intentions to lead the country into chaos and foreign intervention. The content of less humorous forms of political discourse was often echoed in the parodies and satires. For example, one pamphlet—supposedly written by Gamarra and published in July 1834—began, "Citizens: Since I was Prefect of this Department, I loved, it is true, gold and silver." Gamarra's spurious testimony describes his spotty military career, his corruption in Cuzco, the persecution of his enemies, and the placement of his venal supporters in the government and military. As its epigraph made clear ("Our ancestors believed that those places stained by crime required an expiation, . . . I believe that since the land of Cuzco has been stained by so many crimes, it is necessary to purify it through the exemplary punishment of the guilty"), the pamphlet lobbied for a purge of Gamarristas in Cuzco, with jail sentences for as many as possible. It was signed by "Gamarra's Shadow."[85] The pamphlet's accusations against Gamarra for corruption, nepotism, and military incompetence paralleled those leveled by his more renowned critics such as Father Francisco de Paula González Vigil, who condemned Gamarra in a celebrated 1832 speech.[86]

The pamphlets often also specialized in cruel insults. For example, the "New Natural History of Tyranny in Peru," an eight-page pamphlet published in 1834, called Gamarra "an Indian quadruped and an animal," his wife "a hyena so ferocious that it can't be domesticated," and two of his key supporters a pig and an elephant.[87] In a single sentence, the liberal paper *La Aurora Peruana* called the conservative caudillo Salaverry a venal, indolent, cruel, fake, corrupt, seditious, unfaithful, bloody rebel, tyrant, and barbarian. A few issues later it noted how as a youth he liked to "bother domestic animals."[88] With the exception of these particularly nasty invectives, however, the war of the words reflected the terms of the politicized intellectual debates of the period. Liberal writers cast conservatives such as Gamarra and Salaverry as corrupt megalomaniacal despots, and supporters of conservatives depicted liberals as inept, dogmatic elitists. Conservatives were associated with retrograde favoritism and heavy-handedness, whereas liberals were accused of forming exclusionary cliques that were leading the country into chaos. These characterizations emerged not only in grandiose speeches or in erudite editorials, but also in the satirical, personal diatribes that filled the papers and pamphlets of the period. Insults directed at particular caudillos or their supporters reproduced the highly ideological rhetoric of the early republic.

The Gamarra supporters produced more newspapers and pamphlets than the liberals, an indication of their advantage in resources and of their control of the state in most of the early period of the republic. More importantly, they presented a more coherent program, one that resonated well with much of the Cuzco population. Simply put, the liberals failed to translate their program into a Cuzco-specific language.

In sharp contrast to the Gamarristas, the liberal press discussed abstract concepts about the state and society. Liberal writers commented on European debates, reproducing key tracts at great length, and denounced authoritarianism, centralism, and militarism with broad and often listless strokes. They neglected to frame their critique of Gamarrismo and other conservative platforms in terms of the region's language and reality. In general, the liberals were more concerned with ideology and intellectual debates than were their conservative counterparts, so this inability particularly hampered them. Conservatives frequently criticized the liberals for attempting to apply European notions and of not understanding Peru. The dense articles in the liberal press and the inattention to the regional context reinforced the image of liberals as isolated intellectuals, would-be Europeans living in Lima or Cuzco. It was only in the heat of the battle of a civil war, when the attacks became urgent and often quite personal, that liberal ideologues descended into Peruvian reality. Even then, they failed to create a Cuzco-specific program or even to delve into local conflicts. It is not surprising that the conservatives' portrayal of the liberals as a clique composed of Lima and Arequipa elites led by pernicious priests prospered in Cuzco. The liberal press failed to put their doctrine into an idiom acceptable to the Cuzco population.

DISTURBING THE WATER TANK: THE RABBLE AND THE PUBLIC SPACE

Political rituals and publications did not merely serve the propagandistic efforts of the state or particular political groups. In the public, massive celebrations, the lower classes participated in ways not always foreseen by the festivals' promoters. In a city such as Cuzco, where the main plazas held both the residences of the affluent and the social and work centers of the masses, the organizers could not easily exclude the indigenous lower classes. Authorities worried about the lower class's cultural autonomy and its subversive potential. William Miller, José María Blanco, and other travelers noted Indians' attachment to "Inca" dances.[89] The Inca utopia had multiple meanings in this period, as Gamarra's authoritarian version demonstrated. Nonetheless, members of Cuzco's upper classes worried that these representations could form part of an Indian movement. Although they did not attempt to prevent them—which would have been enormously difficult and potentially dangerous—they watched them warily.

From independence until the 1850s, only one riot took place in Cuzco, in 1837 against the Peru-Bolivia Confederation. In his 1848 novel *El Padre Horán: Escenas de la vida del Cuzco*, Narciso Aréstegui describes these events. He indicts his political opponents, both the Gamarristas and the Bolivians who were implementing the confederation, for inciting the lower classes. His account reveals the centrality of regional sentiments against outsiders in Cuzco's political culture. Set around the murder of a young woman by a priest, an incident that shocked Cuzco in the 1830s, this novel depicts with convincing realism the people and streets of the city where Aréstegui grew up. He emphasizes the plebeians' gullibility to the efforts of rabble-rousers and the dangers of unleashing their wrath. He also captures in romantic hues the catastrophic possibilities of war, with widows symbolizing the ravages of the nineteenth century. Although Aréstegui embellishes many aspects of the plot and molds his narrative to fit his liberal scheme, his basic account of the disturbance seems reliable. He lived in his native Cuzco in the time the events took place, and other sources, although scanty, support his depiction.[90]

The Cuzco population resents the presence of Bolivian soldiers, symbolized in the novel by two officers' fresh behavior with a young Cusqueña, the daughter of a veteran of the War of Independence. The same blacksmith who saves the girl from the Bolivians' advances describes rumors ("run runs," an onomatopoeic term for murmurs) that the Bolivians intend to take the image of Señor de los Temblores from the cathedral to La Paz. He reports that "a general preparation, a plot among all the artisans and the people called the plebe" is underway to prevent this, with thousands of knives distributed "behind the back of the government."[91]

Days later, thousands of men and women converge on the cathedral to the sound of the church bells. The author depicts how news of the showdown circulates, prompting people to move "as though a strange force swept them." They occupy the main plaza and proceed to enter the cathedral to verify whether the image has been replaced with a fake. One person, who speaks with the accent of a member of the upper classes, derides the confederation and encourages the crowd to attack the barracks and government offices. Instead, the crowd jams into the cathedral to verify whether the image is authentic. When one person declares it a fake because it is moist, another responds that the moisture is merely the result of the Señor de los Temblores's miraculous ability to cry. The bishop urges them to stop, but to no avail. A man with a straw hat instigates the crowd, directing them to the School of Sciences and Arts, where a sculptor had supposedly crafted the imitation. This agitator turns out to be the evil Father Horán, who staged the riot in order to facilitate his plan to conquer the girl he desired, the same one threatened by the Bolivian soldiers.

The crowd proceeds to ransack the School of Sciences and Arts and to surround the prefect and police officers. Military units attempt to control the rioters, which results in the death of an embroiderer. The crowd returns to the cathedral to rescue the image and place it in the San Francisco Monastery. Peruvian soldiers dressed as civilians encourage broader antigovernment actions, shouting, "This is the moment to proclaim a new government. . . . Down with the Confederation! Let's take the barracks and let's acclaim with enthusiasm the name of our fellow countryman General Gamarra."[92] Members of the crowd denounce the Santa Cruz regime for abandoning Cuzco's industry and raising taxes. They grumble that the politically powerful believe that the people are ignorant. One exuberant participant shouts that the "people are sovereign."[93] A young priest, however, intervenes to calm the crowd and ends the riot, decrying the cost of war and violence. Aréstegui points out that "the Cuzco masses are essentially peaceful, like a water tank that is upset only when a foreign object is thrown into its depths."[94] Thieves take advantage of the moment, though, and break into a number of buildings.

Aréstegui's narrative reflects his liberal project in straightforward and unsophisticated fashion. It also indicates the political and social ambiguities of Cuzco's liberals. Politically, the description of the riot illustrates their quandary regarding the formation of the Peru-Bolivian Confederation. Many opposed it because of the occupation of the region by Bolivian soldiers, their dislike for Santa Cruz, or their animosity toward this grandiose scheme of reuniting Peru and Bolivia. Cuzco liberals, however, had spent years struggling against Gamarra, who led the opposition to Santa Cruz. Aréstegui condemns both projects and instead plots out the need for a strong liberal government like Ramón Castilla's was in the 1840s and 1850s.[95] In his portrayal of the lower-class rioters, Aréstegui emphasizes their superstitious nature and above all their vulnerability to pernicious influences. In the novel, instigators have little difficulty convincing the multitude to attack. Although some of the rioters discuss the burden of taxes and military duty, they ultimately follow the instructions of others.[96] Aréstegui recognizes widespread grievances that could be acted upon in public disturbances such as this riot. Whether the rioters actually follow the urgings of the man in a straw hat and the disguised military officers remains to be seen. The author also points out the danger in fostering such an uprising. In this case, the military kills an artisan, and the rioters ransack Aréstegui's beloved School of Sciences and Arts, where he had studied and taught. Liberals recognize the advantages of mobilizing the lower classes, but remain reticent to do so.

El Padre Horán illustrates how the political struggles of the period were frequently seen as battles between Cuzco and outsiders, which helps explain Gamarra's chauvinism and its effectiveness. Whereas liberals emphasized their cosmopolitanism, conservatives stressed their regionalism and nationalism, usually in harsh indictments of the outsider or enemy. In light of the cult of the region in Cuzco, Gamarristas thus had the upper hand. The novel and other sources from the period hint at interesting gendered formulations. In their emphasis on the conservative's realpolitik, Gamarristas presented a rough-and-tumble Gamarra who waged war throughout the continent. Bullfights epitomized this raw, tough world. Liberals found themselves criticizing these massively popular festivals, casting themselves once again as effete cosmopolitan snobs with no ties to the masses. For example, in a well-known incident, Lucio de la Bellota called his liberal enemy a *maricón* or faggot.[97] Thus, the male Gamarristas confronted the feminine and bookish liberals.

The conflict over the confederation, however, was presented as a clash between men over the female homeland. The riot in Aréstegui's novel begins with two Bolivian soldiers attempting to "take advantage" of an innocent Cuzco girl. Although the novel is not Gamarrista propaganda, it casts Gamarra as the defender of the region's honor against aggressive outsiders. In this unstable period, when residents felt threatened by foreign advances or at least their region's decreasing importance, a certain gender anxiety came to the fore. In representations of this anxiety, Cuzco faced outsiders' aggression, cast as male, with Gamarra coming to its defense. The view of Cuzco versus menacing outsiders was at the core of the contrast made by Gamarristas between themselves, telluric defenders of regional pride, and liberals.[98]

Cuzco's public space was certainly not the meeting ground for rational discussion among diverse social groups, as depicted in Habermas's
utopic vision. In tumultous struggles marked by conspiracy, vitriol, and
occasional violence, people debated and fought over the relationship of
the republican state with civil society and, more precisely, the actual
control of the state. The exclusionary definition of the republic prevailed, however, as liberals and conservatives deemed that the lower
classes were undeserving of a voice in political matters and uninterested in politics, and they codified this vision in policy. Nonetheless,
examining the press, festivals, and other arenas where groups proselytized and protested demonstrates that the political battles of the era
were socially more complex than is often assumed. In Cuzco, urban
lower-class groups followed the debates and skirmishes over the state,
occasionally participating in the riots and revolts that constituted the
groundwork of caudillo politics.

This chapter has examined two related questions: how did political culture change in the republic and who dominated the political
battles of the period? The answer presented here seems contradictory:
the nature of politics transformed with the break from Spain, yet the
group that sought to maintain many elements of Spanish colonialism,
the conservatives, more often than not defeated the liberals. The analysis of Cuzco's hyperactive press indicates that the form and content
of political debates changed with independence. People in Cuzco frequently and fervently discussed ideas about state and society, and a new
republican vocabulary emerged. Although focusing on the antagonism
between conservatives and liberals, and often employing ribald satire or
obscene insults, writers deliberated about the nature of the state. In the
newspapers and pamphlets they used concepts such as freedom and defended constitutions and other republican institutions. The satire and
parodies poked fun at the pompous, often baroque political language
of the period and called attention to the contradictions and unfulfilled
promises of the political groups. The language and pace of politics
changed with independence.

In the colonial period, of course, people—including the lower classes
—did discuss politics. They lobbied, complained, at times rebelled, and
participated in a series of political rituals ranging from celebrations of

the king to the payment of taxes. In the eighteenth century, the Lima press, which predated independence by centuries, published works that questioned Spanish rule. The discussion of political ideas therefore certainly did not begin with independence. The postcolonial debates, however, assumed a more open character and directly addressed the best form of government or most appropriate ruler.

The review of political culture has highlighted the tactics shared by liberals and conservatives. Despite the ideological differences trumpeted in the press, the two groups resembled one another a great deal. Both used inflammatory language, conspired, depended on the armed forces, favored their followers, and expelled the opposition when in power. These practices contradicted the liberals' obsession with institutions and legality. What explains their descent into nitty-gritty caudillo politics? On the one hand, Peruvian reality compelled them. Even before the Spanish had surrendered, coups toppled independent Peru's presidents, and *políticos* abandoned the Constitution. The events of the mid-1820s crushed the liberals' utopian hopes.[99] In the following decades, Peru's intermittent civil and international wars drove them farther away from their political theories. After witnessing the conservatives' willingness to forgo the Constitution and bearing the brunt of their oppressive measures, the liberals returned the favor when in power.

Liberals were also inclined toward caudillo realpolitik. "Reality" cannot be invoked to exonerate them. They shared with the conservatives an extremely narrow notion of who belonged in Peru's political community. Their exclusionary ideology echoed their own restricted membership, as well as their distrust and even fear of the multicolored lower classes. They consistently eschewed building a mass base. For example, they failed to incorporate disaffected groups embittered by the long War of Independence.[100] They also proved themselves quite capable of patronage and self-interest, thus nullifying their critique of the conservatives as venal defenders of the colonial past. Their members fought not only for an abstract good, but for personal (or familial or clan) power and wealth. Undoubtedly, caudillo-led instability induced a cycle of shady political activities, encouraging both sides to plot and punish. The liberals, however, displayed undemocratic and even authoritarian tendencies before the conservatives' success forced their hand. Although ideologies may have differed, conservatives and liberals' political practices resembled one another a great deal.[101]

The liberals remained in the shadow of Gamarra in Cuzco for a number of reasons. Structural factors help explain the predominance of the conservatives. Gamarra was the region's first prefect and thus had the opportunity to build a solid regional base. More importantly, much of the Cuzco population endorsed the conservatives' positions. Similar to Lima, the region had been an important colonial administrative and economic center. Many of its residents—elite and nonelite—missed the halcyon days when Cuzco supplied Upper Peru with cloth, sugar, coca, and other indispensable items, and when the city constituted the undisputed center of the Peruvian Andes. With the decline of the region's importance, explained in part by independence but also by broader economic changes, a nostalgia for its former glory emerged. Conservatives capitalized on this sentiment. Cuzco's main industry, textiles, suffered with foreign competition. The Cuzco population largely favored protectionism, a desire often coupled with xenophobia, which also nudged the region into the conservative camp. Finally, Cuzco's major rival, Arequipa, was the center of early republican liberalism, so Gamarra and others took advantage of anti-Arequipa sentiments.

Yet liberals' efforts, platform, and discourse also need to be examined in order to understand their weakness in the region. They failed to translate their program into a language that resonated in the region. Their dry transcriptions of European ideologues paled next to the Gamarristas' lively satire. Gamarra also outflanked the liberals in the organization of public festivities. The liberals' inability or lack of interest in casting their project in terms of the key political symbol of the region, the Incas, epitomizes their difficulties. Whereas Gamarra and his followers crafted an interpretation of the Tahuantinsuyo that jibed with their authoritarian project, Liberals failed to do so. They frequently complimented the Incas yet never developed them as an icon. Their failure to utilize the region's "glorious past" was not their only glaring omission. They also fell short in addressing and incorporating the majority of the region: the indigenous peasantry. Confronting a strong opponent with firm ties to Cuzco, the liberals did not create a usable past or mobilize the region's majority. Only by expanding the public sphere and by mobilizing could they have defeated the Gamarristas. They failed to do so. Chapter 7 examines a key element behind their downfall: the relationship between the republican state and the indigenous peasantry.

"Since the independence, the condition of the Indians has greatly improved. To
some extent the paths to distinction are opened to them, and though a small tribute
or capitation tax is continued, the injustice and tyranny of the remorseless Spaniards no longer weighs them down in hopeless slavery."—Clements R. Markham,
Cuzco: A Journey to the Ancient Capital of Peru and Lima

Chapters 5 and 6 have shown how caudillo-led political groups
struggled to create republican Peru. The story has involved a
cast of characters that includes the caudillos themselves, textile mill owners, writers, soldiers, urban rioters, and many others. This
chapter scrutinizes a group left out in these chapters (and out of many
other accounts of republican Peru): Indians. The republican state maintained the keystone of Spanish colonialism in retaining the legal division between Indians and non-Indians. The importance of this policy
for modern Peru cannot be exaggerated. Although significant segments
of the Peruvian population descend from Africa, Asia, and various parts
of Europe, the division between Indian and non-Indian continues to
mark society. Indians still remain second-class citizens. This chapter
explores how the victorious anticolonial insurgents maintained racial
hierarchies. It also tells a more interesting story: how Indians managed
to defend their political autonomy and economic resources in the face
of a hostile Creole nation-state. This successful "resistance," however,
ultimately reinforced the division of the nation along the lines of Indians and non-Indians.

Racial definitions in this period were notably fluid. Many people were neither "white" nor Indian but rather a mixture of white, Indian, black, and Asian. Individuals slipped among the fuzzy categories created by the state. Who then were Indians? Clothing, housing, and other cultural markers represented important signs of identity, but none were definitive. Although the use of Quechua as a primary language was an important marker, authorities sometimes referred to "mestizos who don't speak Spanish."[1] Place of residence was also deceptive. Although virtually every resident of Indian communities was an Indian, small towns and cities of Cuzco also counted on a significant Indian population. For example, just less than half of the population of the city of Cuzco was deemed Indian in the early republic.[2] Nor is physical appearance, phenotype, a reliable indication. Many Cusqueños who considered themselves mestizos or whites had similar features to those of Indians residing in rural communities. Yet, although racial definitions were fluid and redefined in everyday practice, the republican state insisted on the category *Indians,* a classification carried over from colonial fiscal practice. Until its abolition in 1854, the Indian head tax anchored ethnic definitions in Peru. Although individuals passed between and perhaps questioned these racial categories, the division of Peruvian society along the Indian/non-Indian faultline grounded relations between state and society and between individuals as well.[3]

Indians constituted some 80 percent of the Cuzco department's population in the late 1820s, and they maintained their strong demographic presence into the latter half of the nineteenth century. In fact, the number of Indians increased in Peru during the nineteenth century.[4] This increase constituted a small part of a larger process. Indians staved off a series of challenges by defending, maintaining, or recovering land, trade rights, relative political autonomy, and their cultural space. This chapter examines their success; it links structural explanations centering on the economy and politics with those that focus on the Indians themselves.[5] In order to analyze this negotiated process between the state and Indians, I examine local, regional, and national political and economic trends, as well as discourse about and by the Indians.

The postindependence arrangement, in which Indians continued to pay the head tax and maintained control of their land and local power structures, was provisional and in some ways circumstantial. It did not represent an enduring solution in which Indians were officially granted autonomy or effectively (and probably brutally) "integrated." Instead, the state and the indigenous peasantry reached an impasse, forging an unwritten agreement that strengthened the paramount division of Peru into Indians and non-Indians. The postindependence decades were not a short aberration, but a defining moment when the faulty foundation of the persistently problematic relations between the national government and the Andean indigenous population was created. Early republican authorities established or maintained the legal, fiscal, and ideological fixtures of Peru's racial divisions, failing to create a more integrated republic. Although authorities changed tax regimes and ideologues developed diverse explanations for Indians' otherness after the 1850s, the underlying mentality of the elite persisted and was reinforced in daily life and state practices: Indians could not and perhaps should not be integrated. The division of Peru along Indian and non-Indian lines endured.

This chapter highlights the disjunction between official ideology and local practice. In this and subsequent periods, Indians often fared better than could be expected even when they were cast as irredeemable "others" by elite groups and were subject to harsh legislation. How and if these racialized codes were put into practice is the key question analyzed here. In answering this question, I stress the efforts of authorities who mediated between the Cuzco and Lima governments and rural society in Cuzco. Despite the power and hubris of the Gamarrista authorities who emphasized their omnipotence in rural society, the Gamarra coalition did not control the countryside. They encountered problems not only collecting taxes and imposing authorities, but also, as I show in the concluding section of the chapter, in mobilizing Indian fighters for the caudillo wars. Moreover, Indians themselves defended their economic and political resources. They sued, bargained, and selectively participated in caudillo politics—practices that would continue well into the twentieth century.

TAXES AND SOCIETY IN RURAL CUZCO

Throughout the Andes, the newly born republics rapidly reinstituted one of the pillars of Spanish rule: the Indian head tax. Shaping relations between Indians and non-Indians, the head tax produced roughly 40 percent of the Peruvian national state's revenues and an even larger percentage of the departmental budgets. One author has called it the

Andean republican governments' "original sin."[6] The Peruvian national state needed income desperately. Not only was it burdened with huge debts from the War of Independence, but, as outlined in chapter 5, two major sources of income for the colonial state—levies on mining and the sales tax—produced little revenue in the early republic. The national and regional states relied above all on the Indian head tax, customs, and various types of loans.[7]

Tax rolls to register the Indian population were almost immediately created after independence. They followed the format of the colonial registrars and listed Indian men between eighteen and fifty years of age and in some cases individuals soon to join the ranks of taxpayers. Some local officials and servants to the priest were exempted. The tax rolls divided Indian society into originarios (landholders) and forasteros (the landless).[8] The Indian head tax produced between 40 and 70 percent of the annual revenues of Cuzco's treasury between 1826 and 1845. Only in 1826 and 1827 did it produce less than 50 percent. Yet incentives for reinstating the head tax were not merely pecuniary. The head tax maintained a relationship that, in the eyes of leaders of the regional and national governments and even according to many Indians, allowed room for negotiation.[9]

Throughout the War of Independence, authorities discussed and tampered with the head tax. The Cádiz Cortes had abolished the head tax in 1811, but Viceroy Abascal reinstated it a year later. By 1815, it was renamed the *contribución,* as it would be called in the republican period. Several early republican leaders endeavored to abolish the head tax. San Martín did so in 1821—a symbolic act because his regime did not control Peru sufficiently to collect it. Simón Bolívar abrogated the head tax on March 30, 1824, and in the following two years weakened two key corollaries of the tax: the office of cacique and Indians' right to corporate lands. In practice and in law, however, the Bolivarian reforms were quickly overturned. Despite the condemnation of the Indian head tax as an odious vestige of Spanish colonialism, legislators reinstated the tax in August 1826. Later that year, the per capita rate was reduced, but in 1828 it was returned to its previous level.[10] Nicolás Sánchez-Albornoz summarized the constant debate and legislation that ultimately changed little: "One step forward and then backward, always in the same direction: toward the Indian head tax."[11]

The failure of the Bolivarian reforms and the paltry income from other taxes led the state to extend the personal head tax to virtually every male between the age of eighteen and fifty-five. On August 11, 1826, the Indian contribution was reinstated and the *contribución de castas* created. Although the Indian contribution largely perpetuated the colonial status quo, the casta tax drastically altered the tax structure because it targeted all non-Indian men. The reforms also included two new categories: the *contribución de predios urbanos y rústicos* (urban and rural property and income taxes) and the *contribución de patentes y de industrias* (professional and artisan taxes). Individuals who paid one tax were exempt from the others, whereas tribute-paying Indians (a redundancy in the state's eyes) were not subject to any of them. Castas were charged 4 percent of their income or, if their income was less than 150 pesos a year, a rate below that of the Indian head tax. In essence, the property income taxes targeted landowners and tenants; the patentes tax targeted artisans; and the caste tax targeted non-Indian laborers and the poor. Until the 1840s, the patente and urban property taxes were collected only in Lima and a few provincial cities. The casta head tax was the most controversial tax until its abolition in 1840.[12]

The legislation defined the castes in purely negative terms, as non-Indians, thus conflating racial, social, and fiscal categories. One authority from Cuzco referred to the castas as whites, mestizos, *zambos* (African, indigenous, and European ancestry) and *pardos* (European and African ancestry).[13] The casta head tax and the term casta itself, however, was associated primarily with Peru's mestizo population. The vast majority of those subject to the tax in the highlands were poor mestizos living outside of the cities in towns and estates and on the margins of Indian communities. On the coast, the percentage of blacks was higher. The people exempt from the property, income, or professional taxes, yet subject to the casta tax, were designated by the original registrars as individuals "without goods or industry." Castas made up approximately 40 percent of the Peruvian population in the early republic, 20 percent in the department of Cuzco (table 2). They, particularly the poorer rural population, are the most overlooked group in Andean historiography. Although much has been written about "white" authorities and elites as well as about Indians, the multiracial poor in the Andes have attracted less attention.

A tax agent of Abancay in 1831 pointed out the wide differences in the wealth of castas. He distinguished two groups: "estate and other prop-

Table 2. The Population of the Department of Cuzco, 1827

Province	Total	Percent Indian
Cuzco City (Cercado)	40,000	46.8
Abancay	35,738	85.3
Aymaraes	18,638	95.4
Calca y Lares	13,097	90.2
Cotabambas	21,979	71.0
Chumbivilcas	19,048	89.0
Paruro	12,126	80.5
Paucartambo	12,929	94.0
Quispicanchis	26,865	87.7
Tinta	36,109	91.7
Urubamba	14,918	63.8
Departmental Total	250,447	79.5

Sources: Gootenberg, "Population and Ethnicity"; Kubler, *The Indian Caste.*

erty owners who are producers and the other people of color who are consumers. The first is of medium fortune, earning enough for themselves and their family through the fruit of their pains, whereas the second is poorer than the Indians who at least have their own land while the caste works for two reales a day, only enough to eat and dress poorly."[14] Many authorities confirmed this description of a wide gap between a small group of relatively prosperous individuals and the majority of poor rural workers. In Quispicanchis, Cuzco, in 1826, 73 percent of the castas were registered in the "without goods or industry" category. The other 27 percent consisted of estate owners or renters, merchants, artisans, employees, priests, and priests' aides.[15] In Cotabambas in 1830, only 11 percent (169 out of 1,472) of the non-Indian taxpayers were declared "with property or industry."[16] The bulk of the nonpropertied castas were *jornaleros* or day laborers, who worked the land under different arrangements. Some had permanent positions on the estates, but others found occasional work or sharecropped. Some toiled their own small plots.

The controversy over the casta tax illuminates the lives of these overlooked people, as well as the ambiguous nature of racial categories in this period. Subprefects and other authorities in the tax network bombarded Cuzco and Lima with complaints about the unfairness of the tax and the extreme difficulties in collecting it. They contended that the Spanish had never extended the head tax to non-Indians and that it targeted the poor, who received nothing in return.[17] They insisted that although Indians maintained the right to hold land in return for the tax, castas gained nothing. Some pointed out that the casta tax was seen as a replacement for the abolished sales tax and therefore shifted the burden from prosperous merchants to the dispossessed. Authorities were at their rhetorical best in describing the poverty of the countryside and the obstacles in collecting the tax.

In 1831, Felipe Infantas, the subprefect of Cotabambas, concluded his explanation of his debts by explaining the impracticality of the casta tax. He argued that it targeted "whites and castes" who were "twice as poor as Indians, who at least have good and bad plots of land, whereas non-Indians have only their labor that can't be used in the province."[18] The former prefect of the city of Cuzco described how he had to put up with the blasphemy and insults of the castas, so poor that they "don't even have anything to wear to bed."[19] A tax agent for the same district in the early 1830s depicted impoverished artisans crying and begging not to have to pay, but also threatening anyone who did pay.[20] Another authority described having to fill the jails in order to coax the castas to pay the tax.[21] Prefect Bujanda called mestizos "a forgotten race, the most persecuted by everyone."[22] In 1829, he defended the suspension of the casta tax by describing the poverty in the towns and villages. He claimed that people did not earn enough to sustain their families or even to buy a single bed or "to cover the nudity of their women and children." In what became a familiar line of argument, he contrasted this situation with the Indians' eagerness and thus ability to pay. Bujanda called collecting the tax "the work of Romans."[23]

The unpopularity and meager revenues of the tax encouraged politicians to herald their opposition to it. In his study of the Indian caste, George Kubler calls the casta tax a "perpetual political toy."[24] Budgets from the period confirm authorities' complaints about the difficulty of collecting it. One national budget claimed that the casta tax would produce 430,000 pesos and the Indian tax 1,040,000 pesos in annual revenues. Yet these numbers were never reached.[25] The casta tax never produced even 10 percent of the income of Cuzco's treasury.

Conservative politics attacked the casta tax and abolished it several times. In mid-1829, General La Fuente eliminated it and compensated by increasing the Indian tax. The Gamarra government unenthusiastically overturned this decree later in the same year.[26] Felipe Santiago Salaverry again abolished the casta tax in March 20, 1835, pronouncing it "odious,"[27] but it was reinstated in the Peru-Bolivia Confederation. After more than a decade of controversy and disappointment over the revenues produced by the casta tax, President Gamarra abolished it on September 25, 1840. The law stated plainly that "the casta head tax has weighed upon miserable people, whose resources barely suffice to provide the basic resources of life."[28] In light of the failure of this radical change in the tax regime, the Cuzco treasury depended primarily on the Indian head tax during the first decades of the republics. This tax not only financed the regional state, but also undergirded relations between non-Indian authorities and Indians. It justified authorities' interventions and allowed Indians room for negotiation, as long as they paid the tax and accepted their place in Peruvian society as Indians. The abolition of the casta tax thus reinforced Peru's racial dichotomy.

RHETORICAL POWER: DISCOURSE ON THE INDIANS

Throughout the early republic, elite political groups avidly supported the maintenance of the Indian head tax. Politicians, ideologues, and journalists contended that the Indians easily raised the money and eagerly handed it over. In his annual presentation to the Congress, the minister of finance, José María de Pando, asserted in 1831 that the reduction of the head tax by one peso in 1826 had "alarmed" the Indians "to such a degree that those of the department of Puno refused this benefit." Invoking tradition, Pando called for a return to the previous, higher rates.[29] An important liberal ideologue, Santiago Távara, refuted Pando's contentions about the willingness of Indians to pay tribute. He argued that in the northern region of Piura "all the Indians have cried out for and continue to cry out for relief from such a disproportionate rate." Távara moreover described the abuses committed by local and regional authorities when collecting the tax.[30] Nonetheless, Pando's argument that the Indian population willingly paid the head tax predominated in Peruvian political circles of the time and was part of the idealized, pastoral view of rural society that circulated among Peruvian elites. Whereas views similar to Pando's were to be found in other political statements and newspaper articles, Távara condemned the tax in virtual isolation.

Support for the Indian head tax was not limited to political groups in Lima. In the years following independence, officials at the regional and local levels in Cuzco opposed efforts to abolish or tamper with the Indian head tax and to prohibit the distribution of land to tax collectors. Local authorities' power derived from the tax system. Collecting taxes offered access not only to capital but also to labor and land. The benefits derived from tax collection constituted a major incentive for individuals who sought governmental posts below the level of the prefecture. Abolition of the Indian tribute would have greatly weakened these authorities and perhaps even rendered unnecessary the positions below the subprefect. Furthermore, alternative direct and indirect taxes did not promise the same levels of income, so Cuzco treasury officials scoffed at the notion of abolishing the Indian head tax. Changes in the tax system were resisted in both the cities and the countryside of Peru, Bolivia, and Ecuador.[31]

Although journalists and political ideologues were largely silent about the rural population, regional authorities were not. In letters and reports, subprefects and their dependents expressed a clear position about the Indians that gradually became the accepted view in regional and national political circles. These officials characterized the Indians as lazy, ignorant, and backward, and argued that they were bound to traditions that impeded spiritual and economic progress. In all of the correspondence and political pamphlets I reviewed, not a single author referred to an Indian as potentially rational or worthy of the rights and obligations of citizenship. Like their colonial predecessors, early republican authorities presented the indigenous peasantry as a distinct and inferior social group. They rarely blamed Spanish colonialism for corrupting or repressing the Indians; instead, they attributed the Indians' purported weaknesses—such as alcoholism, paganism, and indolence—to their inherent defects.[32] Authorities consistently presented the Indians as members of an inferior race that needed to be "protected" by the state.[33]

Gamarrista authorities insisted that if left to themselves, Indians would produce only the minimum needed to survive. They argued that because Indians had sufficient resources, specifically land, to produce the little that they needed, and because they were innately lazy, the state had to induce them to work through taxation. Esteban de Navia, the *fiscal apoderado* (tax agent) of the 1830 Indian tax roll in Quispicanchis, wrote, "The Indians are not capable of improving their agriculture because, since they don't have any other necessities than eating and dressing very poorly, the little that their work produces is enough for them."[34] Another tax agent, José Rueda, exemplified the thinking on Indians. His detailed reports on Calca provided unusually rich information on agriculture and included frank recommendations. He explained that Indians did not use fertilizers (guano) because of the lack of livestock and the distance to grazing areas. He emphasized, however, the Indians' sloth as the key impediment to improving agricultural production. He claimed that "the laziness in which this type of people live during the majority of the year prevents them from having the means to buy plows to deepen their plots' furrows."[35] He blamed the Indians' wretched habitations and clothing ("so miserable that they offend nature") on the fact "that they only work enough to sow their small plots of land, which are not more than two or three *topos*, meaning that working a quarter of the year, they are idle the remaining three-quarters." Rueda asserted that Indians spent most of the day drunk.[36] Agustín Gamarra did not credit Indians with even three months of work a year. In an 1826 letter, he claimed that "an Indian barely uses fifteen days to cultivate his small plot: the rest of the year, he and his family remain idle and suffer in poverty due to the lack of tasks and profitable occupations that would alleviate them."[37] In the same year, a representative of the Cuzco prefecture, Vicente León, wrote the minister of finance that "the Indians or peruanos constitute the most numerous class of the republic, and they lack necessities and tend to idleness. If their taxes were reduced to a proportional contribution, they would pay a trifle that would not force them to work, making them therefore unproductive and a burden on others." He referred to the "sad experience" of 1812 when the Spanish Cortes abolished tribute.[38] Authorities complained not only that the Indians were lazy, but that they wasted their time in drunken festivities, which were more pagan than Christian. In 1831, Juan Angel Bujanda, prefect of Cuzco and a powerful Gamarrista, cited a report from a tax agent on the sorry state of the province of Aymaraes. The authority had reported that the Indians would always remain needy because of "the lack of industry and agriculture, [their] laziness and [the] natural defects of their education, as well as their custom of spending the entire year in popular festivities that, even if they display a superficial worship with a mass and donations to a Saint . . . lead to their absolute depravity in a ten- or twelve-day drunken revelry." He claimed that this behavior caused the "poverty of the towns" and the "needy state" of the Indians.[39] Bujanda also insisted that Indians eagerly paid the head tax: "at the first invitation and decree published by this government, Indians happily came forward obediently and submissively to contribute."[40]

Reminiscent of colonial discourse, postindependence authorities described Andean indigenous people as backward, stupid, and superstitious. In the colonial period, as well as in the early republic, government representatives, the local elite, and priests debated inside and outside the courts about who should "protect" the Indian. They shared one premise: the need to intervene in indigenous society. Little had changed from 1780 to 1840. As described in previous chapters, the more socially liberal sectors had lost both the military and ideological battles. Following the Tupac Amaru rebellion, the colonial state had curbed intermediaries such as caciques and censored alternative views on the Indian population. The Indian-based movements had been defeated in the early phase of the War of Independence and the victorious liberals largely remained silent about the Indians. Therefore, the views of more progressive thinkers or the demands of the southern Andean rebels in the War of Independence did not emerge in the policies and ideologies of the early republic in Cuzco or in Lima. Although authorities used terms such as *freedom* and discussed elections, these discussions never contemplated Indians as possible participants and potential citizens.[41]

The conventional image of the Indian reinforced republican efforts to recreate the colonial relationship between the state and peasant society. Cuzco authorities relayed to their superiors in Lima the subprefects' and tax officials' arguments about the necessity of reimposing the Indian head tax. They insisted that outsiders needed to implement policies to prevent Indians from receding into a subsistence economy. These policies, they believed, would improve production, enhance tax collection, and perhaps fortify the Indian population. Almost all of their correspondence asserted that without the efforts of the authorities, the state would not receive head tax revenues, estate owners would not find indigenous laborers, agricultural production would plummet, and pagan rituals would flourish. They suggested that if their own power were increased and coercive mechanisms to force Indians to work and consume were reinstated or created, the regional and national state, as well as Andean society as a whole, would greatly profit. All firmly believed in the benefits of a "republic of Indians" dominated by the Republic of Peru.

The authorities expressed curious notions about Indians and markets. From local tax collectors to the prefect, Cuzco authorities bemoaned Cuzco's economic decline, describing how demand for its goods had shrunk in recent decades and how previously productive estates and mills lay in ruin. Many recalled the glory days of the eighteenth century when countless teams of mules transported sugar, textiles, coca, and other goods to Upper Peru. The Gamarrista political project, in fact, centered on reviving production in Cuzco. Yet when criticizing Indians for their unwillingness to work, authorities rarely mentioned that there was no demand for laborers. Someone reading these reports could envision estates and textile mills paralyzed because of the scarcity of workers, which was hardly the case in Cuzco in this period. In the eyes of these writers, Indians' purported laziness was innate, not a reflection of the economy. Furthermore, these authorities did not express any confidence that the market could rectify Indians' behavior or ease social differences and tensions. Unlike many liberals who professed Montesquieuan faith about the civilizing effects of commerce, they did not present the market as a panacea. The triumphalist Gamarrista vision of Cuzco recuperating its former dynamism was rarely accompanied by an optimistic view of Indians transforming themselves into more productive members of society. They instead argued that Indians required the visible hand of the coercive state to force them into the economy. According to these authorities, Indians resisted market opportunities whenever possible and thus needed the state to intervene.[42]

These reports extolled the arduous work of the authorities and described countless obstacles in collecting the Indian and casta head taxes. The authors cited the poverty of the region's towns, the deceitfulness and sloth of the Indians, and other causes for delays in delivering revenue. After advocating state intervention in the countryside, they presented themselves as the most suitable candidates for collecting the taxes. As in the colonial and neocolonial "civilizing mission," these reports legitimized the authors' involvement in local Andean society.[43] They therefore often combined somber descriptions of the impediments to tax collection with sanguine estimates of the authors' ability to improve the situation. Emphasizing their leverage in local society, the authors implied that if permitted to conduct business as they saw fit, or if named to a higher office, they would increase tax revenues, maintain order, and even rectify the behavior of the native population. As in any report to a superior, self-interest shaped the content. These authorities no doubt greatly exaggerated their power in local society. Despite their rhetoric, however, they failed to establish themselves as omnipotent intermediaries between rural society and the state.

Many of the authorities devised plans to force Indians to work on estates, particularly on the coca-producing estates to the east. They contended that Indians would benefit economically and morally.[44] These examples suggest that labor coercion formed an integral part of the schemes devised by local authorities to increase agricultural production, raise tax revenues, improve the Indian population, and guarantee laborers for the estate owners. In these plans, the authorities were to oversee the collection of taxes and the distribution of laborers—two activities that had sustained the complex political and economic networks through which colonial authorities mediated between outsiders and the local population. These networks, well-known to students of the eighteenth century, provided profits and important connections, but they also fueled the political discontent of the late colonial era.[45] The authors of the reports emphasized the Indians' purported innate laziness in order to justify their labor schemes.[46]

The officials' opinion should not be understood solely as self-serving justifications of neocolonialism, however. It expressed widely professed beliefs about Indians and the difficulties of integrating them into the economic and political structures of the nascent republic. For example, the author of Cuzco's annual almanac in 1833 characterized Cuzco's Indians as "lazy, disheartened, and given to drunkenness. The majority of them live miserably far away in the highlands and only come to town to go to Mass and buy food on festival days. When they visit the Priest, Subprefect, or another visible person, they take off their capes and after a thousand humiliations, and after kissing the hand of the Priest, they greet each of those present. Those that work in town are a bit rebellious. They work only to pay the contribution, and then they spend all that they make during the week to get drunk on Sunday."[47] Adamant that the Indians could not meet the definition of a "Peruvian," the authorities insisted on the need to maintain colonial caste hierarchies.

It is interesting that almost all descriptions of the "misery" of the Indians condemned their clothing and housing. Rueda mentioned their "offensive" clothing and huts. He claimed that the little work that they did provided "their poor daily food," but little else.[48] Another authority argued that because "eating and dressing very badly" constituted the Indians' only "necessities," they lacked sufficient incentives to work hard.[49] Thus, the authorities were not just objecting to what the Indians wore and where they lived, but criticizing them for not needing commodities that the authorities equated with membership in the Peruvian nation. "Proper" clothing and homes and certain "necessities" therefore represented key elements of the authorities' exclusionary definition of a citizen.[50]

The comments on commodities reflect several related convictions. First, the Indians' seeming ability and eagerness to avoid wage labor frustrated the authorities. As estate owners complained throughout the nineteenth century, Indians refused to work (for deplorable wages, it should be added) because they did not "need" to make money. Coca estates in the disease-ridden lower Andes had particular difficulty in attracting Indian laborers.[51] Second, the authorities' complaints targeted the clothing that the Indians made themselves because they felt that the Indians would bolster the internal market if they bought clothing made by tailors using cloth produced in Cuzco. The authorities thus implied the need for coercive mechanisms to force Indians to work and to consume. Two key colonial institutions that targeted Indians, the mita and the reparto de mercancías, must not have been far from their minds. Nonetheless, the explanation for the authorities' condemnations of Indians' material culture must go beyond the yearnings of those in power to control labor and consumer markets.

The authorities' evident disgust with the Indians ultimately emanated from their exclusionary views on who constituted a Peruvian. Although they blamed the Indians' entrenched traditionalism for setting them apart from the rest of the nation, the Cuzco authorities at the same time attempted to maintain cultural markers that would differentiate Indians from non-Indians. Their descriptions of the Indians mirrored the belief that citizenship—membership in the "imagined community" of Peruvians—required a series of shared cultural codes and artifacts. The authorities defined the grounds for citizenship in completely non-Indian terms. Indians failed to possess these shared symbols (or shared values, if the arguments about work and drinking are considered), so they did not merit incorporation into the republic. The state had to coax, cajole, and control them, but not "include" them. Authorities presented Indians as inherently different, primordial others who would not adopt "Hispanicized" ways. The Cuzco authorities did not believe that the Indians could be converted into "Peruvians" by means of any sort of social or political integration that would include the improvement of their economic well-being through redistribution or education. The belief that the Indians were "different" and thus necessarily to be excluded from the nation endured in non-Indian circles in Peru in the nineteenth and twentieth centuries.

Other sources, however, challenged the Cuzco officials' portrayal of Indians as hopelessly backward primitives who refused to consume Western goods. Instead, they emphasized the early republican elites' efforts to maintain social and economic codes characteristic of the colonial period. In a statistical summary of his native Puno written in the 1820s, José Domingo Choquehuanca sharply contradicted the Cuzco authorities' vision of Indians as traditionalists who would not adapt to non-Indian ways. He described how in Puno in this period authorities prohibited Indians from using increasingly less expensive "European" clothing and, along with priests, discouraged Indians through high taxes from improving their housing.[52] Although they claimed that Indians refused incorporation into "national" society, these authorities in reality prevented them from doing so, thereby maintaining the distinction between Indians and non-Indians in which their power was anchored.

Officials in Cuzco transmitted a cohesive ideology about the relationship between Indians and the republican state. They argued that the Indians' innate backwardness impeded them from "advancing" (*adelantar* was the favored verb in these arguments), which thus required their continuing status as dependents of the state. This neocolonial message implied a great deal about the political and economic situation of the indigenous population. It presented the Indians as divorced from political trends beyond their village and emphasized their adhesion to a backward subsistence economy. Because of their parochialism, the Indians purportedly sought a return to the colonial relationship, in which they paid taxes and fulfilled other obligations in exchange for relative political and economic autonomy. As for the authorities themselves, they contended that they had the ability to establish themselves in Indian society and effectively enforce the demands of the state. Although noting the difficulties, the authors of the letters and reports argued that they could simultaneously enhance tax collection, improve agricultural production, and provide estate owners with laborers. They promised to manage Indian society, resurrecting an increasingly mythologized colonial order.

These officials' opinions help us imagine the difficult everyday relations between representatives of the state and Indians. In these encounters, the officials and their assistants made clear their disdain for Indians. Although not as powerful as they purported in their letters — they had to negotiate and bend much more than they contended — they undoubtedly showed that they had no confidence in Indians as reliable subjects or even as potential citizens. Indians, on the other hand, viewed the officials as pernicious and unreliable outsiders, much like the "non-ethnic" caciques imposed by the late Bourbon state. By putting into practice their views on the Indians, the authorities widened the chasm between the Creole state and the Indian population. The breach would become evident in the civil wars of the 1830s, contributing to Gamarra's failure to remain in power.

CHALLENGING THEIR IMAGINED EXCLUSION:
INDIANS IN THE EARLY REPUBLIC

In their reports and summaries, early republican authorities suggested that the state effectively controlled the countryside. While lobbying for greater latitude in their own activities and even more impositions on the indigenous peasants, they portrayed a victorious state taxing the Indians and gaining access to land and other resources. A study of Cuzco in this period, however, supports other scholars' findings that Indians throughout the Andes did quite well in these decades. They managed to maintain a degree of political autonomy and continued to control land, their key resource. Despite the continuation of the head tax, the republican state effectively demanded less than its colonial predecessor. In general terms, Indians resisted the liberal "assault."

Two types of explanations need to be combined in order to analyze the indigenous peasants' ability to withstand the postindependence attack on their resources. On one hand, broad economic and political conditions favored the Indians. In essence, the stagnant economy discouraged outsiders from attempting to usurp their land. Beset by constant weakness and a dependence on the Indian head tax, the regional and national states could not lead the effort to increase the exploitation of the peasants or decrease their political autonomy.[53] On the other hand, using a variety of tactics, the Indians themselves defended their rights with energy and success. Until recently, the actions of the Indians were all too often left out of accounts of the nineteenth century.[54] This examination of Cuzco in the early republic intertwines the two types of explanations of the Indians' resistance to incursions on their resources, reviewing structural causes, economic and political, as well as the efforts or agency of the Cuzco population—Indian and non-Indian—in shaping the early republican state.

The analysis of the economic situation of the indigenous peasantry must begin with the head tax. In the early republic, Indians by and large paid the tax.[55] Not only do budget records indicate a high rate of payment, but in the abundant documentation on taxes authorities rarely complained about the Indians' resistance to the "contribution." Although scores of letters described the difficulties with the casta tax, few presented the Indian head tax as difficult to collect. Moreover, no case of Indian collective resistance was found from the period between 1824 and 1850. Nor did Indians use a generally more common tactic to evade tax collection: flight. The records do not indicate mass migration in order to avoid the payment of the head tax. All of the evidence leads to the conclusion that Indians paid the tax.

Although the head tax continued after independence, the Indians' general tax burden diminished. They had been freed from the forced purchase of goods, the reparto, and the excise tax following the Tupac Amaru rebellion. As the letters and reports from Cuzco indicate, early republican authorities, particularly conservatives, contemplated the idea of reimposing colonial practices such as the reparto and labor drafts, but the threat of peasant opposition apparently dissuaded them. The burden of the head tax itself decreased after independence. Demographic growth outpaced the increase in Indian head tax revenues. The population of the southern Andes grew 30 percent between 1827 and 1850, but the Indian head tax increased approximately 20 percent.[56] Nils Jacobsen found that the per capita collection declined approximately 30 to 40 percent between the 1790s and 1850.[57] The continual demographic growth of the Indian population according to the tax rolls means that they did not massively elude inscription or pass into another racial category. Although the Indian head tax was larger than, and not as easy to evade as the casta head tax, Indians did not attempt to change their fiscal status.[58] The fact that they did not flee from their role as taxpayers indicates that the head tax did not constitute an unbearable burden.

Indians paid the head tax for a number of reasons. Force is one explanation, but the coercive power of the state should not be exaggerated. Because of the great distances and the small sums collected in each locality, the state could not afford to rely on the military to exact the payment of the head tax. In many cases, the commissioned troops would cost more than the collected revenue. Records in Cuzco and in the military archive do not mention the use of force in compelling the Indians to pay the head tax. The militias might have enforced compliance, but the documentation does not suggest that they routinely did so. A refusal to pay, rather than revolt, constituted the Indians' "strongest weapon against the Treasury."[59] Local authorities could not count on the regional and central governments to back them up, so they were forced to negotiate and, in general, to foster flexible relations with the taxpaying peasantry. Although the threat of force buttressed tax collection, it alone does not explain why Indians paid.

For Indians, payment certainly enhanced relations with the subprefect and his underlings. The more politically and economically influential Indians in particular could bargain for delays and discounts and demand reciprocal favors. Of course, these negotiations did not involve homogeneous peasants amicably dealing with benevolent officials. Indigenous society was stratified, and opportunities for greed, injustice, and sheer exploitation abounded. Indian solidarity should not be exaggerated. More powerful individuals within indigenous society often aligned with economic and political elites to the detriment of the majority of the Indians.[60] However, structural conditions—above all the weakness of the state and the economic decline of the region—favored negotiations over heavy-handed despotism in relations between authorities and the Indians. For the Indians, payment not only allowed them to avoid punitive measures, but also guaranteed better relations with the subprefect.

Tribute payers received two tangible benefits: exemption from military duty and rights to land. Authorities used the promise of military exemption stipulated in the legislation as an incentive for payment. For example, in an edict distributed throughout the Cuzco countryside, Prefect Juan Angel Bujanda decreed that "Indians will be excused from military enlistment when they voluntarily resume paying the half peso increase."[61] However, Indians were frequently impressed into army service regardless of their taxpaying status. In reality, military duty exempted men from paying taxes more often than paying taxes exempted them from the military. In times of civil war, the state preferred a soldier more than a few pesos of revenue. Many authorities petitioned to have their tax bill reduced when their taxpaying subjects were off in the military.[62]

In the early republic, indigenous peasants continued to associate tribute payment with land rights. Although the weak economy and low population density diminished outsiders' demand for Indians' land, disputes nevertheless broke out between Indians over this resource. One document testifies to the relationship between tribute payment and land use. The subprefect of Abancay contrasted the ease of collecting the Indian head tax with the difficulties of collecting from the castas. He noted that in the rare case that an Indian migrated and left his land, "others occupy it and quickly pay the tax or they rent it out, for which there are always candidates, or they cultivate it and thus profit, or the migrant's relatives or debtors benefit from it." The deceased, according to the subprefect, were easily replaced on the Indian tax rolls.[63] Clearly, payment of the head tax fortified an Indian's claim to land rights. If an Indian worked a plot of land and paid the head tax, he believed that the land was his.[64]

The rental, usually in the form of emphyteusis (long-term agreements), or purchase of estates formerly owned or controlled by religious orders prompted the greatest transformation in land tenure in Cuzco in these years. In 1839, prominent men such as Pablo Mar y Tapia and Juan José Larrea held estates in long-term agreements. They rented much more often than they purchased the estates.[65] The documentation on these convoluted agreements indicates the depressed demand for land in Cuzco in the first half of the nineteenth century. Renter after renter complained that the minimal income provided did not produce enough to pay the rent or to interest third parties. In 1827, the administrator of Cuzco's hospital claimed that they would have to discontinue service if they could not collect the rent owed them.[66] These contracts did not infringe on Indian community land. In fact, the decline of some of these estates may have increased Indians' opportunity to use them to graze their animals or in usufruct.

Although the economic situation in Cuzco's distinct ecological zones varied in the early republic, some patterns emerge. The number of haciendas declined sharply after independence. Magnus Mörner tallied 647 haciendas in the Cuzco region in 1785, but only 360 existed in 1845.[67] Indian communities, in turn, fared relatively well in this period. Demographic resurgence is one indication. As mentioned, despite several epidemics, the population growth rate of Indians remained high throughout the nineteenth century. More specifically, the majority of Indians in Cuzco resided in communities rather than migrating to work on estates. In 1845, 84 percent of the Indians in rural Cuzco were registered in communities, with the remaining 16 percent on estates,[68] and the communities maintained control of their land as well as their labor in this period. Toward the end of the century, however, greater internal differentiation, more mestizos in the communities, stronger non-Indian entrepreneurs and the state, and a higher demand for Andean products chipped away at Indians' autonomy and well-being. But in this earlier period, they were able to maintain both.

By actively participating in the regional economy, Indians undercut estates and other producers. In the high upper provinces to the south of Cuzco, they produced wool for the burgeoning English market. Although representatives of foreign trade houses scoured the southern Andes, Indians sold their wool directly in the city of Arequipa or in vibrant annual fairs held in different locations in the southern Andes. The fairs united local producers with the regional, national, and international markets, allowing Indians to sidestep monopsonistic purchasers.[69] They also fostered trans-Andean religious celebrations and other types of communication and exchange. Landowning and commercial elites in the upper provinces faced difficult times as demand for their products declined in Bolivia. Moreover, Arequipa emerged as the key commercial center. But Nils Jacobsen's argument regarding Azángaro just to the south may be applied to the upper provinces and to Cuzco: "as altiplano elites struggled to recover prosperity within trading circuits undergoing major changes, the peasant economy was growing in autonomy."[70]

The areas surrounding Cuzco also suffered from the declining demand for their products in Bolivia. In an extensive section on Urubamba in the Sacred Valley to the northwest, Cuzco's 1833 annual almanac used a nostalgic past tense to describe the area's woes. It noted how "there used to be in this province many cloth factories and many sugar estates where the factories made all sorts of confections. The coca trade was more active."[71] In the reports about the casta tax, subprefects and other authorities described the decline of estates and the difficult times in the countryside. In 1830, José Rueda noted that the food-producing haciendas around Calca were so unprofitable that people often recalled a Quechua saying about the "farmer with a full belly but without underwear." He explained that "the *chacras* [small farms] provide enough to eat but not enough for clothing." Not only noting the low demand for Cuzco's major products, but also describing the region's inadequate infrastructure, he promoted a plan to improve Cuzco's roads, build bridges, and expand education.[72]

South on the Royal Highway, the core area of the department of Cuzco—Quispicanchis—witnessed the decline of its textile industry. Although demand for textiles in Bolivia had decreased, agricultural products from Quispicanchis found markets in the altiplano, specifically in Lampa, Azángaro, and Carabaya to the south. Urubamba and Calca y Lares produced for the city of Cuzco. Farther to the west, in the provinces of Abancay and Aymaraes, sugar production declined precipitously.[73] In Paucartambo to the east of Cuzco, coca production also plummeted. Not only did the demand decrease in Bolivia, but producers faced incursions from Indian tribes from the nearby Amazon basin. Decrying the lack of mules after the War of Independence, a Paucartambo subprefect described the inability to trade and thus the "melancholy" situation of the region.[74] Different colonization schemes in this area failed, and competition grew as coca production greatly increased in Calca and Urubamba in the Lares and Santa Valleys respectively.[75]

The analysis of the peasants' economic situation requires differentiating between their control of resources and their general well-being. Indians were able to maintain control of land and other resources during this period because non-Indians generally fared poorly and did not challenge their control. The depressed economy, state policy, and low population density combined to assure their continual control of land in the early republic. According to one scholar, in the early and mid-nineteenth century, "hacendados were frequently unwilling to incur the trouble and expense of keeping Indians off the land, . . . and Indians were naturally happy to occupy these lands."[76] Furthermore, because of its reliance on the Indian head tax, the early republican state needed to guarantee Indians' continual access to land.[77] The effects on peasant producers of the depressed demand for agricultural products during the postindependence economic crisis are less clear, however.

The only price series for the period refers to corn, which continued to decline in the postindependence decades.[78] In 1827, Gamarra complained to the Treasury Ministry that prices for foodstuffs were "negligible" and that producers could not even cover their rent.[79] Cuzco's depressed economy no doubt hurt peasant producers. Within the bleak panorama, however, positive aspects can be found. In times of depression, peasants' low overhead permitted them to compete well with nonpeasants. Also, they were able to increase the amount of production they consumed in order to protect themselves from depressed markets. Payment of the head tax proved that the Cuzco peasantry did not retreat into a subsistence economy. The fact that the records do not mention that Indians had any great difficulty in obtaining money for the head tax supports this view of their comparative ability to compete. This ability, however, should not be exaggerated. Indigenous peasants were not affluent in this period: poverty definitely marked their quotidian life. Droughts, floods, epidemic diseases, and any other natural or man-made disruption of the agricultural cycle constituted life-threatening tragedies. A meticulous local study would no doubt uncover widespread poverty. Nonetheless, the records do not mention droves of migrating, impoverished Indians.

"FOR THREE HUNDRED YEARS WE HAVE SUFFERED": POSTINDEPENDENCE POLITICAL REALIGNMENTS

The indigenous peasantry did not remain silent in the early republic, but instead participated in the struggles over their economic and political rights. Although authorities professed a cohesive and reactionary view about the indigenous population and their relationship with the state, Indians themselves used a heterogeneous language when dealing with the representatives of the state and members of the elite. The complexity of their language reflects the turbulent course of politics in the southern Andes in the early nineteenth century. In the community of Santo Tomás in the upper provinces, for example, Indians had lodged anticolonial insurgents from a number of rebellions, pro-independence forces, and representatives of both the colonial and the republican governments and probably their armed forces. They had followed and perhaps participated in discussions about Inca revivalism, liberal reform under the Cortes, and a variety of republican caudillos, both liberals and conservatives. After the disheartening defeat of the Pumacahua rebellion and failure of the liberal reforms under the Cortes, many Indians and others simply sought to avoid involvement in the struggle. The kidnapping of Indians to fight for both sides heightened this reticence. In 1826, one tax collector noted that the residents of Marcapata in Quispicanchis were terrified by independence and particularly concerned that they would be drafted once again.[80] The violence and turbulent changes that had marked politics in Cuzco throughout the previous half century intimidated many Indians.

The behavior of the Marcapata Indians, however, was unusual and possibly an invention of the mestizo authority who wrote the memorandum. Instead, Indian representatives in most cases quickly incorporated elements of republican discourse into their rhetorical arsenal. In 1825, caciques from Anta requested the return of land that had been granted to troops involved in the repression of the 1814 uprising. Community land deemed "unused" by the state had been rewarded to soldiers after the defeat of the Pumacahua uprising, which prompted bitter struggles. The caciques pointed out

> the injustice with which the land has been taken from us, based on the assumption that the plots were vacant and that we didn't need them, when to the contrary we are landless, beset by the weight of the enormous head tax, most of us with extensive families who we can't clothe or feed adequately, often forced to sustain ourselves with plants just like animals. And what grief, Sir, that Indians, owners by nature of this land, find themselves deprived and dispossessed by foreign hands! For 300 years we have suffered; we have been treated worse than beasts, lacking everything, without the consolation of being able to complain; now that our brave brothers have freed us from the tyrannical yolk, why wouldn't we demand our rights? It's not possible, Sir, that the Nation tolerate, or that we tolerate, that those who fought so stubbornly for our enslavement maintain the prize for their ignominy, possessing the land granted to them.[81]

Among the fascinating elements of this statement is the contrast between the "foreigners" who deprived them of their land after 1814 and their "brothers" who freed them in 1824. These terms essentially refer to the same people: Peruvian-born non-Indian soldiers. The authors reiterated the essence of Creole nationalism: that the beneficiaries of colonialism had been foreigners and that all members of the Peruvian nation were linked by blood.

These caciques were not alone in presenting independence as a heroic struggle to free Indians from tyranny. In a complaint against their non-ethnic cacique, Indian defendants in Marcacongo, Quispicanchis, began, "All tyranny and despotic oppression should have stopped, particularly for Indians, with the beneficial laws brought to us by the beloved independence." The cacique in question, Mariano Luna, claimed that the complaint was all part of a revenge plot against him and achieved through "seducible and seduced Indians."[82] In another case, a cacique in 1831 cited Bolívar's efforts in Cuzco as part of his claim for land. Don Justo Domingo Vargas argued that as a descendent of one of the Inca rulers, Inca Yupanqui, and as an ethnic cacique, he merited five topos of land in accordance with Bolívar's reforms.[83] In their encounters with the state, Cuzco's Indian population used republican language, specifically a vocabulary that emphasized the promises of postcolonialism. Although they took advantage of the egalitarian strains of republic discourse to advance their demands, they also recognized the hierarchies in the newborn republic. In their negotiations with authorities, Indians emphasized the unfulfilled promises of postindependence ideologies.[84]

Indians maintained a great deal of control over local decision making and influenced outsiders who assumed local office. The republican state could not afford and did not see any pressing need to insert salaried, non-Indian authorities into Indian communities. Therefore, a mixture of locals and outsiders ruled the Indian communities of Andean society in the decades after independence, a pattern that had existed since the partially effective abolition of the cacique office by the Bourbons in the 1790s. Historians disagree about who assumed the different positions in the tribute chain of command and about the relationship these authorities forged with local society. For the case of Cuzco, Víctor Peralta Ruíz argues that Creoles eagerly took the position of subprefect, and mestizos were ready to act as recaudadores.[85] In his study of Otavalo, Ecuador, Andrés Guerrero argues that the postindependence political vacuum created by the abolition of the cacique position and the exodus of many colonial officials forced the republican state to depend on local authorities, generally non-Indians. Outsiders could not be found or were not effective. *Tenientes políticos* slowly replaced caciques and gobernadores de Indios. Like their predecessors, they needed to maintain good relations with the local population in order to fulfill their duties.[86] In the case of Puno, Christine Hünefeldt describes the heterogeneity and general weakness of the local authorities who took the place of the caciques.[87] Nuria Sala i Vila documents the rise of Indian mayors, varayoks, in the final decades of the colonial period, and Roger Rasnake describes two types of authorities simultaneously filling the vacuum left by the abolition of the hereditary *kurakas* or caciques in central Bolivia: Indian authorities and outsiders, usually mestizos, called corregidores. These studies demonstrate that the decline of the cacique office did not necessarily produce the intrusion of abusive outsiders.

An 1829 decree by Cuzco's junta departamental abolishing the cacique office exposed the confusion over who governed local society in the Cuzco countryside. The decree strongly resembled Bolívar's efforts against caciques a few years earlier in that it blamed the caciques for Indians' poverty and oppression. Its preamble described the caciques' pernicious activities and their continued presence despite "various decrees" against them. It contended that, with the abolition of the cacique office, the land these authorities were granted could benefit other public institutions. Also, Indians and rural areas in general would no longer be subject to these authorities and would thus become more productive. The decree stipulated that governors would collect the head tax, keeping 2 percent as compensation. In its final clause, it granted "ethnic caciques" (caciques de sangre) the right to request a plot of land from the junta departamental. The decree concluded by reiterating its basic arguments: that abolishing the cacique office would liberate Indians, thus "impelling them to mix with citizens." It also projected increased revenues for the state.[88]

The prefect office responded that the junta was working from the false premise that caciques continued to "exist." In a memo referring to communications with the minister of finance, who in turn mentioned His Excellency, the president, the author pointed out that Bolívar had abolished the cacique office when he was in Cuzco. It continued, however, that "even if the cacicazgos were to exist, the project needs to be redone, because it conspires against the tax system . . . irreparably damaging public finances." The author argued that the subprefects were in charge of collecting taxes and posting bonds to make sure that payment was made, and that they needed to name tax collectors they could trust. The memo ratified the status quo, which gave subprefects a great deal of latitude in selecting their subordinates. In Cuzco, ethnic caciques, other Indians, and a variety of non-Indians worked as tax collectors.[89]

No single pattern emerged in Cuzco in the decades-long replacement of the ethnic caciques. Indians, mestizos, and whites took the place of ethnic authorities. As argued in previous chapters, authorities named by the central government only slowly and haltingly replaced caciques. The evidence in Cuzco and in other studies on the early republican Andes demonstrates that Indians were able to maintain a degree of political autonomy and to strongly influence non-Indians who assumed local office. Some caciques remained in power, while, in general, the more democratic Indian varayoks became increasingly important.[90] Also, because their livelihood ultimately depended on collecting the Indian head tax, local officials were forced to maintain acceptable relations with Indians. Subprefects could not count on the state or local elites for much support in conflicts with the local population, so political and economic conditions encouraged them and other authorities to sustain good working relations with the indigenous population.[91]

The fate of the caciques and their descendants is unclear. A few became prominent public figures. José Domingo Choquehuanca, the scion of Azángaro's most powerful cacique family, participated in the political and intellectual currents of the early republic. His 1833 book on Azángaro provides a particularly informative and critical perspective on southern Andean society. Justo Sahuaraura published two books in the early 1850s that defended Cuzco's indigenous nobility, underlining their direct ascendance from the Incas, whom he exalted.[92] Descendants of royal Incas in the city of Cuzco continued to consider themselves a special class. One traveler noted "that those who claim to be of the same blood as the Incas assume a haughty manner toward their neighbors, which becomes the Indian as little as other people."[93] Some caciques and their offspring passed into the casta category and thereafter joined the ranks of the locally powerful through their own economic activities and marriage. For example, the descendants of the Sinanyuca and Guambo Tupa families in Coporaque can be found in the casta registrars of Coporaque, Chumbivilcas.[94] Yet in the majority of Cuzco's mid-nineteenth century tax registrars, records of the descendants of cacique families cannot be found in either the Indian or casta category.[95] Some migrated, but those descended from caciques who had supported Tupac Amaru lost their positions or even dropped the use of the cacique surname. The fate of the cacique lines varied, and some individuals remained influential in Cuzco society. But in the early republic, they were not key intermediaries as they had been throughout the colonial period.

In the first half of the nineteenth century, no single group connected peasant society with national political circles, and, in general, the links between these spheres remained weak. Not only were caciques in decline, but another key group that served as cultural brokers in the colonial period—priests—faced a number of challenges. Busy defending their place in the nascent republic, they did not serve as key intermediaries.[96] Nor did outsiders rapidly fill the vacuum left by the demise of the cacique office. Teachers and other representatives of the state did not have a massive presence until well into the twentieth century. As described in the previous chapter, political groups did not energetically campaign in the countryside except when they needed soldiers.[97] The fact that no single group emerged as key intermediaries between rural and national society does not mean, of course, that these ties did not exist. All of these groups—caciques, priests, teachers, politicians, merchants (the ubiquitous muleteers), and others—existed in Cuzco, and many individuals within these groups connected rural towns and communities with broader society. Moreover, Indians themselves forged direct ties with representatives of the nation-state. Nonetheless, the republic's perpetuation of the late colonial impasse over the replacement of the caciques, the stagnation of Cuzco's agricultural economy, and the segregated view of society implemented by the leading political groups maintained the chasm between Indians and the nation-state. Even Agustín Gamarra, the preeminent Cuzco caudillo, could not bridge it.

GAMARRA'S BLACK LAGOON

The caudillos who ruled much of Spanish America in the nineteenth century invariably counted on a mass base to aid them in their frequent wars. In Argentina, Juan Manuel de Rosas had the gauchos; in Venezuela, José Antonio Páez had the mixed-race *llaneros* from the central plains; and in Guatemala, Rafael Carrera had the Indians.[98] For Gamarra, the Indians of his native Cuzco constituted the logical group. Nonetheless, he and other Peruvian caudillos failed to create a mass fighting force from the majority of the region's population, Indians. The indigenous peasantry of the southern Andes resisted fighting in the wars that decided the caudillo struggles. The "misconnection" between caudillos and Indians epitomizes the argument presented here about the state and Indians in the postindependence period.

Gamarristas and others did not target Indians in their extensive proselytizing efforts. They did not consider them citizens, even potential citizens, and thus excluded them from their heterogeneous coalition. Militarily, Gamarra's officers relied on dragooning conscripts, which produced notably unreliable soldiers. When they recruited Indians as guerrilla forces by threatening them and offering money or food, but never by increasing their political rights, they had little success. The indigenous peasantry remained largely detached from the caudillo struggles. Although they took advantage of the weakened state and incorporated republican language into their negotiations, they did not support one side or another. In order to explain the separation between caudillo politics and Indian society, I focus on the civil war of 1835, particularly the Battle of Yanacocha ("Black Lagoon"). At this point, Gamarra had assembled thousands of Indians guerrillas, but their unwillingness to fight doomed his forces.

Three groups fought in the caudillo civil wars: formal military units, militias, and guerrillas.[99] The social origins of the military and militia soldiers varied. Some elite battalions were composed of veterans who expected to be paid on time in return for their loyalty and skills. Most of the foot soldiers were products of the infamous draft, the *leva*. Describing the low standards for soldiers, an official in Cuzco claimed that he could not provide ten replacements for the Zepita Battalion because "I can't find any vagrants or malefactors."[100] The militias were commanded by local notables eager to demonstrate their enthusiasm in order to gain the favor of the caudillo's inner circle (an enthusiasm probably greater in training than in real battle); they were manned by the lower classes, both volunteers and draftees. The military and militia units combined veterans, walk-ons, and young men dragged from work, home, or taverns. In the late 1840s, an anonymous author complained that "Cuzco is only remembered when armies are being formed or resources mobilized for war."[101]

The terms *guerrilla* and *montonero* did not have any social or racial ambiguity in the southern Andes: they meant "Indian." Whereas on the coast guerrillas came from every racial group, in the Andes they were overwhelmingly Indians. They were generally recruited near the place of battle, and they fought with rudimentary weapons, a pattern dating from the War of Independence.[102] In an 1827 letter from Cuzco, Gamarra wrote to La Fuente, requesting horses for the cavalry. He proudly noted that even without his entire cavalry, he could count on "two thousand good men, besides the montonera that will be enormous. I also have between twelve and fifteen thousand Pumacaguas who are steady and resolute."[103] With the term *montonera*, Gamarra referred to individuals incorporated into the military and militia units. Pumacaguas, from the name of the cacique leader of the 1814 rebellion, alluded to Indian guerrillas. The letter to La Fuente greatly exaggerated the number of Indian guerrillas that Gamarra could recruit. Despite major efforts, he was never able to raise a large army of effective Indian soldiers.

Gamarra and his supporters went to great lengths in late 1833 to keep him as president, and in 1834 and 1835 worked to return him to office. In Cuzco, they focused on raising money and recruiting soldiers. For example, the subprefect of Chumbivilcas, Juan Infantas, drafted hundreds of soldiers and built up the militia in late 1833.[104] In March 1834, Prefect Bujanda instructed Infantas to send soldiers for several battalions and to organize guerrilla troops. He also ordered him not to leave any horses or livestock for the enemy.[105] Yet, despite these efforts, Gamarra lost the first round of the civil war with General Orbegoso. On April 24, 1834, Gamarrista troops deposed General Bermúdez in the central Andes and, in the "Abrazo de Maquinhuayo," swore allegiance to Orbegoso.[106]

Even with Gamarra in exile, his supporters continued to prepare Cuzco for war. When the Gamarrista Juan Ceballos became the military commander of Chumbivilcas in late 1834, he was told to "rebuild the montoneros wherever you think necessary and request adequate espionage."[107] An important Gamarra supporter, Juan Rosell, described the months leading up to the Battle of Yanacocha. In a trial about his debts, Rosell noted, "When I was subprefect of the province of Cuzco, an army was formed to oppose the invasion of Santa Cruz. I had orders from the prefect as well as Gamarra to provide food to the troops and to buy war supplies, which I did until the unfortunate moment of Yanacocha."[108] In May 1835, José de la Cuba, the newly installed subprefect of Chumbivilcas, was warned to guard against the incursions of Orbegoso forces to the south. He was ordered to "send guerrillas to distract the enemy and thus impede them from attacking."[109]

When Gamarra returned to Peru in June 1835 and established the

Central State of Peru in Cuzco, military preparations accelerated. At this point, he sided with Salaverry, who instructed him to avoid direct confrontation with Santa Cruz. Nonetheless, when Santa Cruz entered Peru upon the invitation of Orbegoso, Gamarra prepared to meet him in battle. Chafing at his subordination to Salaverry, Gamarra believed that he could defeat Santa Cruz and vie for national power. On June 30, Santa Cruz wrote Gamarra, "They have told me that you are surrounding yourself with all the men who induced you before to commit the mistakes that turned people's opinion against you, that you are giving promotions in your army as though you did not have officials or you had won the Battle of Waterloo, and that you have prohibited the mention of Bolivia in public acts." He reproached Gamarra for increasing expenditures on the military when "the Peruvian treasury is devastated due to the abuse of its employees and the disorder following revolution."[110] A month later, Santa Cruz wrote Orbegoso, "I know for a fact that Gamarra intends to fight a war of positions, basing his strength in Paruro . . . and rousing the Indians."[111]

Gamarra officials organized Indian guerrilla troops throughout the Cuzco countryside. They concentrated their efforts in Paruro and Chumbivilcas in the upper provinces, the mountainous livestock areas to the southwest of Cuzco.[112] Juan Infantas distributed coca leaves to commanders of Indian guerrillas from Urubamba to the north of the city. Authorities from San Sebastián, Maras, Chincheros, and numerous unspecified locations received between 150 and 250 pounds of coca leaves. In all, Infantas dispensed sixty *arrobas* or fifteen hundred pounds. This amount of coca could provide sustenance to thousands of Indians.[113] In a note written on August 11, two days before the Battle of Yanacocha, Bujanda instructed Infantas to pay for "the sixty arrobas that you have bought to distribute to the *immense number of guerrillas*" from whatever source he could as subprefect.[114] On August 8, the head of the Bolivian advance forces wrote to Santa Cruz from Canas, near where the battle would take place five days later, that the Gamarrista subprefects of Canas and Quispicanchis had fled after organizing small guerrilla groups. The author reported that he had gathered sufficient forage, meat, and potatoes for the Bolivian military.[115] Two days later, he sent a letter describing how "throughout the province of Quispicanchis in both the mountain and valley towns, Farfán and Villafuerte have been organizing the *indiada*, who with repugnance and tears have resisted."[116]

Gamarra's forces occupied a gorge overlooking Lake Yanacocha about thirty-five miles to the southeast of Cuzco. They consisted of approximately four thousand soldiers from militia and military units. Historians disagree about the number of Indian guerrillas, with estimates ranging from six to eleven thousand. All accounts agreed, however, that the Indians did little to defend Gamarra's position. Most of the guerrillas ran away when the fighting began.[117] The Santa Cruz forces attacked Gamarra's flanks and then charged the gorge. Santa Cruz supposedly promised a generalship to the first commander to take the peak.[118] After a little more than two hours, the Gamarra forces surrendered. The reports of the battle, as well as the final result, reveal that the guerrilla forces avoided combat and failed to contribute to the Gamarristas' defense, which destroyed Gamarra's chances. Most accounts of the battle tally more than one thousand dead. Santa Cruz had four enemy officers executed,[119] but Gamarra himself escaped and fled to Lima. Salaverry exiled him to Guayaquil, where he left for Costa Rica.

Gamarra's inability to recruit an effective guerrilla force reflects a more general aversion of southern Andean Indians to participation in the caudillo military struggles. No military leader recruited a mass indigenous backing in the southern Andes in the first half century after independence.[120] Numerous factors have to be analyzed in order to overcome interpretations that focus on Indians' purported provincialism or even cowardice. The point of departure for this analysis is that the Indians decided not to participate. Their absence from the political struggles waged in long military campaigns derived from their determination that the costs outweighed the benefits, not because they did not understand the caudillo wars or because the "elite" excluded them. Of course, the "decision" was not always collective, consensual, or conscious. In some cases, entire communities dug in their heels against a subprefect's demand for soldiers, whereas in other communities, individuals simply slipped away from the military. In both cases, however, Indians realized that serving a caudillo ran against collective and individual interests. In order to understand the Indians' reluctance to participate in the caudillo wars, military, ideological, and economic factors need to be analyzed.

At first glance, nonparticipation is odd given the fact that Indians in the southern Andes had a great deal of experience with mass insurrection. The Pumacahua uprising had occurred only twenty years before the civil wars of the 1830s, and the Tupac Amaru and Tupac Katari rebellions only a half century before. Yet, although Tupac Amaru lived on as a symbol of resistance, a symbol appropriated by a broad spectrum of political movements, the memory of the repression also survived. Most Indians in the 1830s had witnessed or at least heard of the high costs of fighting for the losing side of a war. Although the levels of violence of the early republican civil wars never approached those of the late colonial rebellions, the postrebellion repression discouraged Indians from waging war. In the same sense that the defeated rebels had "won"—in that the specter of another uprising deterred exploitative outsiders and helped bring about the fall of the Bourbons—the repressive state had also succeeded in impressing upon the Indians the high stakes of rebellion.

Indians had also learned a great deal from the civil wars that had begun in Peru even before the Spanish were defeated. In the caudillo period, the constant turnover in office, from the presidency to the subprefecture level, impeded long-term alliances between caudillos and social groups such as Indians. Political instability fostered skepticism within civil society. The caudillo did not remain in office long enough to deliver the "benefits" (various forms of favoritism) promised to supporters. More importantly, when the successor of the caudillo (frequently his nemesis) took office, he withdrew these benefits and even punished his predecessor's supporters. For example, Gamarrista supporters faced a hostile state during the Santa Cruz regime. Simply put, Indians received little benefit from actively supporting a caudillo and had to endure the wrath of whoever followed him. Even Gamarra, who in Cuzco created one of the most enduring regional strongholds of the early republic, faced frequent challenges and failed to entrench himself in office. Contrary to the hyperbole about Gamarra's charisma among Quechua speakers (e.g., Paz Soldán's assertion that Gamarra could make thousands of Indians obey with one word), Indians had learned during the first decade after independence that Gamarra was not omnipotent.

Early republican caudillos had little to offer to the Indians. During the 1833–35 civil war, Gamarra promised tax exemptions to those who fought for him, mainly to recruit non-Indians for the militias. However, for Indians, the allure of these promises was limited. As described previously in this chapter, the tax burden in this period was tolerable for the Indians. Furthermore, Gamarra staunchly advocated the Indian head tax and presumably did not want to set a precedent by suspending it. In addition to giving tax breaks, a caudillo such as Gamarra could also aid communities and individuals in resolving conflicts in exchange for mobilization. Yet conditions in the early republic did not encourage this type of patron-client arrangement. Indians' economic and political situation had improved, and tensions ran low. Disputes over land or political authority did not divide rural society. At the same time, the regional state had little legitimacy in local political and economic disputes. In this period, it did not mediate in conflicts between communities. Below the level of subprefect, it remained weak and generally abdicated to local authorities and customs. Not only had tensions diminished following independence, but Gamarra and other caudillos had little leverage (and perhaps interest) in monitoring and solving local conflicts.

The amicable exchange of favors does not, of course, aptly characterize political relations in general in this period. Military recruitment in the nineteenth century did not rely on negotiation and reciprocity. Most soldiers were dragged from their homes in the infamous leva.[121] Choquehuanca called the military campaigns "fatal" for the Indians. Commanders forced them to work as "beasts of burden" and frequently beat and cheated them.[122] The indigenous guerrillas who fought for Gamarra in Yanacocha were primarily draftees or mercenaries. Subprefects paid them or their masters small amounts of money, provided them with supplies such as coca leaves, and promised them spoils of victory such as pillage. Soldiers recruited through coercion and promises of meager economic benefits perform poorly on the battlefield. As part of large units, they need to be monitored and forced into situations where they have to fight.[123] The gorge selected by Gamarra prevented the bulk of his troops from fleeing in the Battle of Yanacocha.

Unlike common soldiers, guerrilla forces—such as those that Gamarra staked his hopes on—require greater independence and mobility. They attack the enemy's front and rear, attempt to cut off supply lines, and pursue the opposition after battle.[124] If motivated, they greatly improve an army. If not, they are almost worthless. In the Battle of Yanacocha, the Indian guerrillas were positioned to the left and right of Gamarra's main forces, covering his flanks. If they had fought well, they would have prevented Santa Cruz from dividing Gamarra's forces and breaking his lines in several places. However, they quickly bolted. Their collapse reflected their poor motivation.

The inability of Gamarra and other caudillos to mobilize guerrillas in the southern Andes can be explained in part by the relatively favorable economic and political conditions enjoyed by the Indians. Their improved economic standing and continuing political autonomy mitigated against mobilization. Individuals who wanted to join the military in order to flee a problem, make some money, or see the world could simply join the military or the militias; they did not need to join guerrilla armies. Opportunities abounded for anyone interested in becoming a soldier. Peru's instability, however, made supporting one faction against another an often costly mistake that further discouraged mobilization. Nevertheless, economic and political factors alone cannot sufficiently explain the Indians' reluctance to mobilize for Gamarra and other caudillos. Indians' role in political struggles dating from the late colonial period and more specifically their relationship with the caudillos need to be addressed.

Factional divisions in early republican Cuzco did not extend far beyond the city. For several reasons, struggles between Gamarristas and Santacrucistas did not characterize politics in Cuzco's ten provinces. Gamarra predominated. Through the measures described in chapter 5, he created a broad base in his homeland. His Cuzco chauvinism emphasized a vague regional favoritism and thus did not divide political factions into clear-cut groups for and against him. A liberal opposition existed but did not develop much of a base outside the city of Cuzco. From the perspective of the southern Andes, Santa Cruz's policies did not differ greatly from Gamarra's. In the mid-1830s, both sought a reunification of Peru and Bolivia, and they held similar social views. Although a liberal in trade policy, Santa Cruz's perspective on the organization of state and society matched the perspective of Peruvian authoritarians.[125] Gamarra had the advantage in Cuzco, though, because he had spent a decade consolidating his support in the region, his homeland. In sum, the liberal/conservative or Santa Cruz/Gamarra divide did not mark politics in rural Cuzco. The liberal opposition to Gamarra had almost no presence in the countryside. The Gamarra forces were stronger but could not count on a mass, Indian base.

Reluctance and even disinterest on the part of the Indians should not be confused with ignorance. The rural population followed political struggles and differentiated between the factions. Although the authority of the state remained weak below the level of the subprefects, its reliance on the head tax required it to maintain a presence in rural society. The Cuzco prefecture produced countless edicts that were placed throughout the region. Indians could not avoid governmental representatives. In the early republic, therefore, statelessness did not characterize the Cuzco countryside.

The level of contact with the state varied from region to region. The half century between the Tupac Amaru rebellion and the 1835 war witnessed a growing localization and even fragmentation of Indian identity. On the one hand, the Bourbons had aimed to weaken Indian identity through the ban on cultural practices, such as dances and books that extolled the Incas, and the dismantling of the cacique office. At the same time, they attempted to reinvigorate laws that separated different caste groups. As described in chapter 3, the political situation varied greatly throughout the southern Andes. The impositions of the Bourbons no longer united Andean society. On the other hand, independence and the subsequent civil wars did not polarize rural society. No new type of Andean solidarity along caudillo lines emerged. The relationship between authorities and Indians, and how both groups perceived this relationship, differed widely. The evidence suggests that, all in all, the rural lower classes understood the constant conflicts over the control of the state and decided not to participate. In retrospect, this decision does not seem to have been a bad one.

CONCLUSION

This chapter has evaluated relations between Indians and the state from a variety of perspectives. To conclude, I would like to link these perspectives. The national state rapidly forewent its liberal ideas about granting Indians the rights of citizens and instead restored the basis of the colonial relationship: the head tax for land rights agreement. They treated Indians not as individuals but rather as members of a corporation, the Indian community. Local and regional authorities in the Andes buttressed this decision by depicting Indians as uncivilized others who required the heavy hand of the state to contribute to the nation and possibly to be considered Peruvians. These retrograde policies and harsh discourse have led some historians to depict an unmitigated loss of political autonomy and control of communal land and thus concomitant economic misery for Indians in the early republic. An explanation, however, that grants Indians agency and follows how these policies and discourses played out in local Andean society provides a more nuanced interpretation.

By and large, Indians maintained control of much of their land and managed to influence local officeholders, Indian and non-Indian. In structural terms, the weak economy and reigning political instability discouraged outsiders from risking their investments and perhaps even their lives in the countryside. They did not count on the economic incentives or a supportive state necessary for such efforts. Clearly, independence did not usher in a widespread assault on Indian land. Indians also used various tactics to resist, taking advantage of special rights historically granted to them as Indians, or noncitizens. They continued to lobby and pressure local authorities, Indian and non-Indian, as they had done for decades. Indian leaders employed the language of freedom and anticolonialism that spread during the long War of Independence. They did not, however, massively participate in the caudillo wars. Caudillos such as Gamarra demonstrated little interest in the Indians except as taxpayers and occasional soldiers. They did not attempt to link their coalitions with local struggles in the Andean countryside. On the other hand, Indians saw little to gain from latching their struggles to those of the caudillo coalitions. In the early republic, the schism between national/regional political movements and Indian society remained enormous. Cultural and social differences, mistrust, and even disdain divided these spheres, and cultural brokers were not to be found.

The gulf between caudillo and peasant politics and the relative success of Indians in defending their resources ultimately reinforced the notion of Peru as a racially divided nation. The story cannot end therefore with this "resistance." Local authorities' discourse, which emphasized the otherness of Indians and the impossibility of their converting into citizens, reinforced exclusionary national ideologies and policies. Even if these authorities were not as omnipotent as they purported, their vision of Indians as inferiors made its way into national and regional circles. In the early republic, the state and its ideologues quickly rebuilt and even raised the dividing wall between Indians and non-Indians. The opposition to an intermediary category, such as castas, reflects these efforts. Indians succeeded in resisting encroachment by relying on their traditional rights, premised on their otherness or even inferiority. Besides harsh rhetoric and occasional recruiting, political movements by and large overlooked the Indian population, excluding them from political circles. This exclusion, more than an assault on Indian resources, constituted the baneful, enduring legacy of the early republic.

"Cuzco. ¡Qué complejo es su destino!"—Jorge Basadre[1]

In November 1841, Agustín Gamarra found himself in battle in neighboring Bolivia. Once again in the presidency, he had led the Regeneration, the staunchly conservative government formed by those who had defeated Andrés Santa Cruz and the Peru-Bolivia Confederation. Gamarra's forces entered Bolivia in order to impede Santa Cruz's return to power and, presumably, to prepare a confederation under Peruvian (and his own) control. On the eighteenth of November, Bolivian troops routed the Peruvians. Gamarra watched his army break down and the cavalry withdraw. He strove to rouse his troops but was shot and killed—perhaps, as many have contended, murdered by one of his own soldiers in retaliation for mistreatment in the barracks.[2]

Gamarra's death coincided with dramatic changes. First, after 1840 Cuzco no longer served as the base for Peru's most significant dissident political projects. In the previous sixty years, a series of conspiracies, uprisings, and short-lived governments had risen up against Spanish colonialism and Lima centralism. Although with different strategies and social bases, participants in these movements attempted to decolonize Peru and hoped to transform an ethnically diverse, highly stratified viceroyalty into an independent nation. Upon independence, rebels fought to locate the republic's capital in the Andes rather than on the coast.

Gamarra's death also marked a more subtle change in caudillo politics. Military chieftains continued to rule Peru for much of the nineteenth century, yet with notable differences from the way Gamarra and his early republican brethren ruled. After the 1840s, border conflicts no longer represented the central activity of military chieftains because the struggles examined in this book had already by and large defined Peruvian territory. Also, after midcentury, caudillos came primarily from the ranks of the coastal upper middle classes. Provincial mestizos like Gamarra, Santa Cruz, and Castilla no longer predominated and stronger political parties emerged. Caudillos continued to vie for power, but with different institutional bases and backgrounds.[3]

Third, the relationship between Indians and the state changed dramatically in the decades following Gamarra's death. The abolition of the Indian head tax in 1854 and the implementation of a liberal constitution ended the arrangement examined here. In the latter decades of the nineteenth century, demand increased for the land held by Indian communities and for Indians' labor. Peasant communities could no longer count on a state inclined to conciliation in return for the taxes they paid. Instead, the state led or at least supported non-Indians' attacks on Indian autonomy to gain access to community resources. The "liberal assault" on Indian communities thus began in earnest in the second half of the nineteenth century.

In light of subsequent developments, the period stretching from 1780 to 1840 may be seen as a long, chaotic interval, after which the flourishing of an export economy enabled the Lima-based oligarchy, less quixotic caudillos, and land-grabbing mestizos to form a fragile but enduring coalition. The period studied here, according to this view, constituted a disorderly preamble to capitalism and the full-scale usurpation of the Andean peasants' resources. Undoubtedly, in the latter half of the nineteenth century, the expansion of the export economy — centered on the extraction of guano, cotton, and sugar — and the increasing codification of racism in the mentality and laws of Peru deepened geographic, ethnic, and class divisions. Centralism and racism were institutionalized under a liberal veneer.

Nonetheless, important continuities can be found between the transitional period examined here and post-1840 Peru. In this conclusion, I review some of my central arguments in light of developments after the mid–nineteenth century. Although pointing out major social and political transformations, I emphasize how the theoretical and methodological arguments of this book can contribute to a deeper understanding of modern Peru.

I have made three central arguments about caudillismo and political instability in Spanish America. Caudillos did not exist in a political vacuum; instead, they created political coalitions and ran fully functioning, albeit unstable, states. Caudillismo is not a synonym for statelessness; consequently, the political structures and administrative units of the caudillo state, as well as the caudillos themselves and their coalitions, have been important in my analysis. I hope this work helps explain the difficult path toward state formation in Spanish America and the persistence of authoritarianism.

The case of Gamarrismo in Cuzco demonstrates that early republican political struggles in Peru should not be understood as a battle between rustic caudillos in the countryside and modernizing elites in Lima, or as senseless infighting between elites and their praetorian proxies. Peruvian caudillos created multiclass alliances. They were neither the dupes of the behind-the-scenes upper classes, nor the masters of the peasant masses. No Peruvian caudillo depended exclusively on the lower classes. On the other hand, no caudillo could forgo having a popular base. The lower classes were neither fully dependent on nor independent of the caudillos. Although every caudillo needed a mass base, lower-class groups proved capable of withdrawing support or even changing sides. Gamarra and the Indians in his native Cuzco exemplify this intricate relationship.

Second, the ideological debates in the caudillo struggles must be taken seriously. As I have shown for the case of Cuzco, discussions about state and society in Cuzco extended far beyond the parlors of elite homes on the Plaza de Armas. These debates shaped the struggles over the nature and control of the postcolonial state, and they influenced subsequent discussions as well. The liberal-authoritarian divide that characterized Peruvian politics well into the twentieth century—and that seems to have regained currency in recent years in light of the unorthodox Fujimori regime—developed in the 1820s and 1830s.[4] Throughout this book, I have attempted to show that civil wars and unstable regimes led by generals did not mean the absence of debate or the lack of political participation beyond the battlefield.

Third, I have stressed the benefits of contextualizing political culture in terms of on-the-ground political struggles. Elections, festivals, the press, and other preferred topics of students of political culture need to be placed within their specific political context. These rituals can be understood only in relation to the tumultuous caudillo-led civil wars. Moreover, they must be historicized. Not only do we need to review the "colonial antecedents" of public rituals, discourse, and the use of space, but we need to consider local traditions and enduring struggles. For example, Gamarra's regime in Cuzco can be understood only in light of the Tupac Amaru and Pumacahua rebellions as well as the Andean utopia or Inca revivalism.

Let us turn to caudillismo in Peru after the death of Gamarra, specifically to certain ramifications of this study. In the last 150 years, the military has continued to play a key role in politics. In the second half of the nineteenth century, military battles rather than orderly elections usually decided who controlled the presidency. Twenty-one out of Peru's twenty-nine presidents from 1841 to 1899 were military officers.[5] In fact, rumors of military coups still haunt Peru in the 1990s. Although the ideologies and social bases of caudillo movements and states have changed over time, one characteristic of the 1820–40 period remained: the caudillos' relatively weak hold on power. Peru's most enduring caudillo, Ramón Castilla, governed Peru for twelve years (1845–51, 1855–62), far less than Juan Manuel de Rosas, Porfirio Díaz, or other Spanish American rulers. No single chieftain left an indelible mark on nineteenth-century Peru. Many created regional and national power bases like Gamarra's, but all proved equally unable to institutionalize their authority.

Yet caudillismo changed in other ways. In the immediate postindependence period, the countryside and small towns played an unusually important role in political struggles throughout Spanish America,[6] but this role changed with the rise of the export economy, the relative institutionalization of politics, and the ascent of cities, particularly the capital, dating from the late nineteenth century. The liberals' failure to build a base in the Cuzco countryside foreshadows these changes. As seen in chapter 6, the urban lower classes participated in the constant political struggles over the control of the state, thus altering political rules and practice. These groups played an important, even if episodic, part in the political turmoil of the long nineteenth century.

The same level of participation did not occur in the Cuzco countryside. Caudillo coalitions such as Gamarra's rarely proselytized outside of the city and medium-sized towns. They recruited soldiers but did not incorporate them into their political movements. The constant, usually impassioned debate about politics that marked the city of Cuzco in this era did not have the same effect in the ten provinces. The terms of national and regional political discussions were not extensively incorporated into discussions in the provinces, and the beliefs and demands from local, rural society failed to influence broader ideological discussions. In Cuzco, the indigenous peasants—the overwhelming majority of the rural population—did not massively involve themselves in caudillo politics. As seen in chapter 7, they rejected the limited invitation to act as occasional mercenaries.

The absence of Indian peasants from caudillo struggles in Cuzco does not mean that politics and society did not change with independence or that the countryside was "apolitical." In fact, the struggles evident in the wake of the Tupac Amaru uprising over who held local office escalated in the nineteenth century. In general, the pivotal cacique office waned, and the Indian mayors, or varayoks, became increasingly important.[7] Non-Indians continued to vie for influence, although their entrenchment as local authorities was not an unbroken process. Yet in the first half of the century, at least, these struggles did not mesh with the caudillo-led battles over the control and nature of the regional and national state. The roots of urban domination in politics can be seen in early republican Cuzco.

What does the study of Gamarrismo contribute to the understanding of the causes of caudillismo? Above all, this book has shown the benefit of linking local, regional, and national politics. Caudillos were not an aberration or an unfortunate reflection of the failure of republican political formation. Instead, caudillo politics constituted a unique type of state formation. Caudillos led broad coalitions, often forging ties with or even representing political parties. With the aid of a network of ideologues and cultural brokers, they promoted influential ideas and platforms about postcolonial state and society. Furthermore, the analysis of lower-class groups, as I have emphasized throughout this book, represents another key element in understanding caudillismo.[8]

The postindependence period shaped the modern Peruvian republic. On one hand, the political system and national borders have largely remained the same. In the late eighteenth and early nineteenth centuries, Peruvians weighed and fought over a variety of political options —above all, different forms of republicanism and monarchism. Republicanism prevailed. On the other hand, there arose a form of nationalism, stronger than many analysts might suggest, that allowed for a sense of unity while permitting diverse notions of what Peru was, is, and will be. Despite the divisions of the caudillo period and the ethnocentric discourse flowing between the different realms of the state, a sense of Peruvianness extended throughout much of the country. Although I stress divisions throughout this book, I do not mean to imply that a Peruvian identity was weak or nonexistent. Instead, I believe that various notions of *peruanidad* circulated, including more inclusionary concepts that contradicted the exclusionary views espoused by the state and national elite.[9]

INDIANS AND THE STATE

After the 1840s, political and economic power shifted away from Cuzco and the Andes toward Lima and the coast. With the abolition of the Indian head tax in 1854, the state no longer had a financial incentive to defend the Indian communities' right to land. Nonetheless, the Indian peasantry withstood challenges to their political autonomy and economic resources. The diverse projects to "de-Indianize" Peru failed. In 1961, "Indians" constituted just less than half of the national population. Indeed, perhaps 35 percent of the population speaks Quechua today.[10] To understand the persistence of Indians as a key social group in the Andes, a number of factors need to be considered: divisions within the elite, structural obstacles to anti-Indian policies, the divergence between ideology and practice, and the active role in politics played by Indians themselves. This book has attempted to provide a holistic explanation of this process.

Throughout the nineteenth century, the upper classes remained divided about the meaning and implementation of liberalism in the Andes. As in the case of the Bourbon reforms, these divisions hindered efforts to change the relationship between Indians and the state. Whereas some governments, such as the *civilista* regime of President Manuel Pardo (1872–76), sought to integrate Indians—that is, to westernize them—the government of Nicolás Piérola (1879–81 and 1895–99) claimed to protect them from pernicious external influences. Intellectuals and politicians largely agreed about the need to de-Indianize the Peruvian population and to expand the market economy. They disagreed, however, about how to achieve this. Although an anti-Indian mentality persisted among elite groups and became more elaborate with the rise of scientific racism, the policies they proposed varied greatly.[11]

But just as this book has shown for the 1780–1840 period, subsequent political divisions cannot be reduced to squabbles between members of the elite class. The tenuous relationship between different social groups and the various realms of the state is central to any analysis. In general, under a tacit agreement with the Lima-based national state, local officials in the Andes largely pursued their own interests, heeding the requests of the *gamonales,* the locally powerful. These authorities guaranteed local order for the party in power and, in most cases, support in elections or even in civil wars. This agreement was frequently broken, however, and in some regions the gamonales or their representatives clashed with the national state. The presence of the Lima-based state in the Andes remained weak, particularly after the abolition of the Indian head tax and the consequent dismantling of the fiscal network. Peru's difficult topography and the lack of transportation and communication widened the gulf between the coast and the Andes.[12]

State formation in the nineteenth century therefore had two fundamental weaknesses. First, different political projects emanating from Lima agreed, explicitly or tacitly, to exclude the lower classes. Well into the twentieth century (and perhaps even until today), the state failed to incorporate the Indian majority into its scheme. Second, connections between the different echelons of the state remained fragile, frayed by the gulf between Lima and the provinces and by the ascendancy of local elites. The national state in nineteenth-century Peru relied upon a makeshift coalition with the locally powerful, which excluded the majority of the population. The consequences became brutally evident in the disastrous War of the Pacific (1879–83) when the Chilean army swept through Peru.[13]

In light of the policies of a hostile state, how can we explain Indian survival? Elite division and governmental inefficacy are only part of the story. The lower classes in Cuzco and throughout the country employed a variety of political tactics to defend themselves and to assure a place in the republic. Indians and other lower-class groups protested not only by rebelling, but also by using the legal system, forming alliances, and challenging the intrusions of outsiders. In fact, uprisings were infrequent until the beginning of the twentieth century.[14] Indians also incorporated and subverted official discourse, bringing to light unfulfilled promises and contradictions. The consequence of their efforts is most evident in what they were able to prevent: the diverse plans to deprive them of their culture and of their political and economic resources.[15]

With increased threats on Indian land and political autonomy, as well as the widespread belief that progress required ridding Peru of Indians, these different forms of resistance apparently succeeded. Yet such a story oversimplifies Andean history. Many communities in fact lost land, many suffered under the tyranny of gamonales, and many saw their members forced to seek work on estates and mines. Indigenous peasants faced economic hardship and political pressure as demand for their labor and land increased. We need to look closely at these processes in order to avoid the "ethnographic thinness" that plagues many works on "resistance."[16] Indians remained noncitizens well into the twentieth century.[17]

Moreover, Indians did not just dig in their heels and defend their rights to be Indians; race and society are much more complicated than this scheme indicates. The sociological messiness continued in the republic. Homogeneous, unified Indians did not confront a monolithic non-Indian "elite." Not only were (and are) dominant political groups divided about what to do with the Indian population, but the lower classes themselves took advantage of and contributed to the fluid definitions of racial categories in the Andes. Since the decline of the colonial and postcolonial state's interest in defining and defending the category *Indian*, various social, economic, and political factors have shaped the meaning of this term. Millions of individuals have abandoned this category to become casta, mestizo, or cholo. Others have slipped from one category to another and back.[18] Nonetheless, I contend that, even faced with an often hostile state and powerful non-Indians who sought their communities' land and labor, Indians continued to be an important part of Peru—a striking achievement indeed.

CUZCO

To conclude, let me return to the focus and inspiration of my study, Cuzco. After 1840, the relative importance of the city and region declined. Although the city of Cuzco had roughly 60 percent of Lima's population in 1830 (30,000 to 50,000), today it has about 5 percent

(320,000 to 7,000,000). It is now Peru's fourth largest city, with tourism replacing production for the Upper Peruvian–Bolivian market as the economic mainstay. Even the staunchest Cusqueño regionalist recognizes that the city and the area cannot compete with the capital for predominance. Yet, although Cuzco no longer represents the primary opponent to Lima centralism, significant dissident movements continue to rise up there. *Indigenismo,* for example, a movement by non-Indians to place Indians at the center of the national agenda, emerged in Cuzco in the early twentieth century. In the late 1950s, the peasant federations organized by Hugo Blanco and others in the La Convención Valley to the north of Cuzco set in motion the radicalism that culminated in the guerrilla movements of the 1960s. Yet all in all, Cuzco's political significance has declined in the last century.[19]

It is not surprising, therefore, that Cuzco's social, intellectual, and political movements have invariably cast an eye to the period studied here, 1780 to 1840, in search of historical symbols and alternatives. Virtually every political force in Cuzco invokes Tupac Amaru and Pumacahua, and Agustín Gamarra merits a statue in the important Plaza de San Francisco. For many, these men were heroes who, although alas defeated, sought to change the course of Andean history by challenging Spanish rule and Lima centralism and thus returning Cuzco to its rightful place. In light of the racial, class, and geographic divisions that continue to mark Peru today, many Cusqueños and others pose the tantalizing question, What would have happened had these men been victorious? Not surprisingly, these speculations provide the heroes with mythical abilities in what is often a heavily chauvinistic "Cuzco First" perspective. Others go further and claim that if contemporary Peru is to be changed, the strategies, goals, and utopias spearheaded by these figures continue to hold the secret to such change. In other words, Tupac Amaru, Pumacahua, and Gamarra are more than symbols of lost opportunities: they are the bearers of alternative paths for Peru.

NOTES

ABBREVIATIONS

ADC	Archivo Departamental del Cuzco
AGI	Archivo General de Indias
AGN	Archivo General de la Nación
AHM	Archivo Histórico Militar
ALF	Archivo de Limítes y Fronteras
ATP	Administración del Tesoro Público
BN	Biblioteca Nacional del Perú
CBC	Centro Bartolomé de Las Casas
CC	Causas Criminales
CDBTU	Colección Documental del Bicentenario de Tupac Amaru
CDIP	Colección Documental de la Independencia Peruana
CLAR	Colonial Latin American Review
CML	Colección Mata Linares
CNDBRETA	Comisión Nacional del Bicentenario de la Rebelión Emancipadora de Túpac Amaru
CSIC	Consejo Superior de Investigaciones Científicas
Doc.	Documento/Document
EEH-A	Escuela de Estudios Hispano-Americanos de la Universidad de Sevilla
HAHR	Hispanic American Historical Review
IEP	Instituto de Estudios Peruanos
INC	Instituto Nacional de Cultura
JLAS	Journal of Latin American Studies
LARR	Latin American Research Review
Leg.	Legajo (archive packet no.)

Unless otherwise noted, all translations of Spanish-language texts are mine.

1 This has been a central tenet of subaltern studies, albeit in reference to quite different "Indians." See Ranajit Guha, *Elementary Aspects of Peasant Insurgency in Colonial India* (Delhi: Oxford University Press, 1983). Much of the historiography of Latin America in the last twenty years, some of it in dialogue with subaltern studies, has emphasized the political agency of the peasantry.

2 Two key works that refute the "primordial" notion of nationalism and emphasize ideology over structural conditions are Benedict Anderson, *Imagined Communities: Reflections on the Origin and Spread of Nationalism* (London: Verso, 1983), and Eric Hobsbawm and Terence Ranger, eds., *The Invention of Tradition* (Cambridge: Cambridge University Press, 1983).

3 Partha Chatterjee, *Nationalist Thought and the Colonial World: A Derivative Discourse*, 2d impression (Minneapolis: University of Minnesota Press, 1993) and idem., *The Nation and Its Fragments: Colonial and Postcolonial Histories* (Princeton: Princeton University Press, 1993). See a number of edited volumes on nationalism, including Geoff Eley and Ronald Grigor Suny, eds., *Becoming National* (New York: Oxford University Press, 1996), particularly the introduction, 3–37, and for an innovative piece on Spanish America, see Julie Skurski, "The Ambiguities of Authenticity in Latin America: Doña Barbara and the Construction of National Identity," in ibid., 371–402. Important work on peasants and nationalism in Latin America includes Florencia Mallon, *Peasant and Nation: The Making of Postcolonial Mexico and Peru* (Berkeley and Los Angeles: University of California Press, 1995), and Peter Guardino, "Identity and Nationalism in Mexico: Guerrero, 1780–1840," *Journal of Historical Sociology* 7 (1994): 314–42. On the concept of nation in nineteenth-century Spanish America, see Mónica Quijada, "¿Qué Nación? Dinámicas y dicotomías de la nación en el imaginario hispanoamericana del siglo XIX," in *Imaginar la nación*, ed. Francois-Xavier Guerra and Mónica Quijada (Hamburg: AHILA, 1994), 15–51.

4 This has been a key question concerning subaltern studies. On this issue, see Florencia Mallon, "The Promise and Dilemma of Subaltern Studies: Perspectives from Latin American History," *American Historical Review* 99, 5 (1994): 1491–1515; and Mallon, *Peasant and Nation;* Peter Guardino, *Peasants, Politics and the Formation of Mexico's National State: Guerrero, 1800–1857* (Stanford, Calif.: Stanford University Press, 1996). The dean of modern Peruvian historians, Jorge Basadre, long addressed this question. See for example, Jorge Basadre, *La inciciación de la república*, 2 vols. (Lima: F. y E. Rosay, 1929).

5 Particularly influential works include Lynn Hunt, *Politics, Culture, and Class in the French Revolution* (Berkeley and Los Angeles: University of California Press, 1984), and Lynn Hunt, ed., *The New Cultural History* (Berkeley

and Los Angeles: University of California Press, 1989); Keith Baker, ed., *The Political Culture of the Old Regime* (Oxford: Pergamon Press, 1987).

6   Thomas Krüggeler helped in this enterprise. Like so many "discoveries" in the Andes, many locals already knew of these sources.

7   For examples, see the essays in the following edited volumes: Lelia Area and Mabel Moraña, eds., *La imaginación histórica en el siglo XIX* (Rosario: UNR Editores, 1994); William H. Beezley, Cheryl English Martin, and William E. French, eds., *Rituals of Rule, Rituals of Resistance: Public Celebrations and Popular Culture in Mexico* (Wilmington, Del.: SR Books, 1994); Beatriz Gonzáles Stephan et al., eds., *Esplendores y Miserias del Siglo XIX: Cultura y Sociedad en América Latina* (Caracas: Monte Avila Editores, 1994); Iván Molina Jiménez and Stephen Palmer, eds., *El paso del cometa: Estado, política social y culturas populares en Costa Rica (1800–1950)* (San José: Porvenir-Plumsock Mesoamerican Studies, 1994).

8   This is my main criticism of the work of Francois-Xavier Guerra, the most influential writer on nineteenth-century Spanish American political culture. See his *Modernidad e independencias* (Madrid: Ediciones MAPFRE, 1992).

9   For an insightful review of the rise of peasant studies, see Steve Stern, "Introduction," in the volume that he edited, *Resistance, Rebellion, and Consciousness in the Andean Peasant World, 18th to 20th Centuries* (Madison: University of Wisconsin Press, 1987), 3–25. For another important examination, see William Roseberry, "Beyond the Agrarian Question in Latin America," in Frederick Cooper et al., *Confronting Historical Paradigms: Peasants, Labor, and the Capitalist World System in Africa and Latin America* (Madison: University of Wisconsin Press, 1993), 318–68. For a series of essays on peasants in nineteenth-century Spanish America, see Heraclio Bonilla and Amada A. Guerrero Rincón, eds., *Los pueblos campesinos de las Américas: Etnicidad, cultura e historia en el siglo XIX* (Bucaramanga, Colombia: Universidad Industrial de Santander, 1996).

10 Nicholas B. Dirks, Geoff Eley, and Sherry B. Ortner, eds., "Introduction," in *Culture/Power/History: A Reader in Contemporary Social Theory* (Princeton: Princeton University Press, 1994), 5. See also the introductory essay by Joseph and Nugent in Gilbert M. Joseph and Daniel Nugent, eds., *Everyday Forms of State Formation: Revolution and the Negotiation of Rule in Modern Mexico* (Durham, N.C.: Duke University Press, 1994), 12–15. Studies that have linked peasants and state formation include Guardino, *Peasants, Politics;* Mallon, *Peasant and Nation;* and Nelson Manrique, *Campesinado y nación: Las guerrillas indígenas en la guerra con Chile* (Lima: C.I.C.-Ital Perú, S.A., 1981). For a review on works on Mexico, see Eric Van Young, "To See Someone Not Seeing: Historical Studies of Peasants and Politics in Mexico," *Mexican Studies* 6, no. 1 (1990): 133–59.

11 Domingo F. Sarmiento, *Life in the Argentine Republic in the Days of the*

Tyrants; or Civilization and Barbarism (New York: Hurd and Houghton, 1868).

12 For an incisive examination of caudillos and their biographers, see John Lynch, *Caudillos in Spanish America, 1800–1850* (Oxford: Clarendon Press, 1992), esp. chap. 1.

13 Richard Morse, "Towards a Theory of Spanish American Government," *Journal of the History of Ideas* 15 (1954): 71–93; idem, "The Heritage of Latin America," in *The Founding of New Societies*, ed. Louis Hartz (New York: Harcourt, Brace & World, 1964). For a review, see Frank Safford, "Politics, Ideology, and Society," in *Spanish America after Independence c. 1820–c. 1870*, ed. Leslie Bethell, *Cambridge History of Latin America* (Cambridge University Press, 1987), esp. 117–18.

14 Tulio Halperín Donghi has examined these factors with particular intellectual and geographic breadth. Tulio Halperín Donghi, *The Aftermath of Revolution in Latin America*, trans. Josephine de Bunsen (New York: Harper Torchbooks, 1973). See also Lynch, *Caudillos*, ch. 2; Guerra, "Identidades e independencia," in his *Modernidad e Independencias*.

15 This explanation begs the analysis of the relationship between politics and economics. See Donald F. Stevens, who concludes that politics shaped the economy more than economics shaped politics. *Origins of Instability in Early Republican Mexico* (Durham, N.C.: Duke University Press, 1991).

16 Lynch, *Caudillos*, chap. 10, 404. Halperín Donghi and Jorge Basadre have also examined these questions.

17 Joseph and Nugent, *Everyday Forms*, 12–15.

18 The spelling of Cuzco has been the subject of much debate in recent decades. In the 1970s, the spelling was officially changed from *Cuzco* to *Cusco* as Quechua specialists argued that the letter z was a Spanish aberration. In 1990, the mayor of Cuzco changed the name once again to *Qosqo* to match even closer the Quechua phonetics. I use Cuzco throughout.

19 See Alberto Flores Galindo, *Buscando un Inca*, 4th ed. (Lima: Editorial Horizonte, 1994), and, for invented traditions, Hobsbawm and Ranger, *The Invention*.

20 Paul Gootenberg, "Population and Ethnicity in Early Republican Peru: Some Revisions," *LARR* 26, no. 3 (1991), esp. 123–35; Thomas Krüggeler, "Unreliable Drunkards or Honorable Citizens? Artisans in Search of their Place in the Cusco Society (1825–1930)," Ph.D. diss. (University of Illinois at Urbana-Champaign, 1993), 27–32.

21 Parts of what is today the department of Puno were transferred to and from Cuzco in the late eighteenth century, whereas the districts of Abancay, Aymaraes, and Cotabambas pertained to Cuzco until the middle of the nineteenth century when they became part of the department of Apurímac. Magnus Mörner, *Perfil de la sociedad rural del Cuzco a fines de la colonia* (Lima: Universidad del Pacífico, 1978), 7–28, and 163–65.

22 On Cuzco's geography, see Mörner, *Perfil,* passim; Victor Peralta Ruíz, *En pos del tributo: Burocracia estatal, elite regional y comunidades indígenas en el Cusco rural (1826-1854)* (Cuzco: Centro Bartolomé de Las Casas, 1991); Pablo Macera and Felipe Márquez Abanto, "Informe geográfico del Perú colonial," *Revista del Archivo Nacional* 28 (1964): 132-247; and Deborah Poole, "Landscapes of Power in a Cattle-Rustling Culture of Southern Andean Peru," *Dialectical Anthropology* 12 (1988): 367-98.

23 Neus Escandell-Tur, *Producción y comercio de tejidos coloniales: Los obrajes y chorrillos del Cusco 1570-1820* (Cuzco: Centro Bartolomé de Las Casas, 1997); and her "Textile Production and Trade during the Colonial Period: Cusco, 1570-1820," Ph.D. diss. (University of California at San Diego, 1993).

24 José Tamayo Herrera, *Historia social del Cuzco republicano,* 2d. ed. (Lima: Editorial Universo, 1981), 46-49; see also, *El Cuzco y sus provincias* (Arequipa: Imprenta Miranda, 1848). The populations of the Amazon basin and the Andes have differed greatly since the Inca period at least. See José Manuel Váldez y Palacios, *Viaje del Cuzco a Belen en el gran para* (Lima: Biblioteca Nacional del Peru, 1971 [1844]).

25 Michael J. Sallnow, ed., *Pilgrims of the Andes: Regional Cults in Cusco* (Washington, D.C.: Smithsonian Institution Press, 1987).

26 Pedro Celestino Florez, *Guía de forasteros del departamento del Cuzco para el año 1834* (Lima: Imprenta de M. Corral, 1834), 59-61.

27 Gootenberg, "Population," 137-40; Peralta Ruíz, *En pos,* 61-62.

28 Gootenberg, "Population," 137-38; Peralta Ruíz, *En pos,* 61. On social geography in the city of Cuzco, see Ramón Gutierrez, *La casa cusqueña* (Corrientes: Universidad Nacional del Nordeste, 1981), 107-97.

29 With the arrival of people from Africa, Europe, and Asia and widespread miscegenation, the division of colonial society in the sixteenth century into separate republics, Indian and Spanish, had transformed into a kaleidoscope of "caste" groups by the eighteenth century. For works that question the notion of closed caste ranks in colonial Spanish America, demonstrating the permeability of these categories, see Patricia Seed, "Social Dimensions of Race: Mexico City, 1753," *HAHR* 62 (1982): 559-696, and R. Douglas Cope, *The Limits of Racial Domination: Plebeian Society in Colonial Mexico City, 1660-1720* (Madison: University of Wisconsin Press, 1994).

30 For a deconstruction of the term *Indian,* see Irene Silverblatt, "Becoming Indian in the Central Andes of Seventeenth-Century Peru," in *After Colonialism: Imperial Histories and Postcolonial Displacements,* ed. Gyan Prakash (Princeton: Princeton University Press, 1995), 279-98. Among many works on race and ethnicity in the Andes, see Brooke Larson, "Andean Communities, Political Cultures and Markets: The Changing Contours of a Field," and Olivia Harris, "Ethnic Identity and Market Relations: Indians and Mestizos in the Andes," in *Ethnicity, Markets, and Migration in the Andes: At the Crossroads of History and Anthropology,* ed. Brooke Larson and Olivia Harris

(Durham, N.C.: Duke University Press, 1995), 5–53, and 351–390; Thomas Abercrombie, "*Q'aqchas* and *la plebe* in 'rebellion': Carnival vs. Lent in 18th Century Potosí," *Journal of Latin American Anthropology* 2, no. 1 (1996): 62–111; Marisol de la Cadena, "'Las mujeres son más Indias.' Etnicidad y género en una comunidad del Cusco," *Revista Andina* 9, no. 1 (1991): 7–29; Zoila S. Mendoza-Walker, "Contesting Identities through Dance: Mestizo Performance in the Southern Andes of Peru," *Repercussions* 3, no. 2 (1994): 50–80.

31 For a concise summary of the differences between Mexico and Peru, see Florencia Mallon, "Indian Communities, Political Cultures, and the State in Latin America, 1780–1990," *JLAS* 24 (1992): 35–53.

32 These families are studied in Scarlett O'Phelan Godoy, "Aduanas, mercado interno y elite comercial en el Cusco antes y después de la gran rebelión de 1780," *Apuntes* 19 (1986): 53–72.

2 THE TUPAC AMARU REBELLION

1 For example, John A. Hall defines nationalism as "the belief in the primacy of a particular nation, real or constructed; the logic of this position tends to move nationalism from cultural to political forms, and to entail popular mobilization." John A. Hall, "Nationalism: Classified and Explained," *Daedalus* 122, no. 3 (summer 1993), 2. John Breuilly offers a very similar definition in *Nationalism and the State*, 2d ed. (Chicago: University of Chicago Press, 1994), 2. For more culturally attuned definitions, see Brackette Williams, "A Class Act: Anthropology and the Race to Nation across Ethnic Terrain," *Annual Review of Anthropology* 18 (1989): 401–44; Katherine Verdery, "Whither 'Nation' and 'Nationalism'?" in Benedict Anderson, ed., *Mapping the Nation* (London: Verso, 1996), 226–34.

2 John A. Armstrong, *Nations before Nationalism* (Chapel Hill, N.C.: University of North Carolina Press, 1982).

3 Anderson, *Imagined;* E. J. Hobsbawm, *Nations and Nationalism Since 1789* (Cambridge: Cambridge University Press, 1990); Eley and Suny, *Becoming National,* introduction.

4 As Steve Stern has noted, the rebellion's "protonational symbols were tied not to an emerging Creole nationalism, but to notions of an Andean- or Inca-led social order." "The Age of Andean Insurrection, 1742–1782: A Reappraisal," in Stern, ed., *Resistance, Rebellion,* 76.

5 Chatterjee, *Nationalist Thought;* for a contrasting view, see Jorge Klor de Alva, "Colonialism and Post Colonialism as (Latin) American Mirages," *CLAR* 1–2 (1992): 3–23.

6 Mallon, "The Promise and Dilemma"; Gilbert M. Joseph, "On the Trail of Latin American Bandits: A Reexamination of Peasant Resistance," *LARR* 25, no. 3 (1990): 7–53.

7 Hall admits historical sociologists' discomfort with Spanish American independence; "Nationalism," 9–10.

8 Boleslao Lewin, *La Rebelión de Túpac Amaru*, 3d ed. (Buenos Aires: SELA, 1967 [1st ed. 1943]).

9 For a sharp review of the ideological basis of the historiography of the rebellion, see Jean Piel, "¿Cómo interpretar la rebelión panandina de 1780–1783?" in *Tres levantamientos populares: Pugachóv, Túpac Amaru, Hidalgo*, ed. Jean Meyer (Mexico: CEMCA, 1992), 71–80. On the Velasco regime, which published the invaluable document collection *Colección documental de la independencia peruana*, see John Fisher, "Royalism, Regionalism, and Rebellion in Colonial Peru, 1808–1815," *HAHR* 59, no. 2 (May 1979): 232–58. Other reviews of the literature include Stern, "The Age of Andean," in his *Resistance, Rebellion*, 36–43; Carlos Daniel Valcárcel, prologue, CDIP, vol. II, no. 1, pp. xv–xxiv; Alberto Flores Galindo, "Las revoluciones tupamaristas: Temas en debate," *Revista Andina* 7, no. 1 (1989): 279–87.

10 John Rowe, "El movimiento nacional inca del siglo XVIII," in *Túpac Amaru II–1780*, ed. Alberto Flores Galindo (Lima: Retablo de Papel Ediciones, 1976), 13–53.

11 See the magisterial work by Flores Galindo, *Buscando un Inca*. On the construction of national pasts, see Hobsbawm and Ranger, *The Invention*.

12 This is one aspect of the otherwise valuable study by Jan Szeminski, *La utopía tupamarista* (Lima: Pontificia Universidad Católica, 1983). Scarlett O'Phelan Godoy and David Cahill criticize Flores Galindo for conflating the memory of the Incas and the Inca Empire itself. I disagree with their assessment. Scarlett O'Phelan Godoy, "Utopía andina: ¿Para quién? Discursos paralelos a fines de colonia," in O'Phelan Godoy, *La gran rebelión en los Andes: De Tupac Amaru a Tupac Catari* (Cuzco: Centro Bartolomé de Las Casas, 1995), 13–45, esp. 25–26; David Cahill, "Una visión andina: El levantamiento de Ocongate de 1815," *Histórica* 12, no. 2 (1988): 133–59.

13 John Phelan, *The People and the King: The Comunero Revolution in Colombia, 1781* (Madison: University of Wisconsin Press, 1978), esp. 79–88.

14 Alberto Flores Galindo, "La nación como utopía: Tupac Amaru 1780," in *La revolución de los Tupac Amaru: Antología*, ed. Luis Durand Flórez (Lima: CNDBRETA, 1981), 60.

15 For an important discussion of whether to categorize the movement as a rebellion or revolution (postulating the former), see Scarlett O'Phelan Godoy, *Un siglo de rebeliones anticoloniales: Perú y Bolivia, 1700–1783* (Cuzco: Centro Bartolomé de Las Casas, 1988); and for a more recent version, her "Rebeliones andinas anticoloniales: Nueva Granada, Perú y Charcas entre el siglo XVIII y XIX," *Anuario de Estudios Americanos* 49 (1993): 395–440.

16 On the Bourbon reforms as a cause of the Tupac Amaru uprising, see O'Phelan Godoy, *Un siglo;* John Fisher, "La rebelión de Tupac Amaru y el programa

imperial de Carlos III," in Flores Galindo, ed., *Tupac Amaru II*, 107-28. For an overview of the Bourbon reforms, see David Brading, "Bourbon Spain and Its American Empire," in *Colonial Spanish America, The Cambridge History of Latin America*, vols. 1 and 2, selections, ed. Leslie Bethell (Cambridge: Cambridge University Press, 1987), 112-162.

17 On jurisdictional changes and the ensuing confusion about the new viceroyalty, the intendancy system, and shifts in the audiencia, see John Lynch, *Spanish Colonial Administration, 1782-1810* (London: University of London Press, 1958), 65-68; John R. Fisher, *Government and Society in Colonial Peru: The Intendant System, 1784-1814* (London: Athlone Press, 1970), 49-50; Carmen Torero Gomero, "Establecimiento de la audiencia del Cuzco," *Boletín del Instituto Riva Agüero* 8 (1969): 485-91.

18 Nils Jacobsen, *Mirages of Transition: The Peruvian Altiplano, 1780-1930* (Berkeley and Los Angeles: University of California Press, 1993), 41.

19 Jacobsen, *Mirages*, 44; O'Phelan, *Un siglo*, 174-221.

20 Scarlett O'Phelan Godoy, "Revueltas y rebeliones del Perú colonial," in *The Economies of Mexico and Peru during the Late Colonial Period, 1760-1820*, ed. Nils Jacobsen and Hans-Jürgen Puhle (Berlin: Colloquium-Verlag, 1986), 146-48; Jürgen Gölte, *Repartos y rebeliones: Túpac Amaru y las contradicciones de la economía colonial* (Lima: IEP, 1980).

21 Nils Jacobsen, "Peasant Land Tenure in the Peruvian Altiplano in the Transition from Colony to Republic," manuscript (1989), 28-29; Charles F. Walker, "Peasants, Caudillos, and the State in Peru: Cuzco in the Transition from Colony to Republic, 1780-1840," Ph.D. diss. (University of Chicago, 1992), 55-57. The data are from John J. TePaske and Herbert Klein, *The Royal Treasuries of the Spanish Empire in America*, vol. 1, *Peru* (Durham, N.C.: Duke University Press, 1982).

22 Jurgen Gölte calculated an average markup of approximately 300 percent. Gölte, *Repartos*, 104-105 and 120. For critiques of Gölte, see O'Phelan Godoy, *Un siglo*, 117-35, Flores Galindo, *Buscando*, 103-04.

23 Among many studies on the declining role of the caciques, see Brooke Larson, "Caciques, Class Structure and the Colonial State in Bolivia," *Nova Americana* 2 (1979): 197-235, and Núria Sala i Vila, *Y se armó el tole tole: Tributo indígena y movimientos sociales en el virreinato del Perú, 1784-1814* (Lima: IER José María Arguedas, 1996). For an interesting comparative case, see Nancy Farriss, *Mayan Society under Colonial Rule* (Princeton: Princeton University Press, 1984).

24 John Fisher, "Imperial 'Free Trade' and the Hispanic Economy, 1778-1796," *JLAS* 13, no. 1 (1981): 21-56.

25 According to Enrique Tandeter and Nathan Wachtel, "the (Tupac Amaru) rebellion exploded at the end of a long period of low prices." See "Prices and Agricultural Production: Potosí and Charcas in the Eighteenth Century," in

Essays on the Price History of Eighteenth-Century Latin America, ed. Lyman L. Johnson and Enrique Tandeter (Albuquerque: University of New Mexico Press, 1989), 271. Others who note this price trend include Luis Miguel Glave and María Isabel Remy, *Estructura agraria y vida rural en una región andina: Ollantaytambo entre los siglos XVI y XIX* (Cuzco: Centro Bartolomé de Las Casas), 429–53, graph on 439; Luis Miguel Glave, "Agricultura y capitalismo en la sierra sur del Perú (fines del siglo XIX y comienzos de XX)," in *Estados y naciones en los Andes,* vol. 1, ed. J. P. Deler and Y. Saint-Geours (Lima: IEP, 1986), 213–17; Jacobsen, *Mirages,* 95–106. On demographic pressures, see Luis Miguel Glave, *Vida símbolos y batallas: Creación y recreación de la comunidad indígena, Cuzco, siglos XVI–XX,* (Lima: Fondo de Cultura Económica, 1992), 93–115.

26 Jacobsen and Puhle, *The Economies,* 23–24.

27 For arguably the most influential work in this interpretative line, see E. P. Thompson, "The Moral Economy of the English Crowd in the Eighteenth Century," *Past and Present* 50 (1971): 76–136, and "The Moral Economy Reviewed," in *Customs in Common,* ed. E. P. Thompson (New York: New Press, 1991), 259–351. For applications of Thompson and James Scott's notions of moral economy, see Brooke Larson, "Explotación y economía moral en los Andes," in *Reproducción y transformación de las sociedades andinas, siglos XVI–XX,* 2 vols., ed. Segundo Moreno Yañez and Frank Salomon (Quito: Abya-Yala and MLAL, 1991) 2: 441–80; and Ward Stavig, "Ethnic Conflict, Moral Economy, and Population in Rural Cuzco on the Eve of the Thupa Amaro II Rebellion," *HAHR* 68, no. 4 (1988): 737–70.

28 Rowe, "El movimiento."

29 Brading calls the publication of the second edition of the *Comentarios* in 1722 "an incendiary event" for the Indian gentry. David Brading, *The First America: The Spanish Monarchy, Creole Patriots, and the Liberal State, 1492–1867* (Cambridge: Cambridge University Press, 1991), 490. I thank John Rowe for clarifying this point.

30 *Tupac Amaru y la iglesia: Antología* (Cuzco: Edubanco, 1983), 276–77. Lewin, *La rebelión,* 382–88; José Durand, "El influjo de Garcilaso Inca en Túpac Amaru," *COPE* 2, no. 5 (1971): 2–7.

31 Flores Galindo, *Buscando,* 106. On Quechua in the eighteenth century, see César Itier, ed., *Del siglo del oro al siglo de las luces: Lenguaje y sociedad en los Andes del siglo XVIII* (Cuzco: CBC, 1995); Bruce Mannheim, *The Language of the Inka Since the European Invasion* (Austin: University of Texas Press, 1991).

32 See the essays in John Lynch, *Latin American Revolutions, 1808–1826: Old and New World Origins* (Norman: University of Oklahoma Press, 1994), esp. part 5, "Ideas and Interests."

33 Cited in Carlos Daniel Valcárcel, "Fidelismo y separatismo de Túpac Amaru,"

in *La revolución de los Tupac Amaru: Antología,* ed. Luis Durand Flórez (Lima: CNDBRETA, 1981), 366.

34   José Antonio Del Busto Duthurburu, *José Gabriel Tupac Amaru antes de su rebelión* (Lima: Pontificia Universidad Católica del Perú, 1981), 93–95.

35   Robert Schafer, *The Economic Societies in the Spanish World, 1763–1821* (Syracuse, N.Y.: Syracuse University Press, 1958), 157; Victor Peralta Ruíz, "Tiranía o buen gobierno: Escolasticismo y criticismo en el Perú del siglo XVIII," in *Entre la retórica y la insurgencia: Las ideas y los movimientos sociales en los Andes, siglo XVIII,* ed. Charles Walker (Cuzco: Centro Bartolomé de Las Casas, 1996), 67–87.

36   This was the case with the uprising of Arequipa discussed below.

37   Antonello Gerbi, *The Dispute of the New World: The History of a Polemic, 1750–1900* (Pittsburgh: University of Pittsburgh Press, 1973); Brading, *The First America,* 499.

38   Juan José Vega, *José Gabriel Tupac Amaru* (Lima: Editorial Universo, 1969), 13–15; Juan José Vega, *Tupac Amaru y sus compañeros,* vol. 1 (Cuzco: Municipalidad del Qosqo, 1995), 3–21.

39   Cited in Cristobal Aljovín Losada, "Representative Government in Peru: Fiction and Reality, 1821–1845," Ph.D. diss. (University of Chicago, 1996), 221. Lewin argues persuasively that there was no contradiction between being both an "Inca aristocrat" and an "Indian muleteer." Lewin, *La rebelión,* 335–36.

40   John H. Rowe, "Genealogía y rebelión en el siglo XVIII: Algunos antecedentes de la sublevación de José Gabriel Thupa Amaru," *Histórica* 6, no. 1 (July 1982): 65–85, esp. 74–75. Rowe cites one of Tupac Amaru's complaints against Viana's exaggerated repartimiento. For an early glimpse of Tupac Amaru's resolution and disgruntlement, see his strongly worded petition against Geronymo (*sic*) Cano, a tax collector working for Viana. CDIP, II, 2, 20–21.

41   For this case, see the rigorous study of Rowe, "Genealogía." For the documentation, see CDIP, II, 2, 39–75.

42   Rowe, "Genealogía," and John Rowe, "Las circunstancias de la rebelión de Thupa Amaro en 1780," *Revista Histórica* 34 (1983–84): 119–40.

43   For the documentation on Moscoso, see CNDBRETA, vol. II, 1980. For the events in 1779 and 1780, see *Tupac Amaru y la iglesia,* 165–201, introduced by Scarlett O'Phelan Godoy, which contains part of the rich documentation found in the archbishop archive in Cuzco. Analyses of these events include David Cahill, "Crown, Clergy and Revolution in Bourbon Peru: The Diocese of Cuzco, 1780–1814," Ph.D. diss. (University of Liverpool, 1984), 216–34; Iván Hinojosa, "Población y conflictos campesinos en Coporaque (Espinar) 1770–1784," in *Comunidades campesinas: Cambios y permanencias,* ed. Alberto Flores Galindo (Lima: CES Solidaridad, 1987), 229–56; Glave, *Vida símbolos,* chap. 3.

44   Publications on the church in the rebellion include Severo Aparicio, "La acti-

tud del clero frente a la rebelión de Tupac Amaru," in Comisión Nacional del Bicentenario de la Rebelión Emancipadora de Tupac Amaru, *Actas del coloquio internacional Tupac Amaru y su tiempo* (Lima: CNDBRETA, 1982), 71–94; Cahill, "Crown, Clergy"; Emilio Garzón Heredia, "1780: Clero, elite local y rebelión," in Walker, ed., *Entre,* 245–271; Jeffrey Klaiber, "Religión y justicia en Tupac Amaru," *Allpanchis* 19 (1982): 173–86; O'Phelan Godoy, *Un siglo,* 237–43.

45 See O'Phelan Godoy, who correlates these changes and number of revolts in *Un siglo,* 177–80.

46 O'Phelan Godoy, *Un siglo,* 177–80.

47 CDIP, II, 2, 111.

48 CDIP, II, 2, 108.

49 Ibid.; Kendall W. Brown, *Bourbons and Brandy: Imperial Reform in Eighteenth-Century Arequipa* (Albuquerque: University of New Mexico Press, 1986), chap. 9; Lewin, *La rebelión,* 156. For analyses of "death to bad government," see Phelan, *The People;* Eric Van Young, "Millennium on the Northern Marches: The Mad Messiah of Durango and Popular Rebellion in Mexico, 1800–1815," *Comparative Studies in Society and History* 28 (1986): 386–413; and his "Quetzalcóatl, King Ferdinand, and Ignacio Allende Go to the Seashore; or Messianism and Mystical Kingship in Mexico, 1800–1821," in *The Independence of Mexico and the Origins of the New Nation,* ed. Jaime O. Rodriguez (Los Angeles: UCLA Latin American Center, 1989), 176–204.

50 Lewin, *La rebelión,* 158.

51 One began, "We are speaking here / of royal officials / who by robbing / want to make a fortune"; Lewin, *La rebelión,* 155. For other examples, see CDIP, II, 2, 127–28 or 108, which proclaimed "Long Live our Grand Monarch / Long Live Carlos III / and Death to all Customs Officers."

52 CDIP, II, 2, 106–12, quote from 110. This verse frequently invoked noblemen and plebeians.

53 David Cahill, "Taxonomy of a Colonial 'Riot': The Arequipa Disturbances of 1780," in *Reform and Insurrection in Bourbon New Granada and Peru,* ed. John R. Fisher, Allan J. Kuethe, and Anthony McFarlane (Baton Rouge: Louisiana State University Press, 1990), 287. O'Phelan Godoy, *Un siglo,* 202–7.

54 CDIP, II, 2, 112–20.

55 Cahill, "Taxonomy," 270–72 and 276–82.

56 Cahill, "Taxonomy," 272–76; Brown, *Bourbons,* 207–8.

57 Cahill, "Taxonomy," 281–282.

58 Lewin, *La rebelión,* 163.

59 Lewin, *La rebelión,* 163. Guillermo Galdos Rodríguez, "Vinculaciones de las subversiones de Tupac Amaru y de Arequipa en 1780," CNDBRETA, *Actas,* 271–78; Galdos Rodríguez cites a verse from Arequipa that calls for Cuzco to follow. He also noted the use of poems from Arequipa in Cuzco, 272.

60　O'Phelan Godoy, *Un siglo*, 207, notes that even their "small loads of hot peppers" were embargoed.

61　ADC, Libros de Cabildo, no. 27, 1773–80, 161–62.

62　Lewin, *La rebelión*, 164–65.

63　O'Phelan Godoy, *Un siglo*, 208–9.

64　Quoted in O'Phelan Godoy, *Un siglo*, 214. Rowe argues that Tupac Amaru "learned from the errors" of this conspiracy. Rowe, "Las circunstancias," 127.

65　On this uprising, see Víctor Angles Vargas, *El cacique Tambohuacso* (Lima: Industrial Gráfica, 1975), and O'Phelan Godoy, *Un siglo*, 207–17.

66　On the Tupac Katari movement, see María Eugenia del Valle de Siles, *Historia de la rebelión de Túpac Catari, 1781–1782* (La Paz: Editorial Don Bosco, 1990); Sergio Serúlnikov, "Su verdad y su justicia: Tomás Catari y la insurrección Aymara de Chayanta, 1777–1780," in Walker, ed., *Entre*, 205–43; Lewin, *La rebelión*, 500–566.

67　Tupac Amaru owed tribute payments and had other debts. Arriaga demanded payment, threatening to harm the cacique and his family. CDBTU, vol. II, 159–60, 223–25; CDIP II, 2, 735.

68　Lewin, *La rebelión*, 442–43.

69　CNDBRETA, I, 502 and 508. Tupac Amaru reportedly told the priest that "he had orders from Sr. Visitador General, authorized by the real audiencia of Lima." CDIP II, 2, 254.

70　CNDBRETA, I, 504.

71　CNDBRETA, I, 508, document from Dr. Don Miguel Martínez, priest and vicar of Nuñoa and Santa Rosa. He based his account on a conversation with Bolaños and a letter from Eugenio de Silva, parish priest of Sicuani. It is indicative of the rebels' knowledge of the fragility of a Indian-criollo alliance that their call for "union and harmony" was followed by "on the contrary, you will be punished."

72　CDIP II, 2, 255.

73　Jorge Cornejo Bouroncle, *Tupac Amaru: La revolución precursora de la emancipación continental* (Cuzco: n.p., 1949), 493, cited in Vega, *José Gabriel Tupac Amaru*, 48, see also 45–54; Lewin, *La rebelión*, 409–12; CDIP II, 2, 277 and 292–93. Magnus Mörner questions these interpretations, *Perfil*, 125–29.

74　Lewin, *La rebelión*, 446. Lewin notes that Tupac Amaru was often slowed down by such seemingly minor tasks, yet contends that letters such as these had important effects.

75　CNDBRETA, III, 69.

76　Lewin *La rebelión*, 447–53; *Tupac Amaru y la iglesia*, 212–15; Alejandro Seraylán Leiva, *Campañas militares durante la dominación española, Historia general del ejército peruano*, tomo 3, vol. 2 (Lima: Comisión Permanente de Historia del Ejército del Perú, 1981), 609–12.

77　CNDBRETA, I, 422–23.

78 CNDBRETA, I, 424.

79 CNDBRETA, I, 432.

80 Tupac Amaru went to great efforts to mend relations with the church and to assure his followers and others that he was a good Christian. Lewin, *La rebelión,* 450–53, includes a letter from Tupac Amaru to Bishop Moscoso dated December 12 explaining his position. Micaela noted that he claimed that the excommunication did not include him and his inner circle because "God knew their intentions." CDIP, II, 2, 716.

81 Lewin argues that Tupac Amaru presented himself this way to Indians, whereas to Europeans he cast himself as a royal Inca; *La rebelión,* 414–15. Leon Campbell notes the vagueness of the proclamations in this early period. "Ideology and Factionalism during the Great Rebellion, 1780–1782," in Stern, ed., *Resistance,* 122–25.

82 Luis Durand Flórez, "La formulación nacional de (en) los bandos de Tupac Amaru," in Durand Flórez, ed., *La revolución,* 29–49; Flores Galindo, *Buscando,* 138–41. Durand Flórez detected a decrease in the number of times the king of Spain was cited in Tupac Amaru's edicts in November and December.

83 Mallon, *Peasant;* Gyan Prakash, "Introduction" to Prakash, *After Colonialism;* William Roseberry, "Hegemony and the Language of Contention," in Joseph and Nugent, *Everyday Forms,* 355–66.

84 Cited by Durand Flórez, "La formulación," 35.

85 CDIP, II, 2, 272.

86 CNDBRETA, I, 432. According to Lewin, the anti-European fervor "was a simplification accessible to the masses of the colony's greatest political-social problem: that of the chapetón, the vilifier of the Indians and monopolist of power and the economy." Lewin, *La rebelión,* 404.

87 See Szeminski, *Utopia,* and "Why Kill the Spaniard? New Perspectives on Andean Insurrectionary Ideology in the 18th Century," in Stern, ed., *Resistance,* 166–92.

88 CNDBRETA, I, 442.

89 CNDBRETA, I, 458. The author also complained of the puerile attitude of the non-Indian population.

90 On the importance of muleteers, see Mörner, *Perfil,* 119–22; Vega, *José Gabriel;* Flores Galindo, *Buscando,* 111–12. On how news about uprisings spread throughout the continent, see O'Phelan Godoy, "Rebeliones andinas anticoloniales," 438.

91 Studies emphasizing the role of chicherías include Jorge Hidalgo Lehuede, "Amarus y cataris: Aspectos mesiánicos de la rebelión indígena de 1781 en Cuzco, Chayanta, La Paz y Arica," *Chungará* 10 (1983): 117–38, and Scarlett O'Phelan Godoy, "Coca, licor y textiles: El calendario rituálico de la gran rebelión," in O'Phelan Godoy, *La gran rebelión,* 139–85.

92 Flores Galindo, *Buscando,* 115–17.

93 *Tupac Amaru y la iglesia,* 204–5, document from May 19, 1781.

94 CDIP II, 2, 329–30. In another letter, she warned that "if we proceed with lead feet, everthing will be ruined" (331).

95 She was executed alongside José Gabriel and Micaela; CDIP II, 2, 341. On Ana Tomasa Condemayta Hurtado de Mendoza, see Juan José Vega, *Tupac Amaru y sus compañeros,* 2: 409–12. Her trial can be found in CNDBRETA, III, 487–517.

96 CDIP, II, 2, 363 and 371.

97 80 percent of the accused were from Canas y Canchis province; O'Phelan Godoy, *Un siglo,* 228.

98 Flores Galindo, *Buscando,* 112–13. See also Magnus Mörner and Efraín Trelles, "A Test of Causal Interpretations of the Túpac Amaru Rebellion," in Stern, ed. *Resistance,* 94–109.

99 Mörner and Trelles, "A Test," 102, rely on O'Phelan Godoy, "La rebelión de Túpac Amaru, organización interna, dirigencia y alianzas," *Histórica* 3, no. 2 (1979): 89–121, as well as on Leon G. Campbell, "Recent Research on Andean Peasant Revolts, 1750–1820," *LARR* 14, no. 1 (1979): 3–49.

100 O'Phelan Godoy, *Un siglo,* 268. See also Leon G. Campbell, "Social Structure of the Túpac Amaru Army in Cuzco, 1780–81," *HAHR* 61, no. 4 (1981): 675–93.

101 CNDBRETA, I, 460; Lewin, *La rebelión,* 404, for anti-Spanish activities.

102 O'Phelan Godoy, *Un siglo,* 277. See also Jan Szeminski, "La insurrección de Túpac Amaru II: ¿Guerra de independencia o revolución?" in Flores Galindo, ed., *Túpac Amaru II,* 201–28.

103 Mörner and Trelles, "A Test"; Flores Galindo, *Buscando,* 108–14; Leon Campbell, "Women and the Great Rebellion in Peru, 1780–1783," *The Americas* 42, no. 2 (1985): 163–96.

104 ADC, Corregimiento, Causas Comunes, Leg. 61, 1780.

105 CDIP, II, 2, 279.

106 CDIP, II, 2, 282–83. On the weakness of Cuzco's defenses at this point, see CNDBRETA, I, 440 and 484. It should be remembered that Moscoso was facing charges that he supported the rebels, so he presented a particularly vehement stance in these letters to his superiors. His disdain toward Indians, though, rings true for the period.

107 CNDBRETA, I, 484; on the panic in Cuzco, see Leon Campbell, *The Military and Society in Colonial Peru, 1750–1810* (Philadelphia: American Philosophical Society, 1978), 107–12.

108 CNDBRETA, I, 470–89; Abancay, 486.

109 CNDBRETA, III, 78–79.

110 Bishop Moscoso lamented that "because of this, we find ourselves in a confusing chaos, as it is very difficult to plan any action without knowing the situation of the enemy." CDIP, II, 2, 363.

111 CDIP, II, 2, 372.

112 Moscoso attributed the "incomplete victory" in Ocongate to the rebels' rapid retreat: "generally, when the rebels find themselves leaderless as was the case

in these skirmishes, they rarely remain united. They attack tumultuously and at the first casualty they escape to the hills." CDIP, II, 2, 373.

113 Campbell, *The Military*, 117-20, and Campbell, "Ideology," 127; Lewin, *La rebelión*, 453-54. I thank John Rowe for clarifying military aspects of the uprising for me.

114 Among other measures, assemblies of Indians were prohibited. Luis Antonio Eguiguren, *Guerra separatista: Rebeliones de Indios en Sur América, la sublevación de Tupac Amaru. Crónica de Melchor de Paz*, 2 vols. (Lima: n.p., 1952), 1: 252.

115 Campbell, "Ideology," 115-16.

116 Campbell, "Ideology," 128.

117 Lewin, *La rebelión*, 456-57.

118 "They retreated from the city of Cuzco because Indians had been put on the front lines of the enemy, and the rebels did not want to offend them, and because the Mestizos who managed the muskets had become frightened." CDIP, II, 2, 468; Lewin, *La rebelión*, 461. For an informed summary of the battle, see Seraylán Leiva, *Campañas militares*, 621-26.

119 On the hunger of the troops as well as in the city, see CDIP, II, 2, 432-33. Many worried about a bad harvest that year due in large part to the destruction and labor disruption of the rebellion.

120 CDIP, II, 2, 464 and 465.

121 Campbell, "Ideology," 126.

122 Flores Galindo, *Buscando*, 123.

123 Iván Hinojosa, "El nudo colonial: La violencia en el movimiento tupamarista," *Pasado y Presente* 2-3 (Lima) (1989): 73-82.

124 CDIP, II, 2, 413-16.

125 CNDBRETA, I, 433-34.

126 Szeminski, "Why Kill," 171.

127 CDIP, II, 2, 426 and 434.

128 Lewin, *La rebelión*, 458-60.

129 Campbell, *The Military*, 128-33.

130 CDIP, II, 2, 466.

131 CNDBRETA, I, 537-39. The quote is from Lewin, *La rebelión*, 469.

132 On the capture, see L. E. Fisher, *The Last Inca Revolt, 1780-1783* (Norman: University of Oklahoma Press, 1966), 212-41; Lewin, *La rebelión*, 468-72.

133 Richard L. Bushman, *King and People in Provincial Massachusetts* (Chapel Hill, N.C.: Institute of Early American History and Culture, and the University of North Carolina Press, 1985); Joyce Appleby, *Capitalism and a New Social Order: The Republican Vision of the 1790s* (New York: New York University Press, 1984).

134 For alternative nationalisms, see Florencia Mallon, *Peasant;* Guardino, *Peasants;* and Manrique, *Campesinado*—all of which begin with the word *peasant*.

135 Cited in Hinojosa, "El nudo," 79.

136 Cited in Lewin, *La rebelión*, 413.

137 Cited by Leon Campbell, "Crime and Punishment in the Tupacamaru Rebellion in Peru," *Criminal Justice History* 5 (1984), 58.

138 One document noted the plan to make him wear a crown with sharp points piercing his skin and with "three burning iron tips that will puncture his head and come out in his eyes and mouth." *Tupac Amaru y la iglesia*, 204, document from May 3, 1781.

139 *Tupac Amaru y la iglesia*, 270–78.

3 SMOLDERING ASHES

1 Lewin, *La rebelión*, 478–79.

2 For an interesting discussion of the state's ability to reconquer former rebel zones, see James Scott, "Foreword," in Joseph and Nugent, eds., *Everyday Forms*, vii–xii.

3 The question of the legitimacy of the state and the legal system is addressed in the essays in Mindie Lazarus-Black and Susan F. Hirsch, eds., *Contested States: Law, Hegemony and Resistance* (London: Routledge, 1995), particularly the forward by John L. Comaroff and the editors' introduction. Also valuable is the review essay by Sally Engle Merry, "Law and Colonialism," *Law and Society Review* 25, no. 4 (1991): 889–922. For a particularly influential set of essays by historians, see Douglas Hay, Peter Linebaugh, John G. Rule, E. P. Thompson, and Cal Winslow, *Albion's Fatal Tree: Crime and Society in Eighteenth-Century England* (New York: Pantheon Books, 1975).

4 CNDBRETA, II, 245.

5 Fisher, *The Last,* 338–83, quote from 379; also cited in Lewin, *La rebelión,* 702–11. The Katarista rebellion sparked equally if not more brutal measures.

6 Real Academia de Historia, Madrid, Colección Mata Linares (hereafter CML), no. 1994, June 22, 1781, "Informe de Don Antonio Martínez al Visitador General D. José Antonio de Areche sobre los excesos cometidos por los españoles en la represión de Tupac Amaru."

7 Reviews of the repression include Flores Galindo, *Buscando,* 138–41; Pablo Macera, "Noticias sobre la enseñanza elemental en el Perú durante el siglo XVIII," *Trabajos de Historia,* vol. 2. (Lima: INC, 1977), 215–301; and Mannheim, *The Language,* 74–77.

8 "(E)vitar que salte alguna chispa de calor a estas cenizas que aún humean" (emphasis mine), CML, no. 1606, June 30, 1783; also Archivo General de Indias (hereafter AGI), Audiencia del Cuzco, Leg. 35, March 14, 1785.

9 Viceroy Teodoro Croix to Minister Sonora, September 16, 1786, cited by Torero Gomero, "Establecimiento," 400.

10 Torero Gomero, "Establecimiento," 400–2. See also CML, doc. 1926 and 2162.

11 Torero Gomero, "Establecimiento," 404. Durand Flórez cites another docu-

ment that heralded "French freedom." Luis Durand Flórez, *Criollos en conflicto: Cuzco después de Tupac Amaru* (Lima: Universidad de Lima, 1985), 129.

12 Torero Gomero, "Establecimiento," 409, 517.

13 Mata Linares to Gálvez, February 21, 1786, quoted by Fisher, *Government and Society*, 48. In 1784 and 1785, in pasquinades threatening Spaniards, rumors were spread about an uprising.

14 They were the superintendancies of Lima, Arequipa, Cuzco, Huamanga, Huancavelica, Puno, Tarma, and Trujillo. Puno was transferred back to Peru in 1796.

15 John Fisher considers the terms *halting, uncertain,* and *inconsistent* more applicable than *smooth, coherent,* and *masterly* for the reforms. "Soldiers, Society, and Politics in Spanish America, 1750-1821," *LARR* 17, no. 1 (1982): 217. Josep Fontana argues that the reforms were coherent, they represented a single-minded effort to increase state revenues. He ridicules the notion of enlightened despotism, which he considers an oxymoron. "Estado y hacienda en el 'despotismo ilustrada,'" in *Estado, hacienda y sociedad en la historia de España,* ed. Bartolomé Bennassar (Valladolid: Universidad de Valladolid, 1989) 125-47.

16 Tulio Halperín Donghi, *Reforma y disolución de los imperios Ibéricos, 1750-1850* (Madrid: Alianza Editorial, 1985), 70.

17 Cahill, "Crown, Clergy," 245-48; Sala i Vila, *Y se armó,* 78-97; Fisher, *Government and Society,* 93.

18 Stavig, "Ethnic Conflict," 757; Luis Miguel Glave, "Un curacazgo andino y la sociedad campesina del siglo XVII," in Luis Miguel Glave, *Trajinantes: Caminos indígenas en la sociedad colonial siglos XVI/XVII* (Lima: Instituto de Apoyo Agrario, 1989), 281-304. Brooke Larson argues that because of the increased pressures by the state and its representatives on community resources, impositions channeled through the caciques, by the mid-eighteenth century "it was no longer possible for the *caciques* to balance colonial extraction against Andean legitimacy." *Colonialism and Agrarian Transformation in Bolivia: Cochabamba, 1550-1900* (Princeton: Princeton University Press, 1988), 161. See also Karen Spalding, "Social Climbers: Changing Patterns of Mobility among the Indians of Colonial Peru," *HAHR* 50, no. 4 (1970): 645-64, and "Kurakas and Commerce: A Chapter in the Evolution of Andean Society," *HAHR* 54, no. 4 (1973): 581-99. For a less critical view of caciques in the eighteenth century, see Thierry Saignes, "De la borrachera al retrato: Los curacas andinos entre dos legitimidades," *Revista Andina* 5, no. 1 (1987): 139-70.

19 Sala i Vila, *Y se armó,* 68-69.

20 Carlos Díaz Rementería, *El cacique en el virreinato del Perú, estudio histórico-jurídico* (Sevilla: Seminario de Antropología Americana, Universidad de Sevilla, 1977), 233.

21 Archivo de Limítes y Fronteras (hereafter ALF), LB 761, 1798, c. 275, and LB 776, 1799, c. 276.

22 The legal scholar Díaz Rementería doubts that this proposal went into effect. See *El cacique*. What is clear is that the surviving supporters of Tupac Amaru lost their jobs, which was not only preventive punishment but also reflected the fact that many of them had lost a great deal of money during the rebellion and its repression and could no longer cover tribute debts, crucial for a cacique.

23 Sala i Vila, *Y se armó*, 54-56 and 68-76. See also Nuria Sala i Vila, "Revueltas indígenas en el Perú tardocolonial," Ph.D. diss. (Universidad de Barcelona, Departamento de Historia de América, 1989), 208-9, and her "Mistis e indígenas: La lucha por el control de las comunidades indígenas en Lampa, Puno, a fines de la colonia," *Boletín Americanista* 41 (1991): 35-66. Sala i Vila's studies and my research on Cuzco thus question Cahill's argument that "from around 1800, then, local creoles were given a green light to enter into the *cacicazgos*, which means they were permitted to exploit the indigenous sector to the extent that they wished." "Una visión," 138.

24 ADC, Libros, no. 244, 1806, Libro Matriz de los Inventarios de Autos, Registros, Libros y demás papeles que existen en esta escribanía de causas de la real audiencia del Cuzco.

25 Among many studies on this, see Glave, *Vida*, 159-173; René Arze Aguirre, "El cacicazgo en las postrimerías coloniales," *Avances* 1 (1978): 47-50; and Sala i Vila, *Y se armó*, esp. ch. 5.

26 ADC, Asuntos Eclesiásticos (tazmías), Leg. 82, 1782-1786; ADC, Intendencia-Provincias, Causas Criminales (hereafter CC), Leg. 120, 1785.

27 Margareth Najarro Espinoza, "El diezmo y la sociedad indígena del Cuzco (1765-1799)," Licenciatura thesis (Universidad San Antonio del Cuzco, 1995), 138-43.

28 Fisher, *Government*, 129; Mörner poses the question whether the war did not have a positive effect by raising the price for certain goods. *Perfil*, 155-56. See also David Cahill, "Repartos ilícitos y familias principales en el sur andino: 1780-1824," *Revista de Indias* 182-83 (1988): 449-73.

29 Enrique Tandeter et al., "El mercado de Potosí a fines del siglo XVIII," in Harris, Larson, Tandeter, eds. *La participación*, 388. Escandell-Tur emphasizes the impact of competition from Cochambamba. *Producción*, ch. 5.

30 Escandell-Tur, *Producción*, 253-317.

31 ADC, Real Audiencia, CC, Leg. 107, 1792. Alexander Von Humboldt called the mills "filthy jails." Lewin, *La rebelión*, 321. On the use of prisoners in obrajes, see Escandell-Turs, *Producción*, 388-91; Ward Stavig, "Ladrones, cuatreros y salteadores: Indios criminales en el Cuzco rural a fines de la colonia," in *Bandoleros, abigeos y montoneros: Criminalidad y violencia en el Perú, siglos XVIII-XX*, ed. Carlos Aguirre and Charles Walker (Lima: Instituto de Apoyo Agrario, 1990), 72 and 85. For the Mexican case, William Taylor, *Drinking, Homicide and Rebellion in Colonial Mexican Villages* (Stanford, Calif.: Stanford University Press, 1979), 100-101.

32 ADC, Intendencia, CC, Leg. 104, 1787. Guaro is located in Quispicanchis.

33 Glave and Remy, *Estructura agraria*, 429–53.

34 Glave and Remy, *Estructura agraria*, 429–53; in "Prices," Tandeter and Wachtel show a similar downward trend for other southern Andean products in this period. See also Glave, "Agricultura y capitalismo," 213–17; Jacobsen, *Mirages*, 95–106.

35 The data for Cuzco come from TePaske and Klein, *The Royal Treasuries*, vol. 1. Jacobsen found an increase by a factor of fifteen in Puno in the same period. Jacobsen, "Peasant Land Tenure," 28–29. See also Walker, "Peasants, Caudillos," 55–57.

36 Mörner, *Perfil*, 20–21; Gootenberg, "Population and Ethnicity," 128. Jacobsen found rapid growth of the Indian population in Azángaro in the middle of the eighteenth century and a more modest growth of one percent annually from the 1780s into the 1820s. Jacobsen, *Mirages*, 20–22.

37 The inefficiency of the system and the dishonesty of the corregidores who had been charged with tribute collection were legendary.

38 The figure is taken from Gölte, *Repartos*, 104–5; for the markup, 120. In a critique of Gölte, O'Phelan Godoy has pointed out that non-Indians were subject to the reparto and that it was often paid in species and labor. O'Phelan Godoy, *Un siglo*, 117–35.

39 See Cahill, "Repartos ilícitos," passim.

40 Quoted by Jacobsen, *Mirages*, 102. Pablo José Oricaín's comments are an excellent source for social conditions in the period. In general, though, depictions of peasants' poverty must be taken with great caution; for outsiders, it is difficult to differentiate between rich and poor peasants or good and bad times. "Compendio breve de discursos varios," in *Juicio de límites entre el Perú y Bolivia: Prueba peruana*, vol. 11, ed. Víctor Maurtua (Barcelona: Imprenta de Henrich y Comp., 1906), 310–77.

41 Oricaín, "Compendio," 327.

42 Enrique Tandeter has analyzed the difficulties faced by peasants in the 1804–1805 crisis in Potosí. The predicament provoked by a drought, epidemics, and the decline of the Potosí mine was only aggravated by fiscal demands. "Crisis in Upper Peru, 1800–1805," *HAHR* 71, no. 1 (1991): 35–71.

43 Jacobsen, *Mirages*, 95–106. Glave argues that in this period "peasants recovered their role as producers of foodstuffs," "Agricultura y capitalismo," 217.

44 Farriss, *Maya Society*, 366–75.

45 Larson notes a similar phenomenon in Cochabamba. She argues that "the strong presence of the state, following the great Indian rebellions, and its renewed effort to intervene in the public domain, probably encouraged some peasants to engage in 'judicial politics' against their immediate overlords, even at a great risk to their own future." *Colonialism*, 201. See also Cahill, "Una visión andina," 138.

46 Stavig, "Ethnic Conflict," 739.

47 Tristan Platt, *Estado boliviano y ayllu andino: Tierra y tributo en el norte de Potosí* (Lima: IEP, 1982), chap. 2; Tristan Platt, "Liberalism and Ethnocide in the Southern Andes," *History Workshop Journal* 17 (1984): 3–18.

48 For analyses of the litigious nature of Andean peasants past and present, see Linda Seligmann, *Between Reform and Revolution: Political Struggles in the Peruvian Andes, 1969–1991* (Stanford, Calif.: Stanford University Press, 1995); Steve Stern, *Peru's Indian Peoples and the Challenge of Spanish Conquest, Huamanga to 1640* (Madison: University of Wisconsin Press, 1982); Franklin Pease, "¿Por qué los andinos son acusados de litigiosos?" manuscript, 1995; Eric Hobsbawm, "Peasant Land Occupations," *Past and Present* 62 (1974), esp. 120–26.

49 Torero Gomero, "Establecimiento," 388. Cutter notes that the establishment of an audiencia was seen as a panacea in northern New Spain in the same period. Charles R. Cutter, *The Legal Culture of Northern New Spain, 1700–1810* (Albuquerque: University of New Mexico Press, 1995), 68.

50 For the creation of the real audiencia, see Torero Gomero, "Establecimiento."

51 For summaries of the colonial legal system, see H. H. A. Cooper, "A Short History of Peruvian Criminal Procedure and Institutions," *Revista de Derecho y Ciencias Políticas* 32 (1968): 215–67, especially 225–39; Colin MacLachlan, *Criminal Justice in Eighteenth-Century Mexico: A Study of the Tribunal of the Acordada* (Berkeley and Los Angeles: University of California Press, 1974); and Woodrow Wilson Borah, *Justice by Insurance: The General Indian Court of Colonial Mexico and the Legal Aides of the Half-Real* (Berkeley and Los Angeles: University of California Press, 1983).

52 These officials did not have authority to try major crimes such as homicide or subversion and could not sentence criminals to obrajes. Stavig, "Ladrones, cuatreros," 77.

53 Because evidence of the local practice of justice appeared in the formal legal system only when this behavior was so abusive as to merit a lawsuit, more benevolent practices are neglected. Clearly, the trials reviewed do not provide a satisfactory portrayal of local justice. In the transcripts of one trial, a reference is made to a jail in the home of one of Cuzco's prestigious families, Doña Marquesa de Rocafuerte. ADC, Real Audiencia, CC, Leg. 125, 1801.

54 Oral history can penetrate criminal behavior and any punishment excluded from the formal, written records. See Ricardo Valderrama Fernández and Carmen Escalante Gutiérrez, " 'Nuestras vidas' (abigeos de Cotabambas)," in *Bandoleros,* ed. Carlos Aguirre and Charles Walker, 307–34. For analyses of crime in late colonial Peru, see Ward Stavig, "Violencia cotidiana de los naturales de Quispicanchis y Canas y Canchis en el siglo XVIII," *Revista Andina* 3, no. 2 (1986): 451–68; and Bernard Lavalle, "Presión colonial y reivindicación indígena en Cajamarca (1785-1820) según el Archivo del 'Protector de Naturales,'" *Allpanchis* 35–36 (1991): 105–37.

55 Taylor, *Drinking*, 91–92. Testimonies therefore can illuminate the subject population's notions about the state, what it wanted to hear, and what it accepted. See also Joseph, "On the Trail."

56 For an interesting critique of historians' decontextualization of trial records— essentially the coercive, foreign environment faced by defendants—see Renato Rosaldo's analysis of E. LeRoy Ladurie's classic *Montaillou*. Renato Rosaldo, "From the Door of His Tent," in *Writing Culture: The Poetics and Politics of Ethnography*, ed. James Clifford and George Marcus (Berkeley and Los Angeles: University of California Press, 1986), 77–97.

57 These percentages consider only the category *abuses*. In many trials, numerous defendents were named, thus explaining why the totals surpass 100 percent. In the category fraud, which I did not include, I have a variety of culprits, including many caciques. I have not included this category because of the heterogeneity of the crimes and the small number of cases.

58 ADC, Real Audiencia, cc, Leg. 142, 1816.

59 ADC, Real Audiencia, cc, Leg. 105, 1790.

60 ADC, Libros, #289, Libros de Tomas de Razón de los Autos y Documentos que se libren por la Suprema Tribunal, Real Audiencia, 1806.

61 ADC, Intendencia, cc, Leg. 107, 1792.

62 ADC, Intendencia, cc, Leg. 112, 1803.

63 ADC, Intendencia, cc, Leg. 142, 1817.

64 Cahill, "Crown, Clergy," 146. See also Scarlett O'Phelan Godoy, "El sur andino a fines del siglo XVIII: Cacique o corregidor," *Allpanchis* 11–12 (1978): 17–32.

65 This rift was due both to the general effort of the state to gain access to a greater share of the church's income, including priests' income, and to local disputes over resources, particularly the indigenous peasantry's. See David Cahill, "Curas and Social Conflict in the Doctrinas of Cuzco, 1780–1814," *JLAS* 16 (1984): 241–76, and his "Repartos ilícitos." Núria Sala i Vila, "Gobierno colonial, iglesia y poder en Perú: 1784–1814," *Revista Andina* 11, no. 1 (1993): 133–61, and Sala i Vila, "Algunas reflexiones sobre el papel jugado por la iglesia y el bajo clero en las parroquias de Indios en Perú (1784–1812)," in *La venida del reino*, ed. Gabriela Ramos (Cuzco: Centro Bartolomé de Las Casas, 1994), 339–62.

66 ADC, Libros, no. 244, Libro Matriz de los Inventarios de Autos, Registros, Libros y demás papeles que existen en esta Escribanía de causas de la Real Audiencia del Cuzco, 1806, 77–79.

67 Ibid., 97–101.

68 ADC, Real Audiencia, cc, Leg. 103, 1789. For some examples of exploitative practices, see Sala i Vila, *Y se armó*, 78–84.

69 Cited in Christine Hünefeldt, *Lucha por la tierra y protesta indígena: Las comunidades indígenas del Perú entre colonia y república* (Bonn: Bonner Amerikanische Studien, 1982), 23. For another example of ayllu members demand-

ing that authorities be selected from the local population, see Stavig, "Ethnic Conflict," 760, document from 1778.

70   ADC, Intendencia-Provincias, cc, Leg. 120, 1785; and Intendencia, cc, Leg. 103, 1784.

71   ADC, Real Audiencia, cc, Leg. 110, 1793.

72   ADC, Real Audiencia, cc, Leg. 110, 1793.

73   ADC, Real Audiencia, cc, Leg. 111, 1793, from which the subdelegate's quote is taken; Real Audiencia, cc, Leg. 114, 1795; Real Audiencia, cc, Leg. 116, 1795; and Real Audiencia, cc, Leg. 120, 1798. For another case involving Aymitumi, see Intendencia-Provincias, cc, Leg. 120, 1786. Other examples of cases against caciques named after the Tupac Amaru rebellion can be found in ADC, Real Audiencia, cc, Leg. 134, 1897; Real Audiencia, cc, Leg. 113, 1794; Real Audiencia, cc, Leg. 111, 1793; and Intendencia, cc, Leg. 109, 1797.

74   Real Audiencia, cc, Leg. 116, 1795; and Real Audiencia, cc, Leg. 120, 1798. This case is also reviewed in Sala i Vila, *Y se armó*, 135-39.

75   ADC, Real Audiencia, cc, Leg. 111, 1793.

76   ADC, Real Audiencia, cc, Leg. 144, 1820.

77   Mark A. Burkholder, *Politics of a Colonial Career: José Baquíjano and the Audiencia of Lima* (Albuquerque: University of New Mexico Press, 1980), 53-54.

78   See Phelan, *The People*, esp. 79-88.

79   ADC, Intendencia, cc, Leg. 109, 1797. See also Ward Stavig, " 'Living in Offense of Our Lord': Indigenous Sexual Values and Marital Life in the Colonial Crucible," *HAHR* 75, no. 4 (1995): 597-622.

80   ADC, Real Audiencia, cc, Leg. 118, 1797.

81   ADC, Intendencia, cc, Leg. 112, 1803.

82   ADC, Intendencia, cc, Leg. 107, 1792.

83   It is impossible to evaluate how much of this was sincere outrage rather than a calculated legal tactic.

84   For an intelligent analysis of the logic of sentencing in colonial Spanish America, see Taylor, *Drinking,* 102. See also Ruth Pike, "Penal Servitude in the Spanish Empire: Presidio Labor in the Eighteenth Century," *HAHR* 58, no. 1 (1978): 21-40; Cutter, *The Legal Culture,* 125-46; Ricardo D. Salvatore and Carlos Aguirre, "The Birth of the Penitentiary in Latin America: Toward an Interpretive Social History of Prisons," in *The Birth of the Penitentiary in Latin America: Essays on Criminology, Prison Reform, and Social Control, 1830-1940,* ed. Ricardo D. Salvatore and Carlos Aguirre (Austin: University of Texas Press, 1996), 1-43.

85   The courts showed little ambiguity in their treatment of participants in the Tupac Amaru rebellion. For any litigant, loyalty during the Tupac Amaru rebellion benefited his or her case, whereas any hint of favor toward the rebels had dire consequences. In 1792, a cacique accused of pocketing tribute money defended himself by stressing his royalist efforts during the rebellion. In the

same year, in a case against a defendant accused of "seducing and perturbing these idiotic and ignorant peoples," prosecutors emphasized his role in the rebellion more than a decade earlier. Some defendants pushed their loyal lineage even farther back. In a case involving Andahuaylas of the Ayacucho area, references were made to its support for the Spanish in the sixteenth century. ADC, Real Audiencia, CC, Leg. 107, 1792; Leg. 108, 1792; Intendencia, Gobierno, Leg. 151, 1816–18.

86 Lazarus-Black and Hirsch, *Contested States.*

87 Gölte found that Indian communities' frustrations with the expensive and protracted lawsuits against abusive officials encouraged more radical, direct actions. Gölte, *Repartos,* 134. See also the splendid essay by Sergio Serúlnikov, "Su verdad."

4 THE ARRIVAL OF SAINT PATRIA

1 Viotti da Costa notes that "Before Independence, the class and racial conflict latent in Brazilian society could be disguised among the revolutionary ranks." Emilia Viotti da Costa, *The Brazilian Empire: Myths and Histories* (Chicago: University of Chicago Press, 1985), 12. For a similar argument regarding what became Argentina, see José Carlos Chiaramonte, "Formas de identidad en el Río de la Plata luego de 1810," *Boletín del Instituto de Historia Argentina y Americana "Dr. E. Ravignani,"* 3d series, 1, no. 1 (1989): 71–92. In Mexico, as in Peru, the divisions emerged immediately.

2 Heraclio Bonilla and Karen Spalding, "La independencia en el Perú: Las palabras y los hechos," in *La independencia en el Perú,* 2d ed., ed. Heraclio Bonilla (Lima, IEP, 1972). Bonilla develops these arguments in "Estado y clase populares en el Perú de 1821," in Bonilla and Spalding, eds., *Independencia,* 2d ed. (Lima: IEP, 1981). Jorge Basadre provides the most sophisticated critique in *El azar en la historia y sus límites* (Lima: Ediciones P.V.L., 1973). Other historians reacted with less constraint (and foundation).

3 Alberto Flores Galindo, *Aristocracia y plebe: Lima, 1760–1830 (Estructura de clases y sociedad colonial)* (Lima: Mosca Azul Editores, 1984), 227. See also Alberto Flores Galindo, "Soldados y montoneros," in *Buscando;* Scarlett O'Phelan Godoy, "El mito de la 'independencia concedida': Los programas políticos del siglo XVIII y del temprano XIX en el Perú y Alto Perú (1730–1814)," in *Independencia y revolución,* 2 vols., ed. Alberto Flores Galindo (Lima: INC, 1987), 2: 145–99. On independence in Spanish America, see John Lynch, *The Spanish American Revolutions* (New York: W. W. Norton, 1973).

4 I would like to thank Peter Guardino for clarifying this point. See his *Peasants* and "Identity and Nationalism." For an incisive critique of teleological views on independence, see Eric Van Young, "The Other Rebellion: A Social Profile of Popular Insurgency in Mexico, 1810–1815," manuscript, 1994.

5   Alberto Flores Galindo, "Los sueños de Gabriel Aguilar," in Flores Galindo, *Buscando,* 144–200; John Fisher, "Regionalism and Rebellion in Late Colonial Peru: The Aguilar-Ubalde Conspiracy of 1805," *Bibliotheca Americana* 1, no. 1 (1982): 44–59.

6   Quoted by Benito de la Mata Linares. CML, no. 3426, "Respuestas fiscales en la causa de la intentada sublevación del Cuzco de 1805, January 14, 1807," 629. The judge also noted that Tupac Amaru had intended to crown an Inca. See Fisher, "Regionalism and rebellion," 54, for a similar quote.

7   ADC, Intendencia, Gobierno, Leg. 147, 1805, 18.

8   ADC, Intendencia, Gobierno, Leg. 147, 1805, 14–16.

9   The state responded to grain shortages in Upper Peru and the southern Andes from 1801 through 1805 with various measures, including the forced sale of harvest to public grain warehouses. Tandeter, "Crisis," 40–43. Nuria Sala i Vila, "La revuelta de Julí en 1806: Crisis de subsistencia y economía campesina," *Revista de Indias* 192 (1991): 343–74.

10 ADC, Intendencia, Gobierno, Leg. 147, 1805.

11 James Lockhart and Stuart B. Schwartz, *Early Latin America: A History of Colonial Spanish America and Brasil* (Cambridge: Cambridge University Press, 1983), 419–23, quote from 419.

12 Halperín Donghi, *Reforma y disolución;* José Carlos Chiaramonte, ed., *Pensamiento de la ilustración: Economía y sociedad iberoamericana en el siglo XVIII* (Caracas: Biblioteca Ayacucho, 1979); Brading, *The First,* part 3; Lynch, *Latin American,* 5–38; 241–85.

13 Among many works on this period, see Jean-Rene Aymes, ed., *España y la Revolución Francesa* (Barcelona: Editorial Crítica, 1989).

14 For an analysis of the term *nation,* see James F. King, "The Colored Castes and American Representation in the Cortes of Cadiz," HAHR 33, no. 1 (1953), 53. See also Quijada, "¿Qué nación?"

15 David Bushnell, "The Independence of Spanish South America," in *The Independence of Latin America, The Cambridge History of Latin America,* vol. 3, ed. Leslie Bethell (Cambridge: Cambridge University Press, 1987), 98. See also O'Phelan Godoy, "El mito," 154–55; O'Phelan Godoy, "Por el rey, religión y las patrias: Las juntas de gobierno de 1809 en La Paz y Quito," *Boletín del Instituto Francés de Estudios Andinos* 17, no. 2 (1988): 61–81.

16 Lynch, *Spanish American Revolutions,* 124.

17 René Danilo Arze Aguirre, *Participación popular en la independencia de Bolivia.* (La Paz: OEA, 1979); Lizardo Seiner, "Economía, sociedad y política en una coyuntura rebelde: Tacna, 1811–1814," *Pasado y Presente* 2–3 (Lima) (1989): 85–99.

18 Fernando Díaz Venteo, *Las campañas militares del Virrey Abascal* (Sevilla: EEH-A, 1948).

19 Fisher, *Government and Society,* 204.

20 Guha, *Elementary Forms,* 251. Throughout this book, I treat rumors and the

relationship between written and oral cultures. On this topic, see Arlette Farge, *Subversive Words: Public Opinion in Eighteenth-Century France* (University Park: Penn State University Press, 1995), esp. 57–58.

21 Pumacahua to Ramírez, CDIP, XXVI, 1, 430. On rumors in this uprising, see Víctor Peralta Ruíz, "Elecciones, constitucionalismo y revolución en el Cusco, 1809–1815," in *Partidos políticos y elecciones en América Latina y la Península Ibérica, 1830–1930*, ed. Carlos Malamud, 2 vols. (Madrid: Instituto Universitario Ortega y Gasset, 1995).

22 CDIP, V, 1, 76–79.

23 ADC, Real Audencia, CC, Leg. 137, 1809.

24 ADC, Real Audencia, CC, Leg. 137, 1809. The author noted that the Spanish and the soldiers expected help from Joseph I.

25 ADC, Real Audencia, CC, Leg. 137, 1809.

26 Although the term *vecino* excluded women, minors, mestizos, and those of African descent, its exact composition was amorphous. On the contentious debates about the voting rights and Americans of African descent, see King, "The Colored Castes."

27 Marie Laure Rieu-Millan, *Los diputados americanos en las Cortes de Cádiz* (Madrid: CSIC, 1990), 48–52 and, for the social composition, 58–68. See also Timothy E. Anna, *The Fall of the Royal Government in Peru* (Lincoln: University of Nebraska Press, 1979), 82–84.

28 Hünefeldt, *Lucha*, 49. David Cahill argues that "despite the limitations and difficulties of communications in the period, Peruvians of all castes and classes were informed about the development of political and military events in Spain and any other part of the empire and especially of the radical reforms of the Courts." Cahill, "Una visión andina," 141; O'Phelan Godoy, "El mito," 154.

29 ADC, Libros de Cabildo, no. 29, 1811–13, 62–63.

30 CDIP, IV, 2, 50–51.

31 In chapter 6, I analyze at greater length views on the Indians. On the "Great Fear" and discourse on the Indians in the interregnum, see Pablo Macera, "El indio y sus interpretes peruanos del siglo XVIII," in *Trabajos de Historia*, 4 vols., ed. Pablo Macera (Lima: Instituto Nacional de Cultura, 1977), 2: 317–24; Cecilia Méndez, *Incas sí, Indios no: Apuntes para el estudio del nacionalismo criollo en el Perú* (Lima: IEP, 1993); and Walker, "Voces discordantes: Discursos alternativos sobre el Indio a fines de la colonia," in Walker, ed. *Entre,* 89–112.

32 Opponents to the inclusion of Indians argued that they were minors, ignorant, dirty, did not know Spanish, and would participate in great numbers. Fray Cesáreo de Armellada, *La causa indígena americana en las Cortes de Cádiz* (Madrid: Ediciones Cultura Hispánica, 1959), 21. See also Rieu-Millan, *Los diputados,* chap. 4; King, "The Colored Castes"; and Hünefeldt, *Lucha.*

33 Rieu-Millan, *Los diputados,* 111–12.

34 A Mexican representative claimed that Newton and Leibnitz "wouldn't have been more than a couple of dullards [*rudos*]" if they received the education provided to Indians. Rieu-Millan, *Los diputados,* 112–13. The Peruvian contingent remained divided on the question whether education could reform Indians, the doubts centering on their rationality rather than on the efficacy of learning.

35 Rieu-Millan, *Los diputados,* 129.

36 Hünefeldt, *La lucha,* 161–64; Sala i Vila, *Y se armó,* 163–90.

37 Cahill, "Una visión," 142–44; Sala i Vila, *Y se armó,* 156–58 and 170–90.

38 Christine Hünefeldt, "Los indios y la Constitución de 1812," *Allpanchis* 11–12 (1978), 35–40. For summaries of the tribute reforms, see Anna, *The Fall,* 53–66, and Brian Hamnett, *Revolución y contrarrevolución en México y el Perú: Liberalismo, realeza y separatismo, 1800–1824* (Mexico City: Fondo de Cultura, 1978), 122–26.

39 Anna, *The Fall,* 61.

40 For a persuasive argument, see Sala i Vila, *Y se armó,* 179–90.

41 For examples, see Hünefeldt, *La lucha,* 165–67.

42 Hünefeldt, *La lucha,* 171.

43 CDIP, III, 7, 3–4. For an analysis of the cabildo-audiencia tensions and the divisions within the rebel forces, see Peralta Ruíz, "Elecciones."

44 Oficio de Pumacahua al virrey de Lima, April 26, 1813, in Jorge Cornejo Bouroncle, *Pumacahua: La revolución del Cuzco de 1814* (Cusco: Editorial H. G. Rozas, 1956), 232–236, quote from 235.

45 Cornejo Bouroncle, *Pumacahua,* 240–43, Mariano Arriago, February 6, 1816; CDIP, III, 7, noticia de lo ocurrido, November 5, 1813, 134–42, and 166.

46 Basadre, *El azar,* 130; Fisher, *Government,* 228.

47 Cornejo Bouroncle, *Pumacahua,* 261–64, letters to the virrey.

48 Ibid., 236.

49 Ibid., 657.

50 Ibid., 658.

51 CDIP, III, 6, 169 and 232–33.

52 Cornejo Bouroncle, *Pumacahua,* 261; see also Peralta Ruíz, "Elecciones."

53 Cited in Cornejo Bouroncle, *Pumacahua,* 361.

54 Cornejo Bouroncle, *Pumacahua,* 369–70. Juan José Alcón, in CDIP, XXVI, 1, 394. For summaries of the military campaigns, see Fisher, *Government,* 201–32; Lynch, *The Spanish American,* 117–26.

55 On Puno, see CDIP, III, 8, 138, testimony by Martin Castillo; also José Fernando Abascal y Sousa, *Memoria de gobierno,* 2 vols., ed. Vicente Rodríguez Casado and José Antonio Calderón Quijano (Sevilla: EEH-A, 1944), 2: 214; Luis Antonio Eguiguren, *La revolución de 1814* (Lima: La Opinión Nacional, 1914), 47–55.

56 CDIP, III, 7, 329–30.

57 CDIP, III, 8, 46.
58 José Rufino Echenique, *Memorias para la historia del Perú (1808–1878)*, 2 vols. (Lima: Editorial Huascarán, 1952), 1: 4–5.
59 CDIP, III, 7, 268–29.
60 CDIP, XXVI, 1, 415–18. Ramírez did note that the rebels had effective new artillery (*vibrones*) cast in Cuzco.
61 Cornejo Bouroncle, *Pumacahua*, 400–404.
62 CDIP, III, 8, 145.
63 Cornejo Bouroncle, *Pumacahua*, 472–474.
64 CDIP, III, 8, 8. Sala i Vila detected increasing violence in this latter stage, particularly against mestizos. See Nuria Sala i Vila, "La participación indígena en la rebelión de los Angulo y Pumacahua, 1814–1816," in *Conquista y resistencia en la historia de América*, ed. Pilar García Jordan and Michael Izard (Barcelona: Universitat de Barcelona, 1992), 273–88, and Sala i Vila, *Y se armó*, chap. 9. The rebellion also continued in Ocongate, Quispicanchis, in 1815. Cahill, "Una visión," 147–56. See also David Cahill and Scarlett O'Phelan Godoy, "Forging Their Own History: Indian Insurgency in the Southern Peruvian Sierra, 1815," *Bulletin of Latin American Research* 11, no. 2, (1992), esp. 140–53.
65 CDIP, III, 7, 166.
66 CDIP, XXVI, 2, 74. The author of the account develops a familiar contrast between dignified, white Arequipa and savage, Indian Cuzco.
67 ADC, Intendencia, Gobierno, Leg. 151, 1819.
68 CDIP, III, 7, 349–51. La Paz had been the site of a violent siege during the Tupac Katari revolt.
69 CDIP, III, 7, 478–79; and Cornejo Bouroncle, *Pumacahua*, 456–77. See also Heraclio Bonilla, "Clases populares y estado en el contexto de la crisis colonial," in *La independencia en el Perú*, 2d ed., ed. Heraclio Bonilla, (Lima: IEP, 1981), 50.
70 Jorge Basadre summarizes some of the "atrocities," *El azar*, 144–46.
71 CDIP, III, 7, 366–68; Bonilla, "Clases," 53–54.
72 Rodríguez Casado and Calderón Quijano, *Memoria de Gobierno*, 193. See also CDIP, III, 8, 79.
73 CDIP, III, 7, 612.
74 Cited in Fisher, *Government*, 230.
75 Virtually every study of the Pumacahua rebellion has made this argument to some degree. See Basadre, *El azar*, 141–44; Bonilla, "Clases," 52–55; Fisher, "Royalism," 255–57; O'Phelan Godoy, "El mito, 168–72"; Sala i Vila, *Y se armó*, 242–45.
76 ADC, Real Audencia, CC, Leg. 111, 1793.
77 ADC, Intendencia, Gobierno, Leg. 149, 1809–14.
78 Quoted by Hünefeldt, *La lucha*, 51.

79   Cornejo Bouroncle, *Pumacahua,* 456–57. I thank John Rowe for pointing this out to me.

80   Cited in Nuria Sala i Vila, "De Inca a indígena: Cambio en la simbología del sol a principios del siglo XIX," *Allpanchis* 35–36, no. 2 (1991): 619.

81   See the critique by David Cahill and Scarlett O'Phelan Godoy in an otherwise valuable article. Cahill and O'Phelan Godoy, "Forging," 132. Flores Galindo responds to previous and much more tendentious misunderstandings of his work in "El rescate de la tradición: Prólogo," in Carlos Arroyo, *Encuentros: Historia y movimientos sociales en el Perú* (Lima: MemoriAngosta, 1989), 9–21.

82   CML, no. 3427, Expediente sobre la permanencia de las tropas del Regimento de Lima en la ciudad del Cuzco y sobre el movimiento de sedición en el partido de Azángaro," Lima, September 10, 1790.

83   For some examples, see Horacio Villanueva Urteaga, "La idea de los Incas como factor favorable a la independencia," *Revista Universitaria* (Cuzco) 115 (1958), 153–57.

84   On the variety of political options considered during the period and the effects of the war itself, see Guardino, *Peasants,* chap. 2; Van Young, "The Other Rebellion."

85   Anna, *The Fall,* 176–238; Lynch, *The Spanish American,* chaps. 4–5.

86   Flores Galindo, *Aristocracia,* 209–16.

87   Jaime Eyzaguirre, "Los sospechosos de infidelidad en la Lima de 1813," *Mercurio Peruano* 35, no. 133 (1954): 951–60; Raúl Porras Barrenechea, *Los ideólogos de la independencia* (Lima: Milla Batres, 1974), 49–114.

88   Works on the guerrilla bands include Ezequiel Beltrán Gallardo, *Las guerrillas de Yauyos en la emancipación del Perú* (Lima: Técnicos Asociados, 1977); Flores Galindo, *Buscando,* chap. 7; Peter Guardino, "Las guerrillas y la independencia peruana: Un ensayo de interpretación," *Pasado y Presente* (Lima) 2–3 (1989): 101–17; Raúl Rivera Serna, *Los guerrilleros del centro en la emancipación peruana* (Lima: P. L. Villanueva, 1958); and the rich documentation in CDIP V, 1–6, edited by Ella Dunbar Temple.

89   Basadre, *La iniciacion,* 76–80; Charles Walker, "The Patriotic Society: Discussions and Omissions about Indians in the Peruvian War of Independence," *The Americas* 55 (1998): 2.

90   ALF, no. 570, 26 August 1817. The French social critic and utopian socialist Flora Tristan provides a lively description of her uncle, Pío de Tristán. Flora Tristan, *Peregrinations of a Pariah,* translated, edited, and introduced by Jean Hawkes (London: Virago, 1986), 76–79. A recent biography of Paul Gauguin, Flora Tristan's grandson, errs in most aspects about the Tristan family in this period. David Sweetman, *Paul Gauguin: A Complete Life* (London: Hodder & Stoughton, 1995).

91   ADC, Intendencia, Gobierno, Leg. 152, 1818–19. Other emotional pleas from beleaguered tax collectors can be found here as well.

92 ALF, no. 612, October 26, 1817.

93 ALF, no. 612, October 26, 1817.

94 ADC, Libros de Cabildo, no. 31, 1813–22, November 1820, 60. See also the report by Don Ignacio de Alcázar y Carbajal who describes the sorry condition of the sugar estates and other haciendas in Andahuaylas, and the severe shortage of mules due to the war. ADC, Intendencia, Gobierno, Leg. 151, 1816–18.

95 ADC, Libros de Cabildo, no. 31, 1833–22, May 22, 1822.

96 Biblioteca Nacional del Perú (hereafter BN), Manuscripts, 1818, D565, "Expediente reservado sobre la revolución de algunos pueblos del Partido de Aymaraes y asesinato del subdelegado de él, Don José de la Paliza, Octubre 1818." Many of the documents included in this packet are reproduced in Hünefeldt, *Lucha*, 215–22. See also Nuria Sala i Vila, "El levantamiento de los pueblos de Aymaraes en 1818," *Boletín Americanista* 39–40 (1989–90): 203–226.

97 ADC, Intendencia, Gobierno, Leg. 152, 1818–19.

98 ADC, Intendencia, Gobierno, Leg. 152, 1818–19, 25.

99 ALF, LB 947, caja 283, Libro copiador del intendente del Cuzco a los intendentes de Arequipa y Puno, 29, September 27, 1818.

100 CDIP, VIII, 2, 238–39, letter from October 13, 1818.

101 Sala i Vila, "El levantamiento," 222.

102 Sala i Vila, "El levantamiento," 222–23.

103 In September 1821, Prieto reportedly commanded two hundred soldiers in Totos in the central Andes. CDIP, V, 1, 371.

104 ADC, Intendencia, CC, Leg. 119, 1824. As the Shining Path demonstrated in the 1980s, the area between Ayacucho and Aymaraes region in the central Andes and Ica on the coast proved to be a convenient corridor for the movement of insurgents.

105 CDIP, V, 1, 426; ALF, CSG, Tristán to Virrey, no. 1350, March 30, 1821.

106 See the case of Isidoro Toro in ADC, Real Audencia, CC, Leg. 143, 1819, and the case of Mariano Quispe Condori, in ibid., 144, 1820.

107 ADC, Real Audencia, CC, Leg. 143, 1819.

108 ADC, Real Audencia, CC, Leg. 143, 1819.

109 ALF, CSG-60, Libro de Correspondencia de MI Sr. Gov. Presidente Don Pio de Tristán con el Ex. Sr. Virrey, desde el 29 de Noviembre (hasta 20 Diciembre 1824), no. 1232.

110 ALF, CSG, Tristán to Virrey, no. 1350, March 30, 1821. On this uprising, see Mariano Felipe Paz Soldán, *Historia del Perú independiente (Primer Periodo), 1819–1822* (Havre: Imprenta de Alfonso LEMALE, 1868), 160–61; CDIP XXVI, 4, 196–99; Manuel de Odriozola, *Documentos históricos del Perú*, 3 vols. (Lima: Imprenta del Estado, 1872), 3: 290–91. Lavín and other leaders had been arrested in Arequipa in September 1820 for a conspiracy and sent to Cuzco.

111 CDIP, VIII, 2, 41, letter from January 29, 1819.

112 CDIP, V, 1, 368.

113 ALF, 1409, letter dated October 8, 1821.

114 CDIP, V, 1, 391–92. Pardo de Zela noted that his troops needed arms and clothing; they couldn't patrol in the evenings because of the cold.

115 ADC, Intendencia, CC, Leg. 119, 1822.

116 CDIP, XXII, 3, 2–3.

117 John Fisher argues that after the Pumacahua rebellion, Cuzco, more interested in its regional demands than national projects, gave up on the independence struggle and sought to gain favor by supporting the viceroy. He does not, however, demonstrate tangible support for the Crown other than the sycophantic invitations of the real audiencia and the cabildo and does not show that the lack of insurgency resulted from a conscious decision rather than the futility of revolt. He is correct in pointing out how authorities rushed to prove their loyalty. John Fisher, "La formación del estado peruano (1808–1824) y Simón Bolivar," in *Problemas de la formación del estado y de la nación en Hispanoamérica,* ed. Inge Buisson (Bonn: Inter Nationes, 1984), 479.

118 For a review of La Serna's key administrators, see the prologue by Horacio Villanueva Urteaga in CDIP, XXII, 3, 5–10.

119 CDIP, XXII, 3, 32–36; 86–128.

120 CDIP, XXII, 3, 17–25.

121 ADC, Beneficencia, Expedientes civiles, penales, administrativos y registros notariales de la Sociedad de Beneficiencia, Leg. 21, 1820–27. Vigil called de León a "consummate uppity cholo patriot" ("cholo patriota alsado consumado").

122 Flores Galindo, *Buscando,* passim.

123 Campbell, *The Military,* 154–88; Cahill, "Una visión," 133–59.

124 The case of José Antonio Manrique exemplifies the peripatetic careers of many Cuzco patriots. In 1814, he quit school to support the Pumacahua rebellion. Upon the rebels' defeat, he left Cuzco, "su patria," and lived as a fugitive. In 1820, he gained the trust of San Martín, who named him captain of the guerrilla forces in the important province of Huarochirí. Various officials confirmed his energetic efforts as a guerrilla leader until the defeat of the Spanish. CDIP, V, 6, 322–25.

125 Bonilla's "Clases" was written for the second edition of the book. For the original center of controversy, see Bonilla and Spalding, "La independencia," in Bonilla, ed., *La independencia,* 70–113.

126 This is one of the primary arguments in O'Phelan Godoy, "El mito."

127 In 1973, Jorge Basadre criticized Bonilla and Spalding's emphasis on the Creoles' fear of the Indians as a determining factor in the defeat of the Pumacahua movement. With characteristic erudition and style, Basadre showed that the Spanish emphasized the disjunction between the leadership and the Indian bases in order to weaken the movement. Basadre, *El azar,* 216–33; Bonilla replied in the second edition, "Clases," 57–59.

128 CDIP, III, 7, 685.

129 Florencia Mallon, *The Defense of Community in Peru's Central Highlands: Peasant Struggle and Capitalist Transition, 1860–1940* (Princeton: Princeton University Press, 1983), 42–57.

5 CUZCO'S BLACK ANGEL

1 Mariano Felipe Paz Soldán, "Brevísimas notas biográficas," *Revista Chilena de Historia y Geografía* 8, no. 12 (1913): 150. Born in Upper Peru/Bolivia, Andrés Santa Cruz studied in Cuzco as a child.

2 For definitions of caudillos and caudillismo, see Safford, "Politics, Ideology," and Lynch, *Caudillos*, chap. 1. The volume edited by Hugh Hamill uses the term as a synonym of *leader* and *dictator*, reducing its descriptive value. *Caudillos: Dictators in Spanish America* (Norman: University of Oklahoma Press, 1992).

3 Every major caudillo had his biographer. The best-known critique is Sarmiento, *Life*. For a more objective biography of Rosas, see John Lynch, *Argentine Dictator: Juan Manuel de Rosas, 1829–1852* (Oxford: Oxford University Press, 1981).

4 For recent analyses of Sarmiento, see the essays in Tulio Halperín Donghi, ed., *Sarmiento: Author of a Nation* (Berkeley and Los Angeles: University of California Press, 1994). Caudillos and the "Great Man" have been constant themes in Latin American literature. In the "boom," Carlos Fuentes's *The Death of Artemio Cruz* and virtually every work of Gabriel García Márquez stand out.

5 Felipe Pardo y Aliaga, "Semblanzas peruanas," *Boletín de la Academia Chilena de la Historia* 33 (1945), 66.

6 José María Valega, *República del Perú* (Lima: Librería e Imprenta Don Miranda, 1927), 16.

7 Luis Alayza Paz Soldán, *El Gran Mariscal José de La Mar* (Lima: Gil, S.A., 1941), 109.

8 For a couple of recent works that have mined previous biographies, see John Charles Chasteen, *Heroes on Horseback: A Life and Times of the Last Gaucho Caudillos* (Albuquerque: University of New Mexico Press, 1995); Lynch, *Argentine Dictator*. Jorge Basadre wrote stirring short biographical essays on the caudillos, many of them collected in Jorge Basadre, *Peruanos del siglo XIX* (Lima: Ediciones Rikchay Perú, 1981).

9 This was the case for Gamarra and Santa Cruz.

10 Halperín Donghi, *Reforma y disolución*, 220.

11 Frederick B. Pike, "Heresy, Real and Alleged in Peru: An Aspect of the Conservative-Liberal Struggle, 1830–1875," *HAHR* 47, no. 1 (1967): 50–74. For the conservative nature of Peruvian liberalism, see Aljovín Losada, "Representative Government," chap. 2; Florencia Mallon, "Economic Liberalism:

Where We Are and Where We Need to Go," in *Guilding the Invisible Hand: Economic Liberalism and the State in Latin American History*, ed. Joseph L. Love and Nils Jacobsen (New York: Praeger Press, 1988), 177–86; Gonzalo Portocarrero, "Conservadurismo, liberalismo y democracia en el Perú del siglo XIX," in *Pensamiento político peruano*, ed. Alberto Adrianzén (Lima: DESCO, 1987), 85–98; Fernando de Trazegnies, *La idea de derecho en el Perú republicano del siglo XIX* (Lima: Pontificia Universidad Católica, 1980).

12 See Charles Hale, *Mexican Liberalism in the Age of Mora, 1821–1853* (New Haven, Conn.: Yale University Press, 1968). I would like to thank Professor Hale for helping me clarify the ideological and social differences and the similarities between political groups in the early republic.

13 Paul Gootenberg, "North-South: Trade Policy, Regionalism and Caudillismo in Post-Independence Peru," *JLAS* 23 (1991): 273–308; and Jorge Basadre, *Historia de la República del Perú*, 7th ed., 11 vols. (Lima: Editorial Universitaria, 1983), 1–2: passim.

14 For biographies of Gamarra, see N. Andrew Cleven, "Dictators Gamarra, Orbegoso, Salaverry, and Santa Cruz," in *South American Dictators During the First Century of Independence*, ed. A. Curtis Wilgus (Washington, D.C.: George Washington University Press, 1937), 289–333; Manuel de Mendiburu, *Biografías de generales republicanos* (Lima: Instituto Histórico del Perú, Academia Nacional de la Historia, 1963); Paz Soldán, "Brevísimas"; Miguel A. Martínez, *El Mariscal de Piquiza, Don Agustín Gamarra* (Lima: Librería e Imprenta D. Miranda, 1946); Alberto Tauro, "Agustín Gamarra, fundador de la independencia nacional," in *Historia del Perú*, ed. César Pacheco Vélez, *Biblioteca de Cultura Peruana Contemporánea*, no. 7 (Lima: Ediciones del Sol, 1963), 507–18. The allegations about Father Saldívar are found in Pruvonena (José de la Riva Agüero), *Memorias y documentos para la historia de la independencia del Perú*, 2 vols. (Paris: Librería de Garnier Hermanos, 1858), 1: 372–73.

15 "Nueva historia natural de la tirania del Perú" (Cuzco, n.p., 1834). I discuss the attacks by and against Gamarra in chapter 6.

16 Cornejo Bouroncle, *Pumacahua*, 366–68. On Gamarra's participation in an 1820 conspiracy, see CDIP, VI, 4, 295–305; CDIP, XVI, 4, 152; Paz Soldán, *Historia*, 1: 111–15. One suspect noted that "La Paz and Cusco were devoted" to Gamarra and the other conspirators. CDIP, VI, 4, 295.

17 CDIP, VI, 2, letter from José de San Martín, February 26, 1821.

18 CDIP, XXVI, 2, 597.

19 ADC, Intendencia, CC, Leg. 119, 1824.

20 José I. Arenales, *Segunda campaña a la sierra del Perú en 1821*, prologue by Pedro de Angelis (Buenos Aires: Vaccaro, 1920), 64–67.

21 CDIP, VI, 6, 11–47.

22 Basadre calls it "the first confrontation between militarism and *caudillismo* on one side and parliamentary utopianism on the other." *Historia*, 1: 18.

23 For Peru in this period, see Anna, *The Fall;* Basadre, *La iniciación;* Fisher, "La formación"; Lynch, *Spanish American Revolutions,* 266-93; and John Lynch, "Bolívar and the Caudillos," *HAHR* 63, no. 1 (1983): 3-35.

24 For an interesting study on monarchism in Ecuador, see Mark Van Aken, *King of the Night: Juan José Flores and Ecuador, 1824-1864* (Berkeley and Los Angeles: University of California Press, 1989).

25 Documents from the 1820s and 1830 overwhelm the reader with complaints about the destruction and financial ruin provoked by the war. On the economic effects of the war, see Alfonso W. Quiroz, "Estructura económica y desarrollos regionales de la clase dominante, 1821-1850," in *Independencia y revolución,* 2 vols., ed. Alberto Flores Galindo (Lima: INC, 1987) 2: 201-267, and Paul Gootenberg, "Paying for Caudillos: The Politics of Emergency Finance in Peru, 1820-1845," in *Liberals, Politics and Power: State Formation in Nineteenth-Century Latin America,* ed. Vincent Peloso and Barbara Tenenbaum (Athens: University of Georgia Press, 1996), 134-165.

26 By 1808, the colonial state rarely mentioned the Tupac Amaru uprising, even in propaganda against rebels.

27 Archivo General de la Nación (hereafter AGN), OL 144, 1826, 311-471. The letter from Agustín Baca and Anselmo Centeno was dated December 12, 1826.

28 I discuss demographics and economics at greater length in chapters 6 and 7.

29 Basadre, *Historia,* 1: 133-36.

30 The department of Cuzco diminished in size throughout the nineteenth and early twentieth centuries with the creation of the departments of Apurimac (1873) and Madre de Dios (1912), largely from Cuzco territory. It also ceded territory to the departments of Junín, Loreto, and Brasil. See Mörner, *Perfil,* 163-65; Félix Denegri Luna, prologue in José María Blanco, *Diario del viaje del Presidente Orbegoso al sur del Perú,* 2 vols. (Lima: Pontificia Universidad Católica del Perú, 1974), 2: 59.

31 Basadre, *Historia,* 1: 203-247. Santiago Távara, *Historia de los partidos,* ed. Jorge Basadre and Félix Denegri Luna (Lima: Editorial Huascarán, 1951), 51-58. Basadre called Bolivia a "time bomb" for Peru, Basadre, introduction to Távara, *Historia,* lxiv.

32 Nationalists in Peru and other nascent republics would have to differentiate their citizens from neighboring nations that shared a common language, religion, race, and, in most case, history—what Francois-Xavier Guerra calls "the American exception." See "Identidades et independencia: La excepción americana," in Guerra and Quijada, eds., *Imaginar la nación,* 93-134, quote from 134. On the definition of Peru's borders, see Jorge Basadre, *La iniciación,* 1: passim; Aljovín, "Representative Government," chap. 5; Alberto Wagner de Reyna, *Los límites del Perú* (Lima: Editorial Universitaria, 1961).

33 On Gamarra's protectionist policies as president, see Paul Gootenberg, *Between Silver and Guano: Commercial Policy and the State in Postindependence Peru* (Princeton: Princeton University Press, 1989), chaps. 3-4.

34 The 1829 pamphlet "La libertad de la patria" claimed that the juntas sought to "demoralize us, corrupt us, make us anarchic, and later sell us." Anonymous, "La libertad de la patria" (Cuzco: 1829). On the juntas, see Raúl Rivera Serna, "Las juntas departamentales durante el primer gobierno del Mariscal Don Agustín Gamarra," *Boletín de la Biblioteca Nacional* 31-32 (1964): 3-18; and Gootenberg, *Between Silver,* 91-93.

35 For an interesting argument about the difficulties in spatial organization of the young republics, see Guerra, "Identidades et independencia."

36 Horacio Villanueva Urteaga, *Gamarra y la iniciación republicana en el Cuzco* (Lima: Banco de los Andes, 1981), 45-84. Fructuoso Cahuata Corrales, *Historia del periodismo cusqueño* (Lima: SAGSA, 1990), 28-29. On the Corte Superior, see Blanco, *Diario,* 184-85.

37 CDIP, XXVI, 4, 313.

38 Henri Favre, "Bolívar y los Indios," *Histórica* 10, no. 1 (1986), esp. 9-13; Blanca Muratorio, "Introducción," in *Imágenes e imagineros: Representaciones de los indígenas ecuatorianos, Siglos XIX y XX,* ed. Blanca Muratorio (Quito: FLACSO, 1994), esp. 12-15. Documents on Bolívar's reforms in Cusco can be found in CDIP, XIV, 1, 546-87.

39 Villanueva Urteaga, *Gamarra,* 39; on Bolívar's silence on Tupac Amaru, see Favre, "Bolívar," 15-16.

40 Orbegoso's efforts are noted in the newspaper *Cuzco Libre* from 1835; see also Blanco, *Diario,* 140-42. In 1832, one authority criticized the plan to merge the orphanage into the hospital, contending that prior to its creation, the orphans were "dumped in the countryside" and left to die. BN, documentos, 1832, D10855, Indicación del Sr. Diputado Don Pablo Mar sobre huérfanos, corridas de toros, y toda clase de alborotos. Cuzco, June 26, 1832. On notions of charity in the early republic, see Quijada, "Qué nación?"

41 Blanco, *Diario,* 1: 259. These hospices declined despite poignant demonstrations of their role in promoting republican values and even in saving lives. For example, in July 1829, an infant was left at the city orphanage with a crudely written note, "I place myself at this door as an orphan without a father or a mother, only protected by my father *la patria* who has created this great institution for the unfortunate, thanks to Sir Great Marshall Gamarra. . . . I am a son of the Peruvian nation." ADC, Beneficencia, Libro 90, Libro de partidos de los niños huérfanos expuestos, 1826-31.

42 Gamarra labeled these scenes from the conquest "the fierce history of those unfortunate ones who for resisting a foreign invasion were stabbed in the back." Ruben Vargas Ugarte, S.J., *Historia de la iglesia en el Perú,* 5 vols. (Burgos: Imprenta de Aldecoa, 1968), 5: 239-240.

43 Villanueva Urteaga, *Gamarra,* 96-114; Kathryn Jane Burns, "Convents, Culture, and Society in Cuzco, Peru, 1550-1865," Ph.D. diss. (Harvard University, 1993), 226-41; Denegri Luna, "Prólogo," in Blanco, *Diario,* 2: 74-79; Fred Spier, *Religious Regimes in Peru: Religion and State Development in a Long-*

Term Perspective and the Effects in the Andean Village of Zurite (Amsterdam: Amsterdam University Press, 1994), 193–98.

44 Villanueva Urteaga, *Gamarra*, 114–30.

45 "Cartas de Bolívar," *Revista Peruana* (Lima, 1879), 2: 522–23; cited by Denegri Luna in Blanco, *Diario*, 2: 78.

46 The speech is found in Bartolomé Herrera, *Escritos y discursos*, 2 vols. (Lima: Biblioteca de la República, 1929), 1: 14–34. On the church and the state in early republican Peru, see Pilar García Jordán, *Iglesia y poder en el Perú contemporáneo, 1821–1919* (Cuzco: Centro Bartolomé de Las Casas, 1991); Vargas Ugarte, *Historia;* Jeffrey Klaiber S.J., *La iglesia en el Perú* (Lima: Pontificia Universidad Católica del Perú, 1988); Spier, *Religious.*

47 Peralta, *En pos,* 36–43; Walker, "Peasants, Caudillos," chap. 5.

48 María Isabel Remy, "La sociedad local al inicio de la república: Cusco, 1824–1850," *Revista Andina* 7, no. 2 (1988): 451–84.

49 The tax system, particularly its political and social implications, is the subject of chapter 5 of Walker, "Peasants, Caudillos." See also Malcolm Deas, "The Fiscal Problems of Nineteenth-Century Colombia," *JLAS* 14 (November 1982): 287–328; Gootenberg, *Between Silver,* chap. 5, and "Paying"; Nils Jacobsen, "Taxation in Early Republican Peru, 1821–1851: Policy Making between Reform and Tradition," in *América Latina en la época de Simón Bolívar,* ed. Reinhard Liehr (Berlin: Colloquium, 1989), 311–339; Linda Alexander Rodríguez, *The Search for Public Policy: Regional Politics and Government Finances in Ecuador, 1830–1940* (Berkeley and Los Angeles: University of California Press, 1985); Barbara Tenenbaum, *The Politics of Penury: Debts and Taxes in Mexico, 1821–1856* (Albuquerque: University of New Mexico Press, 1986); Nicolás Sánchez-Albornoz, *Indios y tributos en el Alto Perú* (Lima: IEP, 1978).

50 Villanueva Urteaga, *Gamarra*, 20.

51 Tamayo Herrera, *Historia*, 44; Tamayo Herrera provides other evidence about Cuzco's growing isolation. Bolívar promoted improvement of the roads between Puno, Arequipa, and Cuzco, particularly for wheeled vehicles. He dreamed of turning Lake Titicaca into a "small Mediterranean Sea." Villanueva Urteaga, *Gamarra*, 33–34.

52 For Cuzco's nineteenth-century economic problems, see Tamayo Herrera, *Historia,* 27–54; Magnus Mörner, *Notas sobre el comercio y los comerciantes del Cusco desde fines de la colonia hasta 1930* (Lima: IEP, 1979); Glave, "Agricultura," 213–43; Thomas Krüggeler, "El doble desafío: Los artesanos del Cusco ante la crisis regional y la constitución del régimen republicano (1824–1869)," *Allpanchis* 38 (1991): 13–65. For the wool economy, see Jacobsen, *Mirages;* Escandell-Turs, *Producción.*

53 See for example, ADC, PL, 1826–30, PL 6-307, 1826. Also, ADC, Libro de Matrículas, Chumbivilcas, no. 1, Castas, 1825, 1831, which documents the decline of the Indian population, blaming the military campaigns and the sterile fields.

54 Krüggeler, "Unreliable Drunkards," 64.

55 On land in the nineteenth century, see Glave, "Agricultura," esp. 218–221; Mörner, *notas,* and "Compraventas de tierras en el Cuzco, 1825–1869," *Estudios Históricos sobre Estructuras Agrarias Andinas,* no. 1, (Stockholm: Instituto de Estudios Latinoamericanos, 1984); also Lorenzo Huertas Vallejos and Nadia Carnero Albarrán, *Diezmos del Cuzco, 1777–1853* (Lima: Universidad Nacional Mayor de San Marcos, 1983).

56 For the argument that caudillos worked within the structures of the state, not outside of them, see Noemi Goldman, "Legalidad y legitimidad en el caudillismo: Juan Facundo Quiroga y La Rioja en el Interior Rioplatense (1810–1835)," *Boletín del Instituto de Historia Argentina y Americana "Dr. Emilio Ravignani,"* 3d series, 7, no. 1 (1993): 31–58. See also José Carlos Chiaramonte, "Legalidad constitucional o caudillismo: El problema del orden social en el surgimiento de los estados autónomos del litoral argentino en la primera mitad del siglo XIX," *Desarrollo Económico* 26, no. 102 (1986): 175–96.

57 Simón B. O'Leary, *Memorias del General O'Leary publicadas por su hijo Simón B. O'Leary* (Caracas: Imprenta de "El Monitor," 1884), no. 23, 164, doc. 793, May 27, 1825. See also CDIP, XIX, I, 524–25, letter dated May 24, 1825.

58 Alberto Tauro, *Epistolario del Gran Mariscal Agustín Gamarra* (Lima: Facultad de Letras, Universidad Nacional Mayor de San Marcos, 1952), 25–26; CDIP, V, 6, 258–59.

59 See CDIP, VI, 9, "Relación de los jenerales, jefes y oficiales del ejército español, tomados por el Ejército unido Libertador en consecuencia de la batalla de la capitulación de AYACUCHO, con espresion de los se van para Europa, y los que se quedan en el pais." Of the 1,350 officers in the royalist army, this document reports 364 destined for Europe and 986 "to their homes in this country [*país*]" (252). Seventy officers had Cuzco as their destiny, including Ramón Nadal and a few others who would play a role in Cuzco politics in the coming years (241–52). I did not find any documents mentioning the departure of Spaniards from Cuzco upon independence or indications of anti-Spanish activities.

60 See ADC, Administración del Tesoro Público (hereafter ATP), Tributación, Leg. 68, 1831–49, case against Don Santos Valer of Canas.

61 José María Pando, *Memoria sobre el estado de la hacienda de la República Peruana* (Lima: José Masías, 1831), 12. Christine Hünefeldt, "Poder y contribuciones: Puno, 1825–1845," *Revista Andina* 7, no. 2 (1989), 375. Gamarra encountered problems filling the position of judge outside of the city of Cuzco. He blamed the hinterland's low population, in particular the predominance of Indians and the scarcity of merchants, which made "judicial activities" unprofitable. AGN, RJ, Cuzco Justicia, Leg. 194, 1825–30, February 18, 1825. See also Távara, *Historia,* for amusing anecdotes about the incompetence of many officials and their bewilderment with republicanism. For a synopsis, see the introduction by Basadre, lxvi.

62 José Serna, *Memoria sobre el curso y progreso de las contribuciones directas del Perú en los años de 1830 y 1831,* in *Tierra y población en el Perú,* compiled by Pablo Macera, 2 vols. (Lima: Seminario de Historia Rural Andina, 1972), 2: 445.

63 Villanueva Urteaga, *Gamarra,* 220-22; "La institucionalización del ejército: Organización y doctrina," manuscript, 1990, 586-91. In 1834, the Milicia Nacional was renamed the Guardia Nacional. For the militias in Mexico, see Guy P. C. Thompson, "Bulwarks of Patriotic Liberalism: The National Guard, Philharmonic Corps and Patriotic Juntas in Mexico, 1847-88," *JLAS* 22, no. 1 (February 1990), 31-68; Mallon, *Peasant,* chap. 4; Guardino, *Peasants,* chap. 4.

64 Juan Angel Bujanda, "Mensaje del ciudadano Juan Angel Bujanda prefecto del departamento a la muy honorable junta departamento," Cuzco, 1831, 17.

65 These trials compose an entire unit of the extensive holdings on taxes in the Cuzco Departmental Archive: "Contentious Affairs" ("Asuntos Contencio-sos"). I follow many of these cases in detail in Walker, "Peasants, Caudillos," chap. 5.

66 October 22, 1830, decree by Minister of War José Rivadeneyra, published in Juan Oviedo, *Colección de leyes, decretos y ordenes publicadas en el Perú desde el año de 1821 hasta 31 de Diciembre de 1859,* 16 vols. (Lima: F. Bailly, 1861-72), 13: 275. Military histories tend to overlook the militias. Much remains unknown about their organization and political-military functions.

67 Archivo Histórico Militar (hereafter AHM), Legajo Especial, "Tesorería, Guardia Nacional, Cuerpos Civicos, 1826-39."

68 AHM, Legajo Especial, "Tesorería."

69 Ibid.

70 AHM, Legajo Especial, "Tesorería," appendix, "Lista de Cívicos, Abancay," 1832.

71 Basadre, *La iniciación,* 1: 148-49.

72 ADC, Libros, August 22, 1827, 268, "Copiador de Correspondencia Oficial que Llevó la Regencia-Presidencia del Cuzco con todas las Autoridades y Corporaciones desde el reestablecimiento de la Constitución."

73 Basadre, *Historia,* 1: 225-27; Távara, *Historia,* 48-52 and 69-70.

74 Tauro, *Epistolario,* 215, letter to La Fuente, December 6, 1830.

75 Pedro Celestino Flórez, *Guía de forasteros del departamento del Cuzco para el año de 1833* (Cuzco: Imprenta Pública, 1833), 56.

76 M. Nemesio Vargas, *Historia del Perú independiente,* 8 vols. (Lima: Imprenta de "El Lucero," 1912), 6: 228.

77 For a list of battalions loyal to Gamarra in mid-1835, see "La institucionalización," 190. Individuals listed include José Santos, Anselmo Vera, Manuel Orihuela, Agustín Rosel, Gregorio Quintana, Felipe Infantas, Gregorio Lugones, Ramón Nadal, Luis Oblitas, José Gavino Concha, and Juan Ceballos. Flórez, *Guía 1834,* 93-94.

78 Archivo Santa Cruz (La Paz, Bolivia), February 12, 1834, to Domingo Nieto;

August 21, 1835, to Orbegoso.

79 ADC, Bandos, February 1836.

80 Basadre gave this description in 1929. Basadre, *La iniciación*, 1: 262; also Basadre, *Historia*, 1: 276–78.

81 Basadre, *Historia*, 1: 276–78. The numerous, often strident publications against Gamarra contradict the notion of a censored press or of a totalitarian political system often associated with military presidents. For a summary of the press, see Basadre, *Historia*, 2: 290–91; Félix Denegri Luna, "Apuntes para una bibliografía de periódicos cuzqueños (1822–1837)," *Revista Histórica* 26 (1964): 106–235.

82 Tauro, *Epistolario*, 213.

83 Dante Herrera Alarcón, *Conspiraciones que intentaron desmembrar al sur del Perú* (Callao: Colegio Militar Leoncio Prado, 1961), and Basadre, *Historia*, 1: 278–79.

84 Vargas, *Historia*, 6: 191–92.

85 ADC, ATP, Comunicaciones, Leg. 108, 1825–26, letter to administradores del Tesoro, September 5, 1826, from Vicente León. In early 1826, Gamarra complained that "the workshops of this city are backward, the artisans lazy, as they must be forced to be more punctual and honest with the point of a sword." AGN, OL 144, 311–471, 1826, letter dated November 12, 1826.

86 When making these requests, authorities often emphasized the nudity of the soldiers. ADC, ATP, Comunicaciones, Leg. 109, December 7, 1827, and Leg. 110, 1828–29. These efforts also gained Gamarra the support of Cuzco artisans. See Krüggeler, "El doble desafio."

87 For a sample of a few of the countless documents involving Lugones, see AGN, OL 131, 320–94, 1825; ADC, ATP, Administración, Leg. 5, 1838–39; ADC, ATP, Comunicaciones, Leg. 109, 1827; and AHM, J-17, Libros Copiadores, Correspondencia con el Prefecto del Cuzco, 1828–1834.

88 ADC, ATP, Comunicaciones, Leg. 116, 1833–34.

89 AGN, RJ, Cuzco Justicia, Leg. 195, 1831–35. Escandell-Turs, "Textile Production," 467.

90 An anonymous official commended Lugones for having "brilliantly" organized the Paruro civic militia by paying for instructors out of his own money. AHM, 1831, no. 990, April 12, 1830.

91 ADC, ATP, Comunicaciones, Leg. 117, 1834–35.

92 AHM, "Documentos Originales de la epoca del Virreynato," 1827, 8, 45, April 12, 1827.

93 AHM, Legajo Especial, Tesorería, Guardia Nacional, Cuerpos Cívicos, 1826–39. The Garmendias ended up owning the Lucre textile factory, thus becoming one of the most important families in Cuzco.

94 Heraclio Bonilla, Lía del Rio, and Pilar Ortiz de Zevallos, "Comercio libre y crisis de la economía andina: El caso del Cuzco," *Histórica* 2, no. 1 (1978), 17.

95 *Acta*, February 23, 1839; and AHM, Legajo Especial, Tesorería, Guardia Nacio-

nal, Cuerpos Cívicos, 1826–39. Nadal commissioned a two-page flier expressing the gratitude of numerous subprefects and Nadal himself for the defeat of Santa Cruz, "the tyrant that enslaved Peru." Another flier was also distributed with the similarly flowery prose for Gamarra in Quechua. In a one-page flier, Gamarra expressed his gratitude to his paisanos, noting that the nation expected their bravery and patriotism to continue being the pillar of order and the safeguard of liberty. Cuzco, May 20, 1839. These documents are found in the Velasco Aragón Collection housed in the Universidad Nacional San Antonio Abad del Cusco.

96 ADC, ATP, Comunicaciones, Leg. 116, 1833–34, letter to sres. adm. del Tesoro público, May 9, 1834.

97 ADC, ATP, Comunicaciones, Leg. 116, 1833–34, letter to sres. adm. del Tesoro público, May 13, 1834.

98 ADC, ATP, Asuntos Contenciososo, Leg. 82, 1836–37, letter dated August 25, 1834.

99 AGN, PL 13–58, 1831.

100 These trials are found in the voluminious "Contentious Affairs" section.

101 Horacio Villanueva Urteaga, "Don Pablo Mar y Tapia, anfitrión de presidentes," *Revista del Archivo General de la Nación* 7 (n.d.): 163–75.

102 Villanueva Urteaga, "Don Pablo," 174.

103 Pablo Macera, *Trabajos de historia,* 4 vols. (Lima: Instituto Nacional de Cultura, 1977), 4: 79.

104 Tauro, *Epistolario,* 51–52, July 26, 1826, to Simón Bolívar.

105 Anonymous, *Sentimientos de justicia de unos amigos del Gran Mariscal D. Agustín Gamarra* (Cuzco: April 1833); and, for the latter two quotes, anonymous broadsheet, Cuzco, June 11, 1833. The three documents were found in the Velasco Aragón Collection.

106 *Cuzco Libre,* February 1, 1839, 1.

107 Anonymous broadsheet, Cuzco, June 11, 1833.

108 *La Aurora Politica del Cuzco,* March 24, 1835, and March 30, 1835.

109 Martín de Concha, *El prefecto del departamento del Cuzco, a sus habitantes,* (Cuzco: March 16, 1835).

110 *El gobierno y la nación* (Cuzco: 1833). See also Méndez, "Incas sí," and the various works of Basadre on authoritarian thought.

111 Agustín Gamarra, *El Gran Mariscal Don Agustín Gamarra a los cuzqueños* (Cuzco: June 9, 1835). He refers to Salaverry's troops who, when occupying Cuzco in mid-1835, were accused of mistreating the population. Upon returning to Cuzco in 1839, Gamarra released a similar statement: "COUNTRYMEN: upon stepping upon the ground of my birthplace, my heart has been moved by both the evidence of your suffering and the demonstrations of joy and enthusiasm." Agustín Gamarra, *El presidente provisorio de la república a los habitantes del departamento del Cuzco* (Cuzco: May 20, 1839).

112 *El Cuzqueño Observador,* Lima, 1827, n.p.

113 "Lima, 17 de Abril de 1831," El Peruano Avergonzado, Valparaiso: Imprenta de Ontiveros, 1831. For more examples of the employment of the Incas in justifying authoritarian rule, see the speech by Father Francisco Zuñiga from February 1825 in Manuel Jesus Aparicio Vega, "Testimonios cusqueños del libertador: La oración de Zuñiga en honor de Bolívar," *Revista del Archivo General de la Nación* 4-5 (1977): 35-53.

114 Samuel Larned to Louise McLane, February 13, 1834, in William R. Manning, ed., *Diplomatic Correspondence of the United States: Inter-American Affairs 1831-1860*, 12 vols. (Washington, D.C.: Carnegie Endowment for International Peace, 1938), 10: 319-320. In another letter, Larned compared Gamarra to Santa Anna in Mexico, arguing that both sought monarchies. Larned to John Forsyth, March 26, 1835, in Manning, ed., *Diplomatic*, 10: 330-32.

115 José Miguel Medina, *El coronel prefecto y comandante jeneral del departamento a sus habitantes*, (Cuzco: June 2, 1835).

116 According to Paul Gootenberg, Cuzco "was not just a protectionist zone; it became a genuine centre of nationalist agitation, at least until the 1830s." Gamarra sought "an industrial Tawantinsuyo." See "North-South," 294.

117 AGN, Sección Republicana del Archivo Histórico de Hacienda, PL 10-9, 1830. This source is cited and discussed in Bonilla et al., "Comercio libre," 19-20, which includes other choice quotes. See also Félix Denegri Luna, "La antigua controversia sobre el libre comercio en el Cuzco de 1829," *Banca* (Lima) 2 (December 1982): 77-81.

118 Anonymous article, "Economía Política," *El Acento de la Justicia*, Cuzco, September 3, 1829, no. 33, 4, cited by Denegri Luna in Blanco, *Diario*, 2: 185.

119 United States, Department of State, Consular Despatches: Lima, 1823-54, National Archives, M154, reel 3, January 22, 1836-July 10, 1838, letter from T. Taylor to John Forsyth, secretary of state.

120 Fisher, "Royalism"; Alberto Flores Galindo, "Región y conflictos sociales: Lima y Cusco en el siglo XVIII," *Los Caminos del Laberinto* 2 (1985): 33-41; and O'Phelan Godoy, "El Mito."

121 Etienne Gilbert Eugene de Sartiges, *Dos viajeros franceses en el Perú Republicano*, ed. Raúl Porras Barrenechea, trans. Emilia Romero. (Lima: Editoral Cultural Antárctica, 1947), 68. Eugene de Sartiges originally used the pseudonym E. S. de Lavandais. For a discussion on the benefits of moving the capital from Lima to Cuzco, see *La Brújula*, no. 2, 1831.

122 Archivo Andrés Santa Cruz (La Paz, Bolivia), 1834 file, June 26, 1834, and July 22, 1834. On the Gamarra-Santa Cruz rivalry, see Ernesto Diez-Canseco, *Perú y Bolivia: pueblos gemelos* (Lima: Imprenta Torres Aguirre, 1952), esp. 130-133; John Frederick Wibel, "The Evolution of a Regional Community within the Spanish Empire and Peruvian Nation: Arequipa, 1780-1845." Ph.D. diss. (Stanford University, 1975).

123 "Cuzco" was not an artificial entity created upon the break with Spain, but

had existed as a political and administrative center for centuries. Throughout the colonial period, people identified Cuzco as their "patria."

6 THE WAR OF THE WORDS

1 Hunt, *Politics, Culture,* 10.

2 Keith M. Baker, "Introduction," in *The French Revolution and the Creation of Modern Political Culture,* vol. 1, ed. Keith Baker *The Political Culture of the Old Regime* (Oxford: Pergamon Press, 1987), xii.

3 Elsewhere, he describes it as "a realm of our social life in which something approaching public opinion can be formed. Access is guaranteed to all citizens. A portion of the public sphere comes into being in every conversation in which private individuals assemble to form a public body." Cited in Geoff Eley, "Nations, Publics, and Political Cultures: Placing Habermas in the Nineteenth Century," in Dirks et al., *Culture/Power,* 297. Besides this fine article, another useful review of Habermas is the introduction in Craig Calhoun, ed., *Habermas and the Public Sphere* (Cambridge: MIT Press, 1992), 1–48.

4 Eley, "Nations, Publics," 298.

5 Keith Michael Baker, "Politics and Public Opinion under the Old Regime: Some Reflections," in *Press and Politics in Pre-Revolutionary France,* ed. Jack R. Censer and Jeremy D. Popkin (Berkeley and Los Angeles: University of California Press, 1987); Hilda Sábato, "Citizenship, Political Participation and the Formation of the Public Sphere in Buenos Aires 1850s–1880s," *Past and Present* 136 (1992): 139–63; Farge, *Subversive Words;* and the essays in Calhoun, ed., *Habermas.*

6 Among critical approaches are Eley, "Nations, Public"; Dena Goodman, "Public Sphere and Private Life: Toward a Synthesis of Current Historiographical Approaches to the Old Regime," *Theory and Society* 31 (1992): 1–20; Margaret Jacob, "The Mental Landscape of the Public Sphere: A European Perspective," *Eighteenth-Century Studies* 21, no. 1 (1994): 95–113; Joan Landes, *Women and the Public Sphere in the Age of the French Revolution* (Ithaca: Cornell University Press, 1988).

7 See, among many studies, Francois-Xavier Guerra, "La difusión de la modernidad: Alfabetización, imprenta y revolución en Nueva España," in Guerra, *Modernidad e independencias,* 277–318, esp. 296–305.

8 On the stubborn refusal of the masses to refrain from political life once mobilized, see Sábato, "Citizenship;" Mallon, *Peasant;* Guardino, *Peasants.*

9 Prakash, "Introduction: After Colonialism," in Prakash, ed., *After Colonialism,* 3–17.

10 Porras Barrenechea argues that "Liberalism was not, organically, a structured party with leaders, a program, and defined terms. It was instead a mysti-

cal tendency, vague and diffuse, and a spiritual attitude whose symbol, rather than the preference for freedom over order, was tolerance." Cited in Carlos Augusto Ramos Nuñez, *Toribio Pacheco: Jurista peruano del siglo XIX* (Lima: Pontificia Universidad Católica, 1992), 157.

11 Basadre, *Historia*, 1–2: passim.

12 Ramos Nuñez, *Toribio Pacheco*, 157.

13 Pike, "Heresy, Real and Alleged."

14 See anonymous, "Sentimientos del pueblo cuzqueño," Cuzco, July 1834; and "Fiel Compromiso," 1834, for a list of liberals. Liberal papers often mentioned teachers as ardent supporters and even martyrs. See *Cuzco Libre*, no. 1, May 22, 1834, which lists five teachers who lost their jobs because they "were liberals." The department's Philanthropical Society inaugurated by President Orbegoso in 1834 constituted a virtual who's who of Cuzco liberalism. See "Acta," 1835, unmarked document found in the Velasco Aragón Collection.

15 Prominent supporters of this view include Eric R. Wolf and Edward C. Hansen, "Caudillo Politics: A Structural Analysis," *Comparative Studies in Society and History* 9, no. 2 (January 1967): 168–79. For a critique of this interpretation, see Frank Safford, "Bases of Political Alignment in Early Republican Spanish America," in *New Approaches to Latin American History*, ed. Richard Graham and Peter H. Smith (Austin: University of Texas Press, 1974), 78–80.

16 Jorge Basadre, *Elecciones y centralismo en el Perú (apuntes para un esquema histórico* (Lima: Universidad del Pacífico, 1980), 13–40; Vincent Peloso, "Liberals, Electoral Reform, and Foreign Intervention in Mexico, 1855–1880," in Peloso and Tenenbaum, eds., *Liberals*, 186–211. For a comparative perspective, see the essays in Malamud, ed., *Partidos Políticos*, and those in Antonio Annino, ed., *Historia de las elecciones en Iberoamérica siglo XIX* (Montevideo: Fondo de Cultura Económica Argentina, 1995). For a list of electoral representatives in Cuzco, see ALF, CC 28, caja 351, "Documentos de los Colegios Electorales." *El Sol del Cuzco* frequently reported on elections and the controversies they prompted.

17 ALF, CJD 281, caja 374, Libro Copiador de Actas de la Junta Departamental, 1829–33.

18 Villanueva Urteaga, *Gamarra*, 114–21.

19 See Richard Warren, "Elections and Popular Political Participation in Mexico, 1808–1836," in Peloso and Tenenbaum, eds., *Liberals*, 30–58; Antonio Annino, "The Ballot, Land and Sovereignty: Cádiz and the Origins of Mexican Local Government, 1812–1820," in *Elections before Democracy: The History of Elections in Europe and Latin America*, ed. Eduardo Posada-Carbó (London: Macmillan, 1996), 61–86.

20 Agustín Iturricha, *Historia de Bolivia bajo la administración del Mariscal Andrés Santa Cruz* (Sucre: Imprenta Boliviana, 1920), 774–78. León attempted to remain in Cuzco as director of the Superior Court. In late 1829, the Gama-

rra government accused him on twenty-six counts, including improprieties as prefect, plans to assassinate Gamarra, and the "snatching" of a girl. AGN, RJ, Cuzco, Justicia, Leg. 194, 1825–30. See also Basadre, *Historia,* 1: 254–58; Diez-Canseco, *Perú y Bolivia,* 111–25; Philip Parkerson, *Andrés de Santa Cruz y la Confederación Peru-Boliviana 1835–1839* (La Paz: Librería Editorial "Juventud," 1984), 52–56.

21 Herrera Alarcón, *Rebeliones,* 96–98.

22 ADC, Cabildos, Libros de Actas de la Municipalidad, Libro 34, 1830; Odriozola, *Documentos históricos,* 10: 161–63, dated August 26, 1830.

23 Herrera Alarcón, *Rebeliones,* 95–120; Távara, *Historia,* 75–76.

24 Although marred by a vehemently partisan perspective in favor of Gamarra and against Santa Cruz, Herrera Alarcón provides the best narrative of the Escobedo uprising. Herrera Alarcón, *Rebeliones,* 95–120, quote from 110. See the description in Odriozola, *Documentos históricos,* 10: 189–90. See also Basadre, *La iniciación,* 1: 191–93; Diez-Canseco, *Perú y Bolivia,* 111–25.

25 Odriozola, *Documentos históricos,* 10: 190–93.

26 *El imparcial cuzqueño. Por desgracia; una inclinación natural lleva comunmente a los que gobiernan al engradecimiento de su poder, y los ciudadanos encuentran enemigos y opresores en aquellos mismos que hicieron depositarios de su felicidad* (Cuzco: July 18, 1834).

27 AGN, RJ, Ministerio de Justicia, Cuzco, Leg. 27, 1825–34. On shifts in attire, see Mark Thurner, "*Republicanos* and *la Comunidad de Peruanos:* Unimagined Political Communities in Postcolonial Andean Peru," *JLAS* 27, no. 2 (1995), 296–297.

28 *Al Público* (Cuzco: September 24, 1834). Nieto's document is dated June 20, 1834.

29 ADC, ATP, Asuntos Contenciosos, Leg. 82, 1836–37, document dated December 11, 1835.

30 Jean Franco, *Plotting Women: Gender and Representation in Mexico* (New York: Columbia University Press, 1989), 79.

31 Indians are the subject of chapter 7.

32 Quoted in Villanueva Urteaga, *Gamarra,* 7.

33 Villanueva Urteaga, *Gamarra,* 7; *El Sol del Cuzco,* no. 4, January 22, 1825.

34 William Miller, *Memoirs of General Miller in the Service of the Republic of Peru,* 2d ed., 2 vols. (London: Longman, Rees, Orme, Brown and Green, 1829), 2: 227–28 and 215.

35 Villanueva Urteaga. *Gamarra,* 19–20. For Bolívar's satisfaction with his treatment in Cuzco, see letter from June 25, 1825, to Antonio de la Fuente, in Vicente Lecuña, *Cartas del libertador* (Caracas: Lit. y Tip. del Comercio, 1929), 5: 14–15. On Bolívar in Cuzco, see Aparicio Vega, "Testimonios Cusqueños," and Horacio Villanueva Urteaga, *Simón Bolívar en el Cuzco* (Caracas: Biblioteca Venezolana de Historia, 1971).

36 CDIP, XIX, 1, 216, letter dated August 15, 1825, from Huancayo.

37 *El Sol del Cuzco*, no. 29, July 16, 1825.

38 Mendiburu, *Biografías*, 95. On the monument, see ADC, Libros de Cabildo, no. 34, 1825-29.

39 *El Sol del Cuzco*, no. 13, March 26, 1825, cited by Cahuata, *Historia del Periodismo*, 32.

40 On festivals in Latin America, see Beezley et al., *Rituals of Rule*. One particularly influential monograph on France is Mona Ozouf, *Festivals and the French Revolution* (Cambridge: Harvard University Press, 1988).

41 De Sartiges, *Dos viajeros*, 117.

42 Tristan, *Peregrinations*, 107-8.

43 Cuzco commemorated not only Christian holidays as well as Inca festivals (Corpus Christi and Inti Raimi respectively stand out), but also local and personal saints and birthdays of major political figures. Calendars from the period squeeze together the myriad festival days, many of them including pilgrimages. David Cahill, "Popular Religion and Appropriation: The Example of Corpus Christi in Eighteenth-Century Peru, *LARR* 31, no. 2 (1996): 67-110. The *Guía de forasteros 1833* and *1834* lists the almost constant religious and civil fiestas in Cusco. On festivals in Cusco, see, among many works, Carolyn S. Dean, "Ethnic Conflict and Corpus Christi in Colonial Cuzco," *CLAR* 2, nos. 1-2 (1993): 93-120; the forthcoming book by Zoila S. Mendoza, *Shaping Society through Dance: Mestizo Ritual Performance in the Peruvian Andes;* Sallnow, ed., *Pilgrims*.

44 On this issue in Mexico, see Adrian A. Bantajes, "Burning Saints, Molding Minds: Iconoclasm, Civic Ritual, and the Failed Cultural Revolution," in Beezley et al., *Rituals*, 261-84; and Van Young, "Conclusion," in Beezley et al., *Rituals*, 343-74.

45 For example, see Agustín Gamarra, *El Gran Mariscal Don Agustín Gamarra a los Cuzqueños* (Cuzco: June 9, 1835).

46 *Descripción de las fiestas hechas en celebridad del feliz cumpleaños de S.E. el Señor Presidente de la República Don Agustín Gamarra* (Cuzco: Imprenta Pública Dirijida por P. Evaristo González, 1832).

47 Ozouf, *Festivals;* on the very different case of Great Britain, see Linda Colley, *Britons: Forging the Nation 1707-1837* (New Haven, Conn.: Yale University Press, 1992), 10-54.

48 Even the avowedly anticlerical novel *El Padre Horán*, discussed later in this chapter, balanced the evil, lascivious Father Horán with the enlightened, altruistic Father Lucas. Narciso Aréstegui, *El Padre Horán: Escenas de la vida del Cuzco* (Lima: Editorial Universo, 1969 [1848]).

49 "Descripción de las fiestas." See also Horacio Villanueva Urteaga, "El Mariscal Don Agustín Gamarra y el Cusco," *Andes* 2 (1995): 227-48.

50 "Descripción de las fiestas." See the invitation from Ramón Nadal for a bullfight honoring Gamarra after the defeat of the Peru-Bolivia Confederation

in 1839, "Exmo. Señor Presidente de la República Peruana Agustín Gamarra" (Cuzco: n.p., 1839).

51 See J. M. Terroba y Soza, *Arenga pronunciada en el primer arco de la caja de la agua por un joven vestido de Inca el dia del arrivo de S. E. el presidente de la república a esta capital el dia 19 de Mayo de 1839, ¡Hatun Apu Auqui!* (Cuzco: Imprenta de la Beneficencia, 1839).

52 BN, Sala de Investigaciones, doc. D10855, 1832, "Indicación del Sr. Diputado Don Pablo Mar sobre huerfanos, corridas de toros y toda clase de alborotos."

53 BN, Sala de Investigaciones, doc. D8893, 1832, "Moción presentada por el Diputado Don Gregorio de la Quintana a fin de que se prohiba la corrida de toros." Flora Tristan wrote that "Cock-fights, tight-rope dancers, Indians performing feats of strength: all of these spectacles draw the crowds." Tristan, *Peregrinations*, 124.

54 A notary transaction from 1813 indicates this decline in the number of bull-fights. The courts accepted the request for a reduction in monthly payments from the owner of a house that previously had been the mint (today the site of the Tourist Hotel) located in front of La Plaza Regocijo. They assented because "most of the house's income came from the considerable revenue from its balconies rented for the continual and frequent bullfights and other public diversions held in the Regocijo Plaza." The owner could no longer keep up payments "because these events have ended due to the decadence of the city." ADC, Notariales, Anselmo Vargas, Leg. 240, 1812, foja 509, November 22, 1813. Gutierrez et al., *La casa*, 99. For a description of late eighteenth-century bullfights, see Ignacio De Castro, *Relación del Cuzco* (Lima: Universidad Nacional Mayor de San Marcos, 1978 [1795]), 108–33.

55 De Sartiges, *Dos viajeros*, 65.

56 For a splendid critique of the liberals' social and intellectual elitism (their *doctrinarismo* and *limeñismo*), see Jorge Basadre, *Perú: Problema y posibilidad* (Lima: F. y E. Rosay, 1931), 100–105.

57 On street names, see Gutierrez, *La casa*, 35–36; on holidays celebrating Bolívar and independence, see Villanueva Urteaga, *Simón Bolívar*. I discussed the controversy about paintings that depict divine intervention favoring the Spanish in chapter 5.

58 Villanueva Urteaga, *Simón Bolívar*, 21. It could be argued that this quote says more about twentieth-century ideologies than about events in the nineteenth century, but contemporaries also noted the continuities from colony to republic.

59 In chapter 7, I discuss Indians' appropriation of anticolonial rhetoric.

60 These periodicals have been the subject of a careful study by Félix Denegri Luna, "Apuntes." Pedro Celestino Florez mentions the books in *Guía (1834)*, 69. The Wars of Independence had stimulated journalism throughout the continent. See Aníbal González, *Journalism and the Development of Spanish*

American Narrative (Cambridge: Cambridge University Press, 1993), esp. 5–15. On the press in the War of Independence in Peru, see Pablo Macera, "El periodismo en la independencia," *Trabajos de Historia*, 2: 325–42, and Asunción Martínez Riaza, *La prensa doctrinal en la Independencia del Perú, 1811–1824* (Madrid: ICI, 1988).

61 Basadre, *Historia*, 2: 297. Basadre insisted that "the history of journalism is much richer and more complex than superficial commentators have affirmed." He used the terms "brilliant and murky" to describe the journalistic orgy of the 1820s and 1830s (286, 297). On the press in early republican Cuzco, see Denegri Luna, "Apuntes," and Denegri Luna, in Blanco, *Diario del viaje*, 2: 163–66; Villanueva Urteaga, *Gamarra*, 233–47; Cahuata, *Historia*. I was fortunate to have access to the fine collection of newspapers and pamphlets housed in the Velasco Aragón Collection of the Cuzco Departmental Archive. The majority of newspapers, pamphlets, and broadsheets cited in this chapter were found there.

62 On the 1823 "Ley de Imprenta," which remained in effect for decades, see Basadre, *Historia*, 1: 45–47; Cahuata, *Historia*, 58–61.

63 Benedict Anderson deemed North America papers "appendages of the market." *Imagined Communities*, 62.

64 The salon culture of public readings had not taken hold, at least outside of the Peruvian capital, Lima. Even *tertulias*, the gatherings of friends and acquaintances for discussions, were not common in Cuzco. On tertulias, see Guerra, *Modernidad*, 92–98; and, for Lima, Basadre, *Historia*, 1: 281–82; Raúl Porras Barrenechea, "Don Felipe Pardo y Aliaga, satírico limeño," *Revista Histórica* 20 (1953): 238–304; Carlos Forment, "The Formation of Civil Society in Nineteenth-Century Peru: Democratic or Disciplinary," manuscript, 1996.

65 On pious books in France, see Michael Vernus, "A Provincial Perspective," in *Revolution in Print: The Press in France 1775–1800*, ed. Robert Darnton and Daniel Roche (Berkeley and Los Angeles: University of California Press, 1989), 124–38.

66 Aljovín Losada cites contemporaries' views that one-third of the population in the larger cities and one-eighteenth in the countryside were literate. This estimate seems extremely high. "Representative," 141. In his work on Mexico, Guerra notes the comparative lack of sources and studies on schooling and literacy in the Andes; *Modernidad*, 105.

67 Florez, *Guía 1834*, 70–74. One traveler in 1834 noted the religious nature of education in Cuzco, indicating the failure of Bolívar's efforts at secularization. De Sartiges, *Dos viajeros*, 77.

68 AGN, RJ, Instrucción, Leg. 193, 1823–46, information from 1835; Villanueva Urteaga, *Gamarra*, 201–15. The 1834 almanac (*Guía de forasteros*) lamented "the absolute abandon" of education, noting that schools in Sicuani, Checa,

Coporaque, Yauri, and other areas suffered from inconsistent governmental support, which suggests that the number of elementary schools was higher than the number listed in the 1835 document, but that the level of education remained low. Florez, *Guía 1834*, 40.

69 José Domingo Choquehuanca, *Ensayo de estadística completa* (Lima: Imprenta Manuel Corral, 1833), 61.

70 Florez, *Guía 1834*, 44.

71 Cahuata, *Historia*, 44 and 59.

72 *Minerva del Cuzco*, no. 36, May 8, 1830. Bujanda referred to the preparations of the Escobedo uprising discussed in this chapter.

73 See Blanco, *Diario*, for an excellent example of how "campaigning" caudillos propagated their ideals and language. Some of these speeches were reprinted in pamphlets. Gamarra's letters collected in Tauro, *Epistolario*, also demonstrate the importance of military campaigns in disseminating political ideas.

74 Guerra, *Modernidad*, 278–318, esp. 296–305.

75 *El prefecto del departamento del Cuzco, Cuzco a sus inhabitantes*, Cuzco: March 16, 1835.

76 *La patria en triunfo* (Cuzco: 1829). Its name, Triumphant Fatherland, was a play on words on the title of the liberal paper *La Patria en Duelo*, "The Mourning Fatherland."

77 Tristan, *Peregrinations*, 157.

78 The feud began with *Breve relación de un homicidio alevorísimo perpetrado por José Cuba en Colquemarca, provincia de Chumbivilcas* (Cuzco: 1839); *Descubierto de las denuncias, y méritos del traidor a su patria Juan Luis Oblitas* (Cuzco: 1839). Antoine de Baecque describes a similar phenomenon for revolutionary France: "One work would appear, another came out in reply, a third would rebut the rebuttal, and so on in a 'paper conflict,' . . . a veritable barbed-wire entanglement for the student." See "Pamphlets: Libel and Political Mythology," in *Revolution in Print*, Darnton and Roche, eds., 124–38.

79 This question is addressed by Jeremy D. Popkin in a review essay on European studies on the public sphere. *Eighteenth-Century Studies* 28, no. 1 (fall 1994): 151–54.

80 At least, I did not find any.

81 Tristan, *Peregrinations*, 79. In a speech for the arrival of Orbegoso in Cuzco, the mayor denounced Peru's "filthy serials." Blanco, *Diario*, 136.

82 On Pardo y Aliaga, see Basadre, *Historia*, 1: 281–82; Porras Barrenechea, "Don Felipe," and for an important recent analysis, see Méndez, "Incas sí." On the name given to Santa Cruz, see Basadre, *La iniciación*, 2: 43.

83 Basadre, *Historia*, 2: 291.

84 *Fiel Compromiso* (Cuzco), 1834, signed by El Fiscal del pueblo cuzqueño. It opened with the epigraph: "Las huellas de Gamarra con espanto / Brotan furor, desolación y llanto / Partidos busca en mar y tierra / Sostener quiere la

injusta guerra / Y los libres del Cuzco responden / Sostener la ley convencional y el orden."

85 *Sentimientos del Pueblo Cuzqueño manifestados por la voz de la justicia en los descargos que Gamarra hace de su inico* [sic] *comportamiento* (Cuzco: 1834).

86 On Vigil, see Basadre, *Historia*, 1: 270–71.

87 *Nueva historia natural de la tirania del Perú* (Cuzco: 1834?).

88 *La Aurora Peruana* 6 (Sep. 15, 1835) and 16 (Dec. 17, 1835).

89 Blanco, *Diario*, 1: 125, 133; Miller, *Memoirs*, 161–62.

90 Aréstegui, *El Padre Horán*. On Aréstegui and this novel, see Efraín Kristal, *The Andes Viewed from the City: Literary and Political Discourse on the Indian in Peru 1848–1930* (New York: Peter Lang, 1987), 42–55; Krüggeler, "Unreliable Drunkards," 158–61; and Mario Castro Arenas, *La novela peruana y la evolución social,* 2d. ed. (Lima: José Godard Editor, n.d.), 45–61, esp. the documentation on the riot found on 49–50.

91 Aréstegui, *El Padre Horán*, 2: 4. On the Lord of the Earthquakes, see de Sartiges, *Dos viajeros*, 70; Victor Angles Vargas, *Historia del Cusco (Cusco colonial)* (Cuzco: Industrial Gráfica, 1983), 2: 129–132; and for a spectacular drawing, Paul Marcoy (Laurent de Saint Cricq), *Travels in South America: From the Pacific Ocean to the Atlantic Ocean,* 3 vols. (London: Blackie and Son, 1875), 1: 308–9.

92 Aréstegui, *El Padre Horán*, 2: 92.

93 Ibid., 92–93.

94 Ibid., 96.

95 Kristal, *The Andes*, 42–43.

96 Aréstegui, *El Padre Horán*, 2: 94.

97 *Al público* (Cuzco: 1835).

98 For a fine example of gendered analysis of public space, see Mary P. Ryan, "Gender and Public Access: Women's Politics in Nineteenth-Century America," in Calhoun, ed., *Habermas*, 259–288. I would like to thank Kathryn Burns for helping me frame these ideas.

99 Basadre, *La iniciación*, chap. 1.

100 On the frustrating fate of the independence guerrillas, see Flores Galindo, *Buscando*, 203–11, and Charles Walker, "Montoneros, bandoleros, malhechores: Criminalidad y política en las primas decadas republicanas," in Aguirre and Walker, eds., *Bandoleros*, 107–36.

101 The best analysis of the significance of the War of Independence on the early republican political groups continues to be Basadre, *La iniciación*, esp. 1–85.

7 FROM COLONY TO REPUBLIC AND FROM INDIAN TO INDIAN

1 ADC, Real Audiencia, Leg. 124, 1815.

2 George Kubler, *The Indian Caste of Peru, 1795–1940: A Population Study Based*

upon Tax Records and Census Reports, Institute of Social Anthropology Publications, no. 14 (Washington, D.C.: Smithsonian Institution, 1952), 65.

3   Studies that underline the importance of the head tax include Platt, *Estado,* and Andrés Guerrero, "Curagas y tenientes políticos: La ley de la costumbre y la ley del estado (Otavalo, 1830–1875)," *Revista Andina* 7, no. 2 (1989): 321–63.

4   The estimate is from Gootenberg, "Population and Ethnicity," 138. See also Kubler, *The Indian Caste,* and Krüggeler, "Unreliable Drunkards," esp. 27–35.

5   See Brooke Larson, "Communities, Cultures, and Markets," in Larson and Harris, eds., *Ethnicity, Markets,* esp. 18–19, for an intelligent summary of the trend to shed "ethnohistorical light" on well-known structural processes. On "re-Indianization" see the works of Tristan Platt.

6   The national figures are from Gootenberg, "Paying for Caudillos," 138. The quote is from Guerrero, "Curagas," 322.

7   Gootenberg, "Paying for Caudillos." On the fiscal crisis of the "republican" government prior to the defeat of the Spanish, see Anna, *The Fall,* esp. chap. 5. For other cases, see Tulio Halperín Donghi, *Guerra y finanzas en los orígenes del estado argentino (1791–1850)* (Buenos Aires: Editorial del Belgrano, 1982); Tenenbaum, *The Politics;* Rodríguez, *The Search;* and Deas, "The Fiscal Problems."

8   On the tax rolls, see Kubler, *The Indian Caste,* 3–8.

9   On the national "treasury," see Gootenberg, *Between Silver,* 100–103. For Cuzco, see Walker, "Peasants, Caudillos," chap. 5. On tributary citizenship, see Tristan Platt, "Simón Bolívar, the Sun of Justice and the Amerindian Virgin: Andean Conceptions of the Patria in Nineteenth-Century Potosí," *JLAS* 25, no. 1 (1993): 159–62.

10 For information on the Indian head tax in the postindependence period, see Kubler, *The Indian Caste;* Jacobsen, "Taxation"; Sánchez-Albornoz, *Indios y tributos;* Basadre, *Historia,* 2: 253–55; María Isabel Remy, "Indios, estados y hacendados: Notas sobre fiscalidad, derechos y sujetos políticos en el siglo XIX," manuscript, 1990; Carlos Contreras, "Estado republicano y tributo indígena en la sierra central en la post-independencia," *Histórica* 13, no. 1 (1989): 9–44.

11 Sánchez-Albornoz, *Indios y tributos,* 192.

12 For summaries of the casta tax, see Kubler, *The Indian Caste,* 6–7, and Remy, "La sociedad local."

13 Cited in Remy, "La sociedad local," 463.

14 AGN, OL 207, 642–870.

15 Remy, "La sociedad local," 469. The list from Abancay in 1836 also includes estate managers, mule drivers, a silversmith, a tailor, and a blacksmith.

16 Kubler, *The Indian Caste,* 7.

17 Efforts were made in the 1770s and 1780s to extend the head tax to mestizos

and others, but the Tupac Amaru rebellion prevented these reforms. Kubler, *The Indian Caste*, 3–6.

18 ADC, Asuntos Contenciosos, Leg. 79, 1832–33.

19 ADC, Asuntos Contenciosos, Leg. 79, 1832–33.

20 AGN, PL, Hacienda, 13–287, 1833. This letter also describes the incoherence of the casta registrars.

21 AGN, OL 207, 1832, 642–870.

22 AGN, OL 207, 1832, 642–870.

23 AGN, RJ, Ministerio de Justicia, Culto, Cuzco, Leg. 148, 1825–45; AGN, OL 144, 1024–1373, 1830. See also AGN, PL, 13–287, 1830. For more subprefect complaints about the casta tax, see ADC, ATP, Asuntos Contenciosos, Leg. 76, 1825–26, Tomás Becerra, Paruro; ibid., Leg. 77, 1827–28, from the subprefect of Abancay; and ibid., Manuel Oblitas Farfán.

24 Kubler, *The Indian Caste*, 6.

25 Emilio Dancuart, ed., *Anales de la hacienda pública del Perú*, 24 vols. (Lima: Librería y Encuadernación Guillermo Solte, 1902), 2: 47, 48–51, analyzed by Remy, "La sociedad local," 467. I examine caste tax revenues in "Peasants, Caudillos," chap. 5.

26 Dancuart, *Anales*, 2: 46–47.

27 Cited in Kubler, *The Indian Caste*, 6.

28 Ibid., 6.

29 Pando, *Memoria sobre el estado*. For a similar justification of the Indian head tax in the name of their adhesion to tradition, see Serna, *Memoria sobre el curso*, 442–43.

30 [Santiago Távara], *Análisis y amplificación del manifiesto presentado al Congreso del Perú por el honorable Señor Ministro Don José María de Pando*, (Lima: José Masías, 1831).

31 Sánchez-Albornoz, *Indios y tributos*, 187–200; Peralta, *En pos*, 36–43; Mark Van Aken, "The Lingering Death of Indian Tribute in Ecuador," *HAHR* 61, no. 3 (1981): 429–59.

32 Frank Safford, "Race, Integration, and Progress: Elite Attitudes and the Indian in Colombia, 1750–1870," *HAHR* 71, no. 1 (1991): 1–33. Of course, views of the internal "other" are also important in noncolonial contexts, where race does not loom so large. For example, James Lehning shows the importance of discourse on the peasantry in definitions of the French. *Peasant and French: Cultural Contact in Rural France during the Nineteenth Century* (Cambridge: Cambridge University Press, 1995).

33 In Cuzco in 1827, the lawyer José Maruri de Cuba proposed fostering racial mixing between whites and Indians to improve the latter. He noted that the mixture is "beautiful" and that education could accelerate the improvement. *El Sol del Cuzco* 146, October 13, 1827. In general, little work has been done on the role of race in the construction of early republican ideologies in Spanish

America. The literature is vast on the final decades of the nineteenth century, when evolutionary theorists—in particular, Spencer—became influential. For an important example that includes an extensive bibliography, see Richard Graham, ed., *The Idea of Race in Latin America, 1870–1940* (Austin: University of Texas Press, 1990).

34 ADC, ATP, Asuntos Administrativos, Leg. 2, 1829–32.

35 ADC, ATP, Tributación, Leg. 67, 1826–30.

36 Ibid. 3.78 topos equals a hectare, or 2.471 acres. Therefore, 2 to 3 topos equals approximately 1.5 to 2 acres. Mörner, *Perfil*, 167–68. When discussing Indians' penchant for alcohol, Rueda referred to men.

37 Tauro, *Epistolario*, 44, letter to Sr. Ministro de Estado en el departamento de Hacienda, March 13, 1826. For a similar view from Gamarra, see AGN, Sección Republicana, PL 6–309, letter from September 26, 1826.

38 AGN, OL 144, 1826. Vicente León to Sr. Ministro de Estado del despacho de Hacienda, August 13, 1826.

39 AGN, OL 207, 1831, September 12, 1831.

40 AGN, RJ, Ministerio de Justicia, Culto, Cuzco, Leg. 148, 1825–45. In a trial over his debts, former subprefect Bujanda argued that payment had become "natural" for Indians. AGN, PL 13–58, 1833.

41 Elsewhere, I follow some of the more progressive thinkers in the late eighteenth and early nineteenth centuries, showing how they became intellectually or politically marginal. See "Voces discordantes," and Macera, "El indio."

42 In *El Padre Horán*, Aréstegui emphasizes the destructive role of outsiders, implying that priests, greedy landlords, and military chieftains prevented Indians from improving themselves. Here, we see the timid beginning of *indigenismo*.

43 Mary Louise Pratt, *Imperial Eyes: Travel Writing and Transculturation* (London: Routledge, 1992), 146–55.

44 ADC, ATP, Tributación, Leg. 67, 1826–1830; Juan Angel Bujanda, "Mensaje del ciudadano Juan Angel Bujanda, prefecto del departamento a la muy honorable junta departamental" (Cuzco: Imprenta Pública Dirijida por P. Evaristo González, 1831).

45 On these networks, see John H. Coatsworth, "The Limits of Colonial Absolutism: The State in Eighteenth-Century Mexico," in *Essays in the Political, Economic and Social History of Colonial Latin America*, ed. Karen Spalding (Newark: University of Delaware Press, 1982), 25–51; Guardino, *Peasants, Politics;* Cheryl English Martin, *Governance and Society in Colonial Mexico: Chihuahua in the Eighteenth Century* (Stanford, Calif.: Stanford University Press, 1996).

46 For a critique of authorities who deemed Indians lazy in order to legitimize their exploitation, see Choquehuanca, *Ensayo de estadística*, 70.

47 Florez, *Guía 1833*, 51.

48 ADC, ATP, Tributación, Leg. 67, 1826–30. For an interesting analysis of "ne-

cessities" in peasant society in Colombia, see Stephen Gudeman and Alberto Rivera, *Conversations in Colombia: The Domestic Economy in Life and Text* (Cambridge: Cambridge University Press, 1990), esp. 116–121.

49 ADC, ATP, Asuntos Administrativos, Leg. 2, 1829–32.

50 See Bujanda, "Mensaje." It is interesting that the authorities did not present language as an important cultural marker. Quechua, in fact, was rarely mentioned. Unfortunately, we have no way of knowing the role of housing and clothing in local identity formation. Did these distinguish individuals who moved between the categories of Indians and castas? In their reports and letters, the Cuzco authorities presented the Indian as an "other" and did not deem it worthwhile to depict local practice.

51 For the argument that the "labor shortage" was social, not demographic, see Gootenberg, "Population and Ethnicity," 119.

52 Choquehuanca, *Ensayo de estadística,* 69–70. The behavior described by Choquehuanca is similar to the Bourbons' efforts to maintain caste distinctions through dress codes. For an interesting discussion of these codes, see Thomas Abercrombie, "Mothers and Mistresses of the Bolivian Nation: Memory and Desire in a Postcolonial Pageant," manuscript, 1991.

53 Leading interpretations along these lines include Halperín Donghi, *The Aftermath;* Jacobsen, *The Mirages,* esp. chap. 3; Herbert Klein, *Haciendas and 'Ayllus': Rural Society in the Bolivian Andes in the Eighteenth and Nineteenth Centuries* (Stanford, Calif.: Stanford University Press, 1993), chap. 5. These authors, of course, do not overlook cultural factors or the efforts of the Indians themselves.

54 By now, Indian agency is a hallmark of the historiography. For examples that include theoretical and historiographical manifestos, see Mallon, *Peasant;* Cecilia Méndez, "Los campesinos, la independencia y la iniciación de la República. El caso de los iquichanos realistas: Ayacucho 1825–1828," in *Poder y Violencia en los Andes,* ed. Henrique Urbano (Cuzco: Centro Bartolomé de Las Casas, 1991), 165–88; Mark Thurner, *From Two Republics to One Divided: Contradictions of Postcolonial Nationmaking in Andean Peru* (Durham, N.C.: Duke University Press, 1996); and the numerous articles by Tristan Platt, particularly "Liberalism and Ethnocide" and the book, *Estado boliviano.*

55 Walker, "Peasants, Caudillos," chap. 5.

56 The population increase is estimated by Gootenberg in "Population and Ethnicity," 128. The head tax figure comes from the records found in the ADC, particularly the Libros Mayores, which are examined in Walker, "Peasants, Caudillos," chap. 5.

57 Jacobsen, "Taxation," 325.

58 Gootenberg, "Population and Ethnicity," 139–41.

59 Josep Fontana makes this argument convincingly for seventeenth- and eighteenth-century Europe. "Estado y hacienda," 136. On the negotiations and conflicts over tribute payment, see Hünefeldt, "Poder y contribuciones."

60 In E. P. Thompson's review of the fate of his term *moral economy,* he discusses the often exploitative and uneven nature of the exchange between peasants and their rulers. He cautions that, as applied to the study of rural society, the term usually refers to "the social dialectic of unequal mutuality (need and obligation) which lie at the centre of most societies," a very different phenomenon from what he examined in "The Moral Economy of the English Crowd." E. P. Thompson, "The Moral Economy Reviewed," 344; see 342–51.

61 ADC, Bandos, June 16, 1829, signed by Juan Angel Bujanda.

62 For example, see ADC, ATP, Asuntos Contenciosos, Leg. 78, 1831, request by Dionisio Dávila, subprefect of Quispicanchis; see also Peralta Ruíz, *En pos,* 98–99. Brooke Larson notes that in nineteenth-century Bolivia, women and other legally exempted groups were often incorporated into the tax rolls to compensate for the declining number of men. "Dimensiones históricas de la dinámica económica del campesinado contemporáneo en la región de Cochabamba," in *Explotación agraria y resistencia campesina en Cochabamba,* ed. Brooke Larson, 2d ed. (Cochabamba: CERES, 1983), 170–71.

63 ADC, ATP, Asuntos Contenciosis, Leg. 77, 1829–30.

64 Glave argues that payment represented a "permanent renovation of the guarantee by the state to their use of the land and their reproduction as a group." Glave, *Vida, símbolos,* 201. See also Thurner, *Republicanos.*

65 AGN, RJ, Leg. 195, Justicia, Cuzco, 1839, "Estado de rentas pertenecientes a la Administración Jeneral de Beneficiencia del Departamento del Cuzco." The beneficencia archive in the ADC includes dozens of detailed accounts of the rental of properties previously owned by the church. For samples, see ADC, Beneficencia/Hospital, Libro de Cuentas Corrientes, 1836; Beneficencia/Expedientes civiles, penales, administrativos y registros notariales, Legs. 21, 1820–27, and 22, 1830–35, which have several tables on land.

66 ADC, Beneficencia, Expedientes civiles, penales, administrativos y registros notariales, Leg. 21, 1820–1827, letter dating from August 22, 1827.

67 Mörner, *Perfil,* 32; Peralta, *En pos,* 60.

68 Peralta Ruíz, *En pos,* 60–61.

69 Jacobsen, *Mirages,* 69–72.

70 Ibid., 75.

71 Florez, *Guía 1833,* 55.

72 "Chacrayoc quiese Juntasca mana guarayoc," ADC, ATP, Tributación, Leg. 67, 1826–30. This is one of the few times that I found Quechua used in a document.

73 Peralta Ruíz, *En pos,* 61–67; Mörner, *Notas sobre,* 9–10; Tamayo Herrera, *Historia social,* 36–43. For the textile industry, Escandell-Tur, *Producción.*

74 ADC, ATP, Comunicaciones, Leg. 108, 1825–26, March 1, 1825. For an example from Paruro, see ADC, PL, 10–569, 1830.

75 Tamayo Herrera, *Historia social,* 46–49. See the anonymous *El Cuzco y sus provincias* (Arequipa: Imprenta Miranda, 1848); Magnus Mörner, "La distri-

bución de ingresos en un distrito andino en los años 1830," working paper, Institute of Latin American Studies (Stockholm, n.d.), 2; and Patricia J. Lyon, "El ocaso de los Cocales de Paucartambo," *Revista del Museo e Instituto de Arqueología-Museo Inka* 25 (1995): 171-79.

76 Geoffrey Bertram, "New Thinking on the Peruvian Highland Peasantry," *Pacific Viewpoint* 15 (September 1974), 103. Gootenberg, "Population and Ethnicity," 135-41; John Coatsworth, "Patterns of Rural Rebellion in Latin America: Mexico in Comparative Perspective," in *Riot, Rebellion, and Revolution: Rural Social Conflict in Mexico,* ed. Friedrich Katz (Princeton: Princeton University Press, 1988), 21-62; Jacobsen, *Mirages,* particularly 144.

77 Jacobsen, *Mirages,* particularly chaps. 2-4.

78 Glave and Remy, *Estructura agraria,* 429-43. In 1836, one official from Urubamba in the Sacred Valley contended that the price for corn was so low that it wasn't worth marketing. AGN, PL, Archivo de Hacienda, PL 19-142, 1836. For prices in nineteenth-century Peru, see Paul Gootenberg, "*Carnero y Chuño:* Price Levels in Nineteenth-Century Peru," *HAHR* 70, no. 1 (1990): 1-56.

79 AGN, PL, Archivo de Hacienda, PL 6-307, 1826, letter from January 1, 1827. On protectionism in Cuzco, see Bonilla et al., "Comercio libre." On Indians' active role in the economy, see Larson and Harris, *Ethnicity, Markets,* passim; Klein, *Haciendas and 'Ayllus,'* 119.

80 ADC, ATP, Asuntos Administrativos, Leg. 2, 1829-32.

81 O'Leary, *Memorias,* vol. 23, doc. 1828, 189-190.

82 ADC, Asuntos Contenciosos, Leg. 76, 1825-26.

83 ADC, Libros de Tomas de Razón, no. 5, 1831-35.

84 On Indians' use of republican language, see among other studies Platt, "Simón Bolívar," and Thurner, "*Republicanos.*"

85 Peralta Ruíz, *En pos,* 39-42.

86 Guerrero, "Curagas," 327-36.

87 Hünefeldt, "Poder y contribuciones," 367-409. For political and economic struggles after independence in more mestizo regions, see Florencia Mallon, *In Defense,* chaps. 1-3; and Brooke Larson, *Colonialism,* 270-321.

88 "Supresión de caciques por gobernadores, 1829," ALF, CJD-36, caja 368, from October 10, 1829.

89 "Supresión de caciques por gobernadores, 1829," ALF, CJD-36, caja 368, from October 10, 1829.

90 Sala i Vila, *Y se armó,* 151-62.

91 Platt, *Estado boliviano,* 110.

92 Rafael José Sahuaraura Titu Atauchi, *Estado del Perú,* notes and edited by Francisco A. Loayza (Lima: Librería e Imprenta D. Miranda, 1944). On this family, see Ella Dunbar Temple, "Un linaje incaico durante la dominación española," *Revista Histórica* 18, no. 1 (1949): 44-77.

93 Wm. Lewis Herndon and Lardner Gibbon, *Exploration of the Valley of the*

Amazon Made under the Direction of the Navy Department, part 2 by Lt. Lardner Gibbon (Washington, D.C.: A.O.P. Nicholson, 1854), 75.

94 Glave, *Vida, símbolos,* 201. Harris also provides a few examples in "Ethnic Identity," in Larson and Harris, eds., *Ethnicity, Markets.*

95 I base this assessment on my review of the Libro de Matrículas found in the ADC.

96 On the church in the early republic, see García Jordan, *Iglesia y poder,* 19–95; Klaiber, *La iglesia,* 59–85.

97 Historians of Native Americans in the United States have emphasized the role of cultural brokers or intermediaries. For particularly rich studies, see Richard White, *The Middle Ground: Indians, Empires, and Republics in the Great Lakes Region, 1650–1815* (Cambridge: Cambridge University Press, 1991), and Daniel H. Usner, *Indians, Settlers and Slaves in a Frontier Exchange Economy: The Lower Mississippi Valley Before 1783* (Chapel Hill: University of North Carolina Press and the Institute of Early America History and Culture, 1992).

98 See Lynch, *Caudillos,* for subtle analysis of these caudillos' popular bases.

99 Women who accompanied the men in the long campaigns provided essential intelligence reports and logistics. Historians have tended to overlook the role of the *rabonas.* For a description of them, see Tristan, *Peregrinations,* 179–81.

100 ADC, ATP, Asuntos Contenciosos, Leg. 76, 1825–26; the quote is from July 3, 1828.

101 *El Cuzco y sus provincias,* 7.

102 This pattern reflects not only the obvious fact that Indians made up the majority of the Andean population, but also that non-Indians—poor urban artisans, for example—joined militias. For guerrillas, see Bonilla, "Clases populares," and idem, "Bolívar y las guerrillas indígenas," *Cultura* (Quito) 6, no. 16 (1983): 81–95. For revisionist views, see Flores Galindo, "Soldados," and Guardino, "Las guerrillas." In the Battle of Yanacocha, discussed later in this chapter, the montoneros relied on slings, stones, and sticks.

103 Tauro, *Epistolario,* 66, letter to Sr. Don Antonio Gutiérrez de la Fuente, Cuzco, March 25, 1827; emphasis added.

104 ADC, ATP, Asuntos Contenciosos, Leg. 80, 1833–34.

105 ADC, ATP, Asuntos Contenciosos, Leg. 84, 1839–40.

106 Basadre, *Historia,* 2: 10–11.

107 ADC, ATP, Comunicaciones, Leg. 117, 1834–35.

108 ADC, ATP, Asuntos Contenciosos, Leg. 81, 1835.

109 ADC, ATP, Comunicaciones, Leg. 118, 1835–36.

110 ASC, letter dated June 30, 1835.

111 ASC, letter dated July 25, 1835. Santa Cruz used the term *indiada.*

112 ADC, ATP, Asuntos Contenciosos, Leg. 86, 1843.

113 In present-day Peru, an Indian takes a small bag of the lightweight leaves for

a dawn-to-dusk day of work. One scholar gauged seven to thirteen ounces a week to be "moderate" coca consumption and more than fourteen "heavy." Thus, if Bujanda provided each Indian guerrilla with three ounces a day, he distributed enough coca for eight thousand Indians for a single day. Roderick E. Burchard, "Coca Chewing and Diet," *Current Anthropology* 33, no. 1 (February 1992), 7.

114 ADC, ATP, Asuntos Contenciosos, Leg. 82, 1836–37; emphasis added.

115 AHM, 1835, 1, 102, from Francisco Alvarez to Señor Presidente de Bolivia y Jefe Supremo del Ejército Unido.

116 AHM, 1835, 1, 101, August 10, 1835. Domingo Farfán was a loyal Gamarrista who had risen in typical fashion: he had been subprefect of Canas, the commander of the Quispicanchis Cavalry, and a representative of Cuzco in Congress. The list of participants in a public ceremony organized by Gamarra for Bolívar in 1825 includes Mariano Villafuerte. It is unclear whether this was the same Villafuerte. Tauro, *Epistolario*, 19. Other documents noted the presence of guerrillas in Quispicanchis. For example, AHM, 1835, 18, 4, August 12, 1835.

117 Vargas, *Historia*, 7: 140–43; Carlos Dellepiane, *Historia militar del Perú*, 2 vols. (Lima: Librería e Imprenta Gil, 1931), 1: 336–37; Basadre, *Historia*, 2: 38; Basadre, *La iniciación*, 1: 382–84; Alfonso Crespo, *Santa Cruz: El condor Indio* (Mexico City: Fondo de Cultura Económica, 1944), 160. For an account of the battle, see "Ejército Unido, Boletín N. 3," in *Colección de documentos y de sucesos notables en las campañas de la pacificación del Perú* (Lima: Imprenta de Eusebio Aranda, 1837), 38–46. The accounts more favorable to Santa Cruz present higher figures; Alfonso Crespo cited more than ten thousand. Jorge Basadre estimated their number at eight thousand, whereas Nemesio Vargas and the military historian Carlos Dellepiane put the figure at six thousand.

118 Crespo, *Santa Cruz*, 160.

119 Távara, *Historia*, 185–86.

120 Santa Cruz himself was frustrated by his inability to raise a guerrilla army in the southern highlands or on the coast. In September 1838, he wrote to José de la Riva Agüero that "I am saddened that the guerrillas are lazy, and I don't understand why they don't do the same as they did in the time of the Spanish as they have even more motives for hating them [the opposition to the confederation]." CDIP, XIV, 1, 899, letter of September 29, 1838.

121 For descriptions of the leva, see Tristan, *Peregrinations;* de Sartiges, *Dos viajeros*, 71.

122 Choquehuanca, *Ensayo de estadística*, 69. Authorities such as artisan guild masters also provided troops, who presumably joined the armed forces with little enthusiasm.

123 For innovative works in military history that focus on how commanders "motivated" soldiers to fight, see John Keegan, *The Mask of Command* (London: Penguin, 1987), particularly chap. 2 on Wellington, 92–163.

124 In the words of the Bolivian historian Alfonso Crespo, Indian guerrillas were "worthless in battle but useful after the victory." *Santa Cruz,* 160. Compare this case with that of the central Sierra guerrillas studied by Manrique in *Campesinado.*

125 Bolivianists are often surprised when scholars of Peru call Santa Cruz a liberal. I thank Nils Jacobsen and Erick Langer for explaining Santa Cruz's role in Bolivian politics.

8 CONCLUSIONS

1 Jorge Basadre, prologue to Tamayo Herrera, *Historia social,* 16.
2 In 1873, a dying Peruvian told Manuel Gónzalez Prada that he, not the Bolivians, had killed Gamarra, a view replicated in Abraham Valdelomar, *La Mariscala: Doña Francisco Zubiaga y Bernales de Gamarra* (Lima: Taller Tip. de la Penitenciaría, 1914), and Alfredo Gónzalez Prada, *Un crimen perfecto: El asesinato del Gran Mariscal Don Agustín Gamarra, presidente del Perú* (New York: H. Wolff, 1941). Jorge Basadre refutes this allegation. *Historia,* 2: 148-52.
3 These arguments can be found in Basadre, *La iniciación,* 1: 126-30. See also Celia Wu, *Generals and Diplomats: Great Britain and Peru, 1820-40* (Cambridge: Centre of Latin American Studies, University of Cambridge, 1991).
4 Jorge Basadre stresses the political and ideological legacy of the early republic. Alberto Fujimori, who trumpets his strong will and efficiency while deriding political institutions, brings to mind Gamarra and other authoritarian caudillos.
5 Some held office more than once. Also, civilian caudillos emerged, such as Nicolás de Piérola. David Scott Palmer, *Peru: The Authoritarian Tradition* (New York: Praeger, 1980), 37-39.
6 Halperín Donghi, *The Aftermath.*
7 Sala i Vila, *Y se armó;* Thurner, *From Two Republics.*
8 Peasants' participation in the caudillo struggles of the nineteenth century varied from region to region. Some Peruvian caudillos did count on a mass, peasant base, such as Andrés Avelino Cáceres's guerrillas from the Mantaro Valley area. Yet these groups were not fully incorporated into the political alliances, and the exclusion of the peasantry continued. In fact, Cáceres betrayed his backers, persecuting them once he became president. See Mallon, *The Defense,* and Manrique, *Campesinado.*
9 My debt to Jorge Basadre for these ideas (as well as for his stubborn optimism about Peru) should be evident to many readers.
10 Mallon, "Indians and the State," 36-37.
11 On the complexities of Indians and the state in the nineteenth century, see Nils Jacobsen, "Liberalism and Indian Communities in Peru, 1821-1920," in *Liberals, the Church and Indian Peasants: Corporate Lands and the Challenge of*

Reform in Nineteenth-Century Spanish America, ed. Robert H. Jackson (Albuquerque: University of New Mexico Press, 1997), 123–70. Other important syntheses include Paul Gootenberg, *Imagining Development: Economic Ideas in Peru's "Fictitious Prosperity" of Guano, 1840–1880* (Berkeley and Los Angeles: University of California Press, 1993); and Larson, "Communities, Cultures and Markets."

12 The relationship between Lima and the provinces was often strained and gamonales did not enjoy absolute, uncontested power. Throughout the nineteenth century, the national and regional state could not offer local non-Indian officeholders adequate military or financial support to allow them to entrench themselves in power, so the gamonales were forced to make alliances. Indians took advantage of local authorities' weak hold on power. Moreover, the sociological complexity of political divisions evident in Cuzco continued. In most regions, Indians could be found on opposing sides.

13 Intellectuals have long presented the War of the Pacific as a symbol of the weakness of the nation (or nation-state), but they disagree about the root cause.

14 See Coatsworth, "Patterns," 21–62; and the various introductions by Stern in his *Resistance, Rebellion*.

15 For a sharp explanation of the significance of "alternative nationalisms" even when defeated, see Mallon, *Peasant and Nation*, 141.

16 Sherry Ortner, "Resistance and the Problem of Ethnographic Refusal, *Comparative Studies in Society and History* 37, no. 1 (1995), esp. 180–83.

17 Compare my reliance on fire metaphors so common in the late colonial period to Mallon's gloomy metaphors on postindependence state formation. For example, she describes the building of the oligarchical state on "corpses produced by repression." Mallon, "Indians and the State," 46.

18 For an overview of race and society in the Andes, see Harris, "Ethnic Identity," in Larson and Harris, eds., *Ethnicity, Markets*.

19 The Shining Path and the Movimiento Revolucionario Tupac Amaru (MRTA) had much less of a presence in Cuzco than in other Andean areas, partly because of the importance that the "repressive forces" of the state have given to Cuzco since the 1960s.

PRIMARY SOURCES

Document Collections

Colección de documentos y de sucesos notables en las campañas de la pacificación del Perú. Lima: Imprenta de Eusebio Aranda, 1837.

Comisión Nacional del Sesquicentenario de la Independencia del Perú, comp. *Colección documental de la independencia del Perú.* Lima: Comisión del Sesquicentenario, 1971–73. 26 vols.

Dancuart, Emilio, ed. *Anales de la hacienda pública del Perú: Historia y legislación fiscal de la república.* 24 vols. Lima: Librería y encuadernación Guillermo Solte, 1902–26.

Manning, William R., ed. *Diplomatic Correspondence of the United States. Inter-American Affairs 1831–1860.* Vol. 10 of 12. Washington, D.C.: Carnegie Endowment for International Peace, 1938.

Maúrtua, Víctor. *Juicio de límites entre Perú y Bolivia.* 12 vols. Barcelona: Imprenta de Henrich Y Comp., 1906.

Odriozola, Manuel de. *Documentos históricos del Perú.* Lima: Imprenta del Estado, 1872.

Oviedo, Juan. *Colección de leyes, decretos y ordenes publicadas en el Perú desde el año de 1821 hasta 31 de Diciembre de 1859.* 16 vols. Lima: F. Bailly, 1861–72.

Quirós, Mariano Santos de, comp. *Colección de leyes, decretos y órdenes publicados en el Perú desde su independencia en el año de 1821 hasta 1854.* Lima: José Masías, 1831–54. 12 vols.

Tupac Amaru y la igesia: Antología. Cuzco: Edubanco, 1983.

Selected Pamphlets

Acta. Cuzco: Imprenta de la Beneficencia por P. Evarista González, 1839.

Al gobierno y la nación. Cuzco: May 18, 1834.

Al público. Cuzco: September 24, 1834.

Breve relación de un homicidio alevorísimo perpetrado por José Cuba en Coquemarca, provincia de Chumbivilcas. Cuzco: 1839.

Bujanda, Juan Angel. *Mensaje del ciudadano Juan Angel Bujanda prefecto del departamento a la muy honorable junta departamento.* Cuzco: Imprenta Pública Dirijida por P. Evaristo González, 1831.

Concha, Martín de. *El prefecto del departamento del Cuzco, a sus habitantes.* Cuzco: 1835. *Descripción de las fiestas hechas en esta ciudad en celebridad del feliz cumpleaños de S. E. El Señor Presidente de la República Don Agustín Gamarra.* Cuzco: Imprenta Pública Dirijida por P. Evaristo González, 1832.

Descubierto de las denuncias, y méritos del traidor a su patria Juan Luis Oblitas. Cuzco: 1839.

El imparcial cuzqueños. Por desgracia; una inclinación natural lleva comunmente a los que gobiernan al engradecimiento de su poder, y los ciudadanos encuentran enemigos y opresores en aquellos mismos que hicieron depositarios de su felicidad. Cuzco: July 18, 1834.

El Veraz. *Al público.* Cuzco: 1835.

Gamarra, Agustín. *El Gran Mariscal Don Agustín Gamarra a los cuzqueños.* Cuzco: June 9, 1835.

Gamarra, Agustín. *El Jeneral Gamarra a sus compatriotas.* San José, Costa Rica: Imprenta La Merced, 1835.

Gamarra, Agustín. *El presidente provisorio de la república a los habitantes del departamento del Cuzco.* Cuzco: May 20, 1839.

Larrea, Juan José. *Amor a la patria y justicia a la verdad.* Cuzco: 1835.

Larrea y Loredo, José de. *Principios que siguió el ciudadano José de Larrea y Loredo en el Ministerio de Hacienda y sección de negocios eclesiásticos de que estuve encargado.* Lima: J. M. Concha, 1827.

La libertad de la patria. Cuzco: Imprenta del Gobierno, 1829.

Medina, José Miguel. *El coronel prefecto y comandante general del departamento a sus habitantes.* Cuzco: June 2, 1835.

Nadal, Ramón. *Exmo. Señor Presidente de la República Peruana Don Agustín Gamarra.* Cuzco: 1839.

Nueva historia natural de la tirania del Perú. Cuzco: 1834(?).

Pando, José María. *Memoria sobre el estado de la hacienda de la República Peruana, en fin del año de 1830 presentado al Congreso por José María Pando.* Lima: José Masías, 1831.

Pando, José María. *Reclamación de los vulnerados derechos de los hacendados de las provincias litorales del departamento de Lima.* Lima: J. M. Concha, 1833.

Sentimientos de justicia de unos amigos del Gran Mariscal D. Agustín Gamarra. Cuzco: April 1833.

Sentimientos del pueblo cuzqueño manifestados por la voz de la justicia en los descargos que Gamarra hace de su inico [sic] comportamiento. Cuzco: July 1834.

Serna, José. *Memoria sobre el curso y progreso de las contribuciones directas del Perú en los años de 1830 y 1831*. In *Tierra y población en el Perú*, 4 vols., compiled by Pablo Macera, 2: 441-54. Lima: Seminario de Historia Rural Andina, 1972.

Sr. Editor. Cuzco: February 18, 1835.

[Távara, Santiago.] *Análisis y amplificación del manifiesto presentado al Congreso del Perú por el honorable Señor Ministro Don José María Pando*. 2 vols. Lima: José Masías, 1831.

Terroba y Soza, J. M. *Arenga pronunciada en el primer arco de la caja de la agua por un joven vestido de Inca el dia del arrivo de S. E. el presidente de la república a esta capital el dia 19 de Mayo de 1839, ¡Hatan Apu Auqui!* Cuzco: Imprenta de la Beneficencia, 1839.

SECONDARY SOURCES

Abascal y Sousa, José Fernando. *Memoria de gobierno de José Fernando de Abascal y Sousa*, edited by Vicente Rodríguez Casado and José Antonio Calderón Quijano. Publicaciones de Escuela de Estudios Hispano-Americanos de la Universidad de Sevilla, ser. 3, no. 1. 2 vols. Sevilla: Editorial católica espaniola, 1944.

Abercrombie, Thomas. "Mothers and Mistresses of the Bolivian Nation: Memory and Desire in a Postcolonial Pageant." Manuscript, 1991.

———. "To Be Indian, to Be Bolivian: 'Ethnic' and 'National' Discourses of Identity." In *Nation-States and Indians in Latin America*, edited by Greg Urban and Joel Sherzer, 111-43. Austin: University of Texas Press, 1991.

———. "Q'aqchas and *La Plebe* in 'Rebellion': Carnival vs. Lent in 18th Century Potosí." *Journal of Latin American Anthropology* 2, no. 1 (1996): 62-111.

Aguirre, Carlos. *Agentes de su propia libertad: Los esclavos de Lima y la desintegración de la esclavitud 1821-1854*. Lima: Pontificia Universidad La Católica del Perú, 1993.

Aljovín Losada, Cristobal. "Representative Government in Peru: Fiction and Reality, 1821-1845." Ph.D. diss., University of Chicago, 1996.

Alonso, Ana. "The Politics of Space, Time and Substance: State Formation, Nationalism, and Ethnicity." *Annual Reviews in Anthropology* 23 (1994): 370-405.

Anderson, Benedict. *Imagined Communities: Reflections on the Origin and Spread of Nationalism*. London: Verso, 1983.

Angles Vargas, Víctor. *El cacique Tambohuacso*. Lima: Industrial Gráfica, 1975.

———. *Historia del Cuzco (Cuzco colonial)*. Cuzco: Industrial Gráfica, 1983.

Anna, Timothy E. *The Fall of the Royal Government in Peru*. Lincoln: University of Nebraska Press, 1979.

Annino, Antonio, ed. *Historia de las elecciones en Iberoamérica siglo XIX*. Montevideo: Fondo de Cultura Economica Argentina, 1995.

Aparicio, Severo. "La actitud del clero frente a la rebelión de Tupac Amaru." In *Actas del coloquio internacional Tupac Amaru y su tiempo*, 71-94. Lima: CNDBRETA, 1982.

Aparicio Vega, Manuel Jesus. "Testimonios cuzqueños del libertador: La oración de Zuñiga en honor de Bolívar." *Revista del Archivo General de la Nación* (Lima) 4-5 (1977): 35-53.

Appleby, Joyce. *Capitalism and a New Social Order: The Republican Vision of the 1790s.* New York: New York University Press, 1984.

Area, Lelia, and Mabel Moraña, eds. *La imaginación histórica en el siglo XIX.* Rosario: UNR Editores, 1994.

Arenales, José I. *Segunda campaña a la sierra del Perú en 1821.* Prologue by Pedro de Angelis. Buenos Aires: Vaccaro, 1920.

Aréstegui, Narciso. *El Padre Horán: Escenas de la vida del Cuzco.* Lima: Editorial Universo SA, 1969 (1848).

Armstrong, John A. *Nations before Nationalism.* Chapel Hill: University of North Carolina Press, 1982.

Arroyo, Carlos, ed. *Encuentros: Historia y movimientos sociales en el Perú.* Lima: MemoriAngosta, 1989.

Arze Aguirre, René Danilo. "El cacicazgo en las postrimerías coloniales." *Avances* 1 (1978): 47-50.

——. *Participación popular en la independencia de Bolivia.* La Paz: Organización de los Estados Americanos, 1979.

Aymes, Jean-Rene, ed. *España y la Revolución Francesa.* Barcelona: Editorial Crítica, 1989.

Baker, Keith. "Politics and Public Opinion under the Old Regime: Some Reflections." In *Press and Politics in Pre-Revolutionary France.* Edited by Jack R. Censer and Jeremy D. Popkin, 204-46. Berkeley and Los Angeles: University of California Press, 1987.

——, ed. *The Political Culture of the Old Regime.* Oxford: Pergamon Press, 1987.

Basadre, Jorge. *La iniciación de la república.* 2 vols. Lima: F. y E. Rosay, 1929.

——. *Perú: Problema y posibilidad.* Lima: F. y E. Rosay, 1931.

——. *Introducción a las bases documentales para la historia de la República del Perú con algunas reflexiones.* 2 vols. Lima: P.L.V. Villanueva, 1971.

——. *El azar en la historia y sus límites.* Lima: Ediciones P.L.V., 1973.

——. *Elecciones y centralismo en el Perú (apuntes para un esquema histórico).* Lima: Universidad del Pacífico, 1980.

——. *Peruanos del siglo XIX.* Lima: Ediciones Rikchay Perú, 1981.

——. *Historia de la República del Perú.* 7th ed. 11 vols. Lima: Editorial Universitaria, 1983.

Basadre, Modesto. *Diez años de historia política del Perú (1834-1844).* Lima: Editorial Huascarán, 1953.

Beltrán Gallardo, Ezequiel. *Las guerrillas de Yauyos en la emancipación del Perú.* Lima: Técnicos Asociados, 1977.

Beezley, William H., Cheryl English Martin, and William E. French, eds. *Rituals of Rule, Rituals of Resistance: Public Celebrations and Popular Culture in Mexico.* Wilmington, Del.: SR Books, 1994.

Berg, Ronald, and Frederick S. Weaver. "Towards a Reinterpretation of Political Change in Peru during the First Century of Independence." *Journal of Inter-American Studies and World Affairs* 20, no. 1 (February 1979): 69–84.

Bertram, Geoffrey. "New Thinking on the Peruvian Highland Peasantry." *Pacific Viewpoint* 15 (September 1974): 89–111.

Beverley, John, ed. *The Postmodernism Debate in Latin America.* Durham, N.C.: Duke University Press, 1995.

Bilbao, Manuel. *Historia del general Salaverry.* 3d ed. Lima: Librería e Imprenta Gil, S.A., 1936.

Blanco, Jose María. *Diario del viaje del Presidente Orbegoso al sur del Perú.* 2 vols. Lima: Pontificia Universidad Católica del Perú, Instituto Riva-Agüero, 1974.

Bonilla, Heraclio. *Guano y burguesía en el Perú.* Lima: Instituto de Estudios Peruanos, 1974.

——. "Clases populares y estado en el contexto de la crisis colonial." In *La independencia en el Perú,* edited by Heraclio Bonilla et al., 13–69. 2d ed. Lima: Instituto de Estudios Peruanos, 1981.

——. "Bolívar y las guerrillas indígenas." *Cultura* (Quito) 6, no. 16 (1983): 81–95.

——. "Continuidad y cambio en la organización del estado en el Perú independiente." In *Problemas de la formación del estado y de la nación en Hispanoamérica,* edited by Inge Buisson, 481–98. Bonn: Inter Nationes, 1984.

——. "The Indian Peasantry and 'Peru' during the War with Chile." In *Resistance, Rebellion, and Consciousness in the Andean Peasant World, 18th to 20th Centuries,* edited by Steve Stern, 219–32. Madison: University of Wisconsin Press, 1987.

——. "Estado y tributo campesino: La experiencia de Ayacucho." Documento de Trabajo, no. 20. Lima: Instituto de Estudios Peruanos, 1989.

Bonilla, Heraclio, and Karen Spalding. "La independencia en el Perú: Las palabras y los hechos." In *La independencia en el Perú,* edited by Heraclio Bonilla et al., 71–114. 2d ed. Lima: Instituto de Estudios Peruanos, 1981 (1st ed. 1972).

Bonilla, Heraclio, Lía del Rio, and Pilar Ortiz de Zevallos. "Comercio libre y crisis de la economía andina: El caso del Cuzco." *Histórica* 2, no. 1 (1978): 1–25.

Bonilla, Heraclio, Guerrero Rincón, A. Amada, eds. *Los pueblos campesinos de las americas: Etnicidad, cultura e historia en el siglo XIX.* Santander, Colombia: Universidad Industrial de Santander, 1996.

Borah, Woodrow Wilson. *Justice by Insurance: The General Indian Court of Colonial Mexico and the Legal Aides of the Half-Real.* Berkeley and Los Angeles: University of California Press, 1983.

Brading, David. "Bourbon Spain and Its American Empire." In *Colonial Spanish America. The Cambridge History of Latin America,* vols. 1 and 2. *Selections,* edited by Leslie Bethell, 112–62. Cambridge: Cambridge University Press, 1987.

——. *The First America: The Spanish Monarchy, Creole Patriots, and the Liberal State, 1492–1867.* Cambridge: Cambridge University Press, 1991.

Breuilly, John. *Nationalism and the State.* 2d ed. Chicago: University of Chicago Press, 1994.

Brown, Kendall. *Bourbons and Brandy: Imperial Reform in Eighteenth-Century Arequipa*. Albuquerque: University of New Mexico Press, 1986.

Buisson, Inge, Günter Kahle, Hans-Joachim König, and Hurst Pietschmann. *Problemas de la formación del estado y de la nación en Hispanoamérica*. Bonn: Inter Nationes, 1984.

Burchard, Roderick E. "Coca Chewing and Diet." *Current Anthropology* 33, no. 1 (February 1992): 1–24.

Burga, Manuel. *De la encomienda a la hacienda capitalista: El valle del Jequetepeque del siglo XVI al XX*. Lima: Instituto de Estudios Peruanos, 1976.

———. *Nacimiento de una utopía: Muerte y resurrección de los Incas*. Lima: Instituto de Apoyo Agrario, 1988.

Burga, Manuel, and Alberto Flores Galindo. *Apogeo y crisis de la república aristocrática*. Lima: Rikchay Peru, 1981.

Burga, Manuel, and Wilson Reátegui. *Lanas y capital mercantil en el sur del Perú. La casa Rickets, 1895–1935*. Lima: Instituto de Estudios Peruanos, 1981.

Burkholder, Mark A. *Politics of a Colonial Career. José Baquíjano and the Audiencia of Lima*. Albuquerque: University of New Mexico Press, 1980.

Burns, Kathryn Jane. "Apuntes sobre la economía conventual: El monasterio de Santa Clara del Cuzco." *Allpanchis* 38 (1991): 67–95.

———. "Convents, Culture, and Society in Cuzco, Peru, 1550–1865." Ph.D. diss., Harvard University, 1993.

Bushman, Richard L. *King and People in Provincial Massachusetts*. Chapel Hill: Institute of Early American History and Culture and the University of North Carolina Press, 1985.

Bushnell, David. "The Independence of Spanish South America." In *The Independence of Latin America, The Cambridge History of Latin America*, vol. 3, edited by Leslie Bethell, 93–154. Cambridge: Cambridge University Press, 1987.

Bushnell, David, and Neill Macaulay. *The Emergence of Latin America in the Nineteenth Century*. Oxford: Oxford University Press, 1988.

Cahill, David. "Crown, Clergy and Revolution in Bourbon Peru: The Diocese of Cuzco, 1780–1814." Ph.D. diss., University of Liverpool, 1984.

———. "Curas and Social Conflict in the Doctrinas of Cuzco, 1780–1814." *Journal of Latin American Studies* 16 (1984): 241–76.

———. "Repartos ilícitos y familias principales en el sur andino: 1780–1824." *Revista de Indias* 182–83 (1988): 449–73.

———. "Una visión andina: El levantamiento de Ocongate de 1815." *Histórica* 12, no. 2 (1988): 133–59.

———. "Taxonomy of a Colonial 'Riot': The Arequipa Disturbances of 1780." In *Reform and Insurrection in Bourbon New Granada and Peru*, edited by John R. Fisher, Allan J. Kuethe, and Anthony McFarlane, 255–91. Baton Rouge: Louisiana State University Press, 1990.

———. "Popular Religion and Appropriation: The Example of Corpus Christi in

Eighteenth-Century Peru." *Latin America Research Review* 31, no. 2 (1996): 67–110.

Cahill, David, and Scarlett O'Phelan Godoy. "Forging Their Own History: Indian Insurgency in the Southern Peruvian Sierra, 1815." *Bulletin of Latin American Research* 11, no. 2 (1992): 125–67.

Cahuata Corrales, Fructuoso. *Historia del periodismo cusqueño.* Lima: SAGSA, 1990.

Calhoun, Craig, ed. *Habermas and the Public Sphere.* Cambridge: MIT Press, 1992.

——. "New Social Movements of the Early Nineteenth Century." *Social Science History* 17 (1993): 385–428.

Campbell, Leon. *The Military and Society in Colonial Peru, 1750–1810.* Philadelphia: American Philosophical Society, 1978.

——. "Recent Research on Andean Peasant Revolts, 1750–1820." *Latin American Research Review* 14, no. 1 (1979): 3–49.

——. "Social Structure of the Túpac Amaru Army in Cuzco, 1780–81." *Hispanic American Historical Review* 61, no. 4 (1981): 675–93.

——. "Crime and Punishment in the Tupacamaru Rebellion in Peru." *Criminal Justice History* 5 (1984): 57–89.

——. "Women and the Great Rebellion in Peru, 1780–1783." *The Americas* 42, no. 2 (1985): 163–96.

——. "Ideology and Factionalism during the Great Rebellion, 1780–1782." In *Resistance, Rebellion, and Consciousness in the Andean Peasant World, 18th to 20th Centuries,* edited by Steve J. Stern, 110–39. Madison: University of Wisconsin Press, 1987.

Castillo Meléndez, Francisco, Luisa Figallo Pérez, and Ramón Serrera Contreras. *Las Cortes de Cádiz y la imagen de América (la visión etnográfica y geográfica del nuevo mundo).* Cádiz: Universidad de Cádiz, 1994.

Castro Arenas, Mario. *La novela peruana y la evolución social.* 2d. ed. Lima: José Godard Editor, n.d.

Censer, Jack R., and Jeremy D. Popkin, eds. *Press and Politics in Pre-Revolutionary France.* Berkeley and Los Angeles: University of California Press, 1987.

Cespedes del Castillo, Guillermo. "Lima y Buenos Aires: Repercusiones económicas y políticas de la creación del virreinato del Río de la Plata." *Anuario de Estudios Americanos* 3 (1946): 667–874.

Chasteen, John. *Heroes on Horseback: A Life and Times of the Last Gaucho Caudillos.* Albuquerque: University of New Mexico Press, 1995.

Chaterjee, Partha. *The Nation and Its Fragments: Colonial and Postcolonial Histories.* Princeton: Princeton University Press, 1993.

——. *Nationalist Thought and the Colonial World: A Derivative Discourse.* 2d impression. Minneapolis: University of Minnesota Press, 1993.

Chiaramonte, José Carlos. "Legalidad constitucional o caudillismo: El problema del orden social en el surgimiento de los estados autónomos del litoral argentino en la primera mitad del siglo XIX." *Desarrollo Económico* 26, no. 102 (1986): 175–96.

———. "Formas de identidad en el Río de la Plata luego de 1810." *Boletín del Instituto de Historia Argentina y Americana "Dr. E. Ravignani,* 3d series, 1, no. 1 (1989): 71–92.

———, ed. *Pensamiento de la ilustración: Economía y sociedad iberoamericana en el siglo XVIII.* Caracas: Biblioteca Ayacucho, 1979.

Chocano, Magdalena. "Ucronía y frustración en la conciencia histórica peruana." *Márgenes* 4 (1988): 55–89.

Choquehuanca, José Domingo. *Ensayo de estadística completa de los ramos económicos-políticos de la Provincia de Azángaro en el departamento de Puno de la República Peruana del quinquenio desde 1825 hasta 1829 inclusive.* Lima: Imprenta Manual Corral, 1833.

Cleven, N. Andrew. "Dictators Gamarra, Orbegoso, Salaverry and Santa Cruz." In *South American Dictators during the First Century of Independence,* edited by A. Curtis Wilgus, 289–333. Washington, D.C.: George Washington University Press, 1937.

Coatsworth, John H. "Obstacles to Economic Growth in Nineteenth-Century Mexico." *American Historical Review* 83 (February 1978): 80–100.

———. "The Limits of Colonial Absolutism: The State in Eighteenth-Century Mexico." In *Essays in the Political, Economic and Social History of Colonial Latin America,* edited by Karen Spalding, 25–51. Newark: University of Delaware Press, 1982.

———. "Patterns of Rural Rebellion in Latin America: Mexico in Comparative Perspective." In *Riot, Rebellion, and Revolution: Rural Social Conflict in Mexico,* edited by Friedrich Katz, 21–62. Princeton: Princeton University Press, 1988.

Colley, Linda. *Britons: Forging the Nation 1707–1837.* New Haven, Conn.: Yale University Press, 1992.

Concolorcorvo. *El Lazarillo de ciegos caminantes.* Paris: Biblioteca de Cultura Peruana/Declée de Brouwer, 1938.

Contreras, Carlos. "Estado republicano y tributo indígena en la sierra central en la post-independencia." *Histórica* 13, no. 1 (1989): 9–44.

Cooper, H.H.A. "A Short History of Peruvian Criminal Procedure and Institutions." *Revista de Derecho y Ciencias Políticas* 32 (1968): 215–67.

Cope, R. Douglas. *The Limits of Racial Domination: Plebeian Society in Colonial Mexico City, 1660–1720.* Madison: University of Wisconsin Press, 1994.

Cornejo Bouroncle, Jorge. *Tupac Amaru: La revolución precursora de la emancipación continental.* Cuzco: n.p., 1949.

———. *Pumacahua: La revolución del Cuzco de 1814.* Cuzco: Editorial H. G. Rozas, 1956.

Cornejo Polar, Antonio. *La formación de la tradición literaria en el Perú.* Lima: Centro de Estudios y Publicaciones, 1989.

Corrigan, Philip, and Derek Sayer. *The Great Arch: English State Formation as Cultural Revolution.* Oxford: Basil Blackwell, 1985.

Crespo, Alfonso. *Santa Cruz: El condor Indio.* México: Fondo de Cultura Económica, 1944.

Cutter, Charles R. *The Legal Culture of Northern New Spain, 1700–1810.* Albuquerque: University of New Mexico Press, 1995.

El Cuzco y sus provincias. Arequipa: Imprenta Miranda, 1848.

Darnton, Robert, and Daniel Roche, eds. *Revolution in Print: The Press in France 1775–1800.* Berkeley and Los Angeles: University of California Press, 1989.

Davis, Natalie Zemon. *Society and Culture in Early Modern France.* Stanford, Calif.: Stanford University Press, 1975.

De Armellada, Fray Cesáreo. *La causa indígena americana en las Cortes de Cádiz.* Madrid: Ediciones Cultura Hispánica, 1959.

De Baecque, Antoine. "Pamphlets: Libel and Political Mythology." In *Revolution in Print: The Press in France 1775–1800,* edited by Robert Darnton and Daniel Roche, 124-38. Berkeley and Los Angeles: University of California Press, 1989.

De Castro, Ignacio. *Relación del Cuzco.* Lima: Universidad Nacional Mayor de San Marcos, 1978 (1795).

De la Cadena, Marisol. " 'Las Mujeres son más Indias.' Etnicidad y género en una comunidad del Cusco." *Revista Andina* 9, no. 1 (1991): 7-29.

De Sartiges, Etienne Gilbert Eugene. *Dos viajeros franceses en el Perú republicano,* edited by Raúl Porras Barrenechea, translated by Emilia Romero. Lima: Editorial Cultural Antárctica, 1947.

Dean, Carolyn S. "Ethnic Conflict and Corpus Christi in Colonial Latin America." *Colonial Latin American Review* 2, nos. 1-2 (1993): 93-120.

Deas, Malcolm. "The Fiscal Problems of Nineteenth-Century Colombia." *Journal of Latin American Studies* 14 (November 1982): 287-328.

Del Busto Duthurburu, José Antonio. *José Gabriel Tupac Amaru antes de su rebelión.* Lima: Pontificia Universidad Católica del Perú, 1981.

Del Valle de Siles, María Eugenia. *Historia de la rebelión de Túpac Catari, 1781–1782.* La Paz: Editorial Don Bosco, 1990.

Dellepiane, Carlos. *Historia militar del Perú.* 2 vols. Lima: Librería e Imprenta Gil, 1931.

Denegri Luna, Félix. "Apuntes para una bibliografía de periódicos cuzqueños (1822–1837)." *Revista Histórica* 26 (1964): 106-235.

——. *Historia marítima del Perú.* 2nd ed. *La república, 1826 a 1851,* vol. 6. Lima: Instituto de Estudios Históricos-Marítimos del Perú, 1976.

——. "La antigua controversia sobre el libre comercio en el Cuzco de 1829." *Banca* (Lima) 2 (December 1982): 77-81.

Deustua, José. *La minería peruana y la iniciación de la república.* Lima: Instituto de Estudios Peruanos, 1986.

Díaz Rementería, Carlos. *El cacique en el virreinato del Perú, estudio histórico-jurídico.* Sevilla: Seminario de Antropología Americana, Universidad de Sevilla, 1977.

Díaz Venteo, Fernando. *Las campañas militares del Virrey Abascal.* Sevilla: Escuela de Estudios Hispano-Americanos, 1948.

Diez-Canseco, Ernesto. *Perú y Bolivia: Pueblos gemelos.* Lima: Imprenta Torres Aguirre, 1952.

Dirks, Nicholas B., Geoff Eley, and Sherry B. Ortner, eds. *Culture/Power/History: A Reader in Contemporary Social Theory.* Princeton: Princeton University Press, 1994.

Dunbar Temple, Ella. "Un linaje incaico durante la dominación española." *Revista Histórica* 18, no. 1 (1949): 44–77.

Dunkerley, James. "Reassessing Caudillismo in Bolivia, 1825–1879." *Bulletin of Latin American Research* 1 (1982): 13–25.

Durand, José. "El influjo de Garcilaso Inca en Túpac Amaru." *COPE* 2, no. 5 (1971): 2–7.

Durand Flórez, Luis. "La formulación nacional de (en) los bandos de Tupac Amaru." In *La revolución de los Tupac Amaru: Antología,* edited by Durand Flórez, 29–49. Lima: CNDBRETA, 1981.

——. *Criollos en conflicto: Cuzco después de Tupac Amaru.* Lima: Universidad de Lima, 1985.

——, ed. *La revolución de los Tupac Amaru: Antología.* Lima: CNDBRETA, 1981.

Echenique, José Rufino. *Memorias para la historia del Perú (1808–1878),* 2 vols. Lima: Editorial Huascarán, 1952.

Eguiguren, Luis Antonio. *La revolución de 1814.* Lima: La Opinión Nacional, 1914.

——. *Guerra separatista: Rebeliones de Indios en Sur América, la sublevación de Tupac Amaru. Crónica de Melchor de Paz.* 2 vols. Lima: n.p., 1952.

Eley, Geoff, and Ronald Grigor Suny, eds. *Becoming National.* New York: Oxford University Press, 1996.

Escandell-Tur, Neus. "Textile Production and Trade during the Colonial Period: Cuzco, 1570–1820," Ph.D. diss., University of California at San Diego, 1993.

——. *Producción y comercio de tejidos coloniales: Los obrajes y chorrillos del Cuzco 1570–1820.* Cuzco: Centro Bartolomé de Las Casas, 1997.

Estenssoro Fuchs, Juan Carlos. *Música y sociedades coloniales: Lima 1680–1830.* Lima: Colmillo Blanco, 1989.

Eyzaguirre, Jaime. "Los sospechosos de infidelidad en la Lima de 1813." *Mercurio Peruano* 35, no. 133 (1954): 951–60.

Farge, Arlette. *Subversive Words: Public Opinion in Eighteenth-Century France.* University Park: Penn State University Press, 1995.

Farriss, Nancy. *Maya Society under Colonial Rule.* Princeton: Princeton University Press, 1984.

Favre, Henri. "Bolívar y los Indios." *Histórica* 10, no. 1 (1986): 1–18.

Feierman, Steven. *Peasant Intellectuals: Anthropology and History in Tanzania.* Madison: University of Wisconsin Press, 1990.

Fisher, John R. *Government and Society in Colonial Peru: The Intendant System, 1784–1814.* London: Athlone Press, 1970.

——. "La rebelión de Tupac Amaru y el programa imperial de Carlos III." In *Tupac*

Amaru-II, edited by Alberto Flores Galindo, 109-28. Lima: Retablo de Papel, 1976.

———. *Silver Mines and Silver Miners in Colonial Peru, 1776–1824.* Liverpool: University of Liverpool Press, 1977.

———. "Royalism, Regionalism, and Rebellion in Colonial Peru, 1808-1815." *Hispanic American Historical Review* 59, no. 2 (May 1979): 232-58.

———. "Imperial 'Free Trade' and the Hispanic Economy, 1778-1796." *Journal of Latin American Studies* 13, no. 1 (1981): 21-56.

———. "Regionalism and Rebellion in Late Colonial Peru: The Aguilar-Ubalde Conspiracy of 1805." *Bibliotheca Americana* 1, no. 1 (1982): 44-59.

———. "Soldiers, Society, and Politics in Spanish America, 1750-1821." *Latin American Research Review* 17, no. 1 (1982): 217-22.

———. "La formación del estado peruano (1808-1824) y Simón Bolívar." In *Problemas de la formación del estado y de la nación en Hispanoamérica*, edited by Inge Buisson, 465-80. Bonn: Inter Nationes, 1984.

Fisher, L. E. *The Last Inca Revolt, 1780–1783.* Norman: University of Oklahoma Press, 1966.

Flores Galindo, Alberto. "Tupac Amaru y la sublevación de 1780." In *Tupac Amaru II–1780*, edited by Alberto Flores Galindo, 269-323. Lima: Retablo de Papel Ediciones, 1976.

———. "El militarismo y la dominación británica (1825-1845)." In *Nueva historia general del Perú*, edited by Carlos Araníbar and Heraclio Bonilla, 107-23. Lima: Mosca Azul Editores, 1979.

———. "La nación como utopía: Tupac Amaru 1780." In *La revolución de los Tupac Amaru: Antología*, ed. Luis Durand Flórez, 55-69. Lima: CNDBRETA, 1981.

———. *Aristocracia y plebe: Lima, 1760–1830 (Estructura de clases y sociedad colonial).* Lima: Mosca Azul Editores, 1984.

———. "Región y conflictos sociales: Lima y Cuzco en el siglo XVIII." *Los Caminos del Laberinto* 2 (1985): 33-41.

———. "La imagen y el espejo: La historiografía peruana (1910-1986)." *Márgenes* 4 (1986): 55-89.

———. "Las revoluciones Tupamaristas: Temas en debate." *Revista Andina* 7, no. 1 (1989): 279-87.

———. *Buscando un Inca.* 4th ed. Lima: Editorial Horizonte, 1994.

Florez, Pedro Celestino. *Guía de forasteros del departamento del Cuzco para el año 1833.* Cuzco: Imprenta Pública, 1833.

———. *Guía de forasteros del departamento del Cuzco para el año 1834.* Lima: Imprenta de M. Corral, 1834.

Fontana, Josep. *La crisis del Antiguo Régimen.* Barcelona: Editorial Crítica, 1979.

———. "Estado y hacienda en el 'despotismo ilustrado.'" In *Estado, hacienda, y sociedad en la historia de España*, edited by Bartolomé Bennassar, 125-47. Valladolid: Universidad de Valladolid, Instituto de Historia Simancas, 1989.

Forment, Carlos. "The Formation of Civil Society in Nineteenth-Century Peru: Democratic or Disciplinary." Manuscript, 1996.

Franco, Jean. *Plotting Women: Gender and Representation in Mexico.* New York: Columbia University Press, 1989.

Galdos Rodríguez, Guillermo. "Vinculaciones de las subversiones de Túpac Amaru y de Arequipa en 1780." In *Actas del coloquio internacional Tupac Amaru y su tiempo,* 271–78. Lima: CNDBRETA, 1982.

García Jordán, Pilar. *Iglesia y poder en el Perú contemporáneo, 1821–1919.* Cuzco: Centro Bartolomé de Las Casas, 1991.

García Jordan, Pilar, and Miguel Izard, eds. *Conquista y resistencia en la historia de América.* Barcelona: Universitat de Barcelona, 1992.

Garzón Heredia, Emilio. "1780: Clero, elite local y rebelión." In *Entre la retórica y la insurgencia: Las ideas y los movimientos sociales en los Andes, siglo XVIII,* edited by Charles Walker, 245–71. Cuzco: Centro Bartolomé de Las Casas, 1996.

Gerbi, Antonello. *The Dispute of the New World: The History of a Polemic, 1750–1900.* Pittsburgh: University of Pittsburgh Press, 1973.

Glave, Luis Miguel. "Agricultura y capitalismo en la sierra sur del Perú (fines del siglo XIX y comienzos de XX)." In *Estados y naciones en los Andes,* edited by J. P. Deler and Y. Saint-Geours, 1: 213–43. Lima: Instituto de Estudios Peruanos, 1986.

———. "Un curacazgo andino y la sociedad campesina del siglo XVII." In *Trajinantes: Caminos indígenas en la sociedad colonial siglos XVI/XVII,* 281–304. Lima: Instituto de Apoyo Agrario, 1989.

———. "Sociedad campesina y violencia rural en el escenario de la gran rebelión indígena de 1780." *Histórica* 14, no. 1 (1990): 27–68.

———. *Vida símbolos y batallas: Creación y recreación de la comunidad indígena, Cuzco, siglos XVI–XX.* Lima: Fondo de Cultura Económica, 1992.

Glave, Luis Miguel, and María Isabel Remy. *Estructura agraria y vida rural en una región andina: Ollantaytambo entre los siglos XVI y XIX.* Cuzco: Centro Bartolomé de Las Casas, 1983.

Godenzzi, Juan Carlos. "Discurso y actos de rebelión anticolonial: Textos políticos del siglo XVIII en los Andes." In *Del siglo del oro al siglo de las luces: Lenguaje y sociedad en los Andes del siglo XVIII,* edited by César Itier, 59–88. Cuzco: Centro Bartolomé de Las Casas, 1995.

Goldman, Noemi, "Legalidad y legitimidad en el caudillismo: Juan Facundo Quiroga y La Rioja en el Interior Rioplatense (1810–1835)." *Boletín del Instituto de Historia Argentina y Americana "Dr. E. Ravignani,* 3d series 7, no. 1 (1993), 31–58.

Gölte, Jürgen. *Repartos y rebeliones: Túpac Amaru y las contradicciones de la economía colonial.* Lima: Instituto de Estudios Peruanos, 1980.

González, Aníbal. *Journalism and the Development of Spanish American Narrative.* Cambridge: Cambridge University Press, 1993.

González Prada, Alfredo. *Un crimen perfecto: El asesinato del Gran Mariscal Don Agustín Gamarra, presidente del Perú.* New York: H. Wolff, 1941.

Gonzáles Stephan, Beatriz, et al., eds. *Esplendores y miserias del siglo XIX. Cultura y Sociedad en América Latina.* Caracas: Monte Avila Editores, 1994.

Goodman, Dena. "Public Sphere and Private Life: Toward a Synthesis of Current Historiographical Approaches to the Old Regime." *Theory and Society* 31 (1992): 1–20.

Gootenberg, Paul. "Beleaguered Liberals: The Failed First Generation of Free Traders in Peru." In *Guiding the Invisible Hand: Economic Liberalism and the State in Latin American History,* edited by Joseph L. Love and Nils Jacobsen, 63–97. New York: Praeger Press, 1988.

——. *Between Silver and Guano: Commercial Policy and the State in Postindependence Peru.* Princeton: Princeton University Press, 1989.

——. "*Carnero y Chuño:* Price Levels in Nineteenth-Century Peru." *Hispanic American Historical Review* 70, no. 1 (1990): 1–56.

——. "North-South: Trade Policy, Regionalism and Caudillismo in Post-Independence Peru." *Journal of Latin American Studies* 23 (1991): 273–308.

——. "Population and Ethnicity in Early Republican Peru: Some Revisions." *Latin American Research Review* 26, no. 3 (1991): 109–57.

——. *Imagining Development: Economic Ideas in Peru's "Fictitious Prosperity" of Guano, 1840–1880.* Berkeley and Los Angeles: University of California Press, 1993.

——. "Paying for Caudillos: The Politics of Emergency Finance in Peru, 1820–1845." In *Liberals, Politics and Power: State Formation in Nineteenth-Century Latin America,* edited by Vincent Peloso and Barbara Tenenbaum, 134–65. Athens: University of Georgia Press, 1996.

Graham, Richard, ed. *The Idea of Race in Latin America, 1870–1940.* Austin: University of Texas Press, 1990.

Guardino, Peter. "Las guerrillas y la independencia peruana: Un ensayo de interpretación." *Pasado y Presente* (Lima) 2–3 (1989): 101–17.

——. "Identity and Nationalism in Mexico: Guerrero, 1780–1840." *Journal of Historical Sociology* 7 (1994): 314–42.

——. *Peasants, Politics, and the Formation of Mexico's National State: Guerrero, 1800–1857.* Stanford, Calif.: Stanford University Press, 1996.

Guardino, Peter, and Charles Walker. "The State, Society, and Politics in Mexico and Peru in the Late Colonial and Early Republican Periods." *Latin American Perspectives* 19, no. 2 (1992): 10–43.

Gudeman, Stephen, and Alberto Rivera. *Conversations in Colombia: The Domestic Economy in Life and Text.* Cambridge: Cambridge University Press, 1990.

Guerra, Francois-Xavier. *Modernidad e independencias.* Madrid: Ediciones MAPFRE, 1992.

Guerra, Francois-Xavier, and Mónica Quijada, eds. *Imaginar la nación.* Hamburg: AHILA, 1994.

Guerrero, Andrés. "Curagas y tenientes políticos: La ley de la costumbre y la ley del estado (Otavalo, 1830–1875)." *Revista Andina* 7, no. 2 (1989): 321–63.

Guevara, Ernesto. *The Motorcycle Diaries: A Journey around South America,* translated by Ann Wright. London and New York: Verso, 1995.

Guha, Ranajit. *Elementary Aspects of Peasant Insurgency in Colonial India.* Delhi: Oxford University Press, 1983.

Gutierrez, Ramón. *La casa cuzqueña.* Corrientes: Universidad Nacional del Nordeste, 1981.

——. *Notas sobre las haciendas del Cuzco.* Buenos Aires: FECIC, 1984.

Hale, Charles. *Mexican Liberalism in the Age of Mora, 1821–1853.* New Haven, Conn.: Yale University Press, 1968.

——. "The Reconstruction of Nineteenth-Century Politics in Spanish America: A Case for the History of Ideas." *Latin American Research Review* 8, no. 2 (1973): 53–73.

——. "The Revival of Political History and the French Revolution in Mexico." In *The Global Ramifications of the French Revolution,* edited by Joseph Klaits and Michael H. Haltzel, 158–76. Cambridge: Cambridge University Press, 1994.

Hall, John A. "Nationalism: Classified and Explained." *Daedalus* 122, no. 3 (summer 1993): 1–28.

Halperín Donghi, Tulio. *Historia contemporánea de América latina.* Madrid: Alianza Editorial, 1969.

——. *The Aftermath of Revolution in Latin America,* translated by Josephine de Bunsen. New York: Harper Torchbooks, 1973.

——. *Guerra y finanzas en los orígenes del estado argentino (1791–1850).* Buenos Aires: Editorial del Belgrano, 1982.

——. *Reforma y disolución de los imperios Ibéricos, 1750–1850.* Madrid: Alianza Editorial, 1985.

——, ed. *Sarmiento: Author of a Nation.* Berkeley and Los Angeles: University of California Press, 1994.

Hamill, Hugh, ed. *Caudillos: Dictators in Spanish America.* Norman: University of Oklahoma Press, 1992.

Hamnett, Brian. *Revolución y contrarrevolución en México y el Perú: Liberalismo, realeza y separatismo, 1800–1824.* México City: Fondo de Cultura, 1978.

Hay, Douglas, et al. *Albion's Fatal Tree: Crime and Society in Eighteenth-Century England.* New York: Pantheon Books, 1975.

Herndon, Wm. Lewis, and Lardner Gibbon. *Exploration of the Valley of the Amazon Made under the Direction of the Navy Department.* Part 2 by Lt. Lardner Gibbon. Washington, D.C.: A.O.P. Nicholson, 1854.

Herrera, Bartolomé. *Escritos y discursos.* 2 vols. Lima: Biblioteca de la República, 1929.

Herrera Alarcón, Dante. "Las rebeliones durante el primer gobierno del Mariscal Gamarra." *Revista Histórica* 23 (1957–58): 246–77.

——. *Rebeliones que intentaron desmembrar al sur del Perú.* Callao: Colegio Militar Leoncio Prado, 1961.

Hidalgo Lehuede, Jorge. "Amarus y cataris: Aspectos mesiánicos de la rebelión indígena de 1781 en Cuzco, Chayanta, La Paz y Arica." *Chungará* 10 (1983): 117–38.

Hinojosa, Iván. "Población y conflictos campesinos en Coporaque (Espinar) 1770–1784." In *Comunidades campesinas: Cambios y permanencias,* edited by Alberto Flores Galindo, 229–56. Lima: CES Solidaridad, 1987.

——. "El nudo colonial: La violencia en el movimiento tupamarista." *Pasado y Presente* (Lima) 2–3 (1989): 73–82.

Hobsbawm, Eric. "Peasant Land Occupations." *Past and Present* 62 (1974): 120–52.

——. *Nations and Nationalism Since 1780.* Cambridge: Cambridge University Press, 1990.

Hobsbawm, Eric, and Terence Ranger, eds. *The Invention of Tradition.* Cambridge: Cambridge University Press, 1983.

Huertas Vallejo, Lorenzo, and Nadia Carnero Albarrán. *Diezmos del Cuzco, 1777–1853.* Lima: Universidad Nacional Mayor de San Marcos, 1983.

Hünefeldt, Christine. "Los indios y la Constitución de 1812." *Allpanchis* 11–12 (1978): 33–57.

——. *Lucha por la tierra y protesta indígena: Las comunidades indígenas del Perú entre colonia y república.* Bonn: Bonner Amerikanische Studien, 1982.

——. "Poder y contribuciones: Puno, 1825–1845." *Revista Andina* 7, no. 2 (1989): 367–409.

Hunt, Lynn. *Politics, Culture, and Class in the French Revolution.* Berkeley and Los Angeles: University of California Press, 1984.

——, ed. *The New Cultural History.* Berkeley and Los Angeles: University of California Press, 1989.

Husson, Patrick. *De la guerra a la rebelión.* Cuzco: Centro Bartolomé de las Casas, 1992.

"La institucionalización del ejército: Organización y doctrina." Manuscript, 1990.

Itier, César, ed. *Del siglo del oro al siglo de las luces: Lenguaje y sociedad en los Andes del siglo XVIII.* Cuzco: Centro Bartolomé de Las Casas, 1995.

Iturricha, Agustín. *Historia de Bolivia bajo la administración del Mariscal Andrés Santa Cruz.* Sucre: Imprenta Boliviana, 1920.

Jacob, Margaret. "The Mental Landscape of the Public Sphere: A European Perspective." *Eighteenth-Century Studies* 21, no. 1 (1994): 95–113.

Jacobsen, Nils. "Desarrollo económico y relaciones de clase en el sur andino (1780–1920): Una réplica a Karen Spalding." *Análisis* 5 (August 1979): 67–82.

——. "Land Tenure and Society in the Peruvian Altiplano: Azángaro Province, 1770–1920." Ph.D. diss. University of California, Berkeley, 1982.

——."Commerce in Late Colonial Peru and Mexico: A Comment and Some Comparative Suggestions." In *The Economies of Mexico and Peru During the Late Colonial Period, 1760–1820,* edited by Nils Jacobsen and Hans-Jürgen Puhle, 299–315. Berlin: Colloquium-Verlag, 1986.

——. "Taxation in Early Republican Peru, 1821-1851: Policy Making between Reform and Tradition." In *América Latina en la época de Simón Bolívar,* edited by Reinhard Liehr, 311-39. Berlin: Colloquium, 1989.

——. "Peasant Land Tenure in the Peruvian Altiplano in the Transition from Colony to Republic." Manuscript, 1989. Spanish translation, "Campesinos y tenencia de la tierra en el altiplano peruano en la transición de la colonia a la república." *Allpanchis* 37 (1991): 25-92.

——. *Mirages of Transition: The Peruvian Altiplano, 1780-1930.* Berkeley and Los Angeles: University of California Press, 1993.

——. "Liberalism and Indian Communities in Peru, 1821-1920. In *Liberals, the Church, and Indian Peasants: Corporate Lands and the Challenge of Reform in Nineteenth-Century Spanish America,* edited by Robert H. Jackson, 123-70. Albuquerque: University of New Mexico Press, 1997.

Jacobsen, Nils, and Hans-Jürgen Puhle, eds. *The Economies of Mexico and Peru during the Late Colonial Period, 1760-1820.* Berlin: Colloquium, 1986.

Joseph, Gilbert M. "On the Trail of Latin American Bandits: A Reexamination of Peasant Resistance." *Latin American Research Review* 25, no. 3 (1990): 7-53.

Joseph, Gilbert M., and Daniel Nugent, eds. *Everyday Forms of State Formation: Revolution and the Negotiation of Rule in Modern Mexico.* Durham, N.C.: Duke University Press, 1994.

Katz, Friedrich, ed. *Riot, Rebellion, and Revolution: Rural Social Conflict in Mexico.* Princeton: Princeton University Press, 1988.

King, James. "The Colored Castes and American Representation in the Cortes of Cádiz." *Hispanic American Historical Review* 33, no. 1 (1953): 33-64.

Keegan, John. *The Face of Battle: A Study of Agincourt, Waterloo and the Somme.* London: Penguin Books, 1976.

——. *The Mask of Command.* London: Penguin, 1987.

Klaiber, Jeffrey. "Religión y justicia en Tupac Amaru." *Allpanchis* 19 (1982): 173-86.

——. *La iglesia en el Perú.* Lima: Pontificia Universidad Católica del Perú, 1988.

Klein, Herbert. *Haciendas and 'Ayllus': Rural Society in the Bolivian Andes in the Eighteenth and Nineteenth Centuries.* Stanford, Calif.: Stanford University Press, 1993.

Klor de Alva, Jorge. "Colonialism and Post Colonialism as (Latin) American Mirages." *Colonial Latin American Review* 1-2 (1992): 3-23.

Kristal, Efraín. *The Andes Viewed from the City: Literary and Political Discourse on the Indian in Peru, 1848-1930.* New York: Peter Lang, 1987.

Krüggeler, Thomas. "El doble desafío: Los artesanos del Cuzco ante la crisis regional y la constitución del régimen republicano (1824-1869)." *Allpanchis* 38 (1991): 13-65.

——. "Unreliable Drunkards or Honorable Citizens? Artisans in Search of Their Place in the Cuzco Society (1825-1930)." Ph.D. diss., University of Illinois at Urbana-Champaign, 1993.

Kubler, George. *The Indian Caste of Peru, 1795–1940: A Population Study Based upon Tax Records and Census Reports*. Smithsonian Institution Institute of Social Anthropology Publications, no. 14. Washington, D.C.: Smithsonian Institution, 1952.

Landes, Joan. *Women and the Public Sphere in the Age of the French Revolution*. Ithaca: Cornell University Press, 1988.

Larson, Brooke. "Caciques, Class Structure and the Colonial State in Bolivia." *Nova Americana* 2 (1979): 197–235.

——. "Dimensiones históricas de la dinámica económica del campesinado contemporáneo en la región de Cochabamba." In *Explotación agraria y resistencia campesina en Cochabamba*, 165–91. 2d ed. Cochabamba: CERES, 1983.

——. "The Cotton Textile Industry of Cochabamba, 1770–1810: The Opportunities and Limits of Growth." In *The Economies of Mexico and Peru during the Late Colonial Period, 1760–1820*, edited by Nils Jacobsen and Hans-Jürgen Puhle, 150–68. Berlin: Colloquium-Verlag, 1986.

——. *Colonialism and Agrarian Transformation in Bolivia: Cochabamba, 1550–1900*. Princeton: Princeton University Press, 1988.

——. "Explotación y economía moral en los Andes." In *Reproducción y transformación de las sociedades andinas, siglos XVI–XX*, 2 vols., edited by Seguno Moreno Yañez and Frank Salomon, 441–80. Quito: Abya-Yala and MLAL, 1991.

Larson, Brooke, and Olivia Harris, eds. *Ethnicity, Markets, and Migration in the Andes: At the Crossroads of History and Anthropology*. Durham, N.C.: Duke University Press, 1995.

Lavalle, Bernard. "Presión colonial y reivindicación indígena en Cajamarca (1785–1820) según el archivo del 'Protector de Naturales.'" *Allpanchis* 35–36 (1991): 105–37.

Lazarus-Black, Mindie, and Susan F. Hirsch, eds. *Contested States: Law, Hegemony and Resistance*. London: Routledge, 1995.

Lecuña, Vicente. *Cartas del libertador*. Caracas: Lit. y Tip. del Comercio, 1929.

Lehning, James R. *Peasant and French: Cultural Contact in Rural France during the Nineteenth Century*. Cambridge: Cambridge University Press, 1995.

Lewin, Boleslao. *La rebelión de Túpac Amaru*. 3d ed. Buenos Aires: SELA, 1967 (1st ed. 1943).

Lockhart, James, and Stuart B. Schwartz. *Early Latin America: A History of Colonial Spanish America and Brasil*. Cambridge: Cambridge University Press, 1983.

Lofstrom, William. "Attempted Economic Reform and Innovation in Bolivia under José de Sucre, 1825–1928." *Hispanic American Historical Review* 50, no. 2 (1970): 279–99.

Lohmann Villena, Guillermo. "Criticismo e ilustración como factores formativos de la conciencia del Perú en el siglo XVIII." In *Problemas de la formación del estado y de la nación en Hispanoamérica*, edited by Inge Buisson, 15–31. Bonn: Inter Nationes, 1994.

Lorente, Sebastián. *Pensamientos sobre el Perú*. Lima: Universidad Nacional de San Marcos, 1967 (1855).

Lynch, John. *Spanish Colonial Administration, 1782–1810*. London: University of London Press, 1958.

——. *The Spanish American Revolutions, 1808–1826*. London: W. W. Norton, 1973.

——. *Argentine Dictator: Juan Manuel de Rosas, 1829–1852*. Oxford: Oxford University Press, 1981.

——. "Bolívar and the Caudillos." *Hispanic American Historical Review* 63, no. 1 (1983): 3–35.

——. "The Origins of Spanish American Independence." In *The Independence of Latin America,* edited by Leslie Bethell, 1–48. Cambridge: Cambridge University Press, 1987.

——. *Caudillos in Spanish America, 1800–1850*. Oxford: Clarendon Press, 1992.

——, ed. *Latin American Revolutions, 1808–1826: Old and New World Origins*. Norman: University of Oklahoma Press, 1994.

Lyon, Patricia. "El ocaso de los cocales de Paucartambo." *Revista de Museo e Instituto de Arqueología-Museo Inka* 25 (1995): 171–79.

Macera, Pablo. *Tres etapas en el desarrollo de la conciencia nacional*. Lima: Ediciones "Fanal," 1956.

——. "El indio y sus intérpretes peruanos del siglo XVIII." In *Trabajos de historia,* edited by Pablo Macera, 4 vols., 2: 303–16. Lima: Instituto Nacional de Cultura, 1977.

——. "El indio visto por los criollos y españoles." In *Trabajos de Historia,* edited by Pablo Macera, 4 vols., 2: 317–24. Lima: Instituto Nacional de Cultura, 1977.

——. *Trabajos de historia*. 4 vols. Lima: Instituto Nacional de Cultura, 1977.

——, ed. *Tierra y población en el Perú*. 4 vols. Lima: Seminario de Historia Rural Andina, 1972.

Macera, Pablo, and Felipe Márquez Abanto. "Informe geográfico del Perú." *Revista del Archivo Nacional* 28 (1964): 132–247.

MacLachlan, Colin. *Criminal Justice in Eighteenth-Century Mexico: A Study of the Tribunal of the Acordada*. Berkeley and Los Angeles: University of California Press, 1974.

Malamud, Carlos, ed. *Partidos políticos y elecciones en América Latina y la Peninsula Ibérica, 1830–1930*. Madrid: Instituto Universitario Ortega y Gasset, 1995.

Mallon, Florencia. *The Defense of Community in Peru's Central Highlands: Peasant Struggle and Capitalist Transition, 1860–1940*. Princeton: Princeton University Press, 1983.

——. "Nationalist and Antistate Coalitions in the War of the Pacific: Junín and Cajamarca, 1879–1902." In *Resistance, Rebellion, and Consciousness in the Andean Peasant World, 18th to 20th Centuries,* edited by Steve Stern, 232–79. Madison: University of Wisconsin Press, 1987.

——. "Economic Liberalism: Where We Are and Where We Need to Go." In

Guiding the Invisible Hand: Economic Liberalism and the State in Latin American History, edited by Joseph L. Love and Nils Jacobsen, 177–86. New York: Praeger Press, 1988.

——. "Indian Communities, Political Cultures, and the State in Latin America, 1780–1990." *Journal of Latin American Studies* 24 (1992): 35–53.

——. "The Promise and Dilemma of Subaltern Studies: Perspectives from Latin American History." *American Historical Review* 99, no. 5 (December 1994): 1491–1515.

——. *Peasant and Nation: The Making of Postcolonial Mexico and Peru*. Berkeley and Los Angeles: University of California Press, 1995.

Mannheim, Bruce. *The Language of the Inka since the European Invasion*. Austin: University of Texas Press, 1991.

Manrique, Nelson. *Campesinado y nación: Las guerrillas indígenas en la guerra con Chile*. Lima: C.I.C.-Ital Perú, S.A., 1981.

——. *Mercado interno y región: La sierra central, 1820–1930*. Lima: DESCO, 1987.

Marcoy, Paul (Laurent de Saint Cricq). *Travels in South America: From the Pacific Ocean to the Atlantic Ocean*. 3 vols. London: Blackie and Son, 1875.

Margadant, Ted W. "Tradition and Modernity in Rural France during the Nineteenth Century." *Journal of Modern History* 56, no. 4 (1984): 667–97.

Markham, Clements. *Cuzco: A Journey to the Ancient Capital of Peru and Lima: A Visit to the Capital and Provinces of Modern Peru*. London: Chapman and Hall, 1865.

Martin, Cheryl English. *Governance and Society in Colonial Mexico: Chihuahua in the Eighteenth Century*. Stanford, Calif.: Stanford University Press, 1996.

Martínez, Miguel A. *El mariscal de Piquiza, Don Agustín Gamarra*. Lima: Librería e Imprenta D. Miranda, 1946.

Martínez Alier, Juan. *Los huacchilleros del Perú*. Lima: Instituto de Estudios Peruanos, 1973.

Martínez Riaza, Ascensión. *La prensa doctrinal en la independencia del Perú, 1811–1824*. Madrid: Instituto de Cooperación Iberoamericana, 1985.

Méndez, Cecilia. *Incas sí, indios no: Apuntes para el estudio del nacionalismo criollo en el Perú*. Lima: IEP, 1993.

——. "Los campesinos, la independencia y la iniciación de la República. El caso de los iquichanos realistas: Ayacucho 1825–1828." In *Poder y Violencia en los Andes*, edited by Henrique Urbano, 165–88. Cuzco: Centro Bartolomé de Las Casas, 1991.

Mendiburu, Manuel de. *Biografías de generales republicanos*. Lima: Instituto Histórico del Perú, Academia Nacional de la Historia, 1963.

Mendoza-Walker, Zoila S. "Shaping Society through Dance: Mestizo Ritual Performance in the Southern Peruvian Andes." Ph.D. diss., University of Chicago, 1993.

——. "Contesting Identities through Dance: Mestizo Performance in the Southern Andes of Peru." *Repercussions* 3, no. 2 (1994): 50–80.

Merry, Sally Engle. "Law and Colonialism." *Law and Society Review* 25, no. 4 (1991): 889–922.

Miller, William. *Memoirs of General Miller in the Service of the Republic of Peru.* 2d ed. 2 vols. London: Longman, Rees, Orme, Brown and Green, 1829.

———. *Memorias del General Guillermo Miller.* Lima: Editorial Arica, 1975.

Molina Jiménez, Iván, and Stephen Palmer, eds. *El paso del cometa: Estado, política social y culturas populares en Costa Rica (1800–1950).* San José: Porvenir-Plumsock Mesoamerican Studies, 1994.

Monguió, Luis. *Don José Joaquín de Mora y el Perú del ochocientos.* Berkeley and Los Angeles: University of California Press, 1967.

Mörner, Magnus. "En torno a las haciendas de la región del Cuzco desde el siglo XVIII." In *Haciendas, latifundios y plantaciones en América latina,* edited by Enrique Florescano, 346–92. Mexico: Siglo veintiuno editores, 1975.

———. *Perfil de la sociedad rural del Cuzco a fines de la colonia.* Lima: Universidad del Pacífico, 1978.

———. *Notas sobre el comercio y los comerciantes del Cuzco desde fines de la colonia hasta 1930.* Lima: IEP, 1979.

———. "Compraventas de tierras en el Cuzco, 1825–1869." Stockholm: Instituto de Estudios Latinoamericanos, *Estudios Históricos sobre Estructuras Agrarias Andinas,* no. 1, 1984.

———. "La distribución de ingresos en un distrito andino en las años 1830." Working paper, Institute of Latin American Studies, Stockholm, n.d.

Mörner, Magnus, and Efraín Trelles. "A Test of Causal Interpretations of the Túpac Amaru Rebellion." In *Resistance, Rebellion, and Consciousness in the Andean Peasant World, 18th to 20th Centuries,* edited by Steve J. Stern, 94–109. Madison: University of Wisconsin Press, 1987.

Morse, Richard. "Towards a Theory of Spanish American Government." *Journal of the History of Ideas* 15 (1954): 71–93.

———. "The Heritage of Latin America." In *The Founding of New Societies: Studies in the Histories of the United States, Latin America, South Africa, Canada, and Australia,* edited by Louis Hartz, 123–77. New York: Harcourt, Brace and World, 1964.

Muratorio, Blanca, ed. *Imágenes e imagineros: Representaciones de los indígenas ecuatorianos, siglos XIX y XX.* Quito: FLACSO, 1994.

Nagengast, Carole. "Violence, Terror, and the Crisis of the State." *Annual Reviews in Anthropology* 23 (1994): 100–136.

Najarro Espinoza, Margareth. "El diezmo y la sociedad indígena del Cuzco (1765–1799)." Licenciatura thesis, Universidad Nacional San Antonio Abad del Cuzco, 1995.

O'Leary, Simón B. *Memorias del General O'Leary publicadas por su hijo Simón B. O'Leary.* Caracas: Imprenta de "El Monitor," 1884.

O'Phelan Godoy, Scarlett. "El sur andino a fines del siglo XVIII: Cacique o corregidor." *Allpanchis* 11–12 (1978): 17–32.

———. "La rebelión de Tupac Amaru, organización interna, dirigencia y alianzas." *Histórica* 3, no. 2 (1979): 89–121.

———. "Aduanas, mercado interno y elite comercial en el Cuzco antes y después de la gran rebelión de 1780." *Apuntes* 19 (1986): 53–72.

———. "Revueltas y rebeliones del Perú colonial." In *The Economies of Mexico and Peru during the Late Colonial Period, 1760–1820*, edited by Nils Jacobsen and Hans-Jürgen Puhle, 340–56. Berlin: Colloquium-Verlag, 1986.

———. "El mito de la 'independencia concedida:' Los programas políticos del siglo XVIII y del temprano XIX en el Perú y Alto Perú (1730–1814)." In *Independencia y revolución*, edited by Alberto Flores Galindo, 2: 145–99. 2 vols. Lima: Instituto Nacional de Cultura, 1987.

———. "Por el rey, religión y las patrias: Las juntas de gobierno de 1809 en La Paz y Quito." *Boletín del Instituto Francés de Estudios Andinos* 17, no. 2 (1988): 61–81.

———. *Un siglo de rebeliones anticoloniales: Perú y Bolivia 1700–1783*. Cuzco: Centro Bartolomé de Las Casas, 1988.

———. "Rebeliones andinas anticoloniales: Nueva Granada, Perú, y Charcas entre el siglo XVIII y XIX." *Anuario de Estudios Americanos* 49 (1993): 395–440.

———. *La gran rebelión en los Andes: De Túpac Amaru a Túpac Catari*. Cuzco: Centro Bartolomé de Las Casas, 1995.

Orbegoso, Luis José de. *Memorias del gran mariscal Don Luis José de Orbegoso*. 2d ed. Lima: Gil, S.A., 1940.

Ordoñez, Pastor. "Los Varayocc: Estudios sobre una forma de gobierno y administración." *Revista Universitaria* (Cuzco) 27–29 (1917): 27–40 and 41–48.

Oricaín, Pablo José. "Compendio breve de discursos varios." In *Juicio de límites entre el Perú y Bolivia: Prueba peruana*, edited by Víctor Maurtua, vol. 11 of 14. Barcelona: Imprenta de Henrich y Comp., 1906.

Orlove, Benjamin. *Alpacas, Sheep and Men: The Wool Export Economy and Regional Society of Southern Peru*. New York: Academic Press, 1977.

———. "La posición de los abigeos en la sociedad regional. El bandolerismo social en el Cuzco en vísperas de la reforma agraria." In *Bandoleros, abigeos, y montoneros: Criminalidad y violencia en el Perú, siglos XVIII–XX*, edited by Carlos Aguirre and Charles Walker, 279–305. Lima: Instituto de Apoyo Agrario, 1990.

Ortner, Sherry. "Resistance and the Problem of Ethnographic Refusal." *Comparative Studies in Society and History* 37, no. 1 (1995): 173–93.

Ozouf, Mona. *Festivals and the French Revolution*. Cambridge: Harvard University Press, 1988.

Pagden, Anthony. *Spanish Imperialism and the Political Imagination*. New Haven: Yale University Press, 1990.

Palmer, David Scott. *Peru: The Authoritarian Tradition*. New York: Praeger, 1980.

Pardo y Aliaga, Felipe. "Semblanzas peruanas." *Boletín de la Academia Chilena de la Historia* 33 (1945): 63–67.

Parkerson, Philip T. *Andrés de Santa Cruz y la Confederación Perú-Boliviana, 1835–1839*. La Paz: Librería Editorial "Juventud," 1984.

Paz Soldán, Luis Alayza. *El Gran Mariscal José de La Mar.* Lima: Gil, S.A., 1941.

Paz Soldán, Mariano Felipe. *Historia del Perú independiente (Primer Periódo, 1819–1822).* Havre: Imprenta de Alfonso LEMALE, 1868.

——. "Brevísimas notas biográficas." *Revista Chilena de Historia y Geografía* 8, no. 12 (1913): 147–60.

Pease, Franklin. "¿Por qué los andinos son acusados de litigiosos?" Manuscript, 1995.

Peloso, Vincent, and Barbara Tenenbaum, eds. *Liberals, Politics and Power: State Formation in Nineteenth-Century Latin America.* Athens: University of Georgia Press, 1996.

Peralta Ruíz, Víctor. *En pos del tributo: Burocracia estatal, elite regional y comunidades indígenas en el Cuzco rural (1826–1854).* Cuzco: Centro Bartolomé de Las Casas, 1991.

——. "Elecciones, constitucionalismo y revolución en el Cuzco, 1809–1815." In *Partidos políticos y elecciones en América Latina y la Península Ibérica, 1830–1930,* edited by Carlos Malamud, 1: 83–112. 2 vols. Madrid: Instituto Universitario Ortega y Gasset, 1995.

——. "Tiranía o buen gobierno: Escolasticismo y criticismo en el Perú del siglo XVIII." In *Entre la retórica y la insurgencia: Las ideas y los movimientos sociales en los Andes, siglo XVIII,* edited by Charles Walker, 67–87. Cuzco: Centro Bartolomé de Las Casas, 1996.

Phelan, John. *The People and the King: The Comunero Revolution in Colombia, 1781.* Madison: University of Wisconsin Press, 1978.

Piel, Jean. "The Place of the Peasantry in the National Life of Peru in the Nineteenth Century." *Past and Present* 46 (1970): 108–33.

——. "¿Cómo interpretar la rebelión panandina de 1780–1783?" In *Tres levantamientos populares: Pugachóv, Túpac Amaru, Hidalgo,* edited by Jean Meyer, 71–80. Mexico: CEMCA, 1992.

Pike, Frederick B. "Heresy, Real and Alleged in Peru: An Aspect of the Conservative-Liberal Struggle, 1830–1875." *Hispanic American Historical Review* 47, no. 1 (1967): 50–74.

——. *The Modern History of Peru.* New York: Frederick A. Praeger, 1967.

Pike, Ruth. "Penal Servitude in the Spanish Empire: Presidio Labor in the Eighteenth Century." *Hispanic American Historical Review* 58, no. 1 (1978): 21–40.

Platt, Tristan. *Estado boliviano y ayllu andino: Tierra y tributo en el norte de Potosí.* Lima: Instituto de Estudios Peruanos, 1982.

——. "Liberalism and Ethnocide in the Southern Andes." *History Workshop Journal* 17 (1984): 3–18.

——. "Simón Bolívar, the Sun of Justice and the Amerindian Virgin: Andean Conceptions of the Patria in Nineteenth-Century Potosí." *Journal of Latin American Studies* 25, no. 1 (1993) 159–85.

Poole, Deborah. "Landscapes of Power in a Cattle-Rustling Culture of Southern Andean Peru." *Dialectical Anthropology* 12 (1988): 367–98.

——, ed. *Unruly Order: Violence, Power and Cultural Identity in the High Provinces of Southern Peru*. Boulder, Colo.: Westview Press, 1995.

Popkin, Jeremy. Review essay on European studies on the public sphere. *Eighteenth-Century Studies* 28, no. 1 (fall 1994): 151–54.

Porras Barrenechea, Raúl. "Don Felipe Pardo y Aliaga, satírico limeño." *Revista Histórica* 20 (1953): 238–304.

——. *Antología del Cuzco*. Lima: Librería Internacional del Perú, 1961.

——. *Los ideólogos de la independencia*. Lima: Milla Batres, 1974.

Portacarrero, Gonzalo. "Conservadurismo, liberalismo y democracia en el Perú del siglo XIX." In *Pensamiento político peruano*, edited by Alberto Adrianzén, 85–98. Lima: DESCO, 1987.

Posada-Carbó, Eduardo, ed. *Elections before Democracy: The History of Elections in Europe and Latin America*. London: MacMillan, 1996.

Prakash, Gyan, ed. *After Colonialism: Imperial Histories and Postcolonial Displacements*. Princeton: Princeton University Press, 1995.

Pratt, Mary Louise. *Imperial Eyes: Travel Writing and Transculturation*. London: Routledge, 1992.

Proctor, Robert. *Narrative of a Journey Across the Cordillera of The Andes, and of a Residence in Lima, and Other Parts of Peru, In the Years 1823 and 1824*. London: Archibald Constable, 1825.

Pruvonena (José de la Riva Agüero). *Memorias y documentos para la historia de la independencia del Perú*. 2 vols. Paris: Librería de Garnier Hermanos, 1858.

Quijada, Mónica. "¿Qué Nación? Dinámicas y dicotomías de la nación en el imaginario hispanoamericano del siglo XIX." In *Imaginar la nación*, edited by Francois Xavier-Guerra and Mónica Quijada. Hamburg: AHILA, 1994.

Quiroz, Alfonso W. "Estructura económica y desarrollos regionales de la clase dominante, 1821–1850." In *Independencia y revolución, 1780–1840*, edited by Alberto Flores Galindo, 2: 201–67. 2 vols. Lima: INC, 1987.

Ramirez, Susan. *Provincial Patriarchs: Land Tenure and the Economics of Power in Colonial Peru*. Albuquerque: University of New Mexico Press, 1988.

Ramos, Gabriela, ed. *La venida del reino*. Cuzco: Centro Bartolomé de Las Casas, 1994.

Ramos Nuñez, Carlos Augusto. *Toribio Pacheco: Jurista peruano del siglo XIX*. Lima: Pontificia Universidad Católica del Perú, 1992.

Rasnake, Roger. *Domination and Cultural Resistance: Authority and Power among an Andean People*. Durham, N.C.: Duke University Press, 1988.

Remy, María Isabel. "La sociedad local al inicio de la república: Cuzco, 1824–1850." *Revista Andina* 7, no. 2 (1988): 451–84.

——. "Indios, estados y hacendados: Notas sobre fiscalidad, derechos y sujetos políticos en el siglo XIX." Manuscript, 1990.

Rieu-Millan, Marie Laure. *Los diputados americanos en las Cortes de Cádiz*. Madrid: CSIC, 1990.

Rivera Serna, Raúl. *Los guerrilleros del Centro en la emancipación peruana.* Lima: P. L. Villanueva, 1958.

———. "Aspectos de la economía durante el primer gobierno de Mariscal Don Agustín Gamarra." *Revista Histórica* 24 (1959): 400–440.

———. "Las juntas departamentales durante el primer gobierno del Mariscal Don Agustín Gamarra." *Boletín de la Biblioteca Nacional* 31–32 (1964): 3–18.

Rodríguez, Linda Alexander. *The Search for Public Policy: Regional Politics and Government Finances in Ecuador, 1830–1940.* Berkeley and Los Angeles: University of California Press, 1985.

Rosaldo, Renato. "From the Door of His Tent." In *Writing Culture: The Poetics and Politics of Ethnography,* edited by James Clifford and George Marcus, 77–97. Berkeley and Los Angeles: University of California Press, 1986.

Roseberry, William. "Beyond the Agrarian Question in Latin America." In *Confronting Historical Paradigms: Peasants, Labor, and the Capitalist World System in Africa and Latin America,* by Frederick Cooper et al. 318–68. Madison: University of Wisconsin Press, 1993.

———. "Hegemony and the Language of Contention," in *Everyday Forms of State Formation: Revolution and Negotiation of Rule in Modern Mexico,* edited by Gilbert M. Joseph and Daniel Nugent. Durham, N.C.: Duke University Press, 1994.

Rowe, John. "El movimiento nacional inca del siglo XVIII." In *Tupac Amaru II–1780,* ed. Alberto Flores Galindo, 13–53. Lima: Retablo de Papel Ediciones, 1976.

———. "Genealogía y rebelión en el siglo XVIII: Algunos antecedentes de la sublevación de José Gabriel Thupa Amaro." *Histórica* 6, no. 1 (July 1982): 65–85.

———. "Las circunstancias de la rebelión de Thupa Amaro en 1780." *Revista Histórica* 34 (1983–84): 119–40.

Rowe, William, and Vivian Schelling. *Memory and Modernity: Popular Culture in Latin America.* London: Verso, 1991.

Sábato, Hilda. "Citizenship, Political Participation and the Formation of the Public Sphere in Buenos Aires 1850s–1880s." *Past and Present* 136 (1992): 139–63.

Safford, Frank. "Bases of Political Alignment in Early Republican Spanish America." In *New Approaches to Latin American History,* edited by Richard Graham and Peter H. Smith, 77–111. Austin: University of Texas Press, 1974.

———. "Politics, Ideology, and Society." In *Spanish America after Independence c. 1820–c. 1870, Cambridge History of Latin America,* edited by Leslie Bethell, 48–122. Cambridge: Cambridge University Press, 1987.

———. "Race, Integration, and Progress: Elite Attitudes and the Indian in Colombia, 1750–1870." *Hispanic American Historical Review* 71, no. 1 (1991): 1–33.

Sahlins, Peter. *Boundaries: The Making of France and Spain in the Pyrenees.* Berkeley and Los Angeles: University of California Press, 1989.

Sahuaraura Titu Atauchi, Rafael José. *Estado del Perú,* notes and edited by Francisco A. Loayza. Lima: Librería e Imprenta D. Miranda, 1944.

Saignes, Thierry. "De la borrachera al retrato: Los curacas andinos entre dos legiti-midades." *Revista Andina* 5, no. 1 (1987): 139-70.

Sala i Vila, Nuria. "Revueltas indígenas en el Perú tardocolonial." Ph.D. diss., Universidad de Barcelona, Departamento de Historia de América, 1989.

——. "El levantamiento de los pueblos de Aymaraes en 1818." *Boletín Americanista* 39-40 (1989-90): 203-26.

——. "De Inca a indígena: Cambio en la simbología del sol a principios del siglo XIX." *Allpanchis* 35-36, no. 2 (1991): 599-633.

——. "Mistis e indígenas: La lucha por el control de las comunidades indígenas en Lampa, Puno, a fines de la colonia." *Boletín Americanista* 41 (1991): 35-66.

——. "La revuelta de Julí en 1806: Crisis de subsistencia y economía campesina." *Revista de Indias* 192 (1991): 343-74.

——. "La participación indígena en la rebelión de los Angulo y Pumacahua, 1814-1816." In *Conquista y resistencia en la historia de América*, edited by Pilar García Jordán, Miguel Izard, 273-88. Barcelona: Universitat de Barcelona, 1992.

——. "Gobierno colonial, iglesia y poder en Perú." *Revista Andina* 11, no. 1 (1993): 133-61.

——. *Y se armó el tole tole: Tributo indígena y movimientos sociales en el virreinato del Perú, 1784-1814.* Lima: IER José María Arguedas, 1996.

Sallnow, Michael J., ed. *Pilgrims of the Andes: Regional Cults in Cusco.* Washington, D.C.: Smithsonian Institution Press, 1987.

Salvatore, Ricardo, and Carlos Aguirre, eds. *The Birth of the Penitentiary in Latin America: Essays on Criminology, Prison Reform, and Social Control, 1830-1940.* Austin: University of Texas Press, 1996.

Sánchez-Albornoz, Nicolás. *Indios y tributos en el Alto Perú.* Lima: Instituto de Estudios Peruanos, 1978.

Sarmiento, Domingo F. *Life in the Argentine Republic in the Days of the Tyrants; or Civilization and Barbarism.* New York: Hurd and Houghton, 1868.

Schafer, Robert. *The Economic Societies in the Spanish World, 1763-1821.* Syracuse, N.Y.: Syracuse University Press, 1958.

Scott, James C. *The Moral Economy of the Peasant: Rebellion and Subsistence in South-east Asia.* New Haven, Conn.: Yale University Press, 1976.

——. *Weapons of the Weak: Everyday Forms of Peasant Resistance.* New Haven: Yale University Press, 1985.

——. *Domination and the Arts of Resistance, Hidden Transcripts.* New Haven: Yale University Press, 1990.

Seed, Patricia. "Social Dimensions of Race: Mexico City, 1753." *Hispanic American Historical Review* 62 (1982): 559-696.

Seiner, Lizardo. "Economía, sociedad y política en una coyuntura rebelde: Tacna, 1811-1814." *Pasado y Presente* 2-3 (Lima) (1989): 85-99.

Seligmann, Linda. *Between Reform and Revolution: Political Struggles in the Peruvian Andes, 1969-1991.* Stanford, Calif.: Stanford University Press, 1995.

Sempat Assadourian, Carlos. *El sistema de la economía colonial: Mercado interno, regiones y espacio económico.* Lima: Instituto de Estudios Peruanos, 1982.

Seraylán Leiva, Alejandro. *Campañas militares durante la dominación española.* Historia General del Ejército Peruano, tomo 3, vol. 2. Lima: Comisión Permanente de Historia del Ejército del Perú, 1981.

Serúlnikov, Sergio. "Reivindicaciones indígenas y legalidad colonial. La rebelión de Chayanta (1777-1781)." Documento CEDES/20. Buenos Aires: CEDES, 1989.

——. "Su verdad y su justicia: Tomás Catari y la insurrección Aymara de Chayanta, 1777-1780." In *Entre la retórica y la insurgencia: Las ideas y los movimientos sociales en los Andes, siglo XVIII,* edited by Charles Walker, 205-43. Cuzco: Centro Bartolomé de Las Casas, 1996.

Skurski, Julie. "The Ambiguities of Authenticity in Latin America: Doña Barbara and the Construction of National Identity." In *Becoming National,* edited by Geoff Eley and Donald Grigor Suny, 371-402. Oxford: Oxford University Press, 1996.

Spalding, Karen. "Social Climbers: Changing Patterns of Mobility among the Indians of Colonial Peru." *Hispanic American Historical Review* 50, no. 4 (1970): 645-64.

——. "Kurakas and Commerce: A Chapter in the Evolution of Andean Society." *Hispanic American Historical Review* 54, no. 4 (1973): 581-99.

——. *De indio a campesino.* Lima: Instituto de Estudios Peruanos, 1974.

——. "Class Structure in the Southern Peruvian Highland, 1750-1920." In *Land and Power in Latin America,* edited by Benjamin Orlove and Glynn Custred, 79-97. New York: Holmes and Meier Publishers, 1980.

——. *Huarochirí: An Andean Society under Inca and Spanish Rule.* Stanford, Calif.: Stanford University Press, 1984.

Spier, Fred. *Religious Regimes in Peru: Religion and State Development in a Long-Term Perspective and the Effects in the Andean Village of Zurite.* Amsterdam: Amsterdam University Press, 1994.

Starn, Orin. "Missing the Revolution: Anthropologists and the War in Peru." *Cultural Anthropology* 6 (1991): 63-91.

Stavig, Ward. "Violencia cotidiana de los naturales de Quispicanchis y Canas y Canchis en el siglo XVIII." *Revista Andina* 3, no. 2 (1986): 451-68.

——. "Ethnic Conflict, Moral Economy, and Population in Rural Cuzco on the Eve of the Thupa Amaro II Rebellion." *Hispanic American Historical Review* 68, no. 4 (1988): 737-70.

——. "Ladrones, cuatreros y salteadores: Indios criminales en el Cuzco rural a fines de la colonia." In *Bandoleros, abigeos, y montoneros: Criminalidad y violencia en el Perú, siglos XVIII-XX,* edited by Carlos Aguirre and Charles Walker, 69-103. Lima: Instituto de Apoyo Agrario, 1990.

——. "The Past Weighs on the Minds of the Living: Culture, Ethnicity, and the Rural Lower Class." *Latin American Research Review* 26, no. 2 (1990): 225-46.

———. "'Living in Offense of Our Lord': Indigenous Sexual Values and Marital Life in the Colonial Crucible." *Hispanic American Historical Review* 75, no. 4 (1995): 597–622.

Stern, Steve. *Peru's Indian Peoples and the Challenge of Spanish Conquest, Huamanga to 1640.* Madison: University of Wisconsin Press, 1982.

———. *Resistance, Rebellion, and Consciousness in the Andean Peasant World, 18th to 20th Centuries.* Madison: University of Wisconsin Press, 1987.

Stevens, Donald F. *Origins of Instability in Early Republican Mexico.* Durham, N.C.: Duke University Press, 1991.

Stoler, Ann Laura. "Rethinking Colonial Categories: European Communities and the Boundaries of Rule." *Comparative Studies in Society and History* 31, no. 1 (1989): 134–61.

Sweetman, David. *Paul Gauguin: A Complete Life.* London: Hodder & Stoughton, 1995.

Szeminski, Jan. *La utopía tupamarista.* Lima: Pontifica Universidad Católica del Perú, 1983.

———. "Why Kill the Spaniard? New Perspectives on Andean Insurrectionary Ideology in the 18th Century." In *Resistance, Rebellion, and Consciousness in the Andean Peasant World, 18th to 20th Centuries,* edited by Steve J. Stern, 166–92. Madison: University of Wisconsin Press, 1987.

Tamayo Herrera, José. *Historia social del Cuzco republicano.* 2d ed. Lima: Editorial Universo, 1981.

Tandeter, Enrique. "Crisis in Upper Peru, 1800–1805." *Hispanic American Historical Review* 71, no. 1 (1991): 35–71.

Tandeter, Enrique, Wilma Milletich, Ma. Matilde Ollier, and Beatríz Ruibal. "El mercado de Potosí a fines del siglo XVIII." In *La participación indígena en los mercados surandinos, estrategias y reproducción social. Siglos XVI a XX,* edited by Olivia Harris, Brooke Larson, and Enrique Tandeter, 379–424. Cochabamba: CERES, 1987.

Tandeter, Enrique, and Nathan Wachtel. "Prices and Agricultural Production: Potosí and Charcas in the Eighteenth Century." In *Essays on the Price History of Eighteenth-Century Latin America,* edited by Lyman L. Johnson and Enrique Tandeter, 201–75. Albuquerque: University of New Mexico Press, 1989.

Tauro, Alberto. *Epistolario del Gran Mariscal Agustín Gamarra.* Lima: Facultad de Letras, Universidad Nacional Mayor de San Marcos, 1952.

———. "Agustín Gamarra, fundador de la independencia nacional." In *Historia del Perú,* edited by César Pacheco Vélez, 507–18. Biblioteca de Cultura Peruana Contemporánea, no. 7. Lima: Ediciones del Sol, 1963.

Távara, Santiago. *Historia de los partidos.* Edited by Jorge Basadre and Félix Denegri Luna. Lima: Editorial Huascarán, 1951.

Taylor, Alan. "The Art of Hook and Snivey: Political Culture in Upstate New York during the 1790s." *Journal of American History* 79, no. 4 (1993): 1371–96.

Taylor, William. *Drinking, Homicide and Rebellion in Colonial Mexican Villages.* Stanford, Calif.: Stanford University Press, 1979.

Tenenbaum, Barbara. *The Politics of Penury: Debts and Taxes in Mexico, 1821–1856.* Albuquerque: University of New Mexico Press, 1986.

TePaske, John, and Herbert Klein. *The Royal Treasuries of the Spanish Empire in America.* Vol. 1, *Peru.* Durham, N.C.: Duke University Press, 1982.

Thompson, E. P. "The Moral Economy of the English Crowd in the Eighteenth Century." *Past and Present* 50 (1971): 76–136.

——. "The Moral Economy Reviewed." In *Customs in Common,* 259–351. New York: New Press, 1991.

Thompson, Guy P. C. "Bulwarks of Patriotic Liberalism: The National Guard, Philharmonic Corps and Patriotic Juntas in Mexico, 1847–88." *Journal of Latin American Studies* 22, no. 1 (1990): 31–68.

Thurner, Mark. "Historicizing 'the Postcolonial' from Nineteenth-Century Peru." *Journal of Historical Sociology* 9, no. 1 (1995): 1–18.

——. "*Republicanos* and *la Comunidad de Peruanos:* Unimagined Political Communities in Postcolonial Andean Peru." *Journal of Latin American Studies* 27, no. 2 (1995): 291–318.

——. *From Two Republics to One Divided: Contradictions of Postcolonial Nation-making in Andean Peru.* Durham, N.C.: Duke University Press, 1996.

Tilly, Charles, ed. *The Formation of National States in Western Europe.* Studies in Political Development, no. 8. Princeton: Princeton University Press, 1975.

——. "Did the Cake of Custom Break?" In *Consciousness and Class Experience in Nineteenth-Century Europe,* edited by John Merriman, 17–44. New York: Holmes and Meier, 1979.

——. "Citizenship, Identity and Social History." *International Review of Social History* 40, supplement 3 (1995): 1–17.

Tord, Javier, and Carlos Lazo. *Hacienda, comercio, fiscalidad y luchas sociales (Perú colonial).* Lima: BPHES, 1981.

Torero Gomero, Carmen. "Establecimiento de la audiencia del Cuzco." *Boletín del Instituto Riva Agüero* 8 (1969): 374–522.

Trazegnies, Fernando de. *La idea de derecho en el Perú republicano del siglo XIX.* Lima: Pontificia Universidad Católica del Perú, 1980.

Tristan, Flora. *Peregrinations of a Pariah.* Translated, edited, and introduced by Jean Hawkes. London: Virago, 1986.

Urbano, Henrique, ed. *Modernidad en los Andes.* Cuzco: Centro de estudios regionales andinos "Bartolomé de las Casas," 1991.

Uriel García, José. "La visita de Bolívar al Cuzco." *Revista del Instituto Americano de Arte* 9 (1959): 9–18.

Usner, Daniel H. *Indians, Settlers and Slaves in a Frontier Exchange Economy: The Lower Mississippi Valley Before 1783.* Chapel Hill: University of North Carolina Press and the Institute of Early American History and Culture, 1992.

Valcárcel, Carlos Daniel. "Fidelismo y separatismo de Túpac Amaru." In *La revolución de los Tupac Amaru: Antología,* edited by Luis Durand Flórez, 361–73. Lima: CNDBRETA, 1981.

Valderrama Fernández, Ricardo, and Carmen Escalante Gutiérrez. "'Nuestras vidas' (abigeos de Cotabambas)." In *Bandoleros, abigeos, y montoneros: Criminalidad y violencia en el Perú, siglos XVIII–XX,* edited by Carlos Aguirre and Charles Walker, 309–32. Lima: Instituto de Apoyo Agrario, 1990.

Valdelomar, Abraham. *La Mariscala: Doña Francisca Zubiaga y Bernales de Gamarra.* Lima: Taller Tip. de la Penitenciaría, 1914.

Váldez y Palacios, José Manuel. *Viaje del Cuzco a Belen en el Gran Para.* Lima: Biblioteca Nacional del Peru, 1971 (1844).

Valdivia, Juan Gualberto. *Memorias sobre las revoluciones de Arequipa desde 1834 hasta 1866.* 3d ed. 2 vols. Arequipa: Ediciones Populibros, 1957.

Valega, José María. *República del Perú.* Lima: Librería e Imprenta Don Miranda, 1927.

Van Aken, Mark. "The Lingering Death of Indian Tribute in Ecuador." *Hispanic American Historical Review* 61, no. 3 (1981): 429–59.

———. *King of the Night: Juan José Flores and Ecuador, 1824–1864.* Berkeley and Los Angeles: University of California Press, 1989.

Van Young, Eric. "Millenium on the Northern Marches: The Mad Messiah of Durango and Popular Rebellion in Mexico, 1800–1815." *Comparative Studies in Society and History* 28 (1986): 386–413.

———. "Quetzalcóatl, King Ferdinand, and Ignacio Allende Go to the Seashore; or Messianism and Mystical Kingship in Mexico, 1800–1821." In *The Independence of Mexico and the Origins of the Nation,* edited by Jaime O. Rodriguez, 176–204. Los Angeles: UCLA Latin American Center, 1989.

———. "To See Someone Not Seeing: Historical Studies of Peasants and Politics in Mexico." *Mexican Studies* 6, no. 1 (1990): 133–59.

———. "Agrarian Rebellion and Defense of Community: Meaning and Collective Violence in Late Colonial and Independence-Era Mexico." *Journal of Social History* 27, no. 2 (1993): 245–69.

———. "The Other Rebellion: A Social Profile of Insurgency in Mexico, 1810–1815." Manuscript, 1994.

Vargas, M. Nemesio. *Historia del Perú independiente.* 8 vols. Lima: Imprenta de "El Lucero," 1908.

Vargas Ugarte, Rubén. *Historia del culto de María en Iberoamérica y de sus imagenes y santuarios más celebrados.* 3d ed. Madrid: Talleres Gráficos, 1956.

———. *Historia de la iglesia en el Perú.* 5 vols. Burgos: Imprenta de Aldecoa, 1968.

Vega, Juan José. *José Gabriel Tupac Amaru.* Lima: Editorial Universo, 1969.

———. *Tupac Amaru y sus compañeros.* 2 vols. Cuzco: Municipalidad del Qosqo, 1995.

Verdery, Katherine. "Whither 'Nation' and 'Nationalism'?" In *Mapping the Nation,* edited by Benedict Anderson, 226–34. London: Verso Press, 1996.

Vernus, Michael. "A Provincial Perspective." In *Revolution in Print: The Press in France 1775–1800*, edited by Robert Darnton and Daniel Roche, 124–38. Berkeley and Los Angeles: University of California Press, 1989.

Villanueva, Victor. *Ejército peruano: Del caudillaje anárquico al militarismo reformista.* Lima: Juan Mejía Baca, 1973.

Villanueva Chávez, Elena. "La lucha por el poder entre los emigrados peruanos." *Boletín del Instituto Riva-Agüero* 6 (1963–65): 112–67.

Villanueva Urteaga, Horacio. "La idea de los Incas como factor favorable a la independencia." *Revista Universitaria* (Cuzco) 115 (1958): 137–58.

———. "La revolución de Lopera y el efímero estado central del Perú." *Revista del Archivo Histórico del Cuzco* 12 (1967): 59–148.

———. *Simón Bolívar en el Cuzco.* Caracas: Biblioteca Venezolana de Historia, 1971.

———. *Gamarra y la iniciación republicana en el Cuzco.* Lima: Banco de los Andes, 1981.

———. "El Mariscal Don Agustín Gamarra y el Cuzco." *Andes* 2 (1995): 227–48.

———. "Don Pablo Mar y Tapia, anfitrión de presidentes." *Revista del Archivo General de la Nación* 7 (n.d.): 163–75.

Viotti da Costa, Emilia. *The Brazilian Empire: Myth and Histories.* Chicago: University of Chicago Press, 1985.

Voekel, Pamela. "Peeing on the Palace: Bodily Resistance to Bourbon Reforms in Mexico City." *Journal of Historical Sociology* 5, no. 2 (June 1992): 183–208.

Wagner de Reyna, Alberto. *Los límites del Perú.* Lima: Editorial Universitaria, 1961.

Walker, Charles. "Montoneros, bandoleros, malhechores: Criminalidad y política en las primeras décadas republicanas." In *Bandoleros, abigeos, y montoneros: Criminalidad y violencia en el Perú, siglos XVIII–XX,* edited by Carlos Aguirre and Charles Walker, 107–36. Lima: Instituto de Apoyo Agrario, 1990.

———. "La historiografía en inglés sobre los Andes. Balance de la década del 80." *Revista Andina,* 9, no. 2 (December 1991): 513–28.

———. "Peasants, Caudillos, and the State in Peru: Cuzco in the Transition from Colony to Republic, 1780–1840." Ph.D. diss., University of Chicago, 1992.

———. "The Patriotic Society: Discussions and Omissions about Indians in the Peruvian War of Independence." *The Americas* 55, no. 2 (October 1998).

———, ed. *Entre la retórica y la insurgencia: La historia de las ideas y los movimientos sociales en los Andes, siglo XVIII.* Cuzco: Centro Bartolomé de Las Casas, 1996.

Weber, Eugen. *Peasants into Frenchmen: The Modernization of Rural France, 1879–1914.* Stanford, Calif.: Stanford University Press, 1976.

White, Richard. *The Middle Ground: Indians, Empires, and Republics in the Great Lakes Region, 1650–1815.* Cambridge: Cambridge University Press, 1991.

Wibel, John Frederick. "The Evolution of a Regional Community within the Spanish Empire and Peruvian Nation: Arequipa, 1780–1845." Ph.D. diss., Stanford University, 1975.

Wightman, Ann. *Indigenous Migration and Social Change: The Forasteros of Cuzco, 1570–1720.* Durham, N.C.: Duke University Press, 1990.

Williams, Brackette. "A Class Act: Anthropology and the Race to Nation across Ethnic Terrain." *Annual Review of Anthropology* 18 (1989): 401–44.

Wolf, Eric R., and Edward C. Hansen. "Caudillo Politics: A Structural Analysis." *Comparative Studies in Society and History* 9, no. 2 (January 1967): 168–79.

Wu, Celia. *Generals and Diplomats: Great Britain and Peru, 1820–1840.* Cambridge: Centre of Latin American Studies, University of Cambridge, 1991.

INDEX

Abascal y Sousa, José Fernando de, 89–90, 95–96, 98, 102, 189
Aguilar, Gabriel, 86–88
Alcabala (sales tax): and Bourbon reforms, 23, 29; Gamarra's use of, 134; and Indians, 95; and "rebellion of the pasquinades," 31; and Tupac Amaru, 35, 43. *See also* Taxes
Alcaldes varayoks (Indian mayors), 63, 71–73, 210–11, 226
Amazon basin, 10, 206
Andean utopia. *See* Inca revivalism; Flores Galindo, Alberto
Angulo, José, 98–100
Antonio de Areche, José: fiscal reforms by, 29, 51; policies abolished, 32; and Tupac Amaru rebellion, 48, 53, 57, 62; as Visitor General, 23, 28
Apasa, Julian, 33, 49. *See also* Tupac Katari rebellion
Arequipa, 9, 10, 41; animosity with Cuzco, 149–50, 185; economy of, 135, 205; and Gamarra, 147; intendency of, 65; riots in, 29–32; sugar production in, 66
Aréstegui, Narcisco, 180–82; *El Padre Horán,* 180–82

Argentina, 122; gauchos of, 212; and José de San Martín, 14, 126; and Tupac Amaru rebellion, 12, 16, 40. *See also* Buenos Aires; Río de la Plata
Arriaga, Antonio de, 28–29, 33–35
Audiencia: cabildo members arrested by, 97; changes in cacique office, 62–63; closed by Gamarra, 131; court cases tried by, 70–83, 91, 113; presidents of, 98, 108–9; procurator of, 144; and Pumacahua rebellion, 101; and Tupac Amaru rebellion, 46; and Tupac Katari rebellion, 33; and War of Independence, 88–89
Ayllus, 64, 69–70, 77
Aymaraes, 10; rebellion of, 110–13. *See also* War of Independence
Azángaro, 90

Baquíjano, José, 79
Basadre, Jorge, 155, 222
Bastidas, Antonio, 33
Bastidas, Micaela: capture, 49; execution, 1, 53; as rebel leader, 27, 41, 45, 47. *See also* Women
Battle of Ayacucho, 85, 107, 114, 121, 128, 136

Battle of Ingavi, 1–2, 122, 222
Battle of Sangararā, 37–39, 43
Battle of Yanacocha, 15, 159, 161, 213–16, 218
Belgrano, Manuel, 100, 102
Bermúdez, Pedro Pablo, 158
Betancur, Diego Felipe de, 27–28
"Black Angel." *See* Gamarra, Agustín
Blacks: as leaders of rebellion, 42; opposed to Spanish rule, 13; population in Cuzco of, 12; population on Peruvian coast of, 190; as slaves, 106–7; Tupac Amaru's recruitment of, 17, 42, 52. *See also* Lower classes
Blanco, Hugo, 230
Bolaños, Santiago, 35
Bolívar, Simón: celebrated in Cuzco, 165–66; expulsion from Peru, 121; reforms by, 132–34, 189–90, 210; in War of Independence, 14, 85, 108, 128
Bolivia, 215; border conflicts, 130; economy, 12, 65–66, 77, 135, 230; fictional account of, 180–82; as independent republic, 10, 135; indigenous movements of, 2; invasion of, 122, 140; political analysis of, 9; and Pumacahua rebellion, 98, 102; relationship to Cuzco, 205–6; reunification with Peru, 219; and taxes, 194; and Tupac Amaru rebellion, 16, 40, 42, 49; and Tupac Katari rebellion, 58; and War of Independence, 89–90, 106, 109, 117–18, 128
Bonaparte, Joseph, 84, 89
Bonaparte, Napoleon, 84, 89
Bourbon reforms, 13, 22–25, 29, 52, 55–68, 227
Bourbons: relationship with Catholic Church, 28; response to rebellions,

57–58. *See also* Bourbon reforms
Buenos Aires, 22–23, 45, 59, 106
Bujanda, Juan Angel: and bullfights, 169; description of mestizos by, 192; description of military by, 138; and Escobedo uprising, 159–60; expulsion from Cuzco, 161; favoritism toward Lugones, 142; relationship with Gamarra, 144, 147; suppression of rumors by, 174
Bullfights, 168–70, 182

Cabildo (city council), 70, 95, 97, 130
Caciques: and Bourbons, 22–24, 61–63; complaints against, 76, 209; and court trials, 72, 74–77; decline of office, 61–63, 74–75, 209–11; economic strategies of, 75; ethnic identity, 24–25, 62–63, 209; exempt from head tax, 11; fate of descendants, 211–12; and Inca revivalism, 25; as intermediaries, 40, 42; local autonomy of, 13, 61; opposed to Tupac Amaru, 52; Pumacahua as, 48. *See also* Indians
Carrera, Rafael, 122, 212
Casanga, Antonio, 110, 112
Casanga, Clemente, 110, 112
Castas: 12, 190–93. *See also* Race
Castelli, Juan José, 89
Castilla, Ramón, 225
Catholic Church: and Battle of Sangararā, 37; Bolívar's reforms of, 132–33; in Cuzco, 28–29; relations with Gamarra, 133–34; role in public culture of, 167; and Tupac Amaru, 17, 38. *See also* Priests
Catholicism. *See* Catholic Church
Caudillismo, 129; civil wars and, 7; re-

lationship to state formation, 2, 224–26; study of, 6–7. *See also* Gamarra, Agustín

Caudillos: biographies of, 123; and civil war, 213–20; ideology of, 4, 122; and Indians, 217–18; and lower classes, 5–7; politics of, 5–6, 157–64, 222–27; and state formation, 135, 224–26. *See also* Caudillismo; Gamarra, Agustín

Charles III, 22, 30

Charles IV, 53, 88–89

Chicherías: as sites for conspiracies, 40–41, 58, 87, 90, 174. *See also* Rumors

Chile, 12, 40, 42, 106

Choquehuanca, José Domingo, 200, 211

Chumbivilcas: and Aymaraes rebellion, 114; as guerrilla stronghold, 101; lack of schools, 174; as livestock region, 10, 215; militias of, 143; political figures of, 176; and Tupac Amaru rebellion, 42, 44, 47

Coca: cultivation of, 10; as Cuzco crop, 23–24, 66, 135; decline, 205–6; and Inca revivalism, 103; and Indian exploitation, 73, 77, 198–99; as sustenance for guerrillas, 215

Colegio de Ciencias y Artes, 133, 174

Colegio de Educandas, 133, 174

Colombia, 16, 21

Comentarios Reales (Garcilasco de la Vega), 25, 58

Comunero rebellion, 21, 79

Condemayta, Tomasa, 53

Condorcanqui, José Gabriel. *See* Tupac Amaru II

Conservatives: ideology of, 124–25, 163; and Inca revivalism, 170; political

tactics of, 184–85; use of press, 178–79. *See also* Gamarrismo; Gamarristas

Constitution (of 1812), 92, 97–98, 107

Corregidores, 23, 27, 36, 60, 210

Cortes de Cádiz, 92–96, 116, 189. *See also* Spain

Cotabambas, 49, 191–92

Counter Reformation, 173

Courts: and Gamarristas, 162; Indian use of, 71–83; and relationship to rebellion, 56. *See also* Crime; Lawsuits; Trials

Creoles: and Battle of Sangarará, 37; and Bourbon reforms, 23; as caciques, 62; nationalism of, 51–52, 208–9; relationship with Indians, 93–94, 96, 118; and state formation, 13; and Tupac Amaru rebellion, 17, 26, 55

Crime, 70–71, 73, 77, 80; punishment of, 81, 113. *See also* Lawsuits; Trials

Croix, Teodoro de, 58

Cultural brokers, 12, 22, 103, 119, 212

Cuzco: and Arequipa, 149–50; Bourbon reforms in, 22–29, 61; and church-state conflict, 28–29; city council, 32; decline, 15, 222, 229–30; elites, 11–12, 23, 157, 164, 224; and Incas, 105, 170; and Indians, 11, 68, 164–65, 187, 191–96, 203; legal system, 56, 70–82; and liberals, 155–57, 181–85; literacy and education, 173–74; lower classes of, 179–82; modern period, 229–30; politics in, 97, 130–31, 145–51, 157–60; population, 9, 11, 67, 129, 191 (Table 2), 229; press of, 156, 165, 172–79, 183–84; provinces of, 9 (map 2); public festivities, 164–72; and riots,

Cuzco (*continued*)
180, 182; rural society, 186–221 passim, 225–26; schools of, 27, 133; social
divisions in, 10–11, 199–201; and
taxes, 66–67, 203, 210–11; and Tupac Amaru rebellion, 36, 45–46, 49,
58; and War of Independence, 84–
89, 108–20, 136. *See also* Cuzco: and
Lima; Economy: colonial Cuzco; republican Cuzco; Political culture: in
urban Cuzco; Violence: and Cuzco
riots
Cuzco: and Lima, 8–10, 60, 70, 85, 185

Economy: colonial Cuzco, 24, 64–68,
109–10, 115–16; and peasants, 206–7;
republican Cuzco, 129, 134–35, 197,
204–6
Ecuador: border conflicts, 130; mod-
ern indigenous movements of, 2;
resistance to tax system, 194
Elections: audiencia control of, 97;
debates over Indian suffrage, 93–
95; and Gamarra, 134, 158; as public
ritual, 5
"El Inca." *See* Tupac Amaru II
England, 31
Enlightenment: as ideology for Tupac
Amaru rebellion, 13, 17, 24, 26; influ-
ence on Bourbons, 22. *See also* French
Revolution; United States
Escobedo, Gregorio, 160
Escobedo uprising, 139, 159–60
Europe, 18, 26, 173

Federalism, 125
Felipe de Betancur, Diego, 27–28
Ferdinand VII, 84, 92, 100, 102, 106–7
Flores Galindo, Alberto: and Inca

revivalism, 104; interpretation of Tu-
pac Amaru rebellion, 21, 42, 47, 52;
notion of the "colonial knot," 53; and
War of Independence, 86
Forasteros, 43, 189
France, 31, 167, 173; intendant system
of, 59. *See also* French Revolution
French Revolution, 19, 50, 88–89
Fuente, Antonio Gutiérrez de la, 124–
25
Fujimori, Alberto, 224

Gamarra, Agustín: as "Black Angel,"
123; career of, 2, 122, 152; and caudillismo, 14; as caudillo, 123; and
church, 133–34, 167; and civil war,
213–19; and Cuzco, 129–51 passim,
159, 164–70, 219, 230; death, 1, 122,
150, 222; early life, 125–26; ideology
of, 123–25, 129, 145–51; and Indians,
212–19; opponents of, 151; recruitment of supporters, 135–37; reforms
by, 130–34, 137, 143–44; use of Inca
past, 147–48, 168; veneration of,
167–70, 230; and War of Independence, 2, 121. *See also* Gamarrismo;
Gamarristas
Gamarra and Bolivia, 1, 129, 149–50,
159, 222
Gamarrismo: and caudillos, 224; description of, 147, 167; and militias,
138; relationship to caudillismo, 129,
150, 226. *See also* Gamarra, Agustín;
Gamarristas
Gamarristas: description of, 5; gendered formulations of, 182; policies
of, 159; relations with Indians, 194–
97. *See also* Gamarra, Augustín;
Gamarrismo

Garcilasco de la Vega, 25–26, 54, 58;
   Comentarios Reales, 25, 58
Goyenche, José Manuel de, 89
"Great Fear, the," 55, 57–59, 80, 93
Guatemala, 122, 212
Guerrillas: and Battle of Yanacocha,
   218; demands of, 108; Indians as,
   213–19; and Pumacahua rebellion,
   100–101; tactics of, 45, 48, 218; and
   Tupac Amaru rebellion, 47–48; in
   War of Independence, 85; weapons
   of, 100. *See also* Military; Militias

Habsburgs, 20, 22, 39, 60
Haciendas, 11–12, 205
Head tax: collection of, 211; debate over
   abolition of, 94–96, 189; dependence
   of colonial state on, 23; dependence
   of republican state on, 188–90, 201;
   Indian payment of, 190–97, 207, 217;
   and racial definitions in Peru, 11–12.
   See also Taxes
Hegemony, 39, 56, 69, 80
Herrera, Bartolomé, 134
Hidalgo y Costilla, Miguel, 84
Huamanga, 98–99, 111–12
Huarocondo, 88, 90–91
Huayna Capac, 104

Inca monarchism, 15, 17, 20
Inca revivalism: as alternative to colonialism, 8, 14–16; in Cuzco, 147–48;
   170; and Gamarristas, 148; and Indians, 104, 207; and political rituals,
   179, 225; and Pumacahua rebellion,
   103–5; and Tupac Amaru rebellion,
   13, 16, 19–21, 24–25, 51, 53; used by
   conservatives, 170; used by liberals,
   170–71; and War of Independence,

117, 119–20. *See also* Flores Galindo,
   Alberto
Incas: empire of, 20; and Gamarra,
   147–48; royal descendants of, 211;
   state repression of memory of, 53–
   54, 56, 58, 104; and Tupac Amaru
   rebellion, 20. *See also* Inca revivalism
Indians: and Bourbon reforms, 23, 56;
   and caudillos, 221, 226; and Cortes
   de Cádiz, 92–97; and court system,
   56, 68–83; definitions of, 11, 186–87,
   229; economic behavior of, 206–7;
   and education, 154, 174; exploitation
   of, 15, 68, 72–73, 76–77, 202; labor
   of, 197–99, 205; and land, 204–6,
   221, 229; and lawyers, 78–79; official
   views of, 78–79, 93, 194–201, 221;
   political autonomy of, 211, 219, 227;
   political behavior of, 2, 201–2, 207–
   11, 216–21; population of, 187, 191
   (Table 2), 205; poverty of, 67–68, 135,
   207; in Pumacahua rebellion, 102–
   3; and republicanism, 2, 120, 209,
   220; rights of, 93–97, 199, 221; as
   royalists, 46, 90, 102; social divisions
   among, 203; as soldiers, 214–17; survival of, 228–29; and Tupac Amaru
   rebellion, 13, 42–43, 52; in War of
   Independence, 86–88, 93, 118–19. *See
   also* Cuzco: and Indians; Guerrillas:
   Indians as; Head tax; Indians: and
   state
Indians: and state, 11, 186–88, 202, 223,
   227–29
Intendancy system: continuity in republican period, 130; creation, 59–60,
   74; criminal cases, 70, 72, 81; function of, 60; and head tax, 63, 96. *See
   also* Audiencia

Invented traditions, 8, 20, 51, 167

Jáuregui, Agustín, 57
Jesuits, 27–28
Juntas departamentales, 130–31, 169, 210

Katari, Tomás, 33, 49. *See also* Tupac Katari rebellion

La Mar, José de, 124, 130, 140, 150, 159
Lampoons. *See* Pasquinades
Land: in Cuzco, 135; elite desires for, 68; Indian struggles for, 68, 204–6, 221, 229
Landa, Tiburcio, 36–38
La Paz: junta in, 89; riots in, 29; siege of, 49, 99–100
Lawsuits: and Bourbon state, 81–82; and Gamarra, 144; and Gamarristas, 162; Indian use of, 56, 69, 72–83; and local power relations, 71. *See also* Courts; Crime; Trials
Legal system. *See* Courts; Trials
Liberals: criticisms of conservatives, 146, 151, 155, 161–62, 169; ideology of, 155–57, 163–64; and Inca revivalism, 148, 170–71; political practices, 108, 124–25, 184–85; use of press, 178–79
Lima: centralism of, 8, 149, 223, 227, 230; growth in modern period, 227–29; Inca revivalism in, 105; press of, 184; and Tupac Amaru, 25–26; and Tupac Amaru rebellion, 41; and War of Independence, 14, 85, 105–8, 114, 136. *See also* Cuzco
Lower classes: and caudillos, 5–7; republicanism of, 108. *See also* Blacks; Castas; Cuzco: lower classes of; Indians

Lugones, Gregorio, 138, 142

Mamacha Belén (Our Lady of Bethlehem), 44
Mantaro Valley, 127
Mar y Tapia, Pablo, 144, 169
Mata Linares, Benito de la, 58–59, 104
Mayan Indians, 68
Merchants, 12, 29, 46, 149
Mercurio Peruano, 26, 93. *See also* Press: and newspapers
Mestizos: as Arequipa rebels, 32; as castas, 190, 192; debate over role in republic, 12; mistrust of others, 13; and Tupac Amaru rebellion, 17, 52. *See also* Castas; Race
Mexico, 2, 11, 84, 158
Military: cultural importance of, 168; draft (leva), 109–10, 213, 218; Gamarra's use of, 14, 126–27, 141–43, 215; social origins of, 213. *See also* Guerrillas
Militias, 138–41; social origins of, 213; tax exemptions for joining, 203. *See also* Guerrillas
Mita (labor draft), 11, 42, 199
Mollinedo, Juan de, 37–38, 40
Montiel y Surco, Miguel, 26
Montoneros. *See* Guerrillas
Moral economy, 69–70
Moscoso, Juan Manuel, 28–29, 33, 38, 44–46
Muleteers: as cultural brokers, 12; and Cuzco economy, 10; mules of, 10, 27, 29. *See also* Rumors

Nadal, Ramón, 142–43, 149
Nationalism, 17–18, 51, 159, 167, 208. *See also* Protonationalism
Nieto, Domingo, 141, 162–63

Obrajes (textile mills): burned by Tupac Amaru rebels, 24, 35–36, 66; and convict labor, 65–66; crimes committed in, 70–71; exploitation of Indians in, 73; favored by Gamarra, 142, 148–49; owners of, 115, 142–43; and Viceroy La Serna, 115; work conditions in, 66. *See also* Textile industry

Orbegoso, Luis José: and charitable organizations, 133; as enemy of Gamarra, 148, 150, 161, 214–15; as military leader, 124–25; as president of Peru, 158, 163

Orihuela, José Calixto, 133–34, 158

Otero, Francisco Paula, 143

Padre Horán, El, 180–82

Paliza y Magón, José, 110–11

Pando, José María de, 193

Pan-Indian solidarity, 57–58

Pardos, 190. *See also* Race

Pardo y Aliaga, Felipe, 177

Paruro, 10, 215

Pasquinades: "rebellion of," 30–32; as vehicle for political criticism, 173, 176–77

Peru: modern period, 19, 222–23, 224–30; population, 9; wars of, 124, 130, 161–64. *See also* Presidents of Peru; Race

Peru-Bolivia Confederation, 142, 143, 158; and casta tax, 193; defeat, 222; implemented by Santa Cruz, 122, 125, 148, 159, 161; opposed by Gamarra, 122, 129, 181; riots in Cuzco against, 180–81. *See also* Santa Cruz, Andrés

Pezuela, Joaquín de la, 106–7, 112, 126

Piérola, Nicolás, 227

Political culture, 4–5, 51, 117; and cau-

dillos, 224–27; definitions of, 153; in urban Cuzco, 7, 15–16, 152–85 passim

Politics. *See* Caudillos: politics of; Cuzco: politics in

Potosí, 10, 23, 28, 65

Prefects, 138

Presidents of Peru, 14, 19, 122, 127 (Table 1), 224–25, 227

Press: and Gamarra, 177–78; and newspapers, 26, 173–78; pamphlets, 176–78; political use of, 115, 146, 175–79; and religious texts, 14–15, 173

Priests: as cultural brokers, 12, 212; election of, opposed by Gamarra, 134; political alliances of, 74; and Pumacahua rebellion, 99; as supporters of Gamarra, 14; and Tupac Amaru rebellion, 28–29. *See also* Catholic Church

Protector de indios, 72, 79

Protonationalism, 13, 17–19, 40, 51–52. *See also* Nationalism

Pumacahua, Mateo García: career, 48, 90, 97–98; execution, 100; as historical symbol, 230; use of Inca revivalism, 103–4. *See also* Pumacahua rebellion

Pumacahua rebellion, 13, 118, 216; and defeat, 100, 102–3, 105; events of, 97–105; ideology of rebels, 101; and Inca revivalism, 103–5; Indian support of, 102–3; leadership of, 98–100, 119; recruitment of rebels, 101; repression in wake of, 105; and Spain, 102; tactics of rebels, 99–100. *See also* Pumacahua, Mateo Garcia; Violence: and Pumacahua rebellion

Puno: complaints against caciques in, 76; economic competition of, 135; Gamarra as treasurer of, 126; Indian

Puno (*continued*)
exploitation in, 200; mail route
to, 10; and Pumacahua rebellion,
98–99; subdelegates of, 94; and supporters of Santa Cruz, 159; transfer
of intendency, 60, 65; and Tupac
Amaru rebellion, 41; weakness of
local authorities, 210

Quechua: and caciques, 76; as cultural
marker of "Indianness," 11; repressed
by state, 54, 58; spoken in modern
Peru, 227; spoken by Tupac Amaru,
27; translated in courts, 72
Quiroga, Facundo, 6, 122
Quispicanchis, 136; economy, 206;
military forces, 140, 143; rebellion
in, 58; support of Tupac Amaru
rebellion, 42; violence in, 48

Race: and casta tax, 190–93; definitions in colonial Peru, 11–12, 186–88,
190–91, 229; and racism, 223; social
divisions caused by, 13, 51, 164, 221;
and War of Independence, 53
Ramírez, Juan, 100, 102, 126
Reparto (forced sales): abolished during
Tupac Amaru rebellion, 23, 40, 46,
50; colonial operation of, 23; Cuzco
dependence on, 24; debate over
reintroduction of, 202; importance to
obrajes, 36; Indians exploited by, 67,
110; and subdelegates, 74
Republicanism: caudillo support of,
4, 172; established in Peru, 2–3, 86;
lower class adherence to, 164; and
symbolism, 170–71; in the United
States, 50
Río de la Plata, 35, 126; creation of
viceroyalty, 22; political discontent

in, 88; products of, 24; and Puma-
cahua rebellion, 99–100, 102; and
San Martín, 84, 106; transfer of
Puno intendancy to, 60, 65; and
Tupac Amaru rebellion, 42, 53
Riva Agüero, José de la, 128
Royal Highway, 10, 12, 28, 42
Rumors: chicherías as site of, 40; and
Escobedo uprising, 159; and oral cul-
ture, 90, 174; in *El Padre Horán*, 180;
and Pumacahua rebellion, 99; and
spread of rebellions, 29, 40, 59, 90,
97, 113
Rural society. *See* Cuzco: rural society

Sacred Valley: economic decline in,
205; opposition to Tupac Amaru, 42
Sahuaraura, Justo, 211
Sahuaraura, Pedro, 32
Salaverry, Felipe Santiago, 161, 178, 193,
215–16
Sangarará, 36–37. *See also* Battle of
Sangarará
San Martín, José de, 14, 84–85, 106–7,
114, 189
Santa Cruz, Andrés, 149, 177; as coup
leader, 127; depicted in *El Padre
Horan*, 181; and Escobedo rebellion,
159–60; and Gamarra, 141, 150, 159,
161, 215–16; as head of Peru-Bolivia
Confederation, 148; importance
to Peru, 121; lawsuits initiated by,
144; ouster of La Mar, 140; political
policies of, 218
Santa Rosa, 57
Sarmiento, Domingo, 6, 122
Señor de los Temblores (Our Lord of
Earthquakes), 44, 180–82
Serna, José de la, 59, 107–9, 129, 173;
last stand in Cuzco, 114–17

United States (*continued*)
    movements, 22, 26, 146; republican-
    ism of, 50
Upper Peru. *See* Bolivia
Urubamba, 10, 140, 206

Valle, José del, 48–49
Velasco Alvarado, Juan, 19
Vilcanota Valley, 42–43
Violence: and crime, 71, 73, 78; and
    Cuzco riots, 45–46, 180–82; and
    Indians, 208, 217; and Pumacahua
    rebellion, 99–102; and Tupac Amaru
    rebellion, 21, 37, 45–50

War of Independence, 84–120 pas-
    sim; and Aymaraes rebellion, 111–12;
    in Cuzco region, 86–89, 108–20;
    Indian participation in, 118–19; in-
terpretations of, 14, 85–86; origins,
86–91; and rebel actions, 110–11; and
regional divisions, 85; and social divisions, 14; victory of liberals in, 108.
See also Gamarra, Agustín; Guerrillas
War of the Pacific, 228
Women: as cacicas, 41; as celebrants,
165; in court trials, 80; men disguised
as, 110; political consciousness of,
154, 159; role in rebellions, 41, 43,
47–48; and urban political culture,
153–54. *See also* Bastidas, Micaela
Written culture, 174. *See also* Press

Yauri, 28, 41

Zambos, 190. *See also* Race
Zapatistas, 2

Charles F. Walker is Assistant Professor of History at
the University of California, Davis. He is the editor
of *Entre la retórica y la insurgencia: Las ideas y los
movimientos sociales en los Andes, siglo XVIII* (1996)
and coeditor of *Bandoleros, abigeos, y montoneros:
Criminalidad y violencia en el Perú, siglos XVIII–XX* (1990).

Library of Congress Cataloging-in-Publication Data
Walker, Charles.
Smoldering ashes : Cuzco and the creation of
Republican Peru, 1780–1840 / Charles F. Walker.
Includes bibliographical references and index.
ISBN 0-8223-2261-7 (cloth : alk. paper).
ISBN 0-8223-2293-5 (pbk. : alk. paper)
1. Cuzco (Peru : Dept.)—History.   2. Peru—History—
1548–1820.   3. Peru—History—War of Independence,
1820–1829.   4. Peru—History—1829–1919.   5. Indians
of South America—Peru—Cuzco (Dept.)—Politics and
government.   6. Caudillos—Peru—Cuzco (Dept.)—
History.   I. Title.
F3451.C9W35   1999
985'.3704—dc21   98-30624 CIP